PENGUIN BOOKS

The Britannias

Longlisted for the Women's Prize for Non-Fiction 2024
Shortlisted for the Edward Stanford Travel Writing Awards 2024

'In *The Britannias*, Alice Albinia tilts the map so that mainland
Britain fades and the archipelago of its surrounding islands
comes into focus . . . lavish research . . . accounts such as
Albinia's – which stress the fragility of feminist gains – are
vital correctives and, indeed, warnings for defenders of
women's rights, past and present' Rachel Hewitt, *Guardian*

'There are books crafted from research, worthy and
informative. And there are books that happen. That need
to happen. That feel inevitable. As if they have always,
somehow, been there waiting for us. The voyages of
Alice Albinia around our ragged fringes range through
time, recovering and resurrecting the most potent
myths. A work of integrity and vision' Iain Sinclair

'A dazzlingly brilliant book. Travelling by boat, swimming
through kelp, riding on a fishing trawler, Alice Albinia takes
us on an extraordinary journey around the British isles,
revealing a liquid past where women ruled and mermaids sang
and tracing the sea-changes of her own heart' Hannah Dawson

'Her sparkling new book . . . inverts long-held assumptions about
the periphery versus the centre and creates a history that is richer
and stranger the further it travels from seats of power'
Gavin Plumley, *Country Life*

'An artful book of waterways and wildernesses, monastic havens
and tax havens. A fascinating demonstration that Britain "singular"
is shorthand for something tectonically, volcanically plural'
Amy Jeffs, author c̓

'A passionate rich work of historical
scholarship and poetic imagination'
Xiaolu Guo, author of *Radical: A Life of My Own*

'A book about Britain's relationship with its outlying
archipelago, from Anglesey to Thanet, Shetland to the Isle of
Wight ... she has been touring the British Isles in search of solitaries
and eccentrics, radicals and rebels ... By looking more closely
at the periphery, we might learn something new about the
centre ... Albinia's prose is impressive ... the main impression
given by *The Britannias* is the uniqueness of our outlying
islands, each one entire unto itself' Guy Stagg, *Financial Times*

'Islands always intrigue, hovering on the horizons of
our imaginations ... [Albinia] makes memorable
connections, meets some engaging people and
offers some salutary observations'
Derek Turner, *Spectator*

'A book which doesn't so much take a prism to
British history as view it through a kaleidoscope'
Barry Didcock, *The Herald*

ABOUT THE AUTHOR

Alice Albinia is an award-winning author of fiction and non-fiction. Her books include *Empires of the Indus: The Story of a River* and *Cwen*, set on an archipelago which comes under female rule, which was shortlisted for the Orwell Prize for Political Fiction and Scotland's National Book Awards. Albinia has worked as an editor and journalist, writing for publications including the *Guardian*, *Financial Times* and *National Geographic*. She has taught Creative Writing in Orkney for the Islands' Council, in London with First Story, and currently teaches with the Royal Literary Fund.

The Britannias

And the Islands of Women

ALICE ALBINIA

PENGUIN BOOKS

PENGUIN BOOKS

UK | USA | Canada | Ireland | Australia
India | New Zealand | South Africa

Penguin Books is part of the Penguin Random House group of companies
whose addresses can be found at global.penguinrandomhouse.com

First published in Great Britain by Allen Lane 2023
Published in Penguin Books 2024
002

Typeset by Jouve (UK), Milton Keynes
Printed and bound in Great Britain by Clays Ltd, Elcograf S.p.A.

A CIP catalogue record for this book is available from the British Library

The authorized representative in the EEA is Penguin Random House Ireland,
Morrison Chambers, 32 Nassau Street, Dublin D02 YH68

ISBN: 978-1-846-14911-5

www.greenpenguin.co.uk

For my mother
her mother
and my daughters
in all your golden ages.

Britannia Island, famed in Greek and in our own records, lies off to the north-west . . . Its former name was Albion; but later all the islands . . . were called the Britannias.

Pliny the Elder, *Natural History*, first century AD

Contents

Contents

Introduction

Here are some voyage tales – *immrama* or *echtrai*, as they were called in medieval Ireland. Here are some stories of what living in,[1] on, or within sight of islands, does to the mind. Here are journeys over waves, to the point where land meets sea again and light glitters differently as it refracts off water. Here are meanders along the margins of misladen texts as fingers trail damp stone. Here is a quest under the moon, between the branches, into the dim antechambers of British history.

But it is not just the past that concerns us. It is also the now. As the tide comes in and the tide goes out, so do humans, back and forth across this salty land, building and destroying wonders. Here, then, are fishermen, nuns, entrepreneurs and musicians, some avowedly local, some far-flung, making their lives and their livings in these water-bound places. Crossing over to an island has long been a ritualistic act; even now it is a statement of intent, occasionally of actively hostile difference.

I first set foot on an island for this book with my baby; she is now just turning ten. During the course of her first decade I walked across Anglesey; up and down Iona; north along the coast to Lindisfarne; high up into the hills of Harris. I lived in Orkney, working as a firefighter, a teacher, a school cook (serving soup every Wednesday to that same sweet daughter). I slept on islands off islands under the stars, head tilted down against the rain, face tilted up to the sun. I rode into Thanet on a horse-drawn cart, into Shetland on a fishing trawler, through the Hebrides under sail, into Westminster on my bike at dawn. I grew up in this country; yet none of these journeys and their discoveries were what I expected of Britain.

*

An island is a place apart: abundant oasis or site of deprivation; for blessed refuge or forced exile; protected and exposed. From London or Edinburgh (or anywhere on the largest British island) these outcrops in the ocean might be easy to ignore – at least until the summer. But all residents of Great Britain, Northern Ireland and the Crown Dependencies are island-dwellers: physically isolated from the European landmass for the past eight thousand years. All but two of the United Kingdom's Overseas Territories are islands. Nowadays, England, in particular, thinks of Britain as 'an island nation' – as if the large island in the centre is what matters. But there are thousands of islands in these waters,[2] a fact that influences all who dwell on the associated land, wherever they live, whatever they think. Islandness has shaped the politics, economy, artistic sensibility, and military arrangements of the overlapping political, geographic entities which make up these nations and their sense of themselves in the world. For most of human history, it was the small islands around the 'mainland' that were the powerful protected places, the first to nurture civilization. It was their innovations which spread inward, to cultivate the now-dominant centre. Island-geography is the pivot upon which these histories turn.

In the beginning, when humans first began to colonize the archipelago, the outlying islands were their first foothold. The islands were prized as jewels: being rich in fish; forming fortresses easy to control and hold; sites from which it was possible to eliminate undesirable animals or people, and introduce others. Thus Neolithic humans came to Orkney and pioneered monumental sun worship; Druids made Anglesey Europe's last place of Celtic sanctity and learning; Christian monks made islands the locus of their new religion. To these people, the 'mainland' was the periphery: an incommodious jungle full of competitors and predators which the smaller islands were blessedly free from.

Foreign empires also made use of the islands' favourable geography. Early Greek explorers, like the Vikings after, viewed this conglomeration of islands through the filter of their own island worlds. Until paved roads made inland travel fast, the secure way to live was liquid: on an island with a boat. This is why ancient Greek travelogues detail the chain of small islands but treat the large island as the sideshow; why Shetland, Orkney, the Hebrides and Man formed the vertebrae of Norse colonization. Even the Romans, a continent-bound people, made sure to sack Anglesey, banish heretical bishops to Scilly and develop Wight as an oasis of native comforts.

It was only during the past millennium that the 'mainland' constructed the idea of itself as the centre, and its smaller island neighbours as the margin. From the twelfth century onwards, mainland monarchs in Scotland and England began to attack the independence of islands. Both the lowland monarchy of Scotland and the subsequent government of Britain battled the islands into submission. Henry VIII's Reformation (and later John Knox's) forcibly dismantled the islands' history and meaning, changing them from ancient sanctuaries to national garrisons. In England, a stubborn attempt at reasserting independence came during the Civil War, when many small islands – being well fortified, and often miles distant from the mainland – held out longest as Royalist, or occasionally Roundhead, strongholds, or switched between the two. Pockets of resistance endured even longer into the nineteenth century in Scotland, where the remote northern islands of Handa and Hirta organized themselves with their own parliaments (as their regular meetings were termed, maybe over-romantically, by outsiders). The Welsh island of Bardsey had a king until 1926. In 1975, Sealand (an anarchic North Sea island made of a Second World War offshore platform) began issuing passports.[3]

Where mainland politics led, culture followed. The final assault on island independence has been linguistic. During the past three centuries, English either killed off, or seriously threatened, the indigenous languages of Britain's islands. Norn died in the nineteenth century, Manx in the twentieth; Jèrriais and Guernésiais cling on among the older generation. Gaelic has huge resources allocated to its survival.

Once vanquished, it is hard for islands deemed 'remote' by the authorities to recover. Some are given over to birds, but there is a long history of islands being used not just as prisons but also as pestilence sinks, leper colonies, for weapons testing, or being cleared of humans and trees in preference for sheep. Genocide has been a feature of island life from the beginning, and throughout their history islands also functioned as laboratories of plant and animal propagation or elimination. During the nineteenth century this culminated in a catastrophe for British biodiversity, with the forced eviction of Scottish islanders eerily mirrored by a bloodbath of native birds and mammals. But many of the islands clung to wildness in ways the mainland couldn't. Today – happily, tragically, depending which way you see it – with their red squirrels, corncrakes, pesticide-free machair and dark skies, islands are precious sanctuaries in our human-dominated landscape.

Islands almost always resisted when the mainland asserted its hegemony – a historical legacy which endures in modern political attitudes. During the 2014 referendum on Scottish independence, all the islands voted No, even those, such as the Western Isles, which have elected the SNP on and off since the 1970s. This does not suggest love of London but resistance to Edinburgh, a legacy of the islands' complete political independence, from at least Viking times until the fifteenth century. After Brexit, almost all Scottish seats went to the SNP, but Orkney again held out against mainstream dominance (the Northern Isles have voted Liberal or Lib Dem since 1950). Historically, the impositions of Scotland's ruling class have been the islands' biggest threat.

Curious constitutional arrangements, meanwhile, link the Channel Islands and the Isle of Man to Britain in interdependent ways. At the moment, they function as low-tax money-pots; as do their doppelgangers in Britain's Overseas Territories – such as Bermuda and Cayman – pilfered during empire, and retained for use as military bases, stop-offs for rendition flights, unorthodox financial centres, or, in the case of South Georgia, for future resource use or settlement: when global warming makes human life possible only at the poles.[4] Nowadays, the government in Westminster periodically portrays these islands as rogue states, fiscally out of line. But it tolerates tax havens and semi-autonomous political entities because it is always useful, if sometimes embarrassing, to have places where extrajudicial events may occur and rich people and multinationals can store their money.[5]

The ambiguous status of the outlying islands is partly the result of the idiosyncratic, organic (bloody) development of the United Kingdom's constitutional arrangements – a nation increasingly bedevilled by its own creation. In our globalized world, as nation-states are stymied by the indifferent power of corporations (their use of island tax havens), or mass immigration from nearby war zones (islands as stepping stones), an instinctive human reaction is to isolate: with borders, politics, religion. Nowadays, in Britain, as elsewhere in the world, ethnic, geographical or political groupings with a longer historical lineage than the nation-state clamour for greater self-definition and political autonomy. In 2014, Cornwall won minority status by emphasizing the fact that it is 'almost an island' (a river divides it from the rest of England; before the Norman conquest, it was a separate country). Jersey's government has drawn up fully costed contingency plans for the independence it will demand if London threatens its freedom to set taxes, that being the basis of its economy. The SNP looks to the independence of British islands for Scotland's future; as one MP I spoke to put it, 'If Man can do it with 85,000 people, Scotland with 5 million would seem to have a reasonable chance.' Orkney councillors just voted to 'investigate alternative methods of governance'. If these places seem to be striving for fracture rather than union it is not surprising, given that the dominant imperial, Anglocentric myth of the past three hundred years has taken everything for granted and not differentiated enough between individual cultures.[6]

There has never been a definitive name for these islands, as Pliny pointed out. Sometimes they were 'the twin Bretanides' (Britain and Ireland). The Welsh epic *The Mabinogi*, a story cycle written down in medieval times from a presumed plethora of oral sources, refers to 'the islands of Britain',[7] as do some of the Arthurian romances. Mostly, however, one island stood in for the whole; so that when in 731 the monk-historian Bede wrote his *History of the English Church and People*, he had to explain (doubly dubitably) that 'Britain, formerly known as Albion, is in an island in the ocean'.[8]

Contemporary commentators, meanwhile, still refer to the 'four nations of the United Kingdom' – ignoring the Crown dependencies and all the Overseas Territories. During the 2012 Olympics, the official branding 'Team GB' ostracized the Northern Irish (who live in the United Kingdom, not Great Britain). The Overseas Territories are managed by the Foreign, Commonwealth and Development Office, even though, as the Governor of the Virgin Islands (UK) pointed out to me, 'They are neither foreign nor Commonwealth.' (The 'British Virgin Islands', as these islands are commonly known, is also a misnomer.) It would be more accurate to follow Pliny's example and name the entire archipelago and its associated islands 'The Britannias'. But that would cause anxiety in metropolitan, mainland circles, where power necessarily radiates out from the centre.

Sentimentally, even the staunchest British centrist likes to retreat to an island once in a while. There are lawless islands, radical ones, and many bastions of inherited, or money-controlled, privilege. Little outcrops in the ocean can be wildly expensive, or comparatively cheap, depending; during the writing of this book I came to know of several people with their own little fiefdoms in the Irish Sea, the Channel Islands, off the east and west coast of Scotland. My grandmother's Scottish family still owns two tiny islands off the coast of East Lothian. Today they are managed as wildlife reserves – but family gatherings often involve a boat trip to see the gannets on their rock; outings imbued with the frisson of nostalgia.

Some islands have been at the vanguard of dramatic social change; others still preserve social hierarchies and religious forms in ways peculiar and discrete. But for many Britons, whoever they are, the small islands which ring the large one represent an escape from the stifling homogeneity of national life. They are the mainland's flattering reflection; a repository of eradicated histories; self-styled sites of resistance to state control.

How island people see such incursions is another matter. Ancient island stories chronicle anarchy and flux: peripatetic islands, submerged islands, islands only latterly peripheral, culturally.[9] Mythology, politics and geography interlace, with some islands reclaimed by the shore, others cut off by the tide, and all once pertaining to other dominions. From the once-Norman south to the once-Norwegian north, island-people share memories of political and economic extremes: self-rule to colonization; emigration in lean times, influx in times of plenty; poverty or piracy to fantastic wealth and private purchase.

Nowadays, we refer with derogatory inflection to an 'island mentality' – but that is the mainland speaking for itself. Smaller-island people, because of their circumscribed territory, have always tended to look outwards – to South African gold mines, Antarctic whaling stations, North Sea oil rigs; just as they have tended, throughout their history, to give welcome to outsiders. The fact of being set apart from the mainland connects these islands to each other, and to places far beyond; Shetland regards itself as 'the biggest roundabout in the world'.

Nevertheless, almost all smaller islands within the realm of the United Kingdom, its Crown Dependencies and Overseas Territories, have their own words to distinguish islanders from visitors. The Manx call themselves 'true-born', while British immigrants are 'come-overs'; people from the British Virgin Islands are 'belongers'; tourists to Lindisfarne are 'interlopers'. It is as if such islanders need to draw an extra, symbolic circle to demarcate themselves from outsiders. Encircled as they are by the sun, moon, sea and rival powers, spheres of influence are central to island symbolism. In prehistoric times people built stone circles with solar and lunar alignments; early Christianity made of these isles a spiritual forcefield; subsequent statecraft adapted this idea with forts, airbases and Martello towers. Today there is tension between the islands' overlapping layers of internal and external control, their fiscal and political autonomy, their individual freedoms and strength as a whole.

Many of us experience that tension in our own lives: the push and pull between the communal and the individual, the lure and lull of the familiar and the foreign. For me, a denizen of Britain's circumscribed geography (born in London, raised in the West Country), there has long been something vital about being submerged in other cultures and polities. I moved to India straight out of university, and it was a second, far more radical education. My first two books, accordingly, were about places very remote from the place and the way I grew up: one tells the history of a great South Asian river; the other inhabits a modern-day Delhi run through with Sanskrit epic.

The idea for this particular book came to me as I trekked back from the source of the River Indus in Tibet and sacred Mount Kailash came into view once more. As my Buddhist companions prostrated themselves, and I knelt beside them, I thought of the journey we had just completed and of the work which lay ahead. First, I had to circumambulate the mountain; after that I had to finish the two books for which it was an end and a beginning. But in the wake of the long journey I had just undertaken, through Pakistan, Afghanistan, India and Tibet, I also thought with a pang of my own homeland. I knew so little, comparatively, of its foundation myths; I had travelled so far to study the history and culture of other lands. While part of me longed to continue travelling and encountering new places, I also acknowledged within myself a curiosity about the islands I'd grown up in, the challenge of their strange and familiar idiosyncrasies.

I am grateful to that high-altitude epiphany. Five years earlier, when I was working for a literary magazine in Delhi, I read Ted Hughes's crazy but inspired book *Shakespeare and the Goddess of Complete Being*. I read it cover to cover, during long bus journeys across the city to work. I had never come across Albina before – the ancient British goddess of art and death, apparently. Had she really existed? It didn't matter. The mere evocation of this matriarchal etymology thrilled me.

But it was only when I began researching the island stories which wind through this book that I discovered how important the name was to Britain. Medieval English chroniclers, needing a national founding myth, took up the story of a Syrian princess, Albina, who was punished, along with her sisters, for rebelling against forced marriage (they killed their abusive husbands). The women, who were set adrift from their country in a rudderless boat, eventually reached the uninhabited island of Britain, where they cultivated the land and populated it with a race of giants, by sleeping with demons.

This surprising story of female power, with its chilling echo of modern migrants, reinforces the point: humans seek refuge in islands. Albina founded Albion. (Of course, Brutus took it from her and refounded Britain.) Who knows what cultures, or states, today's migrants will nourish in Britain. Who knows how soon Britain's Wight and Thanet will become its Rhodes or Lampedusa; already, migration across the Channel has gone up exponentially since I started writing this book. Immigration into this archipelago remains one of the most interesting, dynamic and formative parts of its story.

Milton, and others like him, thought the story of Albina 'gross' and 'absurd' (the women have sex with demons and grow fat from the game they are hunting).[10] That the story survived at all is a miracle. The early history-writers never rushed to canonize stories of powerful women.

Relatedly, midway through the writing of this book I had a crisis. I looked back at what I had researched and written – not just about the islands' histories but about their modern-day avatars in those very same places – and realized that I was swamped by the masculine. The crisis in my work coincided with a personal crisis in my life; they were reflections, no doubt, of each other, and of the state of the world.

My cry for help, which was also a war cry, made me turn to the islands, and it was they who led me to the women. I knew from my earlier work about the Indus that even in the most patriarchal places, women's stories will always out; they are normally the first texts to be jettisoned or hidden or ignored, but it is impossible to suppress them for ever. It is simply a matter of looking harder.

One day in the British Library, I opened Kenneth Jackson's compilation of early poetry from these islands, *A Celtic Miscellany*, to the chapter 'Islands of Earthly Paradise'. I read these lines from *The Voyage of Bran*:

Then she sang:
There is an island far away, around which sea-horses glisten . . .
Begin a voyage across the clear sea, to see if you may reach
   the land of women . . .[11]

This was my second epiphany. Thanks to a few words from one of the earliest indigenous texts of the British Isles, first written down in Irish in the seventh century, I knew what I was looking for. There was a reason I had chosen this topic; *islands of women*. After that, I found them all around me.

From at least the time of the Greek geographer Strabo, Britain was othered as a frozen land beyond the outer ocean, a place so barbarian that women were chosen as leaders: small islands were homes to goddess cults, or inhabited by prophetesses who controlled the climate. Colonial-era Romans, medieval poets, authors of late-medieval potboilers, Renaissance dramatists, Restoration travel-writers, were in turn repeatedly intoxicated, enraged or tantalized by this idea.

It has ancient roots – the Greeks conceived of paradise islands, as did the Celts. For a while I thought that Circe and Calypso, the goddess and nymph of Greek mythology, were the wicked or subversive forerunners of the women Bran sails to – and there may be something in that; it is curious how ideas travel, and how they sometimes turn and turn again. But after I moved to Orkney, where I lived for a year and a day while researching this book, I saw that Britain's island-dwellers had from very early on, explicitly or otherwise, made in islands places of female reverence. There, in huge monuments built with vast amounts of communal time and organization, women in particular were celebrated as the recipients of solar bounty on earth.

It was reassuring to be shown – through the writing of this book about British island history – that patriarchy is only a recent invention. If you peer far enough back into recorded human history, into enough different places, it becomes clear that what sometimes feels like our natural human state – because it is so prevalent – is merely a construction. Before written words encoded male dominance into the very language and texture of holy books, epics and law-codes, different social structures prevailed on earth. Back then, for a while, it made sense to treasure women for their capacity for procreation: still one of – if not the – most important, precious and unpredictable functions of life on earth for all societies. Humans' seasonal rhythms seem to have revolved around finding and celebrating echoes of this in nature.

The subsequent cult of male worship – the most successful of our world religions – traversed culture and class, floating men to the top of the social hierarchy and keeping women as their subservient labour force. Since the populations of men and women are equal, however, this was only ever a delusion (as with most hegemonies). But with each new god or king, the pattern deepened, acquiring the patina of age and the authority of tradition. It only takes a few generations for societies to find natural such things as the generic masculine, whereby anybody hearing the word 'judge', or 'mayor', or 'prime minister', automatically thinks of a man.

Throughout the ensuing history of patriarchal dominance, stubborn golden flashes of an alternative way of living glint through the suffocating prevalence of male egos, like phosphorescence in a bog. In ancient India stories were told in Sanskrit (and retold in Greek) of a land in the northern mountains where women ruled. In ancient Europe, these female holy lands were situated on islands.

Female countercurrents always exist; women always tell stories; and men, too (who have mothers, after all, if not sisters, girlfriends, daughters), have helped transmit these tales. This is what I discovered while writing *The Britannias*: a continuous current of female-focused freedom which winds its way like a silent, secret river through the most egregiously male-fixated of ages. Sometimes the climate is so hostile it is forced underground; at other times it explodes from the earth and the rocks; but mostly it trickles quietly, tenaciously, unobtrusively, through thickets and glades, unnoticed by warring princes and noisy, careless husbands – and yet internalized by them, too, in ways atavistic and uncertain.

It must be this uncertainty which accounts for the reappearance in the seventeenth century of the Roman colonial-era motif of Britannia, the female warrior.[12] That dubious honour: women, conquered, as countries, as ships. But there is something there too – the now lone, brave woman (no manifest female solidarity here), sacrificing herself as a symbol.

If islands also have a quality of *apartness* that makes them the ideal location for experimentation, they can be 'enclosed, inward-looking' (as the artist Cornelia Parker writes of Brexit Britain in *Island*, her 2022 installation at Tate Britain). But Strabo and his cohorts were right: something unusual happens to the mind whenever you set foot on an island. It happened to me. Through this work, I was forced to examine all the certainties I had taken for granted and to ask if I could truly consider myself as liberated as the women I was writing about. From Orkney to Scilly, Anglesey to Avalon – from the early Neolithic through all their multitude of avatars – these women began to symbolize the sisterhood I sought. But I also found that I was unable to hold myself to their standard. Strangely, unexpectedly, therefore, *The Britannias* is also the story of my own journey – and, in part, through the unsettling, exhilarating transformations this passage engendered in me. In ways that I didn't anticipate, and weren't always easy, these islands transformed me, one by one, outside in.

PART ONE

In Which the Author Moves to an Island

Islands are ephemeral, created today, destroyed tomorrow.

Rachel Carson, *The Sea Around Us*, 1950

Orkney

Neolithic (3000 BC)

Darkness covers the island, the sun barely making a show. Nights, everlasting. Darkness out at sea. Darkness, in the mind. And so the people build an edifice to draw the sun back out.

Down on the shore they push wood into fissures in the rock and wait for the swelling to split the stone. They lift out slabs as long as three people and slide them with sledges and ropes, or on beds of seaweed, to the islands' axis, the centre of its bowl of hills. Here they build a sun temple finer than any house, a calendrical gauge of the solar orb at its lowest ebb. Four great standing stones go in first, to demarcate the sacred space. Around them, huge horizontal slabs taper upwards in perfect corbelled curves. Off this central chamber are side-cells, altars for the dead. Outside, a circular ditch is filled with water, making an island of the henge. Yellow ditch clay, smeared over the monument's external masonry, forms a conical mound. Grass skin grows in an echo of the hills.

The key to it all is the passage which protrudes from the south-western side and is constructed to capture a shaft of light from the setting winter solstice sun. The angle is such that for three weeks either side of the solstice, fifteen minutes before sundown a wide band of golden light appears in the passage and creeps towards the inner door. As it hits the back wall just below the room where the dead are laid, a second band of light falls across the chamber floor. When the two rays of light conjoin, the chamber is awash in the solar promise of the time of warmth in the months ahead. Then the sun goes down behind the hills in a blaze of gold, the sky goes red, the hills go grey. Stillness falls. And all is dark.

This particular monument, Maeshowe, built by Neolithic people in Orkney to honour and capture the sun moving through the sky, is a civilizational pivot. It represents the tragedy as well as the glory of culture; specifically, the move from gleaning from nature, as hunter-gatherers do, to harnessing and exploiting it, as agriculturalists have done ever since. The name, Maeshowe, is a slightly mysterious Norse word probably meaning 'meadow mound'.[1] (Vikings mythologized these far older Neolithic remains.)[2] Nobody knows what Maeshowe was called by the people who built it. Most things about the Neolithic era remain mysterious – its language, their gods, their gender relations.

I first go to Maeshowe in April 2014, with my mother and baby daughter. The skies are huge and open. I am transfixed by the relationship the Neolithic people established between the sky, sea and land and the monuments they built, interlacing natural and human phenomena.

When I return alone, eight months later, it is the middle of winter. By now the days are lit by grey; people huddle into their coats as they hurry through town and out in the countryside it is hard to tell the sky from the horizon. I visit Maeshowe four sunsets in a row; on the fourth, the sky clears of clouds and, inside, the chamber of corbelled stone explodes with golden sunshine. It is one of the most extraordinary experiences I have ever had in Britain.

Almost every archaeology book you read explains that Neolithic spaces such as Maeshowe are tombs. And clearly they were built to house the dead in flamboyant and lasting ways. But Maeshowe is more than a family or tribal crypt. Its door is made from a boulder which opens on a pivot and can be closed from the inside. A guide who has worked at the monument for decades told me that before the advent of Health and Safety, and other scruples, she would let visitors open and close it for themselves. 'It's effortless,' she said. 'Even a child could do it.' So the building was designed to be entered, easily, and closed off to outsiders. For most of the year, the central chamber would have been in near-darkness and maybe this was important to the type of rituals, or rites of passage, that took place there: initiation ceremonies, giving birth, sacred dreaming. Nowadays, Maeshowe appears as rounded, breasty;[3] and while nineteenth-century male antiquarians, twelfth-century Vikings or few contemporary archaeologists have remarked on its womb-like interior,[4] as someone who has given birth, twice, it is evident, once your mind adjusts to the significance.

I, too, however, have to have it pointed out to me, the first time. It is the late Kristin Linklater – Orcadian voice coach, free-thinking child of these islands – who tells me: *It is a womb*. As soon as she says it I am amazed – then seriously concerned – that I haven't noticed this on my own.

Thereafter, I think differently. I make connections with the communal menstruation huts that the pagan Kalash women use in north-western Pakistan. I remember the natural childbirth movement's emphasis on 'traditional' or 'indigenous' darkness when pushing out a baby. I acknowledge the importance of divination and dreaming for a culture that relied on inscrutable natural phenomena for survival. I ponder all the unpredictable divine acts that can disturb a good birthing, or a good harvest. I consider the importance, since the dawn of human culture, of public ceremony and seasonal entertainment. I think, finally, of those six weeks each year at Maeshowe, when at dusk (the Celtic beginning of the day) the chamber filled with light, and young or ill, elite or old, may have been healed by the sun's golden touch.

Maeshowe, 'one of the largest burial mounds in Neolithic Europe'[5] – or temple, tribal landscape marker, heavenly observation centre, concert hall, women's communal space – was built on the largest of the seventy or so islands in the Orkney archipelago around 3000 BC, midway through the great flourishing of Neolithic culture that took place on those islands from about 3100 to 2500 BC.[6] Even when it pours with rain outside, inside it is quiet and dry, a weather- and soundproof cocoon against the elements which keep beating Orkney flat of trees. To enter Maeshowe at any time of year is to marvel at the elegance, sophistication and skill of the people who made something that five thousand years of hurricanes and history have not been able to destroy. To witness the spectacle of sunlight-capture – to touch the rock where the sun has set – is to be in the dynamic presence of that ancient intelligence. It feels transcendental.

Although the Vikings broke in during the twelfth century, the Victorians entered through the roof and the entrance passage was rebuilt in the twentieth century, to me, Maeshowe is still almost perfect. The main change is cosmic: the Earth's tilt on its axis; the sun now comes in at slightly different angle. I was told that pollution and global warming mean that the days are cloudier now than they were in 3000 BC, often obscuring the penetrating sun.[7]

To be bathed in Maeshowe's sun in the twenty-first century, therefore, is an especially rare and special blessing. The British Neolithic peoples produced very few images of living things. There is no exuberant, Picasso-like art of the kind painted in the Lascaux caves in 15000 BC France.[8] In Orkney, they carved small, portable, enigmatic stone balls with geometric patterns. They etched abstract things – spirals, chevrons – on to the walls of their tombs, or (strange) into places completely hidden from view, such as the underside of construction stones. Possibly these are schematic, condensed representations of landscapes, beachstones, fingerprints.[9] Maybe the scratches are calendrical: notches to mark the passing of the days. Possibly they are doodlings. To the archaeologist Marija Gimbutas, such marks often denoted the feminine: breasts and vulvas. (Certainly, the V-shapes carved into the wall at the island monument Gavrinis in Brittany looked to me exactly like vulvas, but they were termed 'arrowheads' in the archaeological literature.) It is impossible to say – there is no Rosetta stone of Neolithic language.

Clearly, the preponderance of their artistic effort was public and monumental: scrupulously designed architectural spaces in relationship with both the surrounding landscape, other monuments and the movements of planets across the sky.

As the solstice sun goes down behind the island of Hoy's Ward Hill, it hits the top of a standing stone half a mile away from Maeshowe. A mile to the west, the Standing Stones of Stenness (Britain's earliest stone circle, its construction begun around 3100 BC) frame between the sloping tops of their stone fingers Ward Hill in one direction[10] and Maeshowe in the other.[11] From here, a spit of land leads north-west between two lochs (one salt, a latecomer to the islands; the other sweet, and thought to have originally been a bog). Where the two lochs almost meet, the wide face of yet another standing stone points back to Maeshowe. At the far end of this peninsula, within sight of Maeshowe, is the Ring of Brodgar, one of the largest stone circles in Britain. Things natural, human-made and celestial interact in a dance that is slow, mysterious, complex, exact. This sacred islandscape represents the first known civilization of the British archipelago.

While there is evidence of earlier Mesolithic settlement on Orkney – small, mobile communities who travelled light and left no grand gestures for posterity – it seems likely there was significant immigration northwards to Orkney from all over Europe. Orkney's Neolithic red deer were introduced by 'long distance maritime travel . . . from an unknown source': a place that was neither Britain nor Scandinavia but probably much further south.[12] Somehow the people crossed the rough waters of the Pentland Firth (an hour by today's ferry) with their animals in boats. Wherever they came from, they arrived in Orkney as part of a planned colonization. Unlike hunter-gatherers, who try to conserve resources by keeping the population down, farmers need people. This must be one of the reasons that birth is inscribed into the architecture of Neolithic chambered cairns such as Maeshowe.

And these islands repaid their efforts. They were rich in easy tidal pickings such as shellfish and seal meat, and all the other spew of brightly spangled creation which the sea spat forth. Because the climate was a few degrees warmer than today, and the land low-lying, there were abundant grain harvests. The archipelago lacked other large predators – no bears, no wolves – a scene-shifting advantage for humans herding cows and sheep. So the scrupulous lifestyle of hunter-gatherers gave way to a society which converted food surplus into glorious solar monuments.[13] Few viable weapons have been found in Orkney's Neolithic sites (this was the Stone Age). But large monuments suggest elites, and elites suggest armies. Either that, or a vast and well-organized communally minded society with the sea as defence.

Orkney still has a remnant of the wildwood that once covered the rest of the British Isles from the time of the Ice Age, but the shift from gleaning to farming, combined with the sea-salt winds, means that trees have long been sparse here: small, and bent double. There was plentiful stone, however, and it became currency and creation. Pebbles were picked out from the beach for their colour and pattern, and chipped, sanded and polished into things of form and lustre: red-flint arrowheads, grey-and-white-swirled mace heads, axes like lacquered walnut, or with striations reflecting the clouds overhead.

Orkney's natural stone abundance meant that, in later times, people didn't need to recycle ancient megaliths into houses, querns (to grind grain), churches or mosques, as happened elsewhere in the world. Possibly they were also protected by 'superstition'.[14] The major losses appear to have occurred in Victorian times, with the advent of outsider farmers and Romantic tourists. The *Orcadian* of May 1892 reported that 'Tourists had destroyed many of the Standing Stones of Stenness and many of them had been in the habit of taking away portions of the stones – one stone having been completely broken down.' The traffic to Neolithic sites so annoyed one local farmer that he even knocked down the Odin stone, a megalith with a hole in it near Maeshowe. (Tradespeople and lovers would seal deals and liaison with a lithic handshake.) The farmer was an incomer. No Orcadian would have done that.

But Orkney retains a vast amount of its Neolithic past. The culture that was created here rippled out all over the Britannias: Stonehenge, for example, inherited the giant stone circles and Orkney's distinctive grooved ware pottery; possibly even their cows were descendants of Orcadian ones.[15] And when this culture went inland it took with it a spiritual dimension formed by long exposure to coasts and islands: liminal regions where 'the mystery and power of the boundary between life and death was manifested through . . . the visual impact of the huge daily Atlantic tidal range . . . a place where the dead were returned to the realm of the ancestors'.[16]

To stand inside Maeshowe's deep-cut ditch, within sight of its two stone circles, the waters of the lochs, the hills on the horizon, and the cold touch of the sea beyond, is to feel the dizzying rippling out of islands and their meanings. Neolithic people revered islands. Their concept of life was circular.[17] They saw the relationship between their lives, the shape of their land and the solar disc in the sky above. Every winter, they brought that disc's light into the domed temple of their bounded island realm. And the rest of the Britannias learned from them.

A year after my second daughter is born, in spring 2017, I move my family to Orkney. Our plan is to stay for three months; in the end, we are there for fourteen. The baby is too young to object. But my four-year-old is grave. She gives careful consideration as to which of her books and toys to bring from home, on account of the rationing of space in the car. Each child in her class at nursery has made a drawing for her, and she carries them north, refuses to relinquish them during the time we spend in Orkney, holds on to these childish scribbles even as they become Neolithic in relation to the progress she makes in literacy.

Arriving in the islands is easier than it was but still takes time and thought. The planes are small and expensive. Since, on this occasion, I am the only driver – my husband is in New York, I think – I decide to take the longer North Sea crossing out of Aberdeen. It proves a rough beginning for landlubbers such as we. 'Brisk' is how the captain describes it on the tannoy – a weather front is coming in. (It hits two days later, by which time we are safely in Kirkwall; but still I shiver as I read about it in the *Orcadian*: how the windows in the diner where we had sat eating our mac 'n' cheese were dashed in by waves when the ferry was an hour and a half out of Aberdeen.) It is *brisk*, and the baby doesn't like it. Lying below deck, I breastfeed her in the dark, even though I weaned her weeks before and no longer have any milk. As she sucks unhappily I think of those

Neolithic mothers in their cowhide boats, their babies mewling, as mine is, at their breasts. They were crossing to the promised land, as we are. A rite of passage into a dreamland of plenty. The pain was worth it then – and now.

We arrive at the dead of night, in a snowstorm, a freak occurrence, according to our new neighbour, because in general the sea around Orkney acts as a hot-water bottle (or rather, a tepid one, insulating it from extremes of cold and heat). The next morning we aren't sure if it is snow, at first; we stand looking out at it and wondering, until the flakes fall faster and whiter, unmistakable. I want to taste it, my four-year-old says, so I dress her in her hat and coat and Icelandic trousers and she runs around the house I have rented on a hill in Kirkwall collecting mouthfuls from the path, from the bonnet of the car, from the tiny square of lawn. That afternoon, when the sun comes out, we troop along the cobbles, through the slush, brave explorers, buying blankets, towels, saucepans and an old Kenwood mixer for a few pounds each from the much-frequented charity shops that line Victoria Street and Albert Street, on either side of the red sandstone Norse cathedral. I register my daughters at the doctor's, pay my council tax (expensive), read the electricity meter (astronomical), and take the elder one to nursery at the local school.

The school's logo is a Viking ship, there is a Viking ship mural outside and a painted cardboard Viking ship in reception. A notice explains that Years 3 and 4 have recently given a Viking-style longship burial to the school's pet fish, dispatching it to Valhalla – a warrior fish, then – via a ceremonial burning in the local burn. My daughter is put in a group called Selkies. Her school uniform becomes our badge of belonging as we walk around town. 'Selkies are seals who are also humans,' I say as we queue up for ice cream. (The sun has come out with a vengeance.) She nods: 'I know, Mum.'

My husband arrives, and I apply for seasonal jobs with the council, at local hotels, at the fish factory and a florist's. I have a job waiting for me in the south but I want Orkney to claim me too. Since we are only due to stay in Orkney for a brief interlude, I don't want to take away someone else's livelihood. But as it turns out, in the spring and summer, when the islands fill up with tourists and cruise liners tower over the harbours of Kirkwall and Stromness, like the capricious and emotive islands of legend appearing and disappearing at will, everybody needs extra help.

I haven't done this kind of work for a long time, however, and my CV seems way over the top, and way insufficient. I rewrite it, feeling nervous about how it might feel to go back to doing work that requires physical effort as its primary purpose. Maybe motherhood will make the transition easy for me, involving, as it does, much heavy lifting and many too-soon-repeated tasks.

As it is, with every little gesture towards staying rather than moving on, I can taste happiness. (Or is it adventure, the fact of moving somewhere new and different? I am definitely more nomad-Mesolithic than settler-Neolithic in my tendencies.) Happiness or adventure, I can taste it in my mouth like a shard of cold butter as I peg out our washing using four pegs where in London two would do (the wind), as I pick up utility bills in my name from the porch, and bottles of Orkney milk that are delivered to our doorstep. Orkney has a large dairy industry, a legacy of all the cows that were moved here not only during the Neolithic but also to feed the Royal Navy during the Second World War.

Our house, built one hundred years ago by an Orcadian emigré to Canada who made his fortune in the hotel trade, is whitish with a slate roof and a wooden trim under the eaves. It has an echoey feel, which is partly to do with the paucity of our possessions but partly the dimensions of the place. My daughter loves the feel of the wallpaper, which is differently textured in each room: tartan, snowstorm, rosebuds, bark, and where she sleeps, whorled like a shell. The porch floor is tiled in red, yellow and black; the staircase appears to me hotel-grand, with a banister rounded, solid, made from the pine that was shipped over to Orkney from North America. My landlady tells me that the pine gets better with age. She says, 'It rings if you tap it.' She also says that the rowan in the garden is to keep away evil spirits; that every garden in Orkney should have one. *Rawan*, is how she pronounces it.

A hotel on the harbour is advertising for bar and housekeeping staff. I ring: they ask only for my name and age. There are sixty rooms which need daily hoovering and cleaning, the beds straightening or stripping. I am nervous that first morning too, running downhill into town, my raincoat flapping in the wind, past the red cathedral, along King Street, through an alleyway, scooping up a bit of wifi from the library as I run.

I am not expecting to like it but find at first that I do: the exercise, the satisfaction of manual tasks quickly and easily dispatched, of being part of a stern and silent female team. We are thirteen women; no men. Mostly Orcadians, but also three Hungarians (so I am told), all related, and me. Naively, I find it shocking how the seven-day rota changes every week, making it impossible to make other plans and commitments, or to schedule other work. My thoughts are my own, however. The corridors are long, and I walk miles in a morning. Through my headphones I listen to the *Today* programme, feeling, at this distance, how self-absorbed the capital is; in particular, how out of touch with Scotland.

I listen to the radio because nobody speaks much, or at least not to a *soothmoother*, which is what Orcadians call people from beyond the Pentland Firth. *Ferry-loupers* is another name.[18] Our break is from 10 to 10.20, after the breakfast service is over. We pass through the kitchen, allowed to eat whatever the hotel guests have left. (I am scolded one time too many by the cook for taking a banana.) We sit with our porridge and tea in the gloomy bar, the Orcadians conversing among themselves barely at all.

Camaraderie is lacking; chat occurs by chance. Outside the laundry room early one morning as I wait for a pile of kingsize sheets to emerge in warm folds from the press, one of the Hungarian women, Svetlana, tells me she is returning home soon, after three years in Britain. At home, she says, spring is spring, summer is summer. Here in Orkney – her hands fly around her head – everything is disordered. And the wind!

Another morning in the dingy bar, the Hungarians suddenly open up, sea anemones waving at me from the bottom of the seabed, and

I am surrounded by voices explaining their history: how they aren't, strictly speaking, Hungarian at all: how the land they are from had once been Austro-Hungary, then it was Czechoslovakia, then the Soviet Union, now Ukraine.[19] For one hundred years our people didn't go anywhere and changed country four times, says Svetlana. Like Scotland-England, says her sister, who has a degree in history. Like Orkney, I add. (After it was colonized by Vikings, Orkney was part of Norway, then Denmark, then Scotland, then Britain.) How have they, these three women, survived in Orkney? It must be through the close-knit cohesion of their kinship group – as archaeologists would say of social organization in the Neolithic.

The hotel guests are on the upmarket side: business (oil, renewables), tourists, and I wonder about them briefly as I wipe tables and mirrors, empty bins, vacuum around walking boots, sweep away tea stains and sugar crystals from the thrillers and magazines they keep by their beds. Many of the tourists are on Orkney Archaeological Tours.[20] Many, I guess from the style of their footwear and the clothes hanging in the wardrobes, are older than me. Tidier, too. Little about the way they leave their rooms suggests romance. Rarely are they reading books I want to read. I sum them up for myself in the time that it takes to clean a room (five to six minutes), thinking, as I do, about the conclusions archaeologists come to. Don't they also extrapolate vast inferences about unseen humans from random collections of personal things?

Week after week, as I pull off sheets and plump up pillows, I think about the neat little stone houses that Neolithic Orcadians built themselves, embedded in their own luscious waste heaps (middens). At the famous seaside village of Skara Brae, thirteen or so almost identical Neolithic houses are joined by covered passageways, to avoid the scouring cold.[21] The furniture was Ikea-tidy, made of flat-pack stone slabs, which could be moved around and adjusted to size: a central hearth, a showcase dresser opposite the entrance, neat stone beds. The beds are so small, some archaeologists posit that Neolithic people slept sitting up – which seems crazy, for why would anybody do that? But they were still building tiny stone beds in Orkney into the eighteenth century. Nobody seems to know whether they were for children, or if sleep happened in the foetal position, with adults taking turns. You can see the miniature box beds at the Orkney farm museums. Of all the ideas that seem most remote from life today, with its (sexist) kingsize, queen, double, single beds, it is that of people sleeping sitting up in rows, which seem most alien. Maybe the Neolithic concept of sleep was different: brief, and full of dreams.

By now it is mid-May, and the days are eerily long: bright sunlight at ten o'clock at night. My children refuse to go to sleep at all, and I have to overload their curtains with blankets and towels to keep out the sun. On my days off from the hotel I begin to feel possessed by the work I am doing there, as if, in the wide-open spaces of Orkney I might suddenly run up against the sight of myself polishing a mirror, turn a corner on the beach and bang my leg on a hotel chair, sniff the sea-salt and get a spray of Flash up my nose. I cut my hair over the kitchen bin to get rid of the stink of hotel kitchens, and men's aftershave, which billows out of the rooms whose doors I knock on – *Housekeeping!* – but it clings on somehow. I ask myself if I am experiencing the island claustrophobia that people sometimes report. I had never lived on an island before. Or rather, I correct myself, never on an island of this size, because of course, all Britons are island-dwellers. Is the difference merely one of degree? It seems not. The feeling of longing to belong, and longing to set sail, rises and surges within me, like the coming and going of the tide. When I wake in the night, scenes from the hotel rush in like the sea. The puff of foetid air as I tie shut bin bags in the rooms – sperm at worst, tea bags better; the indistinguishable and therefore unsanitary pile of old hotel towels with which we clean bathroom toilets, glasses, taps; the purple-and-green corridor carpets.

There is an influx of Norwegians to the hotel for 17 May. Every year, Orkney celebrates Norway's 1814 declaration of independence from Sweden. The fact that 'Norwegian Constitution Day' is the most important civic event in the islands' calendar says a lot for Orkney's investment in its ancient Nordic history and the feeling one gets here of being part of neither Scotland nor Britain.

Norwegian flags fly from the cathedral side by side with Scotland's and Orkney's (which is almost identical to Norway's) as the Kirkwall Pipe Band play and the Convenor of the Orkney Islands Council, bedecked in a gold chain, gives a speech about the islands' Norse heritage. Inside the cathedral, local primary-school children sing 'Nobilis humilis', the hymn to St Magnus, the Viking-descended earl murdered by his cousin in whose name the cathedral was constructed nine hundred years ago. The hymn was discovered in a thirteenth-century manuscript at Uppsala University in Sweden in 1911. By chance, eight years later, St Magnus's bones were found during restoration work on the cathedral: the shrine to which numberless pilgrims had once made homage had been carefully dismantled at the Reformation and hidden within a red sandstone pillar.

Next come fiddle players from Kirkwall Grammar School, who perform a mixture of Scandinavian and Celtic traditional music: a Norwegian polska, an Orcadian reel, a Burns song, tunes from Nova Scotia and the Western Isles. Orcadians love their own music and its traditions; on these bipolar islands of dark and light, it draws its listeners through the dark phase of the year.

There is a feeling of renaissance in Orkney at the moment: musical, archaeological, environmental, social. Within living memory, for at least the first half of the twentieth century, the archipelago was a quiet place: the kind that young people tried to leave. The two world wars brought an influx of soldiers, prisoners, entertainment and concrete. The wars made the islands ugly, leaving military debris everywhere. I am told by a woman who grew up here, and whose family later moved south, 'A hurricane in '52 blew the worst stuff away.'

Orkney avoided the dramatic rates of depopulation suffered in the late twentieth century by other remote Scottish places thanks only to the discovery of North Sea oil. From the seventies onwards, the islands became comparatively rich, and now, as in the Neolithic, Orkney is the promised land: a utopia for people from 'depressed parts of Britain who move up in search of a better life' (as one island ferryman told me). He was from Blackpool; others decamp from Glasgow, Bolton, Derby, and don't look back. Some complain that southern benefit scroungers use the outlying islands as an easy way of avoiding the demands of the Job Centre, a boat ride away in Kirkwall; or that retirees from England are pushing up house prices and contributing nothing more than strain on the NHS. But it is also undeniable that incomers of all income levels provide energy, and new ideas. Some islands are dominated by Soothmoothers.

Jo Grimond, for example, leader of the Liberal Party, adopted the islands as his home from the moment he won the constituency in 1950, thus bequeathing to the Lib-Dems so-far unstinting Orcadian loyalty. He once described Orkney as a classless society, free of the 'pursuit of status'.[22] It is true that there are none of the vast landholdings that still exist in mainland Scotland and England and that inequality isn't as palpable here as in other parts of the country. There are no private schools, no private healthcare, no luxury shops. The only thing it is easy to spend money on is heating (if you live in an old, leaky house fuel poverty is a big issue), or travel 'outwith' the islands (a Scots word I love). The plainness of Orkney tastes in everything from architecture to dress contributes to the egalitarian feeling. Almost everybody who lives here claims to love it. It is perhaps only those who arrive on a quest for idyllic emptiness, far from society's corrupting compromises, who find Orkney a disappointment.

June comes, and I feel relief like a physical release. The Ness of Brodgar archaeological site is opening up for the summer and I am to be embedded there as resident writer. I will stand in a field, in a pit in the drizzle, my legs coated in mud, raindrops in my hair, to clean – with a trowel this time – what I come to think of as a Neolithic caravanserai.

The Ness of Brodgar site was discovered only in 2003, when a farmer ploughing the spit of land near Maeshowe between the two stone circles pulled up an incised stone slab. Subsequent surveys thrilled and shocked the world's archaeological community by revealing what the Neolithic people had hidden for thousands of years: a huge walled complex of overlapping buildings on the land that guards the approach to Maeshowe. The space appeared to be neither domestic nor martial. What, then – *sacred*? A ceremonial place of pilgrimage and celebration, of communal eating and singing, praying and fucking (probably), tribal pledges and marriage vows, exchanges of genes and knowledge. There was colour, carving and a vast number of animals, butchered, eaten and then ritually buried, within the walls. The head archaeologist, Nick Card, who now lives next to the Ness, nicknamed the largest building the 'temple'.[23] Others think this site was a place of learning – a Neolithic university, perhaps. Since Maeshowe took an estimated one hundred thousand person-hours to build, maybe the Ness housed visiting workers; a ceremonial feasting hall like the *langar* at Amritsar's Golden Temple, where pilgrims come together to eat after volunteering on site. I think of the Sufi shrines I visited along the River Indus in Pakistan: epicentres of everything, including emancipation and release, in a country without dance halls or pubs. I remember the nights I spent on the slopes of Mount Kailash in Tibet during the three-day circumambulation; how I was kept awake by snow-drips from the roof and the drunken carousing of my fellow pilgrims. Maybe *this* was such a place. A hotel in a sacred landscape.

Orkney's public Neolithic monuments did not cease *in medias res*, like Pompeii. They, too, were deliberately decommissioned: a set of cleaners sent in to erase them from the landscape by infilling every monument with midden. Around the edge of the Ness site, in the entrance passageways, they placed votive deposits: cattle skulls and deer carcasses, the remnants of a giant final feast.

Now all that midden has to be removed. In Victorian times, they did this with shovels. Today it happens with mini trowels.

Midden is lovely when displayed in cross-section, with all its changing layers and colours. Everything that biodegrades turns an intense brown-black. The orange-red bands are peat ash. Charcoal glistens black.

I am supposed to be writing, but instead I dig, at a trench beyond the walls of the main complex, where part of the midden is overlaid by a chaotic jumble of 'hill wash', detritus of Neolithic life and landscape unceremoniously swirled downhill by a rainstorm or river some four thousand years ago. All this needs to be scraped away, layer by layer, to reveal walls, structures, deposits.

Time ripples weirdly in Orkney. First, the original, still-mysterious Neolithic buildings; then the seasonal global caravan of archaeologists trying to fathom them out; plus the hordes of visitors coming to watch the unfathoming. Neolithic people were building up from the landscape, impressing their mark upon nature; archaeology is always downwards, inwards. It can feel strangely reductive, to kneel in the dirt, nose pressed in the mud, scraping through other people's rubbish like a detritivore. *Scrape, scrape, scrape*; excising evocative slivers of rich, dark midden, that semi-ritualized, deliberately deposited rubbish of Neolithic life – a prized substance as late as medieval times in Britain. *Scrape, scrape, scrape*; wondering about the nature and purpose of long-ago-discarded lives –

Until the moment you find something. Then it feels like glory.

The first interesting thing I find is commonplace, though not to me: a little star of flint, chipped off a larger knife or arrowhead. That tiny thing with its milky gleam – waste left by a Neolithic flint-knapper – snags my attention as effectively as the tool it came from must have scraped down cattle hides and divided up portions of the flesh for children. It is addictive, the almost totally random process of finding things, unearthing them from the place where they were laid, or thrown, or lost, so many years ago. A day later, my trowel scrapes something, the earth falls away, and a piece of smooth greyish stone the size of my finger rolls towards me. Behind it, in the soil, is its perfect self-impression. I pick it up slowly, as if afraid that if I blink or cough it might vanish and be lost again, this time for ever.

Where is the word in our language to describe the time travel of a thing from its first life – in this case, the Neolithic – to its second, the present? Or for the feeling that this movement evokes in the finder? (The sense of possession.) For thousands of years, since that stone was first picked up off the shore of the nearby loch in its raw form and whittled into new life as a tool, it had lain in the soil, and then my trowel uncovered it and it became something else. WORKED STONE TOOL, I write on the small-finds bag. Anne, head of finds, speculates that even after it was broken the spatula may have had a 'second life, or second job': she makes me touch it, to feel how it is silky on one side, rough on the other. Perhaps it had been used to smooth down pottery or objects made of wood.

After three weeks on the fringes, I move inside the sacrosanct complex itself, to Trench P (not romantically named), where a curious little anomaly of a building is being uncovered. They have already found many pieces of broken pottery, mostly grooved ware, with its distinctive design of parallel lines (incised in the clay by spatulas such as mine). The soil I am scraping away at has strange indentations. For hours I remove feather after feather of soil with my trowel. At last I ask the supervisor, Claire, to take a look. She thinks it is another piece of pot: probably very thin, and friable, and likely to crumble. She is right. When we lift it out the red disc, barely a centimetre thick, breaks into pieces.

But then, as I am clearing out the soil beneath, I notice two solid chunks of pottery with what seems to me a design in black and red. 'Applied ware,' Claire says when I show her the first piece, but when I bring her the second and she sees how the two pieces fit together, her mind, with its knowledge of the Neolithic's ceramic forms, sees something: a small, shallow piece with a 'waisted' outline. There is a buzz of excitement. Other archaeologists are called over to look and to proclaim. Later, Claire tells me that only four others like it have been found in the country. Two are from Stonehenge. She thinks it is probably an incense burner.

An incense burner . . . While living, humans are earthbound, but smoke represents an escape, a metamorphosis, a change of form, upward; just as, in the opposite transmission, sunlight pours into Maeshowe to mark the turning of the year. That little incense burner perhaps played a ceremonial role at the Ness, helping to mark a ritual progression through the landscape, or incarnating, for humans, the inevitable and anticipated moment of their own metamorphosis. Or maybe it merely made one of those long, stone-roofed rooms smell nice. (In the Neolithic, they burned poppy, hemp, even amber, as medicine, fragrance, narcotics.)[24]

At the end of the summer, Nick hosts a party for the dig at his farmhouse on the Ness site. It is late August, long past midsummer and yet, in retrospect, that evening in that land in the midst of those monuments with their palpable past and the light of the islands falling in our eyes and on our skin is the nearest I have come to the fairy feeling of another dimension breaking through our own. *Simmer dim* is the Shetland phrase for the northern islands' endless summer twilight. It feels surreal.

Nick opens up a barn for my daughters and me to camp in. We go to sleep, the three of us, wrapped in that gossamer of earth and light.

I think about those enigmatic and energetic Neolithic colonizers constantly during the time I live in Orkney. It is impossible not to; the monuments they built as a way of organizing the world are still among the most visible features of Orkney's landscape. Orkney's Mainland has a tomb seemingly for each cardinal point of the year, this one catching the rising spring equinox sun, that the autumn equinox sunset. Neolithic spiritual tourism? Competing clans? Alone, with friends, with my children, I climb hillsides, trek along coasts, edge along clifftops, crawl through entrance passages enpuddled with rainwater. Each tomb is different. Some have vertical drops into the clammy dark interiors; some are rectangular (the early ones); the later ones are round and womb-like. None of them compares to Maeshowe in either space or style. All feel hallowed. Maeshowe alone feels central.

Until very recently – before pylons, tall ships and fast-moving cars – the architecture of Orkney's Neolithic must have bristled with power. And although the timespan between Neolithic monuments can be great, the monuments have always meant something to later generations. During the Neolithic itself, stone circles were sometimes transformed into cairns (as may have happened at Maeshowe; an incorporation of the phallic within the feminine, possibly). The cairns themselves were repeatedly modified by what was put in and taken out: whole human skeletons, lone skulls and thigh bones; the beaks and talons and claws of sea eagles; the remains of dogs and otters.

Often, during the final 'decommissioning', they were sealed up with midden, rubble, or (as in one of the cairns on Papa Westray's Holm) with fish bones and limpet shells,[25] supposedly for ever, for reasons unknown. Perhaps the people moved away; maybe there was famine or climate change or coastal erosion. Maybe new people came in and the monuments needed to be saved from disrespect by being hidden. Possibly, decommissioning represented a monument's death (and therefore lasting fame), as time stopped and memories were enshrined.[26] Time – marked by the passage of the sun and moon, the tides, the harvests, the births and deaths and life stages of the current generation as well as the deep reverence of ancestors – was a constant preoccupation. The stones of circles and cairns may have represented the ancestors themselves. Perhaps they *were* the ancestors. Much later, the great builders of the Iron Age, and even the Vikings, often set their towers and feasting halls alongside, indicating awe and respect.

With every summer excavation the estimate of how many people lived on Orkney during the Neolithic goes up. Archaeologists currently guess at between ten and twenty thousand people[27] – a huge number for the time, as if the islands were Manchester and the rest of Britain were Minchinhampton. While the population of Britain has increased exponentially since then, in Orkney there are still around twenty thousand souls. And although there have been many new influxes since Neolithic times, recent genetic studies suggest that the indigenous population is ancient and discrete – a people apart from others in the British Isles. Orkney has the highest rate of multiple sclerosis in the world, an anomaly once thought to have something to do with paltry winter sunshine at northern latitudes. But Orcadians spend longer outside than people in Glasgow. So the cause is now deemed to be 'multifactor' – meaning 'mysterious' – and connected somehow to isolation. On an island, even an archipelago, it only takes one rogue gene for the statistics of disease to be amplified out of all proportion.[28]

Despite all the population shifts and explosions of the past five thousand years, the question of who is *indigenous* to Orkney is constantly asserted, here, as on other British islands, in ways that feel as primal as they are unsubtle. If there is an elite, it is made up of those who have lived here longest. (Or of all the many archaeologists, maybe.) It is not impossible to become an honorary Orcadian, as Grimond proved; on some islands, the famous Orkney dynamism is driven by incomer enthusiasm. But the transitory nature of some island populations – made up of those who arrive from the south and find it doesn't work – can be destabilizing and annoying. A man on Hoy, where I lived, himself an incomer, spoke only to people who'd lived there for three winters. He never spoke to me.

We move to the island of Hoy during the summer. We are forced to move, because our landlady in Kirkwall has sold the house, but we are glad to go. Archaeologists think that the point of the huge monuments of the Neolithic was the slow, communal process of their construction, giving a community or tribe holy focus and purpose. To my surprise, during the eleven months we spend in Hoy, it is exactly this that I fall half in love with: the intoxicating, suffocating intensity of community life; the great things that are hewn from chance meetings in the shop, on the boat, by the seashore. Like a play, an Elizabethan one in repertoire, economy of population means that everybody has to double up. I experience this myself, becoming a firefighter, school cook and creative-writing teacher. I join the choir, curate public art events, cook for the old people's club at school. Around me, love stories, feuds, hopes, losses, lives, intersect.

It is not just Orkney's Mainland – its outer islands were also branded by the Neolithic. Eday has one of Orkney's tallest megaliths, the lichen-covered Setter stone. Rousay 'has the densest concentration of Neolithic chambered cairns in Britain',[29] all of them outdone by the gigantic communal tomb on the seashore, as huge as a small-island school. On North Ronaldsay there is a standing stone twice my height and pierced by a hole, which is still used, as the Odin stone was, for hand-fasting (marriage) and other New Year's promises. My daughters and I go for the weekend, flying in on one of the tinny, epic island planes, to peep through the stone (the hole too high, they too small, for handshakes) and climb the diamond-like lighthouse. We see the stone dyke as we arrive – so low, it is like being on a magic carpet. A feat from a storybook long ago, it encircles the entire island, annually constructed and reconstructed, even now, by the community, to keep the seaweed-eating sheep on the foreshore.

The adjacent and once-conjoined islands of Westray, Papa Westray and the Holm, meanwhile, echo and enclose each other: a Neolithic seaside village (with Bronze Age sauna), a tidal island used for sacred rites, Europe's oldest standing house (of heartbreaking neatness), and most visible and dramatic of all, an island to the east where only the dead live: of not one but three chambered tombs.

Hoy is the hilly island ('high' in old Norse) with ancient woodland ('the oldest natural habitat left in Orkney', warns a notice titled *WILDFIRE* up on the wall of the fire station office). At one end of this valley is the Atlantic-facing seaside hamlet of Rackwick, a place so transfused with light that the Orcadian poet George Mackay Brown called it a 'resurrection'. He likened Lyness, where we live, and which was the navy's headquarters during both world wars, to a 'Yukon shanty town after the gold rush'.[30] The navy left its mark in a whole portfolio of decaying concrete structures, as well as numberless wooden huts that were gradually requisitioned, or recycled, or allowed to fall apart.[31] (Since we also have the old island dump along the beach from us, the tide washes up all kinds of interesting things – painted pottery, twisted metal; once, a little glass bottle tragically labelled 'Lung Tonic'.)

At the entrance to Rackwick valley, in the shadow of Ward Hill, is a Neolithic chamber, unique in Britain, because it was rock-cut into a boulder. Archaeologists call it a 'tomb' for convenience, but I come to think of it as something else – a sonic healing house, a dreaming chamber. What the Neolithic carvers made was three neat spaces the size of single beds, one slightly raised up above the others, with a stone pillow.[32] The chamber has been known, at least since medieval times, as the 'Dwarfie stone'.[33]

Only when I take my children to the Dwarfie stone that summer do I realize how blasé I have become about the brilliance of Neolithic engineers. The boulder is too high for my four-year-old to climb, but she makes me heave her up and stands astride it like a warrior, to echo her voice up into the hills and down the valley to the ocean. It is the baby, though, who discovers the chamber's resonant acoustic. She can't speak English yet; but we are her echo. As we coo and ahh the rock chamber gives back our noise with a resonance that is surely deliberate.

In September I become a once-a-week cook in my daughter's island school. I try to persuade the kids, some incomers, some Orcadians, to eat the delicious North Sea haddock, cod and pollock that is trucked over to the island weekly for their delectation. The children devour spaghetti Bolognese, beef stew, mince and tatties. Very few will eat anything from the sea.

My husband goes diving for our supper in the calm little bay where we are living, just up from the ferry. When he emerges, shuddering but triumphant, clutching an armful of 'clams', as Orcadians call scallops, it is to argue through chattering teeth that by moving into the vicinity of this abundance we are doing something really ancient: using the seashore as a giant free larder.

Mesolithic humans left shell middens around the coasts of the world as they walked, but from as early as Neolithic times in Orkney there was a drop-off in fish consumption; they ate a paltry amount compared to earlier beachcombers or subsequent deep-sea fishing Vikings.[34] Orkney's rich Neolithic farmers feasted on red meat, by preference. By chance, or geographical continuity (Orkney's still-lush farmland), this holds true today. Weirdly for a coastal nation, Britons do not eat much fish in general and the majority of our deep-sea wealth is exported. Hoy's creel fishermen (there have been women in the past, but not currently) make their living sending green crab to Portugal (for soup and stew), lobster to Spain and female brown crab to China. While we are on

Hoy, China's taste for crab pushes the price up from 89 pence a kilo to £3.50.

Contemporary Orcadians call the food of low tide 'ebb-meat', and it is still associated with poverty: a starvation diet. This attitude seems to be fairly regularly attested throughout British history – as in *The Tempest*, when Prospero threatens Ferdinand with a diet of mussels (freshwater ones, at that). One night, as summer turns to autumn, John Budge, farmer and Hoy pier-master, comes for dinner at our place. He weeps as he remembers ploughing the croft across the burn from us as a young man. His cousins had lived there, and he found that he was turning over not good black earth but mounds of limpet shells. It meant that the family had once fallen on hard times.

John Budge and I are in the island choir. He has a lovely voice, his fisherman brother writes songs, and both perform in island concerts and ceilidhs. I wonder how far back this bit of Orcadian gene-genius extends. In the nineties, an archaeologist called Aaron Watson made some acoustic investigations of Orkney's Neolithic monuments and came up with the theory that the stone circles produced formidable echoes; the human voice seemed to make the Dwarfie stone's 'massive stone block, and the air within it . . . shake vigorously';[35] while Maeshowe itself was probably capable of creating standing waves of sound which mutated and magnified the sound of the human voice. Perhaps the gap at the top of the door-boulder was a sound-box. Maybe there was infrasound, for hallucinations, and smoke pillars, for visual effect.

It's a theory that well suits modern Orkney. It seems apt to see places like Maeshowe and the landscape around it not just as temples to the sun and resting places for the dead but also as carnival spaces for the living. That autumn I invite Sink, a band from Edinburgh, to come over for a 'Neolithic Resonancy' and collaborate with the island choir in a public concert. The Resonancy was born the previous summer, on the northern isle of Sanday, where Quoyness, the magnificent, Maeshowe-type chambered cairn next to the sea, is open day and night. Sink, my baby and I camped on the beach. The tomb was closed up thousands of years ago, the entrance passage sealed shut with earth and stones. When it was excavated in the nineteenth century, the skeletons of ten adults and five children were found. (In the Neolithic, adults lived only to the age of thirty or forty; by those standards, I have already lived beyond my span.) Frustratingly, as at Maeshowe, modern archaeology has interfered with Neolithic design: they smashed through the roof to install a glass light-box, presumably for the benefit of tourists. It's hard to know whether this vandalism has changed the acoustics as well as the quality of darkness.[36] But we entered the murky darkness and as the violin began its music we felt the shape of those damp stones with our minds and hands.

Kristin, who once ran an all-female Shakespeare company, joins with Sink and me to experiment with Maeshowe's acoustics. Early one morning, before the site is open, we crowd in: nine musicians, ten vocal students, Kristin, my baby, two archaeologists and me. As we chant, Kristin closes her eyes and hears the music of the spheres. I think about womb-shaped ceremonial spaces. Sink finds the bass resonance most rewarding. Kristin is transported by the high female notes. George, our archaeologist friend, splits his sides laughing.

These noise experiments become a public concert on Hoy, funded by the electricity generated by the island's community wind turbine and sold back to the grid. The concert takes place – old power meeting new, the departing year inaugurating the following – in the giant 12,000-ton oil tank that Hoy's Scapa Flow Museum uses as an overflow gallery. Erected in 1917, it is the last of the sixteen-strong troupe of tanks left here by two world wars.[37] In this dim metal space, the tank's leaky roof makes sunlight, sub-Maeshowe, into camera obscuras of the passing clouds.

Already, by November, the high Hoy hills are covered in snow; there are wild, thrilling storms, monsoon-esque downpours and frequent rainbows stretching from one nearby island to another. Rain hits the roof of our one-storey house like a thousand Norse arrows. Walking along the pebbly beach of our bay is to tread across artworks of punk seaweed dip-dyed orange, red and yellow and strewn there like the hennaéd beards of a thousand pious hajis. There is more snow in December, and when we walk out in the bright sunshine I find that the car has broken down; my husband is away again and the girls and I are rescued by our kind neighbour, Max. (With hindsight, the serendipity of this burgeoning friendship is almost alarming; Max and his wife, Jill, become the warp and weft of our time on Hoy – and yet our meeting was the product of random proximity.)

A friend from the south comes to stay and goes swimming, naked, in our little bay. So I follow him in: most mornings from then on, rain or snow, one hundred strokes through the seaweed fronds.

There is a storm, and the wind lifts my landlady's glass tabletop and smashes it into a million stars on the terrace. The days swirl with darkness and light as if some god is marbling the sky. The children encounter the elements fearlessly, cheeks red, noses running.

Every day that winter the children and I collect shells and stones: striped, heart-shaped, bespeckled like the Milky Way overhead. My elder daughter takes the stones home and scribbles on them with her crayons, a homage to their beauty that is only a little more untidy than the abstract carvings made over the doors of the cells in one of the cairns on the burial island off Papa Westray. ('Did they write in English?' she asked as we felt our way along this Neolithic hotel corridor of the dead; she was learning to write. 'No one knows if it's writing or not,' I said. 'They did these drawings long before English was invented.' In that still, damp gloom, I felt her sense of the world cracking open to reveal new and unexpected vistas.)

Neolithic artists used Hoy-mined haematite as crayons – yellows, reds.[38] Neolithic tools – flints, mace heads and axes – polished, carved, coloured, are still being found on Orkney's beaches or pulled from its archaeological digs. In the past, Orcadians would hide them in their roofs as protection against Thor's thunderbolts. Today they are displayed in museums: miniature works of art, smooth to hold, intense with beauty.

From the privileged vantage point of our warm, hearth-centric modern wooden house, I am transfixed by the Orkney winter. It is physical: the buffeting by the wind, the visual transformation caused by snow, the careful building of our home fires. But the exhilaration of that winter also has something to do with the sunshine at Maeshowe.

One clear sunny January day three weeks after winter solstice I watch the skies, and then, at ten to two, last chance, I drive the children down to the car ferry and over to Mainland. We reach Maeshowe in an exhilarated flurry. The skies are perfect. As always, I long for the twenty-first century to treat this extraordinary gift from the Neolithic with more reverence. There is a metal railing at the back of the chamber which obscures the passage of the sunshine across the wall; I have to implore the guide to turn off the lights. I wish for the silence and sanctity accorded to concert halls and cathedrals. At last, the guide, the tourists and my daughters walk outside, and for a few moments – barely a minute – I have a visceral sense of how powerful it must have been, five thousand years ago, to be solemnly awash in Maeshowe's winter light.

I sit in darkness for a moment and then, suddenly, a reddish flash of sunlight hits the back wall. It is the 'flashing sun' effect that I had only previously heard about: a last offering from the skies, and the Neolithic engineers, before the Earth turns and sunshine will not enter Maeshowe for another year.[39] It is an omen, surely; a warning; later, I interpret it as a sign of the danger which lies ahead.

From our kitchen I watch the bright light of the Flotta flare, the tower burning waste gases from the oil terminal across the water. When I read George Mackay Brown's first novel, *Greenvoe* (1972), I was convinced that it was written about Flotta: a sinister, unnamed industrial company takes over a small Orkney island, forcing most of its population to leave. Flotta people say that, self-evidently, the opposite occurred: oil brought Flotta people home, it created jobs, it brought in good money. On Burns Night we catch the free boat over to our forlorn-rich island neighbour. Anyway, I am told over haggis, GMB (as the writer is known) is too highbrow for Orkney; his fancy prose suits Soothmoother tastes. Everybody here prefers the comic Willick novels that Davy Sinclair, the Flotta postman, wrote about the coming of the oil-men. But I agree with GMB: what happened to Flotta seems strange to me, unnatural.

It is undeniable, however, that for forty years, the length of a Neolithic life, oil revenue has made the Orkney Islands Council rich. It has provided jobs and prospects and social housing. It has also made Orkney, as the local MP puts it, 'one of the most carbon-heavy communities anywhere in the UK'. All that is changing now. Where the end of the last century drew oil from the sea, the beginning of this has brought riches on the wind.[40] Everywhere you look, white-winged turbines turn slowly on island hillsides, a lofty priesthood dispensing hermetic Neolithic rites. The new fashion is to try and convert tidal or wind-generated electricity into hydrogen-fuel cells for mass local use – to power buses or ferries, for example. While I was working in the hotel in Kirkwall a friend who runs Arcola Energy in London sent his team north to install a hydrogen-fuel cell in the harbour; I could see it from the top-floor rooms. The fuel cell is powered by fifty-nine white cylinders of hydrogen, made via electrolysis from the wind and tidal power produced on the northerly island of Eday (the seas there are rough) and wind from the nearby island of Shapinsay. Ferries transport the hydrogen to Kirkwall, where it is taken either to the harbour-side fuel cell, to be turned into electricity to power ferries at night, or to a nearby refuelling station, to be pumped into council vehicles; hydrogen-fuelled ferries are the next step. Hydrogen production on Flotta itself (Flotta Hydrogen Hub) is now being taken seriously as an option to overcome the trauma of oil decommissioning.

By March the days are beginning to lengthen. I watch the sun passing overhead, and it gives me a dizzy feeling, as if I can feel our island turning. I find that I miss the dark afternoons of winter and the feeling of having been cocooned by the weather. The freezing star-filled nights are rich and glorious and potent. I have become a moon-watcher. But it is easy to appreciate winter from inside a well-glazed house. I am not a farmer, up at first light and back after dark. My neighbour Max built our house from wood and glass. It is full of warmth, all year round.

Max and I climb Ward Hill during a snowfall. He and Jill moved up here as young hippies in the seventies; he learned his building trade on the hoof, repairing houses all over the islands with Nick, who later became head archaeologist at the Ness. Recently, Max pioneered the installation of the island's community wind turbine. The council has proposed putting a giant wind farm on Hoy, and the island internet is ablaze with dissenting opinion. We discuss it as we walk up the steep-sided hill called Cuilags; as we walk down again through the wind, across great patches of snow, past the white mountain hares who barely move as we approach, to the top of St John's Head, the highest sea cliff in Britain. Haematite was mined here during the Neolithic.[41] We walk back through Berriedale, the clump of trees that is Britain's most northerly naturally occurring woodland: rowans, birch, aspen, hazel.

It is disorienting to know a place only by its tarmacked roads; better to explore it on foot. Better (stranger) still to explore by water a place you have known from land. In early spring, when the creel fishing starts again, John Budge's red-haired nephews take me out in their fishing boat. We sail up the west side of Hoy, under its gigantic cliffs; between 8 a.m. and 2 p.m. they haul up numberless pots, spilling the island's wild, unknowable underwater life on to the deck: vivid, lapis-blue lobsters speckled with golden suns.

Since the snowfall, I've been swimming through the tactile fronds of kelp that were surely the 'sluggish, gelatinous seas' that Avienius described in his fourth-century poem and guide to the coasts of Europe from Iberia to Scotland, *Ora maritima* ('And the sluggish water of the inert sea stands still / . . . among the currents').[42] I love the feel of those plants on my skin. But I've heard too many stories from fellow firefighters – of daft, half-drowned tourists – to stray far from shore. Instead I watch the moon emptying out our little bay and filling it once more, and feel awe at the daily spectacle of change and renewal. I watch the weather transform the hills in the north from black charcoal sketches to blue-and-green woodcuts to photographs appearing out of darkroom fluid in bright brown and yellow – beauty occurring right there, in this everyday metamorphosis. But the Budges' deep-sea haul is an art-form no human can make. So island-bound have I been I sometimes wonder if I've got Stockholm Syndrome.

Now it is summer again my husband wants to move back south. He has been travelling out of the islands for work. He wants to take his turn living in a place of his choice – in the English house where he partly grew up. I, in turn, will accrue credit for the next place I want to live; already, I have an idea for a book about Peru. Nevertheless, there is a violence in leaving somewhere you love. I feel a part of myself being ripped away; I have felt this feeling before.

I weep as I pack up all the books, papers and seashore detritus we have accumulated over the year: barnacle-covered bottles, pieces of wave-worn seaglass (it takes forty years to make a piece of seaglass, somebody told me), seashells, seaweed, and mini dolmens decorated by the children. I purge unwanted toys and unread books, give away what I can and take the rest back (in most cases) to the excellent charity shops of Kirkwall. At Skara Brae, the people emptied their houses of belongings when they left in 2500 BC. They left behind what seem to be ritual deposits: the skull of a bull on a bed, a dish of haematite, a jar of hallucinogenic henbane.[43]

What will we leave behind? Only our midden. I wonder how it will be judged, in five thousand years' time: the imported plums and peppers from Lidl in the compost heap, the shell mound of scallops, mussels, cockles, whelks and limpets on the beach. (My baby loves limpets; she can eat twenty of them in one sitting.)

For a week, I vacuum and scour. I rub grubby fingermarks off windows; stains of little hands from furniture and walls.

It is June, and I am almost done decommissioning when a visitor arrives from the south. Héloïse is a composer and singer with the all-female Deep Throat Choir. When I take her to the Ring of Brodgar and the Standing Stones of Stenness, she taps the megaliths to hear the notes they make. Archaeologists say that the stones at Brodgar, geologically distinct from each other, were brought from different parts of Orkney, emblems, perhaps, of different tribes. Certainly they are visually distinct. Some have almost-human profiles. Héloïse says that each stone has a different note. From then on, I imagine them singing.

On the way home through Kirkwall, outside the grocer's shop, William Shearer's, we cross paths with Kristin again. She also has a musician friend staying and when I mention the Dwarfie stone's curious acoustic, Kristin, who is eighty and possessed of an undiminished energy, wants to sing the Selkie Song with us there. This year, we have lived alongside a family of seals in our bay[44] and I want to sing to them too.

Inside the Dwarfie stone the next day, the strange, hypnotic sounds of this melodic love song between a woman and a seal weave around us from rock to air. Kristin sits outside, on the boulder which was the door. Above us, in exhilaration (or parental anxiety) the sea eagles that have returned to Hoy to nest, for the first time in 150 years, fly along the valley.[45]

That night, when the eagles are asleep, Héloïse and I return to the Dwarfie stone with our sleeping bags and mats. We cross the valley on foot in the moonlight. Had not the Neolithic carvers suggested *dreams*, not death, by carving a pillow on one of the body-shaped spaces inside the stone?[46]

Héloïse and I go to sleep that night awed and peaceful, encased in the stone's tranquillity. The chamber faces west, and we gaze down the valley towards Rackwick, watching the hillsides darken to blue and grey and black. I had never before lived in a place where the dreaming and the art, the monuments and thought of one historical age have marked it so completely. I know that I will wake at first light with those dreams in my soul.

PART TWO

She Encounters the Islands of Women

*Even today Britain in its madness practises
magic with such grand rituals,
one would think she gave it to the Persians.*

Pliny the Elder, *Natural History*, first century AD[1]

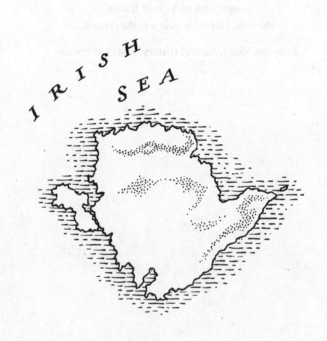

I R I S H   S E A

2.

Anglesey

Druids (200 BC–AD 78)

Now comes history. Now comes text and trauma.

In AD 60, Roman troops marched across Wales, through Snowdonia and over the Menai Strait to conquer the Druids' holy island of Anglesey (known as Mona to the Romans; it is still called Môn in Welsh). Druids were the religious elite of the pan-European Celtic people, whose culture the Roman empire had set out to conquer. The island of Anglesey, in Britain, was particularly apposite for annihilation, because it was believed to be where the Celts sent the Druid leadership for their education. The Druids may have revered other islands – the similarly named Isle of Man or Danish Møn. Plutarch writes that 'many scattered and deserted islands' off the coast of Britain are inhabited by 'holy men who were held inviolate by the Britons'.[1] But Anglesey is the one singled out in Roman report.

It is unclear whether the Druids came to Anglesey from all over Europe for their education, or were indigenous to the island, or descendants of Orkney's Neolithic population – or all of these at once? Probably the latter. The Celts had an excellent and rapid inter-tribe vocal telegraph system,[2] which is probably how Emperor Claudius came to be greeted, upon his arrival on the south coast of Britain, by kings from Orkney. It seems likely that the Druid class was not only 'pan-national' – drawn from across the Celtic tribes of northern Europe – but also pan-historical. Alfred Watkins, who coined the concept of ley lines with his book *The Old Straight Track* (1925), about the legacy of the Neolithic and the Iron Age in Britain's landscape, writes that the 'astronomer priests had the Druids as successors, and all the learning, religion, poetry and science of

35

the community centred around them'.[3] For archaeologist Barry Cunliffe, too, the Druids were 'the inheritors of ancient wisdoms' with 'roots deep in prehistory, possibly as far back as the 2nd millennium'.[4] If the Romans were right, Anglesey was regarded by the Druids much as the early Orcadians viewed their islands: it was their sacred place and stronghold.

Anglesey is a green island, a placid oasis between the mountains and the sea. Like Orkney, it is low-lying, with upland only beyond its watery peripheries. It is especially watery – nowadays studied by geographers on account of being heavily speckled with ponds and lakes. Water seems to have been integral to the function of the Druids' cult, here, and in the rest of Europe. When the Romans conquered southern France, they auctioned off the sacred lakes to entrepreneurs in order that the gold which had been ritually deposited there as part of the Celtic religion could be extracted.[5] What a scandal.

Today there is something supernaturally contented-seeming about Anglesey's tranquil green fields and pretty coastal towns, coming up so unexpectedly after the dark mountain fastness of Snowdon. Isolation on this low level has benefits. There is pride in speaking Welsh first (60 per cent speak it here, compared to 21 per cent in the rest of Wales), and sounding, in English, Scouse. The nearest proper town is Bangor on the mainland, where young people go for dancing, old people for shopping and Anglesey's Muslims for prayers. But while the island is less densely populated than the rest of Wales – meaning fewer road accidents and shorter waits for hospital appointments – there is deprivation: in 2008, the Welsh government reported that in Anglesey 'the majority of its areas are more deprived than the Wales average'.[6]

The Indus journeys I go back to in my head are those I made by foot – through the tribal lands of north-west Pakistan; to the source of the river in Tibet. There is something sacred about walking long distances; the ancient pace brings mental tranquillity. Here, too, I will be walking in: as an outsider – a Roman, a foreign Celt – carrying with me that duality (conquest/preservation), as we all do, as a species, currently.

I am searching for mental tranquillity also because I am living back in England again – a crackerbox country, so it seemed from the vantage point of Orkney. There are aspects of our English life which feel wrong to me, certain stresses, certain strains; but their provenance, their depths, I cannot fathom. It will be good to get away, and think, in the Druids' holy island.

In Snowdonia there is an Iron Age hill fort (or village) called Dinas Emrys, spoken and written of in Welsh mythology. Dinas Emrys means 'Hill Fort of Ambrosia' and it is mentioned in several medieval Welsh compilations of ancient legends, those strange, wonderful, convoluted stories of nation-building, Roman legions and Saxons, of giants, magicians and dragons.[7] In *The Mabinogi* – one of the Britannias' few indigenous literary sources of Celtic lore and culture – Britain is harassed by dragons. The king, Lludd, is told by his brother Llevelys, who is married to the Queen of Gaul, to 'map the country from top to bottom'. He must identify a place to lock the dragons up: that is, Dinas Emrys, either in the actual lake at the foot of the hill or in the mythical pool of mead in the fort itself, the existence of which was pleasingly proven, in the 1950s, by the excavation of a large cistern of Iron Age date.[8] A later tale then has King Vortigern being advised by the boy magician Merlin that his castle keeps falling down because two dragons are fighting beneath the hill – an inherited memory of an earlier tale and its enshrining in folklore.

The settlement guards one of the main passes through Snowdonia and must have been of great strategic value to Iron Age Britons. In *The Ancient Paths: Discovery of the Lost Map of Celtic Europe* (2013), Graham Robb plotted the major Celtic settlements of Iron Age Gaul and Britain according to what he claims is a mathematically precise network of solstice lines. One of these, originating in Oxford, runs right through Dinas Emrys to Anglesey and on to the tiny island beyond which is called Holyhead, an English translation of the Welsh name, its primordial sanctity slipping between languages and ages.

I cut myself a thin but sturdy oak staff from the glade at the bottom of Dinas Emrys and begin to climb the hill. It is sunset and the valley is at peace. My feet crunch hazelnut shells, the hillside glitters with quartz, crows caw as I pass beneath their trees. Down below, in the field I've just crossed, the farmer and his young daughter arrive on a quad bike to check on their pregnant sheep. At the summit, I walk along the narrow flint blade of the fortification, imagining the great vat of mead.

I make my bed in the medieval stone keep of Dinas Emrys, with my oak staff at my side for safety, my head poking out of my bivvy bag. It is a full moon that night. I lie as still as I can in the lucent hilltop silence, but every noise I make – the rustling of my coat, a polite cough – feels clumsy. I gaze up at the stars, thinking of the Celtic practice of head-hunting (the temple at Roquepertuse in southern France had stone pillars and niches specially designed to hold human skulls; Diodorus Siculus describes heads embalmed in cedar oil). But in the middle of the night it is dragons that wake me. There is a thunderous noise and a fearsome orange glow: fighter planes, roaring over the Strait to the RAF airbase on Anglesey. I fall asleep again and, if I dream, it is of dragons' mead. I wake up feeling refreshed and druidical.

It is an easy day's walk north-west towards Anglesey and, before that, Caernarfon, the town with a Roman fort, Segontium, which overlooks the Menai Strait, built after the holy island's conquest. All morning, I tramp in more or less complete silence, through Beddgelert, up the valley past Snowdon: along footpaths, through a nature reserve, and then, in mid-afternoon, when the last tourist steam train passes, along the track of the Welsh West Highland Railway. The parallel lines feel Roman: single-minded, undeviating.

As a child, I was made to recite the Lord's Prayer in Welsh in the primary school in the Gower Peninsula where we lived while my father was studying to be a social worker at Swansea University; and that afternoon, from a shop I pass, I buy a book, *Speak Welsh*. The young woman who sells it to me speaks the prayer for me, and patriarchal and foreign though it is (at least to my Celtic forebears), I feel moved by the music of the language, as if it is stirring some long-ago part of my memory. She compliments my accent in Welsh and I feel the spirit of my four-year-old self warmed anew by her encouragement.

There is a mesmerizing story in *The Mabinogi* called 'The Dream of Maxen'; it has the surreal quality of something gleaned in the hypnagogic state from the colonized hippocampus of British history. The emperor of Rome dreams that he travels across the sea:

> Then it seemed that he came to the fairest island in the whole world, and he traversed the island from sea to sea, even to the furthest shore of the island . . . And thence he beheld an island in the sea, facing this rugged land. And between him and this island was a . . . mountain[9]

This is Britain, and Anglesey, and the mountain Snowdon. 'And at the mouth of the river he beheld a castle . . . and the gate of the castle was open.' Inside is the most beautiful woman in the world – so beautiful that when he wakes and cannot find her he falls into a depression. He sends out messengers all over the world; eventually, after much searching, they follow the line of his dream to Britain, to Caernarfon, overlooking Anglesey. There is the woman, whose name is Helen. The messengers fall at her feet. 'All hail, Empress of Rome!'

So the emperor subdues Britain, marries Helen and portions out the islands according to her wishes: 'for her father, from the Channel to the Irish Sea, together with the three adjacent Islands'. She herself has roads built across Britain.

Seven years pass, and news comes from Rome that the emperor's throne has been usurped. Now it is the Britons' chance to conquer Rome. They cross the seas, lay siege to the capital and take it by cunning. As the Britons return home, they conquer Brittany, remembering in passing 'to cut out the tongues of the women, lest their own British language be contaminated' – remembering, presumably, the contamination of Latin and, later, Anglo-Saxon. I already know about British imperial dominance elsewhere in the world; until now I've barely thought about it from the opposite perspective.

I climb the hill to Segontium, reaching it early in the evening. The fort sits on the crest of the hill, now amid modern housing estates, with a view over the Druids' placid green oasis. I feel relief at being so near. As islands went, Mona (or Môn) probably seemed gods-sent to the Celts: fertile, easy to till and well protected.

I bivvy that night under a tree in what had been the officers' mess. Architecture was circular in Britain, and the Atlantic coast, long into the Iron Age. Rome was rigidly right-angled. Thus Segontium was laid out according to a plan replicated in thousands of forts across the empire, from here to northern Africa.

The empire valued cities; the word 'civilization' means urbanity, an imperial hierarchy topped by the ultra-urbane. The Celts, by contrast, were a nature people who saw divinity all around them, in each breath of air. They honoured wild places, bogs, places ringed by water.

The Celts' Druid elite did not practise writing in any form that has come down to us in a comprehensible way (Robert Graves and others tried hard to parse a tree alphabet from Ogham), and therefore every literary reference to Druid culture, the early Britannias, and the association between the two, comes entirely from Greek and Roman sources. But from the beginning the islands of Britain were associated with mystery and magic.

Herodotus, writing in the fifth century BC, may be the first classical author to mention the islands, although he was far from sure what he was describing: 'I cannot speak with any certainty,' he writes, 'nor do I know of any islands called Cassiterides, whence the tin comes which we use.'[10] (Tin was the major British export, bringing the islands out of the Stone Age.)

A century later, the uncommonly accomplished Greek explorer Pytheas of Marseilles sailed all around Britain, according to Eratosthenes, Pliny and Strabo. He described the moon's effect on the tides and the frozen north, and, according to Pliny, estimated the islands' complete 'circuit' with some accuracy at 4,875 Roman miles;[11] but his text *On the Ocean*, upon which these later descriptions are based, is lost – and Strabo thought him a liar.

The Britannias remained remote, in Greek and Roman minds, throughout the ensuing period of imperial conquest. For Virgil, writing in 33 BC, Britain was still 'totally cut off from the world' – even though Julius Caesar had by then been there twice with his army.[12] Later, Plutarch explained (in the first century AD) that in Caesar's day Britain itself was a matter of dispute among writers, 'some of whom averred that its name and story had been fabricated, since it never had existed'.[13] Herodian, writing at least a hundred years after that, described the Britons as 'barbarians' who swim in swamps and go naked in order to show off their animal tattoos.[14]

It was Julius Caesar, ambitious Roman general – rampaging through independent Gaul like Robert Clive through eighteenth-century India – who furnished the first extant piece of ethnographical writing. Always, during the eight years that he was waging the Gallic Wars, those rebellious northern islands were on his mind, a distant horizon. Rebels 'flee into Britain' or 'send for auxiliaries' from there; 'succours are furnished to the enemy from that country'. But he learned nothing useful about Britain from the Celts in northern France, the Gauls. The Britannias, cut off by 'Ocean', were said to be a mystery to their neighbours.

Therefore, Caesar determined to go and see for himself. He made two autumn visits, in 55 and 54 BC. The first time, the ships he assembled were too large to come close in to that 'mountainous' coast and his soldiers were forced to swim ashore bearing the full weight of their armour, and 'our men did not all exert the same vigour and eagerness which they had been wont to exert in engagements on dry ground'. Four days later, when he tried to return to France again, there was a full moon – which meant a very high, or 'spring', tide – but the soldiers knew nothing of the tides. The ships lost their anchors and cables; 'great confusion arose'.[15] (Confusion on this level happened *thrice* during Caesar's short foray to Britain.) Caesar retreated across the Channel.

A year later, he was back, with eight hundred diverse ships: half his entire army.[16] But this visit, though more assured, was equally brief. As Tacitus put it politely, one hundred years later, 'The deified

Julius, the very first Roman who entered Britain with an army . . . must be regarded as having indicated rather than transmitted the acquisition to future generations.'

The islands remained a daunting prospect. In AD 40, Emperor Caligula marched his troops right up to the northern coast of Gaul, set sail, then turned back; and instead of giving the order to invade, shouted, 'Gather sea-shells!' (Which the troops did, in their helmets.) 'He became greatly elated,' Cassius Dio wrote, 'as if he had enslaved the very Ocean.'[17]

The Romans were keen on reaching 'Ocean' because it linked them to Alexander the Great. The Greek king believed that he'd reached this mythical river which encircles the world when his army waded across the Indus in India. Caesar, Caligula and Claudius had all hoped to be seen as doing something equally epic in their dalliances with the 'water-girt Britons', as Ovid styled them in his *Metamorphoses*.[18]

Of all the emperors, Claudius – physically weak and friendless in the vipers' nest of the Roman Senate – came out best from the potentially hubristic effort of sending his forces into the *'closed island'* (as Pomponius Mela described it that same year, AD 43).[19] He found that a war on that 'exotic', 'whale-burdened' coast at 'the world's end' (Horace, in his *Odes*)[20] was just what he needed to shore up his prestige at home. At first, the invasion was almost scuppered by the troops themselves – who were 'indignant at the prospect of campaigning outside the known world'[21] – but the foray went ahead and was declared to be a triumph. Claudius himself came to Britain – Hannibal-like, with elephants – on a two-week tour. The Senate hailed 'him with the title of *Britannicus*' – a name he in turn gave his son[22] – and voted that two triumphal arches should be erected, one on the northern coast of Gaul,[23] the other in Rome itself, inscribed with the words, 'the first to bring barbarian nations beyond the Ocean under Roman sway'. Colonization had begun.

And so the island of Mona (Anglesey) came into focus. Caesar had mentioned it in passing; but in AD 51 the forces of Claudius captured the British freedom fighter Caratacus – who, although he came from East Anglia (the Catuvellauni tribe) was fighting with the Silures tribe in the territory of the Ordovices (tribes from the south and north of Wales, respectively). The Celts often chose sacred places as battle sites – and hence often lost, as Caratacus did (he likely chose Dinas Emrys because of its position on the solstice grid). With hindsight, it seems that Caratacus was sacrificing himself to keep the Romans away from Mona, as Boudica would do later.[24]

It worked, for a decade. But soon it became clear that Anglesey was a hotbed of anti-imperial resistance; 'a haven for refugees', wrote Tacitus, the very 'place from which the rebels drew reinforcements'.[25]

The Romans hadn't always hated the Druids; indeed, this elite learned class had once been a source of curiosity and respect for Greek and Roman writers. They are barbarian philosophers (Aristotle wrote). They practise divination (opined Cicero). Caesar described in detail how the sect, now dispersed around Europe, originated in Britain and still sent adherents there for their education, fitting them to work as judges and exempting them from taxation and warfare. Strabo claimed that Druids studied natural and moral philosophy; Pliny that they used mistletoe in their magic; Lucan that they professed knowledge of the soul.

The ancient Greeks respected the Druids as philosophers; and even Caesar – as he destroyed their hinterland in Gaul – found them fascinating in an intellectual and almost spiritual way. He had a Druid informer, Diviciacus, who travelled to Rome and stayed with Cicero.[26] (Diviciacus's brother Dumnorix was an anti-Roman rebel.) But within a century of Caesar's army landing in Britain, the emperors who followed him came to regard the Druids as a seditious bulwark against their takeover of Celtic Europe. Emperor Augustus banned Roman citizens from being Druids; Claudius tried to suppress the religion altogether. The authorities knew that a pan-European network of rebellion was building, and annihilation of the Druids' stronghold became the only possible response. As the Romans moved through Europe, absorbing and destroying, the Druids seem to have fled – in a double watery retreat – across the English Channel, and then the Menai Strait, to the island where the revered oak groves were still intact.

By AD 60, the Celts were presumably used to Romans killing their people and disrespecting their culture. Caesar had exterminated some tribes during his conquest of Gaul. But until now, geography had protected the Britannias. Anglesey, in particular, had two natural lines of defence: first the sea, and beyond that, the dark, toothy fortress of Snowdonia.

Rome would wage the bloodiest of its British campaigns in Anglesey, a culminating firestorm of imperial anger under Suetonius Paulinus, Emperor Nero's new British governor (a man who overdid it, Tacitus says, in the violence he meted out to Britons). The governor's particular problem was that Anglesey was inhabited by a 'powerful population', as Tacitus describes it:

> On the beach stood the adverse array, a serried mass of arms and men, with women flitting between the ranks. In the style of Furies, in robes of deathly black and with dishevelled hair, they brandished their torches; while a circle of Druids, lifted their hands to heaven and showering imprecations, struck the troops with . . . awe.[27]

In a tactic used in many colonial missions, the ensuing massacre of this Druid army was justified on the grounds of their evil habits: 'for it was their religion to drench the altars in prisoners' blood'. What they were seeking to eradicate, though, was anti-imperial rebellion.

Until this point, as Tacitus puts it, Rome had prevailed in Britain through the disunity of the tribes: 'Our greatest advantage in coping with tribes so powerful is that they do not act in concert.' Now, in response to this outright attack on their holy island, the Britons rose in a way that was almost cohesive. Their leader was 'Boudica, a woman of kingly descent',[28] who ruled over the Iceni in the south-east (modern-day Norfolk). Shockingly, after her husband died, Boudica was flogged, her daughters raped and her property seized by Roman soldiers. In righteous retaliation at both this outrage and presumably also the one taking place on Anglesey, Boudica's forces destroyed Colchester – Rome's capital in Britain – and burned down the much-hated temple to the deified Emperor Claudius.[29] The huge statue of Victory was toppled. The Iceni had their own victory goddess, Andraste. They erased the fledgling Roman new town, Londonium, and the romanized Celtic settlement, Verulamium, modern St Albans.[30] (Here literary report is verified by archaeology: excavations have shown thick burnt layers in these places.) Paulinus, recalled from Anglesey, met the rebels somewhere in the Midlands (or Cheshire, or possibly the Thames Valley).[31] Despite Boudica's bravery, Rome – with its supremely disciplined and well-trained army – was victor. Tacitus gives Boudica the same self-death by poison as Cleopatra. Cassius Dio reported that she died of sickness.

Eighteen years passed. When Agricola arrived in Britain as governor in AD 78 the very first action of this man who knew Britain well, having done two tours of duty there, was to fight the Ordovices (he almost wiped the Welsh tribe out) and to 'subjugate' the island of Mona. This suggests that the work was not completed by his predecessor, that the island still remained a problem. For this second attack on Anglesey, Agricola took the inhabitants by surprise, swimming over with local auxiliaries 'who knew the shallows and had that national experience in swimming which enables the Britons to take care not only of themselves but of their arms and horses'. It is not written how many people he killed, or how many shrines he burned down.

After that, Agricola set about turning Britain into a peaceable colony. At first it was easy. The Celts were already substantially addicted to Roman wine, and 'step by step', Tacitus wrote, those in Britain 'were led to things which dispose to vice, the lounge, the bath, the elegant banquet. All this in their ignorance, they called civilization, when it was but a part of their servitude.'

But in this most troublesome of colonies nothing could remain peaceful for long. In the sixth year of his governorship, Agricola, grief-stricken by the death of his baby son, decided to conquer the northern barbarian recesses of the country once and for all, by land and by sea. 'The Britons,' Tacitus wrote, 'were confounded by the sight of a fleet, as if, now that their inmost seas were penetrated, the conquered had their last refuge closed against them.' It's a typically sharp insight. The tribes of Caledonia revolted at the sight of their secret ocean knowledge being weighed like so many tin nuggets for export. It is striking how generously disposed Tacitus – son-in-law to Agricola – is to the rebels. He had already given Caratacus and Boudica bountiful gifts of eloquence (the Celts, with their oral culture, were famed for exactly that).[32] Now he had Calgacus, the highland chief, make a speech so disturbing and prescient it should be embossed on the wall of every government office. For it is us – *eliminators of other species* – that he is describing:

> Robbers of the world, having by their universal plunder exhausted the land, they rifle the deep. If the enemy be rich, they are rapacious; if he be poor, they lust for dominion; neither the east nor the west has been able to satisfy them . . . To robbery, slaughter, plunder, they give the lying name of empire; they devastate the world, and call it peace.

This is an extraordinary piece of literature, surprising and subversive; Tacitus as playwright manqué.[33]

The eloquence of the nature people meant nothing in the battle that ensued, however. The literate plunderers of the earth killed as many as they could; the rest melted away into the bogs and forests.

And this is how – in 133 years – Rome conquered Britain.

These evocative, one-sided reports of Rome's colonization of Britain suggest two intriguing – no, fundamental – things about these islands. The first is that the Britannias are sacred, secretive and druidical. The second is that they are associated with female power.

I am ashamed to say that both these facts were new to me: I learned them here first. That is, up until this point in my life, I had either not listened, or had not been told.

By now I knew that islands – also lakes, springs, bogs – were as sacred to the Celts as they had been centuries earlier to the people of the Neolithic. These places, half earth, half water, were in between the known world and that of the gods, who were everywhere and in everything. Chillingly, after Caesar had subdued independent Gaul, he exacted a policy of deliberate cultural appropriation: violating their culture in several ways, by imposing on the people a new council in their name (concilium Galliarum) which was to meet during their sacred midsummer festival in Lyon, where an altar was built to Rome and Augustus on a sacred island.[34] Therefore, when Caesar claimed that the Gauls are completely ignorant about Britain, possibly it is *omertà* he was encountering. This makes sense if the British islands were holy. Anglesey was not the only sacred British island, moreover. Diodorus Siculus, a contemporary of Caesar's, wrote a long description of the 'Hyperboreans' – a mythical northern people who lived (eponymously) 'beyond the point where the north wind blows', and 'beyond the land of the Celts' – just after his section on the Amazons.

The Amazons were an independent female tribe of fighters from the periphery of the Greek world who, whether they existed or not, haunted the imagination of Europe ever after. (The reason the rainforest in South America was named the Amazon in 1542 was because the Spaniards found themselves fighting warrior women there: a landscape that all the patriarchal knowledge of Europe was unable to tame). The Hyperboreans were similar to the Amazons. They had 'in the Ocean', Diodorus wrote, 'an island no smaller than Sicily', where Apollo was worshipped in a 'notable temple adorned with many offerings and circular in shape'.[35]

Apollo was a sun-god, and the Neolithic monuments such as Maeshowe in Orkney were sun-temples of a sort. Apollo took over Delphi, 'womb' of the world and home of the Pythian oracle – a place of female prophecy.[36] Divination and augury were known to be druidic arts; Cicero writes as much in his book on the subject. Boudica, who was possibly a Druid herself, is described as performing a divination ceremony just before her attack on Colchester: she released a hare into the grove of Andraste. (This was not the bloody sacrifice that is sometimes attributed to her – the hare, concealed in the folds of her cloak, ran free between the legs of the opposing Roman soldiers.)[37]

What I hadn't come to realize, until researching this book, was that ancient Greek and Roman texts described other sacred female islands in British waters, numerous times and in numerous contexts, and often to do with female augury. Strabo mentioned – almost in passing – an island 'beside Britain in which sacrifices are performed like those performed in Samothrace in honour of Demeter and Kore [Persephone]'.[38] Samothrace, a sacred island, was the centre of a mystery cult established by Myrina, leader of the Amazons, in honour of the 'Great Mother Goddess'. The cult was unusually inclusive, admitting women, men, slaves and the free: such as Herodotus and the parents of Alexander the Great. There was an island like this, then, in Britain.[39]

Strabo also described the British Cassiterides: ten islands, 'situated in open sea approximately in the latitude of Britain' and 'inhabited by people . . . who resemble the goddesses of Vengeance in the tragedies'. That is, the Furies; *Erinyes* in Greek; three women who served Persephone, goddess of the underworld and spring.[40] In so doing, Strabo identified Britain as a place of powerful female prophecy and magic.[41]

When Pomponius Mela came to write his *Description of the World* in the first century AD, he proffered yet another iteration of this British sacred island theme by naming an island 'in the Britannic Ocean', *Sena*, which, he writes, was inhabited by nine virgin prophetesses, who 'stir up the seas and the winds by their magic charms . . . [and] know and predict the future'.[42] These Circean island witches, nine for the nine Olympian Muses, could be denizens of Île de Sein off the coast of Brittany – that is what French historians posit; the British suggest Scilly. Wherever it was exactly, Sena's trope of a 'ninefold sisterhood' lingered in the imagination of both places: the Bretons have the Korrigan (fairy prophetesses); Geoffrey of Monmouth mentions the nine Morgens in his *Vita Merlini*; while the medieval Welsh story cycle *The Mabinogi* has the nine *gwiddon*, or witches.[43]

A century after Mela, Dionysius Periegetes wrote his own *Description of the Known World* in Greek verse. He, too, attested that:

> Near to Britain are some islands where the women . . .
> Perform sacred rites for Bacchus,
> Wreathed with clusters of dark-leaved ivy.[44]

Four centuries later still, Procopius, writing in Byzantine Greek of the great winter solstice celebrations in the northern island of Thule – a place like Iceland, or Orkney – commented on the islanders' cross-gender cooperation:

> Among the barbarians who are settled in Thule . . . the Scrithiphini . . .
> do not till the land themselves, nor do their women do it for
> them . . . The women join the men in hunting, which is their only
> pursuit . . . For they do everything in common.[45]

Was it possible that these foreign commentators were right? Had there been a cult of female-led worship on Britain's islands? Had it endured in any form? It seemed unlikely – otherwise, why wouldn't it be more celebrated and known? And yet.

Ancient Celtic culture, as it was practised in Britain and in Gaul, had many goddesses, several of whom had more than one consort – sovereignty goddesses, possibly. I sat down and read through Robert Briffault's magisterial investigation of female-centric religions, *The Mothers* (1927), in which he argued that 'In Gaul, before it became Romanised, women occupied a position which is only compatible with pronouncedly matriarchal institutions.'[46] The popular embrace of this possibly extremely ancient, vague and hard to pin down concept still causes annoyance in academic circles.[47] But the contemporary archaeologist Miranda Aldhouse-Green is emphatic: Celtic culture was more inclined to gender equality than Rome, and it was Britain's particular 'position on the edge of the world' which allowed it 'to diverge from mainstream androcentric political ideologies'.[48] To me, this was a solace and a revelation. I also felt bewildered (and angry).

Caesar himself believed that in Britain, specifically, women were polyandrous (each wife, he claimed, had ten or twelve husbands).[49] Patriarchal cultures generally try to suppress polyandry when they encounter it. But polyandry automatically keeps population levels low (when practised in families) and, unlike polygamy, conserves resources. Thus it is sometimes responsible for female empowerment and leadership.[50] I knew this already from Ladakh and Tibet. I also knew that patriarchal men always condemn polyandry or are scared of it.

Perhaps it had been true of ancient Britain. Certainly, the Roman accounts of their colonization of Britain make clear that from the very first phase, governors and generals found that they were having to contend with a surprising number of indigenous female leaders and soldiers. It has just been proved that the Iron Age warrior buried in the Isles of Scilly was a woman. The Romans had long noted the bravery of Celtic women – in part as a way of othering the barbarians. Ammianus Marcellinus took delight in explaining how Celtic men and women fight alongside each other: 'A whole troop of foreigners would not be able to withstand a single Gaul if he called his wife to his assistance who is usually very strong'.[51] If there were Gaulish female leaders, however, none was mentioned by name in the colonial texts, whereas the Britons were so used to female leadership that when the delegation of the captured tribal leader Caratacus was brought before Emperor Claudius in Rome the Britons shocked bystanders by also bowing down, as one, to Empress Agrippina.[52]

As Tacitus explained, the Britons 'admit no distinction of sex in their royal successions'.[53] In Britain there was Cartimandua, ruler of the northern Brigantes tribe, a woman with both husband and lover. She chose to side with Rome: when Caratacus sought refuge with her, she sold him to the enemy. And there was tall, deep-voiced, golden-haired, widowed Boudica – who fought against Roman imperialism and spoke out against it too, in Tacitus' words:

It was customary, she knew, with Britons to fight under female captaincy; but now she was avenging her ravished realm and power, not as a queen of glorious ancestry, but as a woman of the people: her liberty lost, her body tortured by the lash, the tarnished honour of her daughters.[54]

The Roman governor Suetonius Paulinus, when it was his turn to speak, cheered on his troops by pointing out there were more women than men in the barbarian British battle lines. But in truth, if Tacitus was right, the Romans found the 'frenzied' British females they met in battle extremely scary.[55] Rome still hadn't got over being briefly bested by Boudica, even by the time Cassius Dio was writing, a century and a half later. 'The island was lost to Rome,' he wrote. 'Moreover, all this ruin was brought upon the Romans by a woman, a fact which in itself caused them the greatest shame.'[56]

All three of the major British rebellions – those led by Caratacus, Boudica and Calgacus – seem to be cogent indigenous responses to Rome's attacks on their sacred islands, and island learning. But in the end, Roman patriarchal culture prevailed and has endured. Everything that Mona stood for was subdued, if not quite destroyed.

In the Roman town of Aphrodisias in south-west Turkey there is a stone carving of Claudius's defeat of Britannia (the islands now personified as a subdued woman). The Greeks loved depicting their martial domination of the Amazons: triumphant men pitted against rebellious, half-naked women. This statue takes up that theme: Britannia is prostrate, breast bared; Claudius straddles her. It's a rape scene.[57]

I leave the Roman fort and walk down the hill towards the Druids' island to meet two men and a dog, who are joining me on my walk into Anglesey. The Celts saw significance in numbers and liked the number three especially. They also loved hounds. The Britons were famed for their hunting dogs, one of their luxury exports to Rome, after slaves and tin.

The dog's owner, Will, has walked all over Britain, sometimes for years on end, an ancient wanderer. He reads maps like poems. When we meet to walk into Anglesey, he is running the very proper British Pilgrimage Trust with Guy, his business partner. They've come carrying with them what they think is one of the most ancient Welsh songs, 'Pais Dinogad', a lullaby a bit like 'Bye, Baby Bunting'. Its words are evocative of those times when humans and animals lived closely together, hunter-hunted, wild-domesticated. The tune has been lost, but over the next five nights, as we walk from Caernarfon to Caergybi (head to head: head of the Arvon to the holy-head), Will and Guy seek it out.

> Dinogad's coat is speckled, speckled,
> I made it myself from martens' pelts –
> Whistle, whistle, a-whistling;
> I used to sing to him, the eight slaves used to sing to him.
> When your father would go hunting
> With the staff on his shoulder and club in his hand,
> He would call his hounds,
> Giff, Gaff, catch! Catch! Fetch! Fetch! [dally dally, dourg dourg]
> He would kill a fish in his coracle . . .
> None would escape if it were not on wings.[58]

The song is said to be sixth century, hailing from the borderland between England and Scotland, when Welsh was the language spoken all over these isles. It seems to be a dirge – a lament for the dead father. Distressing, too, the mention of slaves, singing. And the pine martens, killed for their skins, and now near extinction.

We walk down through Caernarfon and along a footpath that runs beside the Strait. An old man stops me to compliment my oak staff; he carries his own hazel rods cut from the River Tavy (in Devon) to 'Stick Conventions'. 'But oak is best,' he says, and I feel disproportionately pleased by the approval.

Anglesey is one of those islands which, like Thanet and Skye, nature or engineering has partially absorbed into the mainland – in this case Thomas Telford's 1826 suspension bridge. Thus, one island leads seamlessly to yet another: beyond Anglesey, conjoined, is the island of Holyhead. 'An island off an island off an island, on the way to Ireland,' as the woman frying chips in a café there describes it to me later that week. (The Dublin ferry leaves from Holyhead.)

For the next four days, over the April Easter bank holiday, we will walk north along Anglesey's western coastline. There are several Neolithic monuments on this path, and many early Christian churches, but Mona's Iron Age culture manifests itself very discreetly by contrast. Probably all of Anglesey was sacred to the Druids, in ways that are now intangible and have left little trace in the archaeological record.[59]

Across the bridge, for example, the first religious site we come to is Christian, but it is probably more ancient than it seems. Church Island is dedicated to St Tysilio, one of the many Christian saints who came to Anglesey (in AD 630) in the wake of the Roman empire's endorsement of Christianity, and its subsequent disintegration. St Cybi built his church on Holyhead (or Holy) Island within the defunct Roman fort; St Seriol built a church next to a more ancient holy well at Penmon. Here are continuities which we can only speculate about.

Inside the chapel, Guy bows his head by the altar and recites a long list of names; slightly sheepishly, he explains that Will and he have received some money for this journey from one of their aristocrat patrons and, in exchange, they are to pray for the souls of the woman's deceased Welsh forebears. (Saying prayers for the dead was abolished in England and Wales under Edward VI.) I like this unsought cultural throwback. After all, I am used to it; I was raised a Catholic; I'm familiar with the idea of purgatory and the soul's torturous trajectory through the afterlife. These ancestor prayers also mean we will eat very well this week – unrepentantly Chaucerian pilgrims – in Anglesey's finest pubs.

The Greeks and Romans made much of the druidic belief in the transmigration of the soul, as did early Christian writers; there was some discussion about whether they got it from Pythagoras (Hippolytus), or he from them (Clement of Alexandria). What it mostly seems to have done is to have made the Celts fearless of death, which is perhaps why they fought so well. Iron Age interest in the afterlife, and in particular in the afterlife of their sometimes very-distant ancestors, is well attested in the archaeological record. All over the Britannias, Neolithic burial mounds became the focus for subsequent worship. On the Orcadian island of Rousay, Iron Age people broke into the huge Neolithic chambered cairn, but they did not touch the burials. Instead they built one of their brochs, monumental fortified communal quarters, right beside it.

Anglesey's most celebrated Neolithic burial mound is Bryn Celli Ddu ('Mound in the Dark Grove'), and we reach it late at night, walking over fields in the bright light of the waning gibbous moon. Guy and Will, reverent as always, insist on circling the tomb – 'At least one circumambulation is necessary to avoid a bad result,' Will explains – and then chanting a prayer they have written:

'We come as guests and thank our hosts living in this place;
Singing here we honour you, please bless us with your grace.'

Only then do we enter the darkness of the inner chamber. I sleep right inside the chamber itself, in the womb where previous pilgrims have left offerings of money, daisies and a scallop shell, and where the people of the Neolithic carved slightly hypnotic spirals. Will and the dog sleep in the birth passage, along which sunlight creeps at dawn on midsummer solstice. Guy, spooked and claustrophobic, sleeps outside. He wants to sleep on top of the mound, but Will tells him that is a very bad idea, on account of 'the energy' of the site; its ancient spirits.

Neolithic chambered cairns were probably used as dreaming spaces, including by the Iron Age Celts. The ecologist David Abram describes a world once full of augury, with humans communicating with other species at a level beyond human language, and argues that we must seek 'a new way of speaking, one that enacts our interbeing with the world, rather than blinding us to it'.[60] And so I lie down to sleep, optimistic for omens. But since I became a mother

I sleep differently: hyper-alert around my children, hyper-hyper-somnolent when alone.

I recall nothing of my dreams but wake, refreshed, to the sound of voices. It is 7 a.m. and, outside, two slightly grumpy archaeologists are arriving through the dew, with takeaway coffee in Costa cups, to continue their geophysical survey of the site (that summer, the new radiocarbon dates they gather will prove that the site was used for at least a thousand years).

And then, comically, from the other direction appears a caravan trail of cheerfully chattering adults: a film crew from Los Angeles on a tour of British chambered cairns for the American reality TV show *Expedition Unknown*. 'Josh Gates is over there,' one of them says, gesticulating to a rugged, TV-genic-looking man in a dark fleece.

Wales's national archaeologist, Dr Ffion Reynolds, claims that this particular site once had water flowing past it on both sides, during the Neolithic – a little island. The stream would have eroded the schist, making the waters speckled and spangled with gold mica. She showed me a photograph taken during excavations: her friend's hand, glittery and golden with mica. 'The water would have shimmered.' Iron Age people loved gold things. Metalsmiths may have been magical figures (an early medieval prayer in Ireland wards off the spells of 'blacksmiths, Druids and women'). Hundreds of Celtic golden torcs – the necklaces denoting leadership – have been found in Britain. Those from Snettisham in Norfolk, where Boudica came from, are twisty and intricate and fabulous. She wore a 'great twisted golden torc' when riding into battle, according to Cassius Dio.

We leave the TV crew and the archaeologists and walk back south to the Menai Strait. When we reach the water, I stand and look across to Caernarfon. The mountains of Snowdonia loom over everything, resplendent, a promise of safety. As Will and Guy sing their English-Welsh song I wonder again about the black-clad women of Tacitus's description calling down curses on the Romans; were they warriors, or Druids? Was this moment also the death of women's social parity with men in Britain, or did older social forms persist and prevail?

Clearly, Celtic gods and goddesses often translated into saints in Christian times: most famously, Brigit, said to have been a Celtic solar goddess, became the beloved Irish saint Bridgit (even the Christian hagiographies have her raised by Druids). Sometimes, a practice that was common in Celtic times was continued in Christian ones. That night, for example, we stay on the tidal island of Ynys Llanddwyn, which was one of Anglesey's most popular pilgrimage sites until the Reformation. St Dwynwen, who died in 465, was the beautiful daughter of King Brydan Brycheiniog. She rejected the advances of a man called Maleon (possibly she was raped) and has recently been reborn as the Welsh patron saint of lovers. Like St Triduana/Tredwell, from Papa Westray in Orkney, she became so popular with lovesick pilgrims that even one hundred years after her church had its meaning ripped from it by the Protestant ban on pilgrimage (which was thought to encourage a 'vagabond life'),[61] people were still coming here, to light candles in the ruined porch and use her well for augury.[62] Thus the journey to St Dwynwen's shrine – to an island off an island off an island – performs some kind of ritualized landscape magic.

We bivvy that night, in the rain, against St Dwynwen's Church porch, and superstitious as we have become in each other's company, light candles to cure our lovesick hearts; the next morning, which is Good Friday, we drink water from her well (having cleared it of rubbish). Will tells me stories of the shocking filth he has discovered in Britain's holiest water sources. Dog-poo bags; half-eaten burgers. In order to drink from these places without disgust, he bought himself a water purifier. He passes around the vial of now cleansed holy water.

'Delicious,' says Guy.

'The best ever,' says Will.

There are sacred sites, and royal ones – often they are the same – all along Anglesey's southern and northern coasts. We walk through Aberffraw, where the early-medieval Welsh monarchs had a palace, possibly of prehistoric origin, overlaid with a Roman military installation. The story of Branwen fills my head as I walk around the Roman-style rectangular layout of the palace (the Celtic fashion for roundhouses did not survive the Roman invasion). Branwen suffered for so many years, trapped in her marriage in Ireland. She was rescued by her brother Brân – he of the islands of paradise, in a new iteration.

On the nearby clifftop promontory, where a Bronze Age cairn overlays a Mesolithic campsite (from about 7000 BC), we prostrate ourselves on the earth, as if saying namāz. The smells of plantlife and soil fill my nostrils. I think: *How greatly this land has been loved; how dense it is with meaning.*

A little further up the rocky coast is the little church of St Cwyfan, known as the Church in the Sea, which is also a tidal island, a tiny, church-sized one. That night, as the tide comes in to cut us off from Anglesey, we sing the British Romany Easter carol 'Leaves of Life', with its poignant mixture of pagan and Christian symbolism and, running through it all, the mother's grief for her son:

> Oh peace, mother, oh peace, mother,
> Your weeping does me grieve;
> For I must suffer this, he says,
> For Adam and for Eve . . .
> Oh, the rose, the gentle rose,
> The fennel it grows so strong.
> Amen, sweet Lord,
> Your charity is the ending of my song.

There are no visitors to the church at this time of night from whom to collect alms. It is stormy and we pitch our tarp on the east-facing side, which means that when we wake it is with sunrise on our faces; but it is cold in the night. Will has his dog for warmth; Guy has merino-and-silk underwear; but the wind gets up to 14mph – nothing if you have lived in the winds of Orkney – but still, I am restless with discomfort.

In the bright morning, Easter Saturday, I look out at Bardsey Island – home of twenty thousand saints. Three pilgrimages to Bardsey were equivalent to one to Rome; one glance at the island worked like a charm (or a 'darshan', as Hindus call these holy sights). It is a sunny holiday and the coast throngs with weekend walkers. At midday, while Guy and Will walk on to a beachside pub for lunch, I stop at Barclodiad Neolithic tomb, where Keith, the local postman, unlocks the gates for me and points out the chevron patterns which define the entrance ('like the road markings outside a police station'). Keith is used to visits by neo-pagan and Druid groups; he says he likes the ceremonies they perform. His kindness makes me reflect that although people jeer at the neo-Druidry which goes on at places like Stonehenge for being anachronistic, surely this misses the point. If there was a Bronze Age cemetery at Bryn Celli Ddu, I bet there were Druid ceremonies at Barclodiad too. In the Neolithic they cooked a magical stew of toad, frog, fish, eel and snake – a recipe somehow transmitted through the ages to the witches of *Macbeth*.[63]

Keith and I discuss the Welsh language. Neither of us speaks it – he came to Anglesey as a joiner from Liverpool twenty years ago – but we both feel, in a vague outsider way, that it would do everybody in this Disunited Queendom good, if, instead of English always, we were all better acquainted with the ancient languages (and modern), their literature, myths.

I rejoin the men and their hound and we walk on up the beach and reach the RAF airbase called Valley. Beyond here is a lake or marsh which was the centre of Druid rites and their hopes for delivery from Rome.

During the Second World War, when the British government was constructing this airbase (imagining it, in their turn, as a stronghold against invasion), one of the most important votive deposits in Iron Age Britain was found here. Trapped in the peat of the former marsh was a massive deposition of ornate Iron Age metal: embossed shields, slave-gang chains, a chariot decorated with a swastika, blacksmith's tools, a trumpet, a cauldron, a sceptre. Votive offerings were part of the religion of the ancient world. But the sheer volume of this deposit was extraordinary. It represented the offering up of an incredible store of riches and wealth; as if every woman in India had thrown her gold jewellery into the Ganga; as if all the City of London's bankers had simultaneously plunged their bullion into the Thames. (And indeed, the Thames also received significant Iron Age offerings from around the time of the Roman invasion.)

Iron Age rulers sought out watery island sites as a channel of communication with the other world. The intricate metalwork thrown into Llyn Cerrig Bach seems to date from one particular historical epoch – a submission to the gods provoked by an overwhelming crisis.

The Romans (having only recently outlawed human sacrifice themselves) made much of the bloodiness of druidic practice. This may or may not be colonial propaganda. Despite the slave-gang chains, no bodies were dredged up from Llyn Cerrig Bach in 1942 (it is possible the chains were thrown in to symbolize freedom). Subsequently, however, several Iron Age ritual killings have been uncovered in the British Isles. These sacrificial bodies were found in states of preservation so complete that just looking at them gives a weird time-travel feeling: even their facial expressions survived two millennia in a bog. The Lindow Man, found in Cheshire in the 1980s (possibly the site of Boudica's last stand against the Romans), has a trimmed beard and nails; his skin is tattooed with greenish-blue paint. Before death, he had eaten a charred oat bannock containing four grains of mistletoe pollen. Mistletoe was sacred to the Druids, according to Pliny. (Mistletoe is toxic, but the pollen tastes delicious, as I discover for myself when I pick and dry some – like mango, with a starry massage of the tongue.) The Lindow Man was naked but for an armlet of fox fur; had been stunned by a blow to the head, garrotted, his throat cut. Carbon-dating narrowed down the date of his death to around AD 60.[64] Tacitus wrote that, in Germany, cowards and shirkers were drowned in miry swamps. But this man seems grander than that: a willing sacrifice to the gods; no scapegoat he; possibly a 'Druid prince'.[65] The two bog-deposited men discovered in Ireland also seem to have led cosseted lives. The ancient Old Croghan Man was six foot four, had dined on buttermilk and finely milled flour and done very little physical labour. Cloneycavan Man had long hair styled into a top knot with an expensive pine-resin hair gel imported from France or Spain, giving him the spiky Celtic hairstyle which Diodorus Siculus describes being sported by Gaulish fighters, also seen in the depiction of a British warrior embossed on a fragment of Iron Age pottery from Colchester.[66]

Llyn Cerrig Bach is inconspicuous now, with its ducks and bulrushes. It's been sunny all day, and Guy immediately strips off and wades in, clutching a rosary from Westminster Abbey and two silver pins of Will's (I have told them to bring something for a ritual deposition). At about thigh deep he lies down until the water covers him completely and then he rises and immerses himself three times. It is plausible as a Druid ritual.

Iron Age people often deliberately broke the things they deposited, or they made them in the shapes of real weapons but with a low metal content so that they would have been useless for real fighting. They lived and died in symbols. I walk to the other side of the lake and throw in one of my many broken wooden wedding rings. For twenty years now, my husband and I have had wooden rings made from offcuts from my grandfather's lathe, because love is organic and grows like trees. But the rings break, and recently I have begun to doubt our chosen symbolism. I watch the little wooden half-moons disappear into the water, watch the waters close over them.

It is something I have been giving a lot of thought to. Too much thought, too much thinking. In the end, as it turns out, it is the body that knows.

If the Roman invasion was a cataclysm beyond anything that Anglesey's Iron Age society had known before, the lake's riches also lend credibility to the myth of an ancient Welsh king called Arthur, who, as he was dying, relinquished his power by throwing his sword, Excalibur, into a lake on the isle of Avalon. The lake's waters are dark and stormy. I think of Alexander the Great, who tried to pacify the Indus river-in-spate by pouring a libation into its waters from a gold bowl as he uttered the names of its tributaries. I think of the gods the Druids were trying to reach. What were they like? Why did they abandon the Britons? I think of the men and women who stood here in Iron Age times and watched as their leaders threw away their wealth, watched as the dark waters of the marsh closed over everything which was most precious to them after life itself.

We cross the tidal inlet which separates Anglesey from Holyhead Island and spend that night in the porch of St Gwenfaen's Church in Rhoscolyn. She was born on the Isle of Man – from which she was chased by Druids – and her well water nearby, which we visit the next day, is said to cure mental illness if you offer two quartz pebbles – another sacred deposition or exchange. Will has an ill friend, for whom he has gathered quartz pebbles from Llandwyn Island, and he throws them in and carefully collects and purifies some water. A year later he emails me to say that the friend began to get better the day he received and drank St Gwenfaen's water.

Will and Guy consult the Tarot cards, as they often do when unsure of something, such as which path to take. They want to know whether they should go to church, as it's Easter Sunday. The cards (published by Philip Carr-Gomm, until recently head of the Order of Bards, Ovates and Druids)[67] emphatically say *No*. Instead we buy an ice cream and walk on up the coast. Will's sheepdog, crossing a field ahead of us, inadvertently divides a lamb from its mother, and as we follow in her wake there is a pause, a suspension, an intake of breath as the baby and its mother, tragically separated, assess the danger we pose; and then, bravely, run towards each other, and turn, facing us down – naked Celtic warriors with gel-spiked hair, set against the mechanistic power of Rome. Only after we reach the far end of the field does the lamb have a vigorous, cele-bratory drink of milk. Or maybe it is only I, away from my own babies during these days, who feels it like that.

We stop at the Neolithic burial chamber of Trefignath at noon, with its three chambers, one aligned northwards, and two east-wards. We sing in the east-tomb, where the stone is starred with a huge jewel of quartz, Guy facing east, Will south, and me west, towards Ireland.

The sun is shining by the time we reach the beach at Porth

Dafarch. Will strips off first, and runs into the sea. Guy and I follow. As we emerge from the cold waves I see a group of twenty people gather on the shore. The beach rings with their excited voices. It is an Elim Pentecostal baptism. A young woman who was once, so a friend of hers tells me, a high priestess in a witch's coven, is submerged beneath the salt: pushed backwards beneath the water by two men. 'And now she is Jesus's daughter and he is her father. I led her to the lord; a God-incidence that you are here.' The woman comes up sputtering and choking, looking briefly as if she's been assaulted.

We walk through rain for the rest of the afternoon, towards Holyhead Mountain, on the summit of which we will bivvy for the night as we end our journey.[68] We climb slowly higher, westward, and the clouds clear. There, distant but distinct, is Ireland: Hibernia, as the Romans knew it, an island that they never conquered, and surely where the Druids fled after the conquest of Mona.[69]

The Roman fort in Holyhead town marks the western limit of Roman rule in this part of the world. For all the trouble they went to in sacking Anglesey, the Romans did very little with the island thereafter. In 2011, archaeologists excavated a Roman trading settlement on the opposite side of the Menai Strait from Caernarfon, with a Roman road built over what seems to have been 'a preexisting Iron Age trackway'.[70] But the Romans had no interest in settling Anglesey itself. This was a military zone. No villas, or temples, or any other signs of Roman colonization have ever been discovered. It seems the attack on Anglesey was strategic and symbolic.

In August's blazing sunshine I return to Anglesey, by bus, for the Eisteddfod, the celebration of Welsh language and culture which rotates each year between the north and south of the country and has only been held on Anglesey thrice before, since it began in 1861.

I stop in a teashop on the north coast of the island. Twenty old ladies are having a lunch party. They speak in a mellifluous ripple of Welsh, then switch to English for my sake.

'You get on the bus in Anglesey and go anywhere in the country for free –'

'But you can't get back.'

'The young people have all gone away. They find themselves an Englishman or Scotsman and that is that.'

'All our fathers and uncles worked at sea. Some in the merchant navy, some as volunteers for the RNLI, the lifeboats.'

'Frieda's uncle was coxswain.'

'Betsy's Dad was first engineer.'

'My grandfather came home from sea every nine months. Single mothers are criticized now, but that's how it was. Our mothers managed everything.'

'They called us Moelfre herrings.'

'There was only one road down into Moelfre.'

'If any lad came from another village, the men chased him away.'

'You've got to be very careful who you are related to.'

'She's related to Charles Dickens.'

'Wrong side of the blanket.'

'Don't put any of that down,' they joke, their words emphasizing at every swerve their pride as an island people, at standing apart from the rest of Britain.

At the Eisteddfod itself, hardly anyone speaks English. I understand very little of what is being said, therefore; it is eye-opening and exhilarating. In the arts pavilion, Peter Finnemore is exhibiting a film about the colonial imposition which was the Investiture of the Prince of Wales in 1969; Charles was crowned in the castle at Caernarfon (he may as well have been crowned in the Roman fort). Finnemore quotes *The Townley Geographical Reader* (*c*.1885): 'When speaking of England, it is understood that Wales is also meant'; 'The Britons worshipped false gods and their priests were called Druids. So a wise Roman general sent an army to Anglesey and he destroyed the Druids.' When Finnemore won the gold medal for visual arts at the Eisteddfod in 2005, he came to the ceremony dressed as a Druid. He was made a bard the following year.[71]

These modern gatherings are based around an ancient poetic

competition known of at least as far back as the sixteenth century and drawing on bardic tradition dating to pre-literate times. But the Druid elements of the Eisteddfod were added by Iolo Morgannwg, an ex-patriate Welshman living in London, in 1819, and the organizational and aesthetic aspects – the costume, in particular – he freely based on colonial classical sources (Strabo, Caesar, Pliny).[72]

I go backstage at the Gorsedd of the Bards. Penri Roberts, the Recorder, gives me a tour. The ceremony is due to begin in forty-five minutes and there are Druids wandering around in their underclothes and young girls practising their clog dances in the corridors; in the costume department, rows and rows of polycotton costumes hang, freshly ironed, from long rails. The muted blues and beiges remind me a bit of the standard Pakistani male costume of shalwar kameez (also almost always immaculately pressed). Penri Roberts, like everyone else, is keen to stress that 'there is no link of the Druids then and now'. But I think they are underselling themselves a bit. There is a link – and it is here, in the geography of this island.

Penri introduces me to the first woman arch-Druid of this modern order, Christine James, Professor of Welsh at Swansea University, and points out Urig Salisbury, a preoccupied bard sitting beside that year's chair, still composing or revising his poem to greet this year's prose winner, whose purple gown (to be worn with a crown of gold oak leaves) is being ironed by the costume mistress, Ella. Red is for officials; blue for science, maths and sports; green for the arts. Ella also shows me the horn of plenty, to be carried by the woman representing the 'mother' of the area, and the floral bouquet carried by the 'maiden'. Then the current arch-Druid appears, clad toe to knee in really quite covetable cream-coloured boots. He hasn't put his robe on yet, which is white, naturally, with a big necklace. Penri says that, unfortunately, they no longer use real stone circles because of health and safety. The one outside is fibreglass.

For the ceremony itself I collect a headset from the hall. This is one of the Eisteddfod's few public events with simultaneous translation into English. (I went to an entire geology lecture in Welsh, and when I asked afterwards for a translation they looked as pleased as they were apologetic.) *A oes heddwch?* ('Is there peace?'), the arch-Druid asks the audience in Welsh, and we all shout back, *Mae heddwch* ('There is peace').

Afterwards, Maggi Noggi, a TV drag queen and entertainer, 'seven foot two in my stilettos', meets me in the media pavilion. Her wig and eyelashes are flamboyantly outsized. Her multicoloured sequin dress was made by a woman in Liverpool. Out of drag, Maggi worked as an NHS mortician; she has been a drag queen for twenty-six years and a Druid for slightly longer. Now, as head of the Anglesey Druid Order, Maggi dresses in a cream robe, with a cloak and a replica torc based on those found in the Snettisham Hoard in Norfolk, performs solstice ceremonies at Bryn Celli Ddu and teaches Druidry on weekend courses. 'Islands are sanctuaries, inspiring places,' she says. 'As soon as you cross the bridge to Anglesey it feels like you are in a different place. The voices of the past are contained here. Ritual is the act of stopping. Of noticing yourself as part of the landscape.'

The most important ceremony, for the Anglesey Druid Order, is their memorial of the invasion of Anglesey at Halloween (the Celtic festival was called Samhain). They meet on one of the little islands in the Menai Strait and burn effigies of a wolf (symbol of Rome) and a boar (that of the Twentieth Legion, which marched on Anglesey).[73] Then they proclaim, *'Dani yma o hyd.'*

'What does that mean?' I ask.

Maggi Noggi smiles; her lipstick glimmers.

'It means "We are still here." '

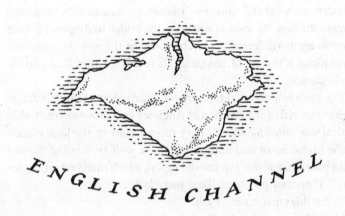

3

Wight

Romans (AD 250–330)

By the mid-third century AD, the south of Britain is settled with Roman garrisons, towns and paved (or re-paved) roads. The empire's writ also extends into the north. But there is no escaping the fact that the Britanniae (for so they are called still)[1] is a hardship posting. The sea between the islands and Gaul is a chilly cloak, a grim barrier between civilization and barbarity. The food sits in the stomach and descends to the bowels with all the enthusiasm of Proserpina visiting the underworld. It takes ages to get it out, and as they wait the wind whips the soldiers' bared bottoms and reminds them how far they are from home. At night they dream of sunshine and grapes, of familiar forests, of continental might.

It is no coincidence that the greatest concentration of Rome's domestic energies and wealth happened in the south of the Britannias, where the weather was less awful, where there was tin, for trading, which made the people easier to govern and consequently more civilized (more Roman). While Boudica's tribe in Norfolk, the Iceni, 'deliberately set their faces against innovation from outside', the more southerly tribes, such as the Trinovantes, lapped up Italian imports.[2] As Caesar observed, the maritime part of southern Britain was no longer purely indigenous; tribes from the continent had long ago rampaged across, lured over 'for the purpose of plunder and making war'.[3] Coastal Britain – inhabited by Gaulish immigrants ready to do business – eased the way for Rome. Emperor Claudius used as a pretext for his own invasion the direct appeal for help from Verica (or Berikos), a Romanized ruler of Hampshire, Surrey, Sussex. Verica may even have been educated in Rome as a young man – just as, from the seventeenth century, Highland chiefs would be sent to London to erase their Gaelic mother tongue and, in the centuries after that, imperial education would trample native languages.[4]

In AD 43, the Roman commander Vespasian took control of *insulam Vectem*.[5] (The Latin term for Wight was *Vectis*). The island became a blueprint in miniature of everything Rome wanted from a colony. The island's forested north had boar and deer. The salty creeks gave fish, oysters, swan and duck. There were sheep on the southern-central chalk hills and beef herds in the foothills. There was plentiful building-stone down by the shore. Vectis was somewhere a visiting Roman might have felt optimistic about the empire's prospects in the region.

And so the Romans – or their Britannic imitators – forged a domain apart, an oasis of familiar comforts. They built a series of villas, each a mini imitation of an Italian country estate. In every house there were bathing suites, with hypocausts heating the rooms through underfloor vents. Since it was possible to grow vines on Vectis, they managed to press (as well as import) drinkable wine.[6] Because there were no wolves and foxes, it was easy to catch deer; and the Britons' hunting dogs were already famous throughout the empire. Situated on the trade route to France, Vectis eventually became a net exporter of wheat; possibly also the loading point for tin. For a brief moment, lasting barely a century, Rome created a little haven of peace on Vectis, a retreat from the tiresome bureaucracy of empire. That nothing is known of the inclinations of the tribes on Vectis themselves strongly suggests quiescence: a time of hush, amid the rain and the turmoil.

Because of this silence, it was thought by eighteenth- and early-nineteenth-century antiquarians that Rome had ignored the Isle of Wight completely. References to Vectis, Ictis and Mictis in Roman sources were taken to indicate some other island; the modern name 'Wight', it was noted, came from the Old English *wiht*, 'person'.[7]

Then, in 1840, the first of the island's eight known Roman villas was discovered. Naturally, this was balm to inquisitive Victorians, for whom the Roman military conquest of the Britanniae crucially presaged their own imperial conquests in foreign lands. Thanks to their queen with her Latin name, Victorians quickly learned to love the Isle of Wight. Victoria and Albert, looking for an island refuge from the island empire they governed, bought a small lodge in a piece of coastal parkland in the north of the island near Cowes in 1845. The purchase annoyed Victoria's ministers, who suspected the queen and her consort of deliberately making themselves inaccess- ible to government business, but it transformed the fortunes of the island itself. Julia Margaret Cameron, the pioneering photographer, moved there, as did Tennyson, the poet laureate (apparently because Keats had written on the island); he composed his poem 'Crossing the Bar' in a boat over the Solent in 1889.[8] But the island soon became too busy for him in the summer (besieged by fans).

With the island's upturn in Victorian times came a renewed inter- est in its ancient history. Archaeologists (or antiquarians) descended on the island like locusts. At Rock, to the west, thieves denuded the villa of all its finds. At Carisbrooke, in the centre, the villa was delib- erately exposed to the winter frost by the vicar, who, fed up with strangers traipsing through his shrubbery, allowed the delicate fres- coed walls, painted in umber and ochre, to crumble.[9] At Gurnard, not far from the queen's house in the north, the villa discovered on a cliff edge gradually fell into the sea.[10] A great effort was made with the largest villa of all, at Brading in the east – its 'State Room' was considered by one post-war commentator to be 'one of the most important Roman apartments ever discovered in Great Britain'.[11] But the excavators threw out bucket-loads of material in their fer- vour, and much evidence was lost.

One of the larger of the Isle of Wight's Roman farmhouses – re- buried now, beneath rolling downland – is Combley, to the north of the island, where patches of ancient woodland are the last remnants of the resource which the Romans loved. With its brick kilns and underfloor heating, the Roman lifestyle required a ready supply of wood wherever they settled. This was one reason why wooded Vectis suited them so well (and perhaps why newly deforested Anglesey didn't). The villa at Combley was an aisled farmhouse supported by large wooden piers; it had a two-room bath suite with floor tiles decorated with a comb pattern. There was a big collection of locally made pottery, fired in a brown, burnished glaze. In the dining room was a bronze spoon, a blue prismatic bottle and a phallic pendant. (Brading, too, had phallus-adorned pottery.)[12]

Judging by the standards of this, and its other villas, Roman society on Vectis was comfortable, even complacent. The island was not fortified, and the people who lived here had resources to spend on aesthetic and bodily pleasures: hot baths, large dining rooms, lovely views and smart mosaics.

In the twenty-first century, chancers still come with metal detectors to Combley. Andrew Groves was born and continues to live in the handsome brick-built seventeenth-century farmhouse adjacent to the villa (the two buildings are not dissimilar; British vernacular architecture took almost a millennium to catch up with Roman standards.) We walk across his fields, where Bestival, the music festival, was held until recently, all the ring-pulls making metal-detecting a frustrating pastime. Still, 'there was a guy who found a load of coins, with emperors on them earlier than the archaeologists had been expecting'. He seems pleased. There's prestige in being a repository of Roman tourist relics.

Groves is less enamoured of what the mainland has done to his farm and his profession. During his sixty years he has seen the government pass some 'stupid laws' regarding the countryside. National supermarkets have been allowed to systematically undermine island life. Cheap supermarket meat has made island living almost impossible for beef farmers like him. The influx of Tesco and its ilk means that local butchers have disappeared and the last slaughterhouse to supply them shut down twenty-six years ago. Groves has to take his beasts over to the mainland to join the centralized meat-packing supply chains. Nobody on the island eats island meat. The supermarkets have strangled the island's own foodchain.

His children still live here – one runs a festival fast-food business; the other rents out the farm's ponds for fishing – but plenty of other youngsters have moved away. 'Who can blame them? What is there for those who remain?' Groves laughs as he speaks, but there is nothing upbeat in the story he tells. It is true that what is good for middle-class pensioners is not necessarily healthy or attractive for the island's younger generation. The island's schools have been termed among the worst in the country.[13] The suicide rate is consistently above the national average.[14] In 2016, the Ofsted chair drew attention to the island's 'mass of crime, drug problems, huge unemployment' – and was lambasted for it.[15] The island didn't like the adverse attention.

'You know that people from the Island used to make their money from wrecking,' Groves goes on. (If 'mainland' has a small m, 'the Island' – as local people call it – always has a capital I.) 'They would take out horses with lights around their necks on stormy nights to lure in merchant ships.'

Whether or not they deliberately caused a ship to be wrecked, picking up salvage from boats was for centuries a cottage industry for British islanders. There is still an official position within the Maritime and Coastguard Agency, 'Receiver of the Wreck', appointed by the Secretary of State.[16] As recently as 1997, the wreck of the *Cita*, a container ship bound for Ireland, bequeathed to Scilly a lifetime's supply of computer equipment, toys and trainers. 'A lot of our big families made their wealth that way. Well, wrecking is in the past now, but young people still get mixed up in smuggling.' His wife gasps and tries to shush him, but Groves is enjoying his tale – and the look on my face – too much to stop. 'Container ships from South America drop their cargo in the shallow water near the Needles, then a local boat goes out. A bloke my son knows is still in jail. The idiot used his own phone to ring the Albanian contact.'

As Groves speaks, he stands with his feet apart, hands behind his back. In his corduroys and hat, English sartorial shorthand for gentility, he could be a farmer out of Trollope. We look out at the land over which he has dominion: chalky English downs, oak woods, ponds, storm clouds. But this is no normal part of England; geography has made all usual forms of trade more difficult. Where the villa once stood, Roman debris and modern festival rubbish intermingle.

Over at the fishing ponds the clouds dance on the water.

'Are the fish tasty?' I ask.

'Oh, nobody *eats* them,' Groves says. 'They just catch them and throw them back.'

As in the Neolithic, Iron Age Britons ate comparatively little fish, according to the archaeological record. Possibly, this is because of the sacredness of water – as a deity, as a place between worlds, as a site for religious ritual deposition. Possibly it is because the sea was where the human dead were sent.[17]

The Romans, by contrast, loved fish – smothered in sauce.[18] Along with wine and olive oil, garum, a fermented fishy sauce, was one of the main things they shipped around their empire, including to Britain. A Latin shopping list from AD 100 found at the commander's residence in the Vindolanda fort on Hadrian's Wall reads: 'chickens, twenty, a hundred apples, if you can find nice ones, a hundred or two hundred eggs, if they are for sale at a fair price . . . 8 sextarii of fish sauce . . . olives'. In Rome, meanwhile, oysters imported from Britain became a delicacy.[19]

With the wild-food forager Fergus Drennan, I return to Brading, the Roman villa. Brading now sits far inland; the marshy foreshore was reclaimed in the late nineteenth century.[20] But when the Romans were there it is likely that there was a wide lagoon and that 'vessels would have been able to moor at about 250m from the villa'.[21] The small wood above the villa is still called Centurion's Copse. This 'high ground . . . was thus another island, which, in case of need would form a "keep" for the Roman garrison.'[22]

At low tide, Fergus and I go down to the seashore and pick limpets off the rocks. Back home, we boil and ferment them in the Sicilian sea salt I collected from rock pools outside the Neolithic island caves I visited – Sicily was a 'centre for the culinary arts' in the classical world and an influence on Roman cuisine[23] – and make our own double-island garum.

In the fields around Brading itself, we pick mushrooms to make the ketchup the Romans were fond of. There were vines, herbs, vegetables in the Roman-era deposits,[24] and the hedgerows around Brading are still full of the species that archaeologists found among the charred plant remains (things that were eaten): fat hen, orache, sorrel.

At this most extensively excavated of villas, archaeologists have been able to prove that the inhabitants, whoever they were – no names are recorded – spent their money on wine from south Gaul and olive oil from southern Spain.[25] (A luxury habit that died out pretty quickly after the Romans left, and only really became commonplace in Britain again in the past half-century.) Their cuisine was served up on imported pottery from central and east Gaul. They ate a lot of oysters and the endemic Celtic fava bean (milled into a flour, presumably mixed with olive oil and possibly flavoured with fermented fish sauce, as per the first-century recipe book known as *Apicius*). They cooked both with the indigenous wheat strain called emmer, as well as spelt, the imported variety.[26]

Seafaring trade was obviously crucial to Rome's interest in Britain, and Britain's barbarian natural wealth was famous from at least the time of Strabo.[27] Tacitus put Britain's 'gold and silver and other metals, as the prize of conquest'.[28] British historians have long argued over the location of Britain's 'tin islands' (Cassiterides) – crucial to the manufacture of bronze. Diodorus Siculus's description of the island of 'Ictis' to which tin was conveyed on carts at low tide is tantalizingly vague. While the Isle of Wight ('Vectis') *sounds* like Ictis, St Michael's Mount is geographically similar (unlike the Isle of Wight, it is currently fordable at low tide), while the peninsula of Mount Batten in Devon has the most plentiful evidence of settlement and trading since long before Roman times.[29]

The Isle of Wight thesis seemed (to me) to receive new fuel at the turn of the millennium, when oyster fishermen alerted archaeologists to the wealth of ancient artefacts they were dredging up from the seabed, thanks to their new (seabed-scraping) trawling equipment. In 1999, divers were sent down and discovered, off

Bouldner on the island's north coast, a number of amazing things. First, they saw a lobster pushing Mesolithic worked-stone tools out of its burrow – 'the first known Mesolithic archaeological excavation by a member of the lobster community', as the Isle of Wight's county archaeologist David Tomalin put it wryly in the report he wrote up later.[30] They also saw what was clearly a submerged forest: 'notable were the silver birch, the bark of which occasionally retained its silver sheen, indicating the well-preserved nature of the drowned lands'.[31] That is, the whole of the Solent – now a famously treacherous tidal channel – was once a 'sheltered valley' entwined with rivers and streams and lived in by humans. At some point 'before 2500 years BC', the sea eventually eroded the land on the western side and broke through, making the valley uninhabitable, but possibly still fordable at low tide,[32] as Diodorus Siculus described in 30 BC:

> The inhabitants of Britain . . . are especially friendly to strangers and have adopted a civilized way of life because of their interaction with traders and other people. It is they who work the tin into pieces the size of knucklebones and convey it to an island off Britain, called Ictis . . . [where] merchants buy the tin from the natives.[33]

But later, in a detailed study for English Heritage, Tomalin concluded that 'the severance event would be a Neolithic one lying in either the later 4th or the later 3rd millennium cal BC.'[34] A valley wandered by Neolithic humans, possibly; Roman-era ones, unlikely.

Nevertheless, if some of Britain's offshore islands were places of sacred rite and learning, others may have been places of supranational trade into Roman times: a bit like twentieth-century Hong Kong, or twenty-first-century Man or Cayman.

The most significant of all Rome's imports *into* Britain was literacy. Obviously, this was a brutal swap: liberty lost, text-based culture gained.[35] This was the Celts' tragedy: their culture was easy to eliminate. When the Romans left Britain, they left behind a people literate in Latin, on the cusp of the development of their own hybrid language; able to record their own histories, legends, thoughts and ideas. It was, undeniably, a revolution; but also a trauma: the evisceration of something ancient and ancestral.

The Roman villas on the isle of Wight take us into the very *oikos* of this trauma. Here, in the domestic sphere, the results of romanization played out in the most intimate of ways. Probably, as Caesar remarked, access to Roman luxuries (rather than civilization) in the 'Province' had corrupted the Gauls.[36] This became deliberate Roman policy; including creating a class of *obsides*: hostages sent to Rome to be 'inculcated . . . during their early years'.[37]

Whoever these people on Vectis were, there is much we don't know about them – how they exercised, what languages they spoke in privacy, whether they enjoyed their sex lives, practised meditation, or felt themselves completely compromised by colonization, either as subject or ruler. What we do know is how they organized their domestic space, what they ate and how they chose to represent aesthetically the colonial mishmash of art, mythology and religion, proffered or forced upon them.

Roman mosaics, being exotic, durable and instantly palpable examples of personal taste, have always thrilled and perplexed in equal measure. The Anglo-Saxons named some of their villages after Roman 'patterned pavements'.[38] For a faraway province beyond Ocean, the Britannias had some excellent examples: in Somerset, 'the *only* mosaic yet known in the Empire which illustrated scenes from the Aeneid'[39] (beautiful, naked Dido, showing to the viewer what is surely one of early art's most expressive bums); in Fishbourne Roman palace, an entire sea-themed floor with Cupid riding a bucking dolphin; references to Virgil and Ovid at Lullingstone; more dolphins, scallops and Cupids in Bignor; Bacchus at Thruxton;[40] a room dedicated to the cult of Orpheus at Brading and at Withington, Gloucestershire.

Of all the mosaic series in Roman Britain, that in Brading villa has proved hardest to interpret, giving rise to numerous theories. As at Fishbourne, there is a marked maritime theme: the entrance panel depicts 'nereids [sea nymphs] . . . being carried over the sea, through the realm of Neptune to the Isles of the Blessed', according to the historian of Roman art in Britain Martin Henig. This emphasis on Britain itself as the locus for the Graeco-Roman belief in the Isles of the Dead is much discussed in classical literature and, it seems, by Britons themselves. On the coins they began minting after the conquest, Romano-British rulers played up their exotic, trans-Ocean status: depicting hybrid creatures from Graeco-Roman myth such as Pegasus (child of Neptune) to speak to Romans symbolically of Britain's edge-iness. A kind of self-imposed 'Hyperboreanism', or 'Zenithism', as I have begun to think of it.

Roman-type hybridity was also familiar to the Britons: their own, endangered Druidic code seems to have included shamanic-religious shapeshifting as part of its system of beliefs.[41] Because the Romans were so phenomenally disciplined as soldiers and administrators, it is easy to forget sometimes that they, too, were superstitious and believed in magic. Henig understands the villa itself, with its unfolding of classical themes from one room to the next, as a 'veritable sacred way' designed for cult processions (a bit like the processional landscape around Maeshowe).[42]

The owners of Brading Roman villa were interested in Orpheus, Hercules, Bacchus and Attis – all patrons of Roman salvation mystery cults. But there is also Ceres: Rome's Demeter, the goddess whom several centuries earlier Strabo had described as being worshipped on one of Britain's small islands.

The most argued over of the mosaics shows a human figure (usually assumed to be a man on account of his stolidness and girth) with a cockerel's head. John and Frederick Price, who were the first to properly catalogue the mosaics, identified him in 1881 as the gnostic deity Abraxas – seeing him as some sort of mystic initiation figure.[43] Subsequent commentators agree, broadly. For Miranda Aldhouse-Green – who with her husband, Stephen, authored a book on ancient Europe's quasi-shamanic beliefs – he is a shape-shifting local shaman. Henig admirably changed his mind several times, at one point deciding the figure was 'probably a satyr' of

Bacchus; or Hermes (Mercury); or 'the god Iao'. He has more recently concluded that 'the Brading guardian is in fact the syncretic Graeco-Egyptian god Hermes Trismegistos . . . god of wisdom' – not a cockerel but a badly done ibis. There are prosaic explanations for most human habits of the past, as observed through the foggy lens of time by archaeologists, but it is indeed very hard to see how a human with a bird's head is anything less than a magical creature. Possibly the mosaic evokes a very ancient shamanic symbol indeed; the paintings in Lascaux include a bird-headed figure.[44]

The Brading bird-headed human puts the other mosaics in a magical frame too. What about the mosaic which arguably shows Achilles derobing himself from his female costume (his mother, Thetis, has disguised him as a woman on the island of Skyros in order to avoid the Troy-draft)? Or is this a portrait of a woman, Daphne, or Arethusa, having her clothes ripped from her by an aggressive god – a rape scene suitable for a colonized country? There are other mosaics here, too, of male aggression: Lycurgus attacking Ambrosia, and Neptune trying to rape, or rescue from being raped, or both, Amymone (one of the sisters from Aeschylus's *Suppliants*).[45]

But in addition to the scenes of violence against women there is also the mosaic of Ceres, who appears with Triptolemos – thricefold, a priest of the Eleusinian Mysteries, which celebrate the separation and reunion of mother and daughter and the turning of the seasons. When he was a baby, Ceres breastfed him back to health; when he was older, she taught him the art of agriculture. And at the centre of it all is Medusa – herself a terrifying agent of metamorphosis, a sculptor – and in recent feminist interpretation, powerful returner of the male gaze.[46]

It is possible that the owner of Brading villa merely picked some designs out of a pattern-book – ones that they thought looked nice, or prestigious, or which showed off their learning – much as you or I might do when choosing floor tiles for the bathroom or a paint colour for the kitchen. But given their collective mythic complexity, it seems more likely that the mosaics were commissioned and executed to advance a particular religious sensibility. This was no ordinary part of Britain, after all: it was an island off an island, a liminal place of the type long worshipped as a means to access the spirit world, a place a shaman might go to for inspiration.[47]

Roman culture was patriarchal, and despite the figures of Ceres and Medusa in the Brading mosaics, it would be hard to argue that the scenes depicted present an overt challenge to this new system. (The bird-headed figure may, of course, be a woman.) But what is there here that we do not see? What do we not realize in our interpretations, even about ourselves? How we understand the past changes from age to age. How we see ourselves, too, changes from phase to phase of our lives.

The Romans, like any colonial power, seriously damaged native culture in Britain. Some parts of it were killed off completely. There is a terrifying lacuna in the archaeological record for the presence of the Iceni tribe, Boudica's people, which can only mean one thing: they ceased to exist from the time of her last battle.[48] The Druids lived on elsewhere: in Ireland, where their presence is palpable throughout the ensuing period of text-based Christianization. And the Britons in general – those who weren't killed – continued to eat and reproduce and follow their own form of public worship, as evidenced in the hot-spring sanctuary to Sulis-Minerva at Bath and the dream-interpretation temple of Nodens in Gloucestershire: Celtic gods taking precedence over Roman ones in both cases.

Private cult ritual is more difficult to trace, and subversive or insurrectionary practice might by definition be expected to be well hidden, but the archaeologist Eleanor Scott has examined burials and well depositions in Roman villas on the British mainland and posited a theory of a 'female-led revitalization movement against patriarchal dominance in Roman Britain'[49] at around the time that the Brading mosaics were laid in the third or fourth century AD.

Scott doesn't write about Brading Roman villa, but the key traits she picks out elsewhere are in evidence here too: sacred depositions, it is presumed, by women, often of the recent dead, secretly interred within wells or water sources near the dwelling places. Scott notices that this happens around the time that the villas themselves – semi-public, semi-private buildings, with their cult mosaics possibly forming an overt sacred way – also become more fortress-like:

> Villas became more closed with elaborate facades and enclosed by walls and/or earthworks, tightly controlling the movements of not only visitors but also the occupants, possibly women in particular.

She speculates that through these 'depositions', women 'sought greater control', also pointing out, first, that Britain's Celtic culture is set apart from Gaul's – with its own 'long history of distinct types of ritual behaviour'; animal depositions in buildings being known of in Britain since at least the Neolithic – and, second, that 'archaeologists, especially Romanists, are not recognizing ritual activity in the archaeological record', especially where it pertains to women.

Was there any ritual activity at Brading? Victorian excavators discovered a 24-metre-deep well within the villa's second-best bathhouse, probably used by the estate workers – presumably a native underclass.[50] About the second century AD, people began to throw things into the well: some southern Gaulish glassware, a bowl stamped with the mark DIVIVATUS (from the mid-second-century reign of emperor Hadrian), animal bones, floor tiles. Ten metres of clean earth went in next. Six metres from the top, a whole layer of oyster shells, animal bones and nails was deposited, then some tiles with extraordinarily vivid handprints, footprints (both barefoot and in sandals) and the pawprint of a dog. Four metres from the top a young man was entombed with three young dogs. This well and its depositions are only briefly analysed in the major report on Brading Roman villa from Cunliffe in 2013, but Tomalin writes about it at length in his catalogue of Roman Wight. 'Such finds,' he concludes, 'must provide food for all but the most barren imaginations.'[51]

Tomalin doesn't suggest what, but thanks to his work, and Scott's, and that of archaeologist Martin Carruthers – who has suggested a range of esoteric activity in relation to the cult properties of earlier subterranean Iron Age dwellings in Orkney – it is possible to imagine that the depositions may represent a form of protest, probably female-led and (literally) underground. Throughout history, many movements against state power have begun with female protest, from the October Revolution in Russia to 2022's insurrection against the clergy in Iran.[52] There were female-led rebellions across Europe in Roman times too. It was not just Boudica in Britain – Tacitus has a long discussion about German respect and reverence for women, and their famous prophetesses: Veleda, and earlier, Aurinia: 'The Germans traditionally regard many of the female sex as prophetic, and indeed, by an excess of superstition, as divine.'[53]

Since at least Roman times, women and their narratives have been easy for society to marginalize and ignore. But this wasn't how it had been, until then, in Britain.[54] If you gather together the little seeds of evidence that remain from Romano-British times and allow them to bloom, the brief defiance of these wild flowers can transform the landscape: *Black-clothed women beseech their divinities. Boudica's hare dashes through the legs of the Roman legion. Medusa turns her gaze upon us at Brading Roman villa. A woman lays the body of a young man in the well of her bathhouse.*

The evidence can only take us so far. After that we have to surrender ourselves to the lost possibilities, to reflect on everything that was deliberately or inadvertently repressed, to dream of alternative dimensions.[55]

For many years, it was easy for scholars of the British Iron Age to ignore or overlook – or just not *see* – the presence and meaning of female power, particularly as it manifested in goddesses and heroines of popular religion and storytelling. As late as 2013, a British academic, already irritated by what he saw as unscholarly attempts to reconstruct a 'sovereignty goddess' for the Iron Age, would assert, 'There is no trace of a widespread cult of Epona in Britain . . . and no solid evidence for a native British horse goddess.'[56]

The nineteenth-century Welsh academic Edward Anwyl was one of the first to connect the mythical figure of Rhiannon in the Welsh story collection *The Mabinogi* to the archaeological evidence in Europe of a native horse goddess called Epona.[57] Now it seems that he was right: recently, excavations from the unusual hexagon-shaped temple of Meonstoke, near Winchester, have revealed that, buried at the centre of the temple was the complete skeleton of a female horse, along with her perinatal foal, 'laid out very carefully, their heads pointing in different directions'.[58] Here was the worship of the horse goddess that *The Mabinogi* hinted of – a native belief system almost lost from sight.

Next door to the temple was a bathhouse with wall plaster of a river goddess or nymph, emphasizing the sacredness of water and rivers as female deities. Epona herself, from whose name we get the word 'pony', was a Celtic mother goddess, a goddess of fertility, and later a goddess of cavalry for soldiers in the Roman army.

The Romans were quick to appropriate local custom, and they did so fifteen miles to the south, at another sacred place: Hayling, a small, marshy (and now heavily built up) island facing the Isle of Wight. Prior to and during Roman times, British devotees brought animals to Hayling from the mainland to be fattened for some days on the island's grassland before being offered for worship not to a goddess (unfortunately for me) but to a 'Mars type tribal god'.[59]

Today, the site of the temple stands beneath a broad-branched oak tree in the middle of farmland. My nearest experience of temple sacrifice was the festival of Durga Puja in Kolkata, India, when I saw devotees bring goats for the goddess, watched the Brahmin priests cutting their throats, was fascinated by that holy place, red and sticky. Undoubtedly, Hayling too was once red and sticky.

Something draws me back to the island. We take our children there, one bank-holiday weekend. The children love the funfair, a rickety, jolly place by the sea emphatically called FUNLAND. On the beach we pick sea beet and swim in the cold water of the Solent. My husband goes off for a meeting; I sit huddled on the shingle, watching my daughters jumping in and out of the sea. The island has shown me something that I haven't wanted to see: the night before, I woke up in our seaside apartment and realized a truth. In the morning, it seems that I am mistaken, but the feeling of that midnight moment lingers: that I am living with obscurity, if not obfuscation.

Two thousand years earlier, I would have interpreted this revelation as a direct communication by the god, or goddess. That afternoon, sitting on the beach, I simply feel upset by my instinct that something is wrong. I look out over the water to the Isle of Wight. By now I have lived on one island and walked across another. But the very first island trip I ever made was to the Isle of Wight, with my eldest, when she was a baby, back when I knew nothing about islands and was learning everything I could about daughters. The journey was iconic. We were in love. I had only just learned to drive, she to walk; we drove and walked all over the island together. We visited the sites of each of the island's eight villas – one in the car park of an industrial estate (the villa 'buried under a metre of hardcore');[60] another in a water-logged field (I took a photo of her happy face from over my head, smiling from a sling on my back); in the centre of the island in a village and on farmland; on its north and south coast; the eighth being Brading itself.[61] We visited the Benedictine monastery of Quarr – from early times a quarry; its stone was used in the Tower of London.[62] I took a photograph of her sitting under a huge, ancient oak tree, a temple with three trunks. (Later, when I look at it, I see me and my two daughters.)[63] On the very southern tip of the island we walked down the steep cliff path to St Catherine's Lighthouse in the wind and sun. I have memories of her lovely burgeoning in all of these places.

It was the apex of our golden age. I was still all hers; she completely mine.

4.
Iona
Christ (AD 563)

In the centre of the Inner Hebrides, the pollen of its petals, is Iona. Such is the island's draw today, it is possible to catch a train from Glasgow to Oban, which meets the ferry to Mull, where, upon arrival, a bus is waiting to take you across the island to board the passenger boat to Iona. And lo, five or so hours after you set off, you have arrived: to such a speck of a place you can walk around it in an afternoon. Even though the history of the British Isles is full of counterintuitions, Iona is distinct: an island the influence of which is out of all proportion to its size.

Nothing is spoken of this iota of land amongst others until 563 – and then history explodes with its reputation. This was the year when Columba, scion of Irish royalty, arrived from Ireland in a hide-skinned currach. His parents, despite being pagans, were modern in outlook: they'd had their child fostered with a priest and trained up in the new religion. But their son was hot-tempered, and in his forties (ancient for the times) he spurned his native land, escaping with several companions (hagiographers later claim twelve) to the islands on the opposite coast. After negotiation with the local king, they settled Ioua, as it was known until the eighteenth century, when a scribe copying out *Vita Columbae* wrote an 'n' for a 'u'.

It is interesting that they chose an island as their spiritual power-base – a discrete world, yet one sociable and interconnected. For a first-generation Christian like Columba, establishing his mission on an island like Iona was not an act of isolation. It put him at the centre of things. Proximity was the point. In the sixth century, the water which surrounded the landmass was its highway. Of course, there were hermits who sought *eremus* – spiritual retreat in the 'deserts of the sea' – on island stacks and remote outposts such as Iceland, Skellig and Sùla Sgeir. But the Inner Hebrides were not that; they were a thoroughfare. And Iona, while small, was fertile; it had its own measure of independence. If the Druids concentrated their core power and energy in one large productive island – Anglesey – Columba and his ilk dispersed it democratically between many little islands. Rival brotherhoods soon sprang up on nearby Eigg and Lismore, but it was Columba's particular influence that looped around Ireland, Scotland, Wales and England. Until the Reformation, Britain was ringed by a forcefield of monk-inhabited islets.

The Roman empire was no more, but thanks to Constantine the religion it had chosen to promote disseminated the empire's patriarchal ethos via one imperial language and social code. A king's fortune, meanwhile, turned on the god he chose to honour – and the priest employed to do it.

Columba – who adopted his Latin name, Dove, following his conversion; his pagan name was Fox – was not a wandering hermit. He was a pragmatic, energetic promoter of the new solo God. It is not clear why the foreign message of Christ triumphed so quickly in Ireland, his native land. Perhaps its simplicity appealed like a beacon in the thronging mist of Celtic proliferations. Maybe the stories were better. Possibly it was the thought of being accepted, regardless of caste or class, and watched over, and forgiven.

That's what I once thought. Now I see in Christianity a potent, greedy mixture – not even a refinement – of all the different traditions and texts which have gone into its creation. And although the stories are good – especially the one about the baby – they are also familiar: the central sacrifice, the dying/reborn king, his watchful mother and judgemental father. I now think that the thing which stands out – the really revolutionary thing that Christianity brought to these islands – was technology: writing. This was the paradigm shift.[1]

The idea of caste-free, democratic writing was resisted for a long time by the Druids, but Christianity had no loyalty to the local dogma. Christian monks knew that the copying down of texts, sacred and secular, from other writers had long been practised by Greeks, Jews, Romans. The inhabitants of the Britannias learned stone carving and inscription during the Roman colonization, just as, some centuries earlier, Gandharan art in India flourished in the wake of contact with soldiers from Greece and traders from Europe. But what the Christians brought next was even simpler and easier: Latin, written on wax tablets or with ink on parchment. For Britain, at the time, it was as significant as the invention of the printing press, the phone, or the Internet. Writing wrought a revolution.

Columba and his companions became absolute masters of this modern technology of book production in the monastery they established on Iona. The Druids outlawed writing but probably used Ogham – inscriptions have been found all over the British Isles. Although the Romans' literary output in these islands appears to have been largely functional and ceremonial – monumental inscriptions, shopping lists, letters – the language they introduced, Latin, would later flourish like fennel in the monastic context.

In a very short space of time, literary production – via scriptoria – became the backbone of monastic life, with the writing and copying of ancient texts (both local and foreign) as one of the monks' sacred purposes. It was Irish scribes who 'introduced word separation and systematic punctuation', eventually making 'Old Irish and Old English the earliest western vernaculars to be written down'.[2]

The monks' literacy in Latin also ensured that posterity was granted to their leaders and heroes. Columba, in particular, achieved fame across Europe thanks to Adomnán, his learned successor on Iona and his biographer. As Adomnán put it (modestly quoting a fifth-century prophecy by St Mochta): 'a son will be born whose name Columba will become famous through all the provinces of the ocean's islands'.[3]

As well as Columba's biography, *Vita Columbae*, Adomnán was the author of a book on the holy places of Christendom, *De locis sanctis*, which he wrote – it seems unbelievable, but this is the claim – after interviewing Arculf, a Gaulish monk-bishop who landed on Iona only by chance, during his return home from Jerusalem, when a storm pushed his ship off course. *De locis sanctis* is a travelogue, describing Jerusalem – in all its glory and filth – for those who have no chance of going there. Arculf visits the very fig tree from which Judas hanged himself, and saw the cloth which Mary wove.[4] There are vivid speculations about Jesus's sepulchre, which Arculf measured himself and 'found to be seven feet'.[5]

Most of the monastic writers of the time display an intimacy with Biblical material, quoting the Old Testament prophets as if they were alive last week; namedropping Jesus, Paul and Jerome as if they lived on neighbouring islands. (Jerome: who thought the people of these isles utterly barbaric and sexually suspicious; cannibals who dine on 'buttocks and nipples'; who do not even 'have individual wives, but . . . indulge themselves like beasts, as if they had read Plato's *Republic*'.[6] That's right: Plato's *Republic* as medieval pornography.) The monks also read, wrote and copied the format of medieval hagiographies coming over to Britain from the continent. Soon they had become so very adept at reading and writing about completely foreign people, themes and places that it was their European colleagues who were coming to them for their learning: to Ireland itself, or to Iona, or to any of the throng of monastery islands in the watery borderland between Ireland and Scotland.

The monks who worked in Iona's scriptorium seem naturally to have woven in pagan-Celtic mythology and artforms, both visually and verbally. Works such as the *Book of Kells* (possibly produced on Iona) and the *Lindisfarne Gospels* (created by a brother-monastery) – with their elaborate margins coloured by local pigments (white seashells, blue woad, yellow arsenic), populated by exotic Syrian desert beasts, familiar island sea birds, as well as bearded saints in gaudy tights (I love male medieval hosiery) – preserved an ancient oral culture from oblivion.

Much of the impetus for writing in Latin and promulgating the Christian faith came out of Ireland. Until Christianity, Druid culture continued there, and Columba and abbots like him took on roles previously performed by Druids. Columba deploys a range of druidical/Biblical magic tricks, the first and most important of which (in Adomnán's eyes) is prophecy. He can also cause the weather to change at will, like those nine priestesses Pomponius Mela described as living on Sena. Weather control is a most ancient, useful and widespread form of public magic. Columba is also good at water-divining, body healing, political diplomacy and powerbroking. This magic survived death, with books that Columba had written being carried over to the island to nourish it in times of drought. Indeed, it is clear from the texts, as from the archaeology, that for a long time the Celtic religions promulgated by Druids and the new religion promulgated by Celtic Christian monks met and mingled. It's hard to fix the point at which Druidism stopped and Christianity began. Some Christian saints coexist with the Druids, or the magicians; some challenge the old priests with new magic.

Iona's monastic community was a melting pot of Britannic nationalities: English, Scots, Irish. Ethnicity is no bar here, and nor is mother tongue for Latin is the lingua franca. (Adomnán emphasizes this: punning flamboyantly on the name of the island in Irish and Latin and pointing out that Columba's Latin name, and the prophet Jonah's Hebrew one, both mean dove.) Columba, meanwhile, is a frequent traveller off the island: forever getting into boats to visit other monasteries on nearby islands, or to attend Irish synods, or to make tours of Pictland, or to talk with mainland kings. He entertains visiting dignitories as ambassador of his religion. He also ordained the kings of Dalriada, the coastal kingdom of which Iona was a part.

The capital of Dalriada is believed to have been Dunadd, a hill fort not far from Oban (now the mainland departure point for Iona). Inhabited from the Iron Age, it reached the peak of its magnificence during Columba's day. It was composed of a series of fortified terraces built over the natural shape of the hill: layers of protection for the citadel at the top. It was an international place. Gaulish merchants traded here: pottery has been found from all over Europe. There was a sophisticated indigenous metal-working industry. The kings who ruled Dalriada also left their impress in the rock. Of their sacred-regal carvings, several still exist. There is a carving of a boar, an as yet undeciphered message in Ogham script, a bowl-indentation (presumably for oblations, possibly symbolizing an island or its loch), and two footprints. I climb through the fort, and there, where the ceremonies happened and the seascape opens up, I place my foot. The shoe fits. The Dunadd kings, like me, wore a European size 38.

Dunadd represented the old way, how it had been done for centuries. There are ancient kingship inauguration footprints carved into stone all over Scotland and Ireland. One of the last things I did before leaving Orkney was to drive down to the island of South Ronaldsay, borrow the key of St Mary's Church from the local post-mistress[7] and stand in the gloom at the back of the abandoned building with my bare feet in the footprints carved two thousand years before into a sea-worn boulder. (A portable inauguration stone.) The cold of the intervening ages seemed to steep upwards through my feet, and maybe that was what monarchs were supposed to think about too: the weight of their responsibility, the heavy, watchful nature of their lineage.

Adomnán gives a laboured description of how an angel appeared to Columba, commanding him to choose Áedán as king and striking him with a whip when he disagreed (the scar 'remained with him for the rest of his life'). 'I am sent to you by God,' the angel emphasized. And so Columba sailed back to Iona, where he met Áedán and 'ordained him king in accordance with the king's command'. This long-drawn-out description suggests some form of argument between the monks and the local monarchs. Columba had been involved in a fight with kings before, in his homeland; he was exiled on this account. And thus, although Adomnán is keen to stress the Biblical overtones to the new process, he is vague on the details. How much of local tradition was condoned? Was there some form of portable footprint stone for Áedán to stand on, as in Orkney? Iona's graveyard was said to be the source of 'the old Druidic Stone of Destiny . . . taken to . . . Scone, where the last of the Celtic Kings of Scotland was crowned on it'.[8] In 1296, a sandstone block measuring 66 x 42 x 27 centimetres was taken to England (stolen) by Edward I and placed within the Coronation Chair at Westminster Abbey; Elizabeth II sat on it in 1953, but duly gave it back in 1996. It was borrowed again for Charles.

Columba also appears to have changed how things were done. There were ancient pagan practices which were explicitly outlawed. Adomnán makes it clear that the eating of mare's flesh was prohibited, for example. Mare's flesh had been eaten by new kings in Ireland's most ancient rite: a complicated ceremony in which the new king mated with, killed, ate and bathed in the broth of a white mare. There was a certain tolerance for the old ways, but not for all of them.

Columba was marking a new beginning. Clearly, he was boundlessly energetic and charismatic. He had a tireless team of scribes on his side, and soon European literature was awash with his name and that of his island. He was lucky to have sat at the peak of a century of exploration and change, of what really was an adventurous age, characterized by an absolute restlessness of endeavour.

Columba's immediate predecessor in this field was St Brendan, whom he may or may not have met – but whose actual, folkloric and literary example (in the Irish and Latin biographies) probably influenced his every move. Brendan, if he existed, would have been quite old when he visited Columba in Scotland (according to the *Vita*). It was said in one of his genealogies that he was descended from Queen Medb, the mythological Irish warrior queen herself. If so, he was semi-sacred. Whatever his antecedents, during his life it is said that he went on an extraordinary set of voyages across the Atlantic, visiting at least fourteen plausible islands, as well as one that was divine – making Columba's own hop across the Irish Sea look trifling by comparison. In so doing he both expanded geographical knowledge and co-opted the age-old classical Greek and Celtic myths of the western Isles of the Blessed (beyond the setting sun) into the new, fragrant Christian paradise.

Otherwordly islands to the west had tantalized the classical and Celtic mind since myth-making began – the Greeks called them the Fortunate Isles, *Tír na nÓg* in Irish (island of eternal youth). Brendan's particular cultural coup was to have restyled this ancient, sacred concept as a Christian island of paradise, a place of saintly Edenic rest.

The *Life of Brendan* (*Vita Brendani* in Latin, *Betha Brennain* in Irish)[9] begins with the saint gazing out 'upon the vast and gloomy ocean on every side' and dreaming of a 'beautiful noble island with the ministering of angels thereon'. The angel of the Lord promises to take him there, but the island is hard to find: the journey involves visits to various islands which appear to be variations on paradise itself – a monastic, vegetarian island; an island where three classes of saints live ('St Brendan, leaving the boat, walked about the island, where the fragrance was like that of a house stored with pomegranates'); as well as some hellish visions with Judas Iscariot and volcanoes. Although Brendan is finally shown the actual paradise island by the angel, he soon returns home, bearing its smell with him ('Do you not know, by the fragrance of our garments, that we have been in the paradise of God?').

The thing about paradise is that to visit it, you normally have to die, and thus descriptions of it are irrefutable. I once spent several hours on a bus in northern Pakistan while a young Islamic cleric made us listen to a taped sermon about paradise, on repeat. In addition to the usual houris it was the preponderance of fruit that struck me. Brendan's travelogues go on about fruit, too. There must be something about perpetual harvests that speak deeply to our hungry inheritance.

Such was the popularity of Brendan's biographies and travelogues in medieval times – they were translated into Middle English, French, German, Flemish, Italian, Provençal and old Norse[10] – that by the time of Columbus's voyage to America, the completely imaginary idea of an 'island of St Brendan' was a standard feature of European geographical knowledge. The island is there on Martin Behaim's globe of 1492, some distance from the Canaries. For centuries the islanders thought they could see it and numerous state-endorsed expeditions were launched to find it.

Many of the descriptions of the islands Brendan went to *do* sound very much like eyewitness descriptions. Both the Irish *Life*, and the Latin travelogue, *Navigatio sancti Brendani Abbatis* (*Voyage of St Brendan the Abbot*), have the saint visiting the 'sheep islands' (believed to be Faroe), volcanic islands (possibly Iceland), as well as various hermit outposts in the sea. He also travelled to Brittany, Orkney and the Hebrides, of course visiting St Columba on Iona.

Monks such as Brendan reckoned – as Adomnán writes – that 'they had passed beyond the range of human exploration' in their oceanic travels.[11] But they were only following in the sea-tracks of innumerable anonymous 'seafarers, fishermen and solitary pilgrims'.[12] And indeed, by the time that Christian monks began making real voyages across the seas, to proselytize, explore and forge ever-more-outlying centres of meditation and prayer, early vernacular literature – which was oral – was already spinning its own wonderful adventure stories on the ocean. Thus, St Brendan's voyage was written up, using the local literary form of *immrama* or *echtrai*, voyage tales. (Which is what this is.) An *immram* was a sea voyage with a Christian context; an *echtra* mythological and pagan.[13] At the time that Adomnán was writing *Vita Columbae*, other scribes were copying down older tales than that. What the monks bore witness to – were agents of – was a strange and wonderful literary overlap between the explicitly religious and definitively secular subject matter.

Bards, singers and storytellers continued to be employed by Welsh, Scottish and Irish rulers into early modern times. Shakespeare's fools are a remnant of this tradition. But since monks were the only ones producing written literature in early-medieval Britain and Ireland, it is as cheering as it is surprising that quite a bit of native magic gets into literature that styles itself wholly Christian.

There was once a Celtic god – not Brendan – but *Bran*. His name – which means 'raven' – associates him with the otherworld, prophecy and music. That much is surmise, for nothing from this time was written down. And when the stories about Bran are eventually made incarnate in words, the ancient gods have become mythical heroes. In *The Mabinogi* he becomes the giant and good king Brân who loses his head after the disastrous marriage between his sister Branwen and the king of Ireland. Following his instructions, Brân's head was buried by his followers at Whitehill in London (at the Tower, with its ravens), as a talisman against outside invasion.

In Irish texts, Bran has more fun: lured across the seas, with a ship full of companions, by a woman who holds out an apple branch, and the promise of the island of women that I read of that day in the British Library. Bran and his companions are helped on their voyage not by angels but by his half-brother Manannán, god of the sea, and they spend many years in that lovely island where 'splendours of every colour glisten' and 'treachery is unknown'. Then one of them gets homesick and begs to return to Ireland. The women warn them not to go, but Bran and his friends do not listen. When they near the Irish coast, they see some people gathered on the shore. Bran calls out to them, 'I am Bran,' expecting them to greet him with tears and joy. But the people do not recognize him. Then they add – and this bit always makes me shiver – 'But we have heard your name in our ancient stories.'

Impatiently, one of Bran's companions leaps from the coracle and swims to shore, whereupon he instantly becomes a heap of ashes. From the boat, Bran tells the Irish 'of all his wanderings from the beginning until that time. And he wrote these quatrains in Ogham, and then bade them farewell. And from that hour his wanderings are not known.'[14]

Until Brendan (often known as Brandon) came along, this prior Bran was Ireland's most famous wanderer-god. Just as St Bridgit took or was given the name of an ancient Irish fire goddess, so it was perhaps natural for St Brendan to take the name and attributes of the pagan god-king. Of course, it is not convenient for Christians to acknowledge this. And nor do they need to, for the old pagan religions have no scriptures, churches, funds or establishment support.

There is a very telling central difference between Bran's story and Brendan's: *women*. I began to wonder if the apple branch that the woman holds out to Bran could symbolise a feminist retelling of Eve. Certainly, the island she takes him to is a paradise; one where women live on their own terms.

It seems to be exactly this aspect of Bran's story that Brendan sought to overcome. A fourteenth-century Low Saxon edition of the life apparently opens with a description of the saint's impatience with old tales:

Brendan, having read a book full of miraculous stories, so strange and incredible, waxed indignant at such extravagancies, and threw the book into the fire.[15]

The ancient story is burned – and Brendan embarks on a new, male-centric voyage that will reconfigure ancient European thinking about the islands. Brendan's paradise is not an island of women but an island of male saints. A patriarchal coup.

If in Celtic civilization and mythology 'the high prestige of women' is a characteristic feature, the same cannot be said of Christianity. 'Do not take this learning from women or virgins,' St Ita tells her foster-son Brendan, 'lest you give occasion for reproach.' Whether or not this attitude grew out of Middle Eastern Christian culture or was exacerbated by being refracted through Rome, Christianity provided men who didn't want to be bothered by women with holy purpose. Later, in the Anglo-Saxon mainland there were 'double monasteries' – religious houses headed by abbesses – where monks and nuns coexisted, living separately, but under one roof and one aegis. That was not the case in Iona. Celibacy was not obligatory for ecclesiastics at the time, but it is clear that this was Iona's practice; and clear, too, that virginity was almost mandatory for holy women. In the realm of Brendan, as of that of Columba, women have little influence. In this monastic waterland – the isles of Whithorn, Iona, Lismore, Tiree – they are not even welcome.

That Columba himself had little use for women is clear from the *Vita Columbae*, which portrays an entirely male-dominated society. Under Columba's auspices, Iona is now inhabited only by monks – as becomes obvious at his funeral, when storms prevent laypeople coming over and disturbing his funeral rites, just as he had hoped. During his life, his interactions with women are largely perfunctory. In Book I of the *Vita Columbae* our hero disillusions a man of his mother's virtue by making her confess her 'secret sin . . . that she is unwilling to admit to anyone' (even the reader); confronts a man for sleeping with his mother; reproaches another for sleeping with whores; and consoles a man who fears that his wife will kill him with witchcraft. (*Women: lying, sinful, sin-creating.*) In Book II, a woman (who has no name) is mentioned in a positive light after she advises her husband, Findchán, to listen to Columba; and there follows a series of incidents in which Columba helps various men's daughters, sisters, an Irish slave-girl, a woman in childbirth (his relative). But when a woman on Rathlin Island goes on sex strike because her husband is so ugly, Columba forces her to submit by quoting Jesus and St Paul. (*Women: obedient, helpless, coercible.*) In Book III, Columba's mother dreams that an angel takes from her a beautiful cloak, for she is unworthy of 'glorious honour' but will bear a famous son. (*Women: necessary but undistinguished.*) This is no longer the culture of Boudica speaking boldly and fearlessly to Rome's power.

Adomnán himself became well known for his 'Law of the Innocents', a major legislative innovation designed to prevent the deaths of women, children and priests during war, and which he managed to get over fifty kings to sign at a conference in Ireland.[16] This is usually presented by historians as a sign of his thoughtfulness and empathy towards the weaker sex, a diplomatic coup on a par with brokering the UN's COP. But there is a counterargument, that Adomnán is also – consciously or not – enshrining in Irish law the Roman view of women: as alien to the battlefield, thus overturning centuries of local tradition, which saw women as warriors.[17]

Iona's *Book of Kells* (if it is Iona's) contains several portraits of men – lovely and languid, their bodies interlaced like the birds and beasts who also populate these pages, holding each other's beards, and stroking each other's tattooed faces. (Men, painting each other's love.) There is one picture of a woman. She is the Virgin Mary – full frontal, severe, enrobed in cloth and haloes – the first portrait of her in Western Christendom (only Coptic depictions are older).[18] Pictorially, the book implies a world where men are the status quo; women, remote and unfamiliar.

Why this is so is not clear, unless one views religious celibacy as an extreme form of contraception. Polyandry for the ancient Britons; abstinence for the Christians. Such considerations are, after all, pertinent in the finite landscape of islands. Whatever the truth of Columba's attitude to women, the idea that he disapproved enough to banish them entirely has entered the folk-language of the place. There's a mean little saying attributed to him, that he banned both cows and women from the island, for (as everybody knows) 'where there is a cow, there is a woman, and where there is a woman, there is mischief'. It is not quoted by Adomnán but appears much later; the Hebridean scholar Alexander Carmichael copies it into his field notebooks when gathering material for his hugely important collection of Gaelic folklore (and pagan remnants), *Carmina Gadelica*, at the end of the nineteenth century. Thereafter it obtained widespread currency; and although the part about the cows is clearly not true in practice – the monks kept cows for milk – monastic life did ban women from the island.

Why cows should be included in the legend seems mysterious today, for we no longer worship cows, as they still do in India. But we did once – the Great Mother, Europa, the Moon-Cow, after whom 'all Europe was named'. Columba, at the vanguard of pagan banishment, would have known that too. The feminist author Barbara Walker links cows etymologically and symbiotically with cowries, the shells known as groatie buckies in Orkney, and which 'everywhere represented the divine vulva'.[19] By 'everywhere', she means India, Egypt, Japan, Sudan, ancient Rome and Greece, Polynesia – but they are also in Britain.

There is now little archaeological trace of Columba's life and times on Iona. His wooden monastery was burnt by Vikings and the site buried by its modern replacement, and a museum has displaced the interlaced stone crosses inside on account of the weather. Only the ditch, or vallum, enclosing the early-medieval monastery is still partly extant. From the waste that was chucked over the ditch, archaeologists have been able to deduce that in the sixth century there was a 'strong preference for prime cuts of beef' – cows again – 'with whole haunches of venison next in popularity'.[20] No Brendanian vegetarian regime on Iona.

The island's premier artistic product, meanwhile, whether created on Iona or at the Abbey of Kells, ended up in Dublin; just as the *Lindisfarne Gospels* are now in London – the islands' jewels, pocketed by their mainland masters. Even the specific monastic rule of Columba was over and done with, on Iona, within a few centuries of the founder's death.

In 1207 or 1208, a nunnery was built on Iona, dedicated to St Mary or St Oran.[21] So holy women were eventually allowed in. Upon arriving at Iona by ferry, this medieval structure, made from pink granite, a ruin full of wild flowers, is one of the first things you see.

Not only that: the nunnery preserves in its structure one of the more extraordinary relics of pagan antiquity to have survived the onslaught of medieval Christianity: a symbol of female sexuality. This sculpture – called a Sheela-na-gig, and which unlike the crosses, has been left to the elements – is quite worn now, but it shows a naked woman, legs crossed, hands playing with genital folds.

I had never seen a Sheela-na-gig before I lived in Orkney, but there is one there too, high up on a pillar behind the altar in the cathedral; Kristin Linklater took me to see it. Sheela-na-gigs persist especially in the islands. Later, I would see them on the Isle of Man, at Penmon in Anglesey, in plain sight at Holy Cross Church in

Binstead on the Isle of Wight, at St Clement's Church in Rodel, Harris. People haven't had very nice things to say about them, until recently; Tom Muir, writing on the sculpture in St Magnus's Cathedral in Orkney, isn't unusual in finding it 'grotesque', 'a squatting female figure with open legs, displaying her genitals'.[22] The usually excellent Canmore website has a slightly panicky description of the Rodel carving as a 'nude female nursing a child and in a crouching attitude' – the entry is from July 1923 and hasn't been updated since. Even the twenty-first-century website Undiscovered Scotland advises that the ' "sheela na gig" should probably not be viewed too closely by anyone of a sensitive disposition (and is not shown on this page for the same reason).'

Sheela-na-gigs were once widespread in medieval Britain and Ireland. Why exactly, nobody knows: maybe they were cures for illness or infertility, or lucky charms for childbirth, or graphic demonstrations to a sexually timid people of the wonders that could be theirs, erotically. For Marija Gimbutas (inevitably hated/loved, quoted/misquoted in equal measure), these sexually explicit icons are direct descendants 'of the ancient frog goddess, the great regeneratrix' who 'ruled all water sources: lakes, rivers, springs, wells and rain clouds'. They certainly speak loudly of the complexity which is medieval Christianity in the British Isles. That these pornographic statues bedeck the churches of these isles suggests a robust and arguably glorious refusal of total folkloric memory loss; 'proof of the living cult of a pagan goddess'.[23]

The Sheela-na-gig at Iona is embedded in the outside wall of the nunnery, looking down over the busy thoroughfare that leads up from the port. (A public sexual-health campaign, perhaps.) The sculpture has been smoothed away by Scotland's acid rain, and by the hands of pilgrims who maybe once rubbed it to conceive a child. The neglect seems purposeful: to save pious pilgrim blushes.

It is a curious fact that despite being robbed of material wealth, both Iona and Lindisfarne have seen their spiritual power grow, not diminish, in recent times. While Lindisfarne is still strongly associated with Christianity, Iona's aura, oddly, has become a bit free-floating.

Neo-pagans come here (there are ley lines joining Iona to Glaston-bury, St Michael's Mount and Jerusalem). So do modern-day Druids, who presumably draw on the stories of Columba's antagonistic inter-actions with Druids for inspiration. Somebody on Iona told me that the exquisitely-carved Iona crosses were once Neolithic-cum-druidic standing stones, and this doesn't seem unlikely – why wouldn't the Christians deliberately reconfigure pagan worship-stones in this way?[24] There are more than enough stories in the canonical texts about Columba speaking with angels, raising the dead and practising more local forms of magic (he cured the King of Pictland's wizard with some Neolithic-sounding stone broth) to feed those with a new-age bent.[25]

It was only when I met a woman who'd done a 'vision quest' on Iona under the guidance of a North American shaman – she stared at a seashell for twenty-four hours until she saw infinity – that I real-ized how authentically Celtic-monastic such modern quests for enlightenment are. Celtic monks who went on retreat (*eremus*) in the trackless ocean – as Adomnán describes it – were on vision quests too. In 'the bosom of an isle, from the peak of a rock, that I might often see there the calm of the sea . . . its ebb and its flood-tide in their flow', says St Columba mystically in a twelfth-century Irish poem, 'Island Hermitage'.[26]

In addition to its modern spiritual side, Iona also has political and cultural cachet. It was the burial place of Scottish kings for centuries – as Shakespeare mentions in passing in *Macbeth* (Ross: 'Where is Duncan's body?' Macduff: 'Carried to Colm-kill / The sacred store-house of his predecessors / And guardian of their bones'). This legacy continues today: the most recent political figure to be buried here (in Relig Odhráin, the medieval graveyard next to the restored Benedic-tine Abbey on Iona) was John Smith, in 1994, leader of the Labour Party before Tony Blair.

Columba, who was Irish, transmogrified over the centuries into a Scottish nationalist hero (just as Patrick, who was British, became Ireland's patron saint). Apparently it's not about where you were born but where you end up. By the fourteenth century, the monks of Inchcolm, an island on the other side of Scotland that took Columba's name, were calling him 'Mouth of the dumb, light of the blind: O Columba, hope of the Scots'.

When English tourists began visiting Iona in the eighteenth century, they made much of the island's decrepitude. Rather in the way that Arculf emphasized the rot and dirt of Jerusalem, Samuel Johnson, Boswell, Wordsworth, all bewailed Iona's ruin. Johnson wrote melodramatically that 'The Island, which was once the metropolis of learning and piety, has now no school for education, nor temple for worship, only two inhabitants that can speak English, and not one that can write or read'. In 'Iona' Wordsworth describes the island in the lofty, aghast way of the contemporary-English in India:

> How sad a welcome! To each voyager
> Some ragged child holds up for sale a store
> Of wave-worn pebbles, pleading on the shore . . .
> Yet is yon neat trim church a grateful speck
> Of novelty amid the sacred wreck.

Of course, Romantic tourism such as this exactly presaged Iona's renaissance. The proximity of picturesque Staffa – 'discovered' for mass tourism in 1772 by Joseph Banks and made iconic by Mendelssohn and Walter Scott thereafter – meant that the steamship company MacBrayne was soon running tours taking in both islands. Tourism did not help Iona's farming tenants, who were cleared off the island in the nineteenth century by the landowner, the Duke of Argyll, to make way for sheep; even Columba could not protect them from the price of wool.

But there are 130,000 visitors a year today.[27] Agriculturally, also, things have returned towards how they were in Columba's day. The land, a mixture of peat upland and strips of seashell-fertilized machair along the shore, once more supports twelve crofts.[28] There is a strong political character to modern crofting – 'it fills the gap between the cooperation of the clan structure and Socialism', says crofter and island resident John Maclean. The Scottish government emphasizes that this form of landholding, 'unique to Scotland', 'resulted in a strong culture of community and common purpose'[29] – a stunning transformation, therefore, of an agricultural practice which landlords originally adopted as a form of extortion (poor-quality tenanted crofts replaced the better communal runrig land that landlords took away from their tenants to give to sheep). Modern crofting pays self-conscious homage to Columban self-sufficiency; 'you feel you are part of something ancient'. The mainland authorities work hard to reverse depopulation and decline on this, their flagship island. Thanks to Columba, 'Iona punches above its weight.' The island's name has spread across the world. Even after a millennium and a half, Columba still controls the food chain, drawing in the spiritual tourists upon whom the island's residents feed and prosper.

Many times, while writing this chapter, I tried to imagine what it must have been like for these men, to live together without women: the evolution from weird and sad, to defiant and normal. Then I began thinking that I ought to be like a Celt and go on an island retreat. A female one; as in, a retreat to the island of women. I never dreamed that anybody would have the cheek to do so in the actual island from which Columba banned women.

But the Findhorn Foundation did. An alternative-living community in eastern Scotland, it owns a house in the island: the women's retreat was planned there for April. At the time, I was still living in Orkney. It seemed like the perfect education for me. I was curious to know what it felt like, to live among only women on a once-male-only island. My sister and I grew up with three brothers and a plethora of male cousins; I went to a mixed school and a mixed college. The nearest I ever got to a female community was the nunnery to which my London primary school was attached, and a female madrassah which I visited once, when I lived in Delhi. I still remember the sweet, cloying aroma of female bodies living in close proximity with each other; the inquisitive faces. Maybe, I thought, the retreat will have that same undercurrent of mischief that you get wherever there are women. Or cows.

The retreat was full, but I joined the waiting list, and forgot all about it.

Then, out of the blue – a boat appearing on the distant horizon – the Findhorn Foundation emailed to say that a last-minute space had come up. I must tell them immediately if I can do it.

And so I say yes. It is now or never.

I arrive in Iona in May, an auspicious month. The 16th of May was St Brendan's death-day, my own late father's birthday. The 19th of May was the day Columba himself arrived in Iona (he died in June). Everything happens in the spring, in these northern islands, when it is at last possible to move around again by boat, after the winter.

I walk up from the port, breathing in the delicious smell of wild flowers, and exalting in the ubiquity of the sea. When Boswell and Johnson visited Iona in 1773, nobody mentioned the Sheela-na-gig, but the men did have 'Nuns' Island' pointed out to them. They were told that stone for building Iona came from there.

I was intrigued, on first reading of this island, but though I look on my maps I can't see it marked. 'Where's the nun island?' I ask on the ferry, on the pier and in the shop. Nobody knows what I am talking about.

Eventually I knock on the door of a man who does charter sailing trips in his Danish boat with its rust-red sails. He is out, but his wife says, 'Oh, you mean Eilean naBan?' She points it out to me, across the water: tiny, rocky, barren – but significant. She says to come back in the evening and ask her husband myself.

In the meantime, I set out to find the female retreat centre. The house is down a long track, facing the island of women across the water. Upon arrival, there is much unpacking and arranging of lotions and make-up, hairdryers and dresses. (I am sharing a room with three others.) We are respectful around each other, in the kitchen, bedroom and the bathroom, hanging up the bathmat, swilling toothpaste away, not leaving the toilet seat up or shaving into the sink. We share in the cooking, which is vegetarian, possibly vegan; I find the whole thing very relaxing.

During the day, we build labyrinths on the seashore out of seaweed and walk them, chanting. We perform the 'crane dance' (this is, essentially, made up) on the beach, invoking St Columba (for the reason that Adomnán tells how he once predicted the arrival of some tired cranes from Ireland). We gather pieces of green Iona marble from the bay where Columba first landed; and if I remember rightly, we massage each other with them, in some form of healing ritual. We even have the 'Stargate' pointed out to us – those squeamish about modern-day spirituality should look away now – which is a portal to the otherworld. After a while, I realize that at least one of our number is away with the fairies. The fairies, or antique goddesses of this land, are speaking to her in their ancient language, which they then kindly translate into Dutch and she transcribes into English. She emails me the transcription later.

Somebody in my room turns out to be a travelling saleswoman of essential oils; she has an oil for each ailment in her suitcase. But the fairy woman announces herself to be highly allergic to all essential oils; it is a stand-off. The little bottles have to be taken out furtively and sniffed. The air begins to crackle with sedition.

At night, slightly bored with the talk of fairies, I begin to wonder about my own impatience at being alone with other women. By then I have read Maggie Nelson's *The Argonauts* and had my life changed by its depictions of casual female solidarity (and uncasual sex). I wonder why it is that women need to be taught to claim their own space, their own room, their own island; why they so readily submit to something lesser.

So, I submit myself again to the gentleness of my fellow females' rhythms. I reflect that diversity of age and background are strengths in a community. Life shouldn't be run like a Cambridge college; I don't need to be discussing political theory or imperial iterations. I am here to open myself up to something different. It is good to be open-minded and empathetic. I listen to the essential-oil woman and find that I learn something helpful (knowledge I still value); I read a book published in Glastonbury, my local hippy town as a child, about labyrinths (which I quote in this book). I learn how to ferment and cook gluten-free seed bread. (I haven't done that since, but I will, one day.)

Despite my studiously acquired inner peace, I look out at the women's island opposite every now and then. Nobody on the women's retreat has mentioned it yet: but there it is, visible at all times in its harsh red crossness, just across the water. I feel a little rude for pointing it out, but I decide it is good to be honest and so I express my opinion that Saint Columba is said not to have liked women that much; is it weird to be here, on his island, obediently discussing his slightest, mundane sayings? Would anybody mind if I visited the women's banishment island across the water? Nobody would. Indeed, they encourage me gladly in my process.

Eilean naBan, proximate as it is to Iona, is not on the tourist boat routes. One evening, I walk back to the port to call on the man with the Danish sailing boat whose wife I spoke to. He comes to the door, slightly weary, and we have a long chat. He grew up in Glasgow, and when he moved here it was to be completely reborn as an islander. His grown-up son is now the island's creel fisherman, and it is the father-and-son team who take me out to Eilean naBan when the charter boats won't. There is at least one false start on account of the weather – he doesn't believe me, clearly, when I claim fantastic sea-legs on account of having lived in Orkney. (Orcadians are farmers, even now; every Hebridean knows that.) He is marginally more impressed when I say I'm in the fire service. He is in the fire service on Iona, as is his son. They invite me to a training night.

Eilean naBan is tiny, as I find when they drop me there. It has no natural water. The beach to the south is awash with rubbish – plastic bottles, string, bags. (A report came out while I was living in Orkney which showed that Scapa Flow had as much microplastic pollution as the Forth or Clyde). It would have been insane to have banished anybody here, then or now. But the legend, for all its exaggeration, is stating something obvious about male monastic communities and their attitudes to women.

That night, my last on Iona, I walk out to the beach at Iona's north coast, with the retreat convenor. She has shown me, I see now, a different way of looking at – and rescuing something from – the past: in a manner less didactic, more instinctive; less historical and more empathetic.

During the day, as I'd contemplated Iona from the island of women, I wondered if the sea was the way to understand these islands. What can the land tell you, after all? It has neither the velvet grandeur of Mull next door, nor Jura's famous skyline breasts, nor the industry of Islay. There's not much to it, once you've wandered across its Lewisian gneisses, as I had done, through the sweet-honey scent of heather, past bog cotton's acid splashes.

Talking to father and son that morning in the boat, I'd discovered that in the age of tarmac and combustion it is still quicker to follow Columba's route from Iona to Oronsay (a subsidiary monastery) than it is to go the long way round by car. Once you submit your mind to the rhythm of the tides, it is the logical way to travel. But having never been sailing before, I could only imagine how it might feel: the wind pushing itself taut in the canvas, the salt on the planks beneath my feet, the crowding thoughts of island monks, many of them poets, whose journeys continue to inspire poetry long after they are dead, their sacred words crisscrossing the water.

Apparently, it would take a day to reach Oronsay – Adomnán says this too – with its fourteenth-century priory dedicated to St Columba. I remember that priory and its island from family holidays when I was a child. We walked across the strand to Oronsay when the tide was out, stepping in our bare feet over lugworm casts, collecting cowrie shells, athrill with the thought that the tide might cut us off from the neighbouring island. It never occurred to me then that these remote islands were once as important as London or Edinburgh.

Together, we two women reach the beach where, in the daytime, the retreating tide reveals a long spit of sand like a bar of light. For now I can only imagine such a journey. I step into the sea, feel the cold waves around my ankles, then my knees, then my thighs. Anchored in the ocean, I look back at Iona. I feel comforted, suddenly, by this week in the company of other women. I think about their warmth, emotionally, the hot blood circulating around their bodies. I feel the warmth of our companionship, through the experiences and words and cooking we have shared.

The sea is cold. But here on the island, together, we are warm. I know that I still have a lot to learn. But maybe this week of sincere engagement with my own sex has engendered the metamorphosis which I know I need.

Hopefully, Iona is just the beginning.

5

Thanet

Augustine to the Angles (AD 597)

We, the *horse-drawn*, approach the island along tarmac roads. I, whom they are allowing along for the ride, sit in the final of the three vehicles, a smartly painted cart, watching, feeling, tasting the rapid accumulation of traffic and bad temper. It is rush hour in Kent. Earlier, I walked back along the traffic jam, eating blackberries, losing count at around fifty cars. From where I am sitting now, the hedges are fecund, the lanes narrow, my stomach a churn of blackberry jam, and because the traffic is at bay and I can suddenly hear birdsong it's as if I've entered a new realm of perception – the low, maternal coo of a wood pigeon, the pig-grunt of a raven, the shrill song of a robin. I could be a farmworker in a Thomas Hardy novel, hitching a ride. The commuters behind me must be cursing Google for sending them home this way. Most likely, though, they're cursing us.

My cart is being driven by a dark-haired sixteen-year-old girl called Erin. Her blonde mother, Annette, who wears a stetson and an elaborate riding jacket cut from embroidered cloth, suggests anarchy in her aspect. Both women ignore the car drivers; they seem serene and secure in their disruptive status as conductors of a now-defunct mode of transport. The Highway Code is on their side, for now, as is history. And anyway, the unrightful ire of the people at the helm of gas-guzzling combustion engines is as nothing to the temper of the man at the front of our procession. SANGER'S STAGE SHOW, it says on two sides of his caravan, the letters painted in red and gold. He, Dave Sanger, skinny as a rake and irascible as a goat, has a brain loaded high with the stress of this entire expedition, like a pile of o'toppling plates. They set out from Stonehenge at summer solstice and, the further east they've gone, the more choked the roads have got; it is making his body shake. He, too, wears a hat, and dead-tight trousers, and a leather waistcoat over a tanned torso. I try not to look but am sure I can see his ribs.

Dave is descended from the great Victorian circus impresario 'Lord' George Sanger (he ennobled himself), who started, among other things, the beachside fairground which would later become the twentieth-century amusement park Dreamland on the Isle of Thanet. Thanet, known to fifth-century Constantinople as an Isle of the Dead, is where we are headed, to lead the Margate summer carnival.

'Showmen', I learn, are different from Romany Travellers. Damian Le Bas, in *The Stopping Places*, describes them as 'our mutually suspicious cousin group'.[1] Annette lives in Somerset during the winter, but in the summer she is peripatetic; all of this crew seem peripatetic by nature. They incarnate the original human condition for the rest of us, and in so doing they seem to be unwitting vectors of settled peoples' anti-Traveller rage, which has possibly existed ever since the Neolithic.

I joined the Sanger processional just as they entered Kent. They'd put on their travelling circus show at an animal sanctuary that afternoon – Dave is a vegan – and had set up camp already by the time I arrived that night. I was collected from Folkestone station by Pete, one of Dave's long-term collaborators and self-declared 'king of biodiesel'. We stopped at the village shop on the way back so that I could buy something for the party – Strongbow and Special Brew, at Pete's suggestion.

The entourage consists of five ponies, one magician in a bus, two teenagers, an impresario, five dogs, three singers, two wooden caravans, one cart, two camper vans, a fixer, a car-driving logistics man and several hangers-on. That's just the road crew. Meeting us in Thanet are a giant on stilts, twin acrobats, a circus act, the costume van, three make-up artists and an acoustic techno band. Sitting up front with Annette is young Robyn, who has rings on her fingers and bells on her toes and wears extravagant corseted dresses and huge eye make-up and a multitude of spangles in her big, reddish dreads.

Sitting in the cart with me is even younger Finn, sixteen years old, who, like Erin, has grown up on and off the road. There's a whole host of middle-aged practical- to mystical-minded men who come and go; a couple in a caravan who feed me non-vegan sausages and Smash my first night; a musician who once played bass with Ringo Starr's son Zak. But the one person I've been in touch with before arriving, Dave's partner, is absent, having split up with him in Hampshire. She has taken his baby and the car straight to Thanet.

Dave has a metal plate in his arm from a fight with a man who hit him with a spade and is missing the end of two fingers, which were bitten off by a horse. His grandfather was a pugilist and his father and seven sisters grew up singing for their supper. The result of this childhood destitution was that his father joined the merchant navy and wanted his son to join the Royal Navy. But the call of the road was strong. The nineties rave scene, free festivals, gave Dave a taste for travelling with a troupe. He met Annette, his calm colleague of the road, at a London squat, or Reclaim the Streets, or during the poll tax riots, or the 1992 Earth Summit, or at the Big Green Gathering. 'We are all natural-born nomads and anarchists,' says Annette. She and Dave call each other Paddy. Neither of them is Irish; it's an in-joke that I don't get. 'All right, Paddy?' 'You OK, Paddy?'

It is clear that I will be cold in my tiny tent. They are all kind and concerned; without question and judgement, they have welcomed me in. Pete gives me his army ditch-suit to wear and Robyn extracts from her blue camper van (all bedecked with her multi-coloured clothes) a pink-and-green crochet blanket. She also lends me 'Lord' George Sanger's memoir, *Seventy Years a Showman: My Life and Adventures in Camp and Caravan the World Over*, which was first published in 1908. It describes a completely itinerant life, as used to be normal in Britain. The 1926 edition has a foreword by Kenneth Grahame, who wrote *The Wind in the Willows* (a book which now reads like a paean to bachelor, female-free life). By the end of his life, Sanger was quite a rich and respectable man. But he writes, 'I have still my theatres at Ramsgate and Margate, so I am not quite cut away from old associations.' He is buried in Margate cemetery.

It takes us five hours to travel the eight miles to Bramling Common, where we are to camp that night. Along Kentish hedgerows, past oast houses, and chalky-flint fields, Robyn and Annette reminisce about the counties they have passed through since June. Somerset was full of rednecks (I grew up in Somerset), but Hampshire was nice. Sussex was difficult on the A272 with the traffic, but Kent has been worse. The police have already visited them twice and issued them with a charge sheet mentioning 'zero tolerance in Kent'. At this point in their story we are passing a big house with a field, across which a woman in jodhpurs and a hard hat is cantering on a shiny auburn horse. She shrieks with joy upon seeing us – not us, the five Gypsy cobs. 'Where are you going?' she yells. 'Margate.' 'Where have you come from?' 'Stonehenge.' Ululations of the Kentish type.

At teatime, in Lower Hardres, a bald man in underpants comes out and begs Dave to let his granddaughter sit up in the cart. He gives Dave a couple of pounds and we have to stop for a while by the road so the whole family can pet the horses. They, too, are going to Margate carnival that weekend and they chatter with star-struck excitement. Dave is a showman: he has to respond to his public. But it means that it's late when we reach Bramling Common. Wheatfields stretch into the distance, but near at hand is a field of potatoes on one side, from which we glean, and a wood on the other, where we gather firewood. I have picked rosemary and oregano from hedges and gardens during our journey, and I cook supper for everyone on Robyn's little gas stove. My effort is received politely. We're almost back to civilization now – just a day away – and then it will be straight into the kebab shop.

Round the campfire, Crumbs the magician, who is driving the blue bus and has a 'Jamaican' Labrador–Staff cross called Kaiser ('he eats peas and rice') enters a wild reverie about his magical career: a bit of escapology, sleight of hand, comedy. He got his Covent Garden performer's licence at sixteen, but it's too expensive to perform there now; parking alone is £16 an hour. Pete changes the subject: he thinks the government's proposal to ban petrol and diesel cars by 2040 is a conspiracy to take us back to a feudal society where it's too expensive for normal people to drive, and so once again they'll be restricted to a 150-mile radius of where they were born and raised. Annette speaks of the different Traveller communities she's known. She's a new-age hippy; neither her clan nor Dave's will mix with the Romanys or the Irish – who keep to themselves, and fight, they say, among themselves. She would never go to the Appleby Horse Fair. Gary, who is sleeping in a car-top tent, speaks of his musical career with the men from Wings (Paul McCartney post-Beatles) and how he made music for TV documentaries. TV people really rip you off.

I keep the tent flaps open under the starry sky and fall asleep to the sound of Robyn's sweet voice lifting above her guitar. The air is alive with the dry smell of ripening wheat and the rustling of small creatures in the long grass. Tomorrow we will cross into the Isle of Thanet – the latest in a long line of immigrants and invaders.

By the time St Augustine landed in Thanet, in 597 – the year Columba died on Iona – the island was outsiders' premier route into Britain. Thanet was divided from England proper by the River Wantsum, which silted up only in the seventeenth century. Caesar was presumably following in the wake of other prior invaders when he chose this island off an island as his landing point; Claudius seems to have copied him a century later. As the Roman priest-historian Orosius explained to his mentor, Augustine of Hippo, in his fourth-century *History against the Pagans*: this part of Kent 'affords the nearest landing place for those who cross the water'.[2] Even before the Romans left, the Germanic tribes were in turn using Thanet (and Sheppey) for this purpose.[3]

The Old English Chronicles bristle with mentions of 'barbarians' wintering in Thanet as late as 851, 969, 1046. Of course, the chroniclers themselves were barbarian invaders once – descendants of Woden. By the time the *Beowulf* poet came to memorialize their ancestors across the seas in Old English, that heroism was water-worn, looking back across the 'sea-lanes', 'gannets' bath' and 'whale-road' to the Anglo-Saxons' origins in northern Germany and southern Scandinavia. All the prowess of the people is in their mastery over water: from the 'whorled prows' that carry presents and tokens from one people to another; to the boat burials they perform for their leaders; to the imposing barrow they construct on the headland for Beowulf, their 'hero's memorial', 'a marker that sailors could see from afar . . .' The sea is everywhere in this poem.[4]

But given time, every invasion has a chance of becoming a sanctified migration. By 1874, when the historian J. R. Green published *A Short History of the English People,* he was positively sentimental about the early Anglo-Saxons:

> It is with the landing of Hengest and his war-band . . . on the shores of the Isle of Thanet, that English history begins. No spot in England can be so sacred, to Englishness, as that which first felt the tread of English feet.[5]

Perhaps. For St Augustine, the island of Thanet was the second in a series of false starts. In the late sixth century he was sent by Pope Gregory the Great to proselytize to the English. Gregory, as the English liked to boast ever after, had a special thing for their race:

> there came to Rome certain people of our nation, fair-skinned and light-haired. When he heard of their arrival he was eager to see them; being inspired by God, he received them and asked what race they belonged to. (Now some say they were beautiful boys, while others say that they were curly-haired, handsome youths.) They answered, 'The people we belong to are called Angles.' 'Angels of God,' he replied. Then he asked, 'What is the name of the king of that people?' They said, 'Aelli', whereupon he said, 'Alleluia, God's praise must be heard from there.'[6]

That was the flattering version put about by an anonymous nun or monk at the abbey of Whitby, in about 704 AD (it was a joint monastery, then run by Abbess Aelfflaed, who may or may not have been the author, or editor).[7] The prolific Bede ('the only

Englishman mentioned by Dante', as they say in the north) repeated it with equal care some thirty years later when writing his *History of the English Church and People*, adding the embellishment that the blond Englishmen were slaves.

But this was not how Gregory himself told it. In a letter to his friend Eulogius, the Bishop of Alexandria, written soon after Augustine has arrived in England, Gregory described how 'The English, a people shut up in a little corner of the world, have been up to this time unbelievers, nay, worshippers of stocks and stones.'[8] In his *Moralia*, a commentary on the Book of Job, Gregory rejoiced that Britain, which 'once could make only barbarous noises, had now begun to sing the Hebrew Alleluia in its divine praises'.[9]

The point is that despite those long centuries of Roman rule, Britain was still – as Gregory put it – 'at the end of the world'. Procopius, official historian of Emperor Justinian in mid-sixth-century Constantinople, has a garbled yet revealing story to tell about Britain, and in particular the Isle of Thanet. Despite all those tracts on Britain written by the Romans, he is confused even about the islands' names, calling the biggest island 'Bretannia' and writing at length about a nearby island, 'Brittia'. Procopius seems to base his account about Brittia on reports he was given by 'some of the Angili' who were dispatched to Constantinople on an embassy to Emperor Justinian from the King of the Franks, who was seeking the emperor's support to his claim over 'Brittia'.

Procopius's section on Brittia opens with an unusual love story about a fierce young woman of the island who is betrothed to a man from the continent but is later spurned on account of the 'long and arduous journey' from his home to hers (choosing a woman from across the Rhine was easier). Outraged by this slight, Brittia 'took up the duties of a man and proceeded to deeds of war'. She assembled four hundred ships and one hundred thousand warriors, and in this way, Boudica-like, won her lover back.

Procopius then tells of the island's ancient wall that cuts the island in two, dividing east – the good side – from the west, where only snakes can live. Most probably he is thinking of Hadrian's wall, or the Antonine wall, both of which divide the island the other way, north from south.

Procopius's third and final story is about migration in and out of the island. It is clear that in the sixth century, as in Caesar's time, there is much traffic to and fro, between 'Brittia' and the continent. But Procopius goes on to describe another form of migration that even he considers utterly untrustworthy – 'it bears a very close resemblance to mythology'. But he doesn't want to leave it out of his account in case 'I gain a lasting reputation for ignorance of what takes place there.' The story appears to be a garbled recasting of the ancient Greek and Celtic myth of the western Isles of the Dead. Here, the legend is given a contemporary twist, with Frankish fishermen conveying the souls over to Britain at night:

> They say, then, that the souls of those who die are always conveyed to this place . . . they are aware that the boats are burdened with a large number of passengers . . . they themselves, however, see no one, but after rowing a single hour they put in at Brittia.

In 1955, A. R. Burns argued in the *English Historical Review* that Procopius's Brittia was probably Thanet. First, Procopius is rehashing ancient classical stories about supernatural Britain, in particular Plutarch's account of the traveller Demetrius's tale of the holy men and spirits who live unmolested on British islands. In trying to locate this island of Brittia, he puts it not in the west, as was usual, but in the east – site of constant migration between the continent and England. The specific place he chose was the island with the deathly-name: for *Thanatos* means 'death', in Greek, an Isle of the Dead.

Isidore of Seville, whom everyone believed, writing in the late sixth century AD, was even more explicit about Thanet's death-meaning. In *Etymologies* he describes how

> Thanet is an island in the Ocean in the Gallic channel, separated from Britannia by a narrow estuary, with fruitful fields and rich soil.

It is named Thanet (*Tanatos*) from the death of serpents. Although the island itself is unacquainted with serpents, if soil from it is carried away and brought to any other nation, it kills snakes there.[10]

This is how myths are made and stories transmitted – murkily, randomly. For Isidore, Procopius's snake story merges with Thanet's uncertain etymology to become a meditation on death. For medieval Irish annalists, it is co-opted 'for the greater glory of St Patrick' (Ireland has no snakes because their patron saint killed them).[11] Others suggest that what is meant by this is the expulsion of the Druids – once known as 'serpents of wisdom'.

Even now, Thanet's name continues to provoke debate among linguists, with the most interesting recent intervention coming from the German professor of historical linguistics Theo Vennemann, who posited an entirely different and distant origin-name for the island. He asserted that classical writers were entirely misled in assuming a connection between Thanet and death: a false, though 'learned', 'folk-etymology'. 'Thanet', Vennemann suggested, is actually derived from the Phoenician name for their goddess Tanit, patron of Carthage, and a fertility goddess associated with Demeter. Many classical writers attest to the Phoenicians' control of the ancient trade in tin – out of Iberia and Britain, predominantly. Vennemann argued that Phoenician traders used Thanet, a 'bridgehead' island, as a means of controlling the 'tin eldorado of Britain'; and, as many European colonial powers would do subsequently, they named this useful little island after one of their 'foremost deities'.[12] They are also probably responsible for the common *y* suffix to British island names, for this was the Semitic noun for island.

This, then, was the history of Thanet when Gregory despatched Augustine as apostle to the English: *dead men and fertile goddesses, immigration in, and export out.* Hindsight is useful: how Anglo-Saxon culture treated their women seems glorious compared to what came later. Professor Stephanie Hollis writes of Augustine's landing in Kent as 'among other things, the harbinger of an authoritarian regime'.[13]

Augustine and his companions had to muster all their courage to make the journey to England. In 595, Pope Gregory had written to a priest he knew, asking him to buy English teenage boys in the slave markets of Gaul, 'so that they might be trained in Roman monasteries, presumably to be sent back as missionaries to England'.[14] But this strategy, if it was ever executed, does not seem to have borne fruit. Halfway along in France, such was the bad report the missionaries heard of the 'English' (the violent Anglo-Saxons) that Augustine's companions refused to go on. Bede wrote that they 'were appalled at the idea of going to a barbarous, fierce and pagan nation, of whose very language they were ignorant'. Augustine was forced to leave them on the southern French island monastery of Lérins and return to Rome to seek guidance from the Pope. The guidance was clear. Pope Gregory ordered Augustine back to fulfil his 'holy task'.

So Augustine disembarked in Thanet – a marshy island, wreathed in fog. The land beyond was indistinct. He spent three days waiting in a cloud of indecision as the local king deliberated whether or not to come and meet him – an early-medieval version of a twenty-first-century immigration centre. When the king eventually appeared he insisted on speaking out in the open, where England's fresh air would protect him; he would not step inside Augustine's tent in case he was smothered by his magic. The king's Frankish wife, Bertha, was already a Christian, but the king was a suspicious and fearful pagan.

Augustine's mission to England was twofold: designed by the Pope to save the souls of those beautiful blond-haired English youths and as a challenge to the anarchic power of Celtic monks such as Columba. The Celtic Church did not recognize the supremacy of Rome. Much like the assertion of monolithic Roman power a few centuries earlier, the papal legate set foot in England with the authority to forge from these scatterings of island monasteries a single church for all the Britannias, one which would report directly to the mother church in Rome. Augustine's mission was as much to correct the mess made by British Christians as to convert the newest wave of pagans.

Augustine knew that he was not the first Christian to these isles.

Long ago, in the glory days of Emperor Constantine, the presence of Christianity was so strong a myth arose that these islands were converted by the apostles Peter and Paul, who had arrived on the urging of Claudia, daughter of the exiled British chieftain Caratacus.[15] But since then, British Christianity had evolved in shocking ways. Like Darwin's finches with their island-specific beaks, British Christians diverged, autonomously deciding on their own date for Easter. This sounds like a petty thing to argue about now, but for centuries it was a huge source of tension in British monastic communities, with the British faction insisting on following their own method of calculation – and refusing to follow the directives of Rome. (So too in Pakistan today Eid is almost always called early by an independent group who see the new moon before others.) As Bede illustrated at great length in his work *The Reckoning of Time*, how to calculate Easter was immensely complicated, given the variance between solar and lunar calendars, Jewish and Christian holidays, and the fact that the Resurrection was always to be celebrated on one particular day of the week.[16]

Barbara Walker believes it came down to gender, with the British faction following the 'peasants' unofficial, lunar, Goddess-given menstrual calendar' and the Roman lot preferring to follow the official solar calendar.[17] It is true that 'Easter' comes from the Celtic fertility festival, Eostre.

But these weren't the only differences: the Celts also tonsured monks in an eccentric fashion, from ear to ear, instead of the 'crown of thorns' favoured by Rome. The schisms which these disagreements provoked are also a reminder of the fact that the Reformation, a thousand years later, and Brexit, five hundred years after that, merely followed local tradition. Now, as then, British islanders were experiencing the power of two intractable forces: the empire without and independence within.

Trying to resuscitate correct practice on these corrupted isles, Augustine made repairs to a British-Christian church built centuries before by imperial Romans – St Martin of Tours, which Queen Bertha used for worship, and which, amazingly, still exists, in part.

(It stands in Canterbury, 'the oldest church in continuous use in the English-speaking world'.)[18] Augustine reported to the Pope that the tomb of Mary, mother of God, was to be found in a church on an island off the west coast of Britain. The modern author Graham Phillips has argued that this western island was none other than Anglesey – a tantalizing theory, if impossible to prove. What the story does bear out, however, is the enduring power of Britain's trope of sacred female islands.[19] Thanet, too, became associated with holy women in the centuries following Augustine's advent.

In its early years, the English church was ruled by royal abbesses such as Ely's Aethelthryth. Hilda (614–80) was particularly influential; daughter of King Edwin, she was converted by Paulinus, who had come to England with Augustine. She founded or was in charge of monasteries at Monkwearmouth, Streanaeshalch [Whitby], Hartlepool, Tadcaster and Hackness; convened the seismic Synod of Whitby in 664; and discovered and promoted the poetic spiritual talent of Caedmon, who, unlike most famous (aristocratic) church-women and men at this time, worked as a lowly cowherd before joining the monastery.

In fact, were it not for the women who supported him, then and afterwards, Augustine's mission may have come to nothing. Augustine had a hard time in England. He did a great deal of work in trying to bring the wayward British Christians into line. He first convened a conference under an oak tree (shades of the Druids) on the border between the Hwicca and West Saxon peoples. This was a failure, and a fuller meeting was planned, with 'seven British bishops' from the monastery of Bangor. But the British-Christians refused to be bullied by a man from Rome. They found him unbearably arrogant; he answered them with threats.[20]

Augustine wrote despairing letters to Pope Gregory, complaining that the local Christians stupidly venerated the relics of a spurious saint called Sixtus. Copious ink and thought were also devoted to the sexual habits of the Anglo-Saxons.[21] Augustine wrote anxiously, legalistically; Gregory returned patient, generally tolerant answers. Qu: *Can they be allowed their cousin-marriage?* Ans: *Do not punish them for sins committed in ignorance.* Qu: *Are women allowed to enter church during their monthly courses?* Ans: *The workings of nature should not be considered culpable.* Qu: *Should their pagan temples be destroyed?* Ans: *Destroy the idols but asperse the temples with holy water, set up altars: deposit relics.* The correspondence was preserved for posterity in a text which was a bestseller in medieval Europe. King Alfred had a copy made in the ninth century.

King Aethelbert eventually allowed human curiosity and hospitality to prevail over a ruler's innate caution. The kindest lines in Bede's history belong to him. He tells Augustine that

> Your words and promises are fair indeed; but they are new and uncertain, and I cannot accept them and abandon the age-old beliefs that I have held together with the whole English nation. But since you have travelled far, and I can see that you are sincere in your desire to impart to us what you believe to be true and excellent, we will not harm you. We will receive you hospitably and take care to supply you with all that you need.

Imagine if modern rulers spoke to travellers from afar like this.

Aethelbert's kingdom of the south Saxons was huge, extending as far north as the River Humber. But the land he granted Augustine for his new church was at Canterbury, in the south, 'the chief city of all his realm' (according to Bede) and the first place you get to once you cross the River Wantsum between Thanet and England.

In the short term there were serious setbacks: King Aethelbert's son reverted to paganism upon his father's death, for example. (It must have been difficult to be weaned of dependence on Woden.) Nor was the division between British Christians and Rome one which Augustine was able to heal in his lifetime; it continued to provoke recrimination, and accusations of insularity, until the Celts compromised at the Synod of Whitby in 664, when Wilfrid argued for the Roman cause and against the will of 'one remote corner of the most remote island' (by which he may have meant Iona).[22]

It is in the island of Lindisfarne, a century later, that the directives of Rome, the mythology of Ireland and the ink of the Anglo-Saxons eventually found their greatest artistic expression.[23] But the ballast of all that was Canterbury – the English church which Augustine established, and which survives to this day as Anglicanism's 'mother-church'.[24]

Every small British island has subtle and not-so-subtle ways of distinguishing belongers from outsiders. Thanet became capital of England's little-islander mentality because of deprivation and an imagined clash between recent immigrants and the descendants of Angles (who landed there a millennium and a half ago). In 2015, Nigel Farage, noisy leader of the United Kingdom Independence Party (UKIP), which campaigned for Brexit, chose to stand in Thanet South because, as he claimed, 'there are areas of Thanet which are no-go for English people'. He was talking about Cliftonville, a once-genteel part of the seaside town of Margate, out beyond the Turner Contemporary art gallery. From the mid-1990s onwards, Rwandans, Bosnians, Afghans and Iraqis were sent there to occupy street after street of large, bow-windowed, brick-and-flint-built B&Bs. The reason was due to Augustinian geography: many of the immigrants who came to Britain illegally did so by boat, or (from 1994) through the Channel Tunnel in Kent; they were processed by asylum authorities in Canterbury and offered the nearest available housing. In the following year's Brexit referendum, Thanet voted with a 64 per cent majority to Leave.[25]

Bede had attested that (in the wake of Augustine) his country was now

> in harmony with the five books of the divine law, five languages and four nations – English, British, Scots, and Picts. Each of these have their own language; but all are united in their study of God's truth by the fifth – Latin – which has become a common medium through the study of scriptures.

Once beloved of Londoners, Margate emptied of tourists when cheap flights took Britons overseas for their tans. Until the refugees arrived, the shops in Northdown Road, Cliftonville's main shopping street, looked like they'd been bandaged. Now the street is an advert for Margate's Bede-like transformation: halal butcher, followed by Polish supermarket, next door to hipster bicycle shop, cheek by jowl with African and Afro-Caribbean vendors of yams and Cypriot coffee shop. *Five tongues; plurality of peoples; hospitality.* The plurality of peoples is Britain's strength.

Long before travelling to Margate with the horse-drawn, I visit by train. It is April 2015, and days before the general election (when UKIP is hoping to take over the seat). The sun shines down on all of England but its eastern coast, where fog wraps up Margate's chip vans, beach huts, lolly sticks on the sand, the pride-of-town Primark store, the UKIP posters. I walk along the seafront, huddled into my overcoat, thinking of the teenage Tracey Emin dancing at Margate's Dreamland fairground (it has since been saved from destruction and refurbished for the twenty-first century; Emin herself, who moved back to Margate to make work and set up an art school, artist residencies and a museum, has been honoured as a 'Freewoman of Margate' by Thanet Council).[26] Out on the pier, three teenagers are drinking Heineken, a fisherman is making repairs to his boat and a family are chatting to each in a language that turns out to be Romani as they try to make the best of the weather, freezing in thin cottons.

In the Northern Belle, I sit at the bar and listen to the conversation about incomers and locals. 'Incomers always have a story to tell,' says Bert, a carpenter from the Isle of Sheppey who married a Thanet girl. 'It's the local people who are brain-dead.'

'Ramsgate rednecks, Margatian morons,' adjoins Dick the Fish, an old man from Camberwell as thin as a hoe in a potting shed.

'This place has the second-highest unemployment rate in the country,' continues Bert, 'but I've never been out of work. Thirty per cent of the people here don't even know where Faversham is. I met someone the other day who's never been to France – it's twenty miles away. They think it's a day out to go to the Co-op.'

Bert is from Sheppey's Traveller community: 'the most picked-on people in the world'. Sheppey people still get called 'swamp monsters'.

'I'm a Gorga,' he says.

'A what?'

'GORGA. Traveller who lives in a house.' His hand jabs his neck. 'Gorged-up.'

(Only later do I learn that the word is Romani: *gorjie* – a derogatory term for non-Romanys.)[27]

'My people work hard,' he goes on. 'We don't take injuries. We're men. People from Thanet do fuck all, and loads of it. When I need to hire someone I have to find a fella from nearly forty miles away. They're inbred. They're swindlers. They're fraudulent, wonky people all trying to nick a shekel. Every leader of the council has ended up in jail. Like that UKIP woman who got The Hoy [the pub next door] to give her a receipt for four grand. They're all on benefits. No respect for the poke—'

'The what?'

'The mazuma, to give it its correct legal term. The reds.' He turns towards me, pushing his hand along the bar for emphasis. 'God, you've led a sheltered life.'

I laugh and offer to buy him the next pint, but there is a collective inhalation, seven male tuts, part joke, part serious. At the time, I assume they are being sexist. Later, I realize that it's because Bert himself owns the pub. He also owns the pub next door. And a host of other places, apparently.

'I'm not being funny,' Bert goes on, 'but a lot of people here work their bollocks off – the Polish, good as bloody gold – Pakistanis I know work hard. It's the locals cause the problem.'

'The government sends all the scum down here. Drug heads.'

'London scum.' In the eighties, they explain, Margate was known as 'Dole-gate' on account of the unemployed Londoners and Liverpudlians who moved into the dirt-cheap accommodation created as hotels emptied. The talk turns to life-long tax avoidance, then the dividing line between Thanet and the world. Dick the Fish (ex-London himself) takes me outside to point out Reculver, with its famous towers, across the bay. We squint into the sunset.

'It's the defensive line at the end of the Wantsum Channel,' says Bert when we get back to the bar. 'It's what the Romans sailed up to do their business. There's still water in the Wantsum, which still makes Thanet, technically, an island.'

The Reculver towers epitomize Thanet's changing fortunes. They stand amid the ruins of a Roman fort, built around AD 200 and billeted by men from western Germany. By the fourth century, the fort was running naval patrols to try and control the depredations of other, more disobedient Germans: Saxon raiders. The fort was eventually abandoned in 407, and stayed so until 669, when (as on Holyhead) a post-Augustine priest established a monastery in its midst. That was abandoned in its turn, but Trinity House, the lighthouse keepers, bought the ruin and rebuilt the towers to stand as a navigational aid for shipping. 'Local upcycling', as they say in the King Ethelbert pub at Reculver. Black-and-white photos on the walls show this exact patch of the coast's glory days as a caravan park. It, too, was until recently the holiday destination of choice for gorged-up Londoners.

Images of Kent – in maps prior to the twelfth century – show Thanet completely encircled by the sea. The Wantsum was six hundred metres wide then: a shipping channel, the quick and sheltered route from the Channel into the Thames Estuary. Medieval monks hastened the encroachment by draining the salt marshes. Gradually the channel silted up, and the last vessel to sail down it was a boat delivering bells to the Church of St Clement's in London in 1672. But, as Bert says, the Wantsum still exists. It's about three metres wide now, still too much to jump; home to swans and ducks, who navigate its placid waters among the fields of rape which stretch across this part of Kent like the dayglo picnic blankets of lazy giants.

If the Wantsum proves that Thanet is still an island, the people who live here never let you forget it. They still refer to 'the isle' and call themselves islanders. The land itself emanates islandness: the silt made it fertile, and today it is a centre of horticultural production. Massive greenhouses churn out 13 per cent of Britain's tomatoes, cucumbers and peppers, undermining what was once Jersey's market niche. Production is year-round because of Thanet's 'vast island skies'. (Turner returned again and again to paint in Margate because, as he famously told Ruskin, 'the skies over Thanet are the loveliest in all Europe'.) The chairman of Thanet Earth, the island's biggest horticultural group, explains that he chose Thanet because, being 'almost surrounded by the sea, it has outstandingly high light levels' – as well as 'a ready supply of local unemployed people'.

I walk the streets of Cliftonville with Aram Rawf, who is standing as one of Labour's three candidates in the Cliftonville West ward of Thanet District Council. Down Athelstan Road, up Ethelbert Road, leaflets through the doors in Harold Road and Dane Road: patriotic names that display their origin as clearly as Hassan Barber's and Nasza Biedronka grocers do.

Aram came to Britain in 1999 as a seventeen-year-old. He is a Kurd. After a jihadi group in his hometown in northern Iraq imprisoned him for refusing to become a suicide bomber, his sister paid to have him smuggled out. One agent took him to Iran, another to Turkey, and the third gave a lorry driver £3,000 to drive him all the way to England. For a week he sat in the back of the lorry eating biscuits and peeing into a bottle. He didn't know where he was when the driver let him out on the M20. The police picked him up; the immigration authorities sent him to a hotel in Cliftonville; he's been in Thanet ever since.

'It's amazing what British people have done to save my life,' he says. It's amazing what he's done for Britain (working as a translator at the Dover detention centre, the Kent Refugee Support Group and a homeless shelter; making history by being the first asylum seeker to volunteer for St John Ambulance). Farage and friends succeeded in stirring up resentment towards immigrants who 'don't speak the local language'. But the complaint is ironic. In his ninth-century *Life of Alfred*, Bishop Asser refers to Thanet as 'the island, which is called in the Saxon tongue, Tenet, but Ruim in the British language'.[28] Ruim? Those lost local names. What did 'Ruim' mean to its people?

'Thanet, it's always been known for its immigrants,' Aram says. He came here alone, and in sixteen years has contributed more to British civic life than I, or most other Britons, ever have. 'Are you homesick?' I ask him. He looks surprised, then withdrawn, then determined. 'This is my home now.'

I know now that this was the wrong question.

Which is worse: asking the wrong questions, or not asking them at all? That having one's national history inscribed and reinscribed by medieval monks may result in an absence of strong female roles should be – but rarely is – one of the first things pointed out about this particular form of cultural teleology. By the time Augustine arrived in Thanet the prominence of women in the Neolithic and Iron Age had long waned, thanks partly to those Christian monks and their Roman inheritance. Gildas, for example, the spirited, angry monastic who wrote *De excidio Britanniae* ('Concerning the Ruin of Britain') on an island in the Bristol Channel in AD 540, called Boudica – British freedom-fighter – 'that deceitful lioness'. (Some see this as a backhanded compliment.) He also saw the *islandness* of Britain as its weakness: making it prone to invasion, cultural dilution, wilfulness and vice.[29] UKIP's anxiety is ancient.

Reading Bede, too, one might think that women played a negligible part in Christianity's spread north through England from Kent; that his 'near silence on the activities of reigning queens and his scanty, unforthcoming coverage of the double monasteries' not only under-represents 'women's social participation' but reflects 'an aspiration towards their actual marginalization'.[30]

Female patronage and female religious leadership were hugely important to the conversion of the Anglo-Saxons. Double monasteries – 'miniature kingdoms ruled by women'[31] – were a feature of English Christianity until the Norman invasion. The virginal, segregated view we have of nuns today was not necessarily that of the Anglo-Saxon era.

To my joy I discover that there was once a particularly interesting double monastery on Thanet, run by a succession of eminent women – all of whom Bede must have known about. He writes extensively on Kentish Christianity, having corresponded with his friend at Canterbury, the abbot called Albinus. However, he mentions none of these women.

The first abbess on Thanet, Domne Eafe, was a descendant of Augustine's first royal convert, King Aethelbert. She acquired the land from the king, Egbert, as part of a *wergild* – a blood debt; for he had killed her brothers. She asked for as much land on the island of Thanet that her 'hind would run around in one circuit'.[32] Since Domne Eafe's hind was tame, it followed her as she rode around the island, and thus she claimed almost all of Thanet. The king, though he felt tricked, was obliged to honour his promise. (His pagan minister, Thunor, tried to diddle the abbess, but the earth opened and swallowed him up.) The hind motif of the abbess's land grant may have been a 'female counterpart of the stag from Sutton Hoo' – the grand Anglo-Saxon boat burial from East Anglia: a pagan symbol of territorial claim and power.[33] She ruled a domain set apart from her cousin's and controlled trade along the Wantsum; she established a house of perpetual prayer for the peace of the kingdom. That Domne Eafe chose an island as her cult place puts her in a hallowed tradition of independent women controlling their own destinies by controlling small islands.[34]

Domne Eafe's daughter-successor in Thanet was equally potent. An entire cult centre built up around Mildrith, who sizzled with such sanctity that the footprints she left on a rock near Ebbsfleet acquired their own cult following. They were famed for their healing powers; a chapel was built over them.[35] Mildrith's body, meanwhile, was found to be undecayed when her coffin was opened up – it even exuded a sweet fragrance.

That was in the seventh century. Following the harrying of Thanet in 980 by the Danes, the community of nuns probably moved to Canterbury, which was considered safer. But Mildrith's cult was eventually re-established in Thanet by monks and became so lucrative that in 1030 King Cnut gave Abbot Aelfstan permission to 'translate' her – remove her body to Canterbury itself. Ostensibly, this was in order to promote her elsewhere, but arguably he ended up stripping the island of its female potency. As it happened, 'he met with fierce resistance from the Thanet people'. They were right to object. Abbot Aelfstan left behind some 'dust from her body' to console the islanders, but he took away Mildrith's body *and* the nail from the true cross which she brought back from Gaul.

During the eleventh century, her relics were displayed at the high altar in Canterbury, and the monks travelled back to the island annually on her feast day in July, which was 'accorded the highest rank'. When a 'newly founded priory fraudulently claimed to possess Mildrith's relics' the monks commissioned the Flemish writer Goscelin to refute these 'bogus allegations' and to write a new life, *Vita Mildrethae*. This describes in detail the healing cult associated with Mildrith's footprint stone at Ebbsfleet, which was 'white marble and very hard, yet Mildrith's footprints showed as though printed in fresh snow or clay'. 'Scrapings of the stone' cured fevers. Thus Goscelin created a Kentish Christian version of the footprints Jesus left on the Mount of Olives; but also of the more ancient footprint stones from Dunadd and all over the islands.[36]

In the early fifteenth century, a monk at St Augustine's wrote a history of the institution, *Speculum Augustinian*, and painted two illustrations. One was a delicately coloured map showing Thanet surrounded by bright blue water. Bounding on to the island (seemingly from the sea, like Julius Caesar) is Domne Eafe's hind. A green wiggly line traces the route she took across Thanet. The other was a picture of the high altar at Canterbury, with its fifteen shrines, including that of St Augustine himself in the east – and also, the only woman, 'Sta Mildreda, virgo'. According to the picture, her shrine, to the north of the church, traced in blue, red and ochre, was one of the three largest in the abbey. Like Abbot Hadrian's opposite, it was two storeys high, with numerous windows and elaborate roof tiles.[37]

Mildrith was reverenced after her death, but female monastic learning was not. Either female monastics were not encouraged to be bookish, or female-scripted books and the archives of female communities were more vulnerable than men's and did not survive.[38] Late Anglo-Saxon nuns tend to be known for their embroidery rather than their letters.[39] After the Normans, nuns cease to wield power as their predecessors did.[40]

Being rich, St Augustine's was one of the first religious houses to be ransacked at the Reformation and has been in ruins ever since. As in Orkney, it seems that the relics of abbots and saints were hastily packed up – in this case, sent for safekeeping to the continent. In modern times, English Heritage placed marker stones in the abbey indicating the location of Augustine's grave, and that of several abbots and Anglo-Saxon kings. But there is no marker stone for Mildrith. Her island rock was still being talked of in the eighteenth century, but there is no trace of either the footprints, the chapel, or its healing cult in Thanet now.[41]

One of the first Anglo-Saxon burial sites to be excavated in Britain was that of Ozengell on the Isle of Thanet.[42] The person buried there had a metal, sword-shaped object and so was assumed to be a man. Later it was proved that the bones were those of a woman: so the 'sword' was reclassified as a 'weaving stick'. Still, gendered assumptions are being painstakingly unpacked; slowly, the thought process swung round again, and at last it is possible to conceive of a woman buried with a sword, a weaving stick or even a deliberately 'trans-gender' weaving sword.[43]

Thus, although much evidence points to Thanet as an island of revered women – an Anglo-Saxon iteration of the earlier indigenous tradition reported by Romans and attested in Celtic legend – through deliberate misrepresentation in literature (Bede), physical removal of relics (Aelfstan) and modern misunderstanding (nineteenth- and twentieth-century archaeology), this interesting and potent history dissolved as quickly as an ice cream melts in the hot Thanet sun. It is enough to make a woman weep.

Holy women did in time return to Thanet, however. When Europe's late-nineteenth-century antiquarian fervour spread to monasteries, they began opening up their relic stores and subjecting them to historical analysis. The church of Saint Lebuinus in the

Netherlands duly discovered that, interred with the off-white silk-sheathed bones of their two male founding saints were some 'more delicate bones, wrapped in faintly pink silk'. Documents showed that they belonged to St Mildrith herself. A 'great big leg bone' was promptly packed up and sent over to England, to bring its Catholic community some rare cheer. For the next hundred years, Mildrith's purported femur lived a peripatetic existence, drifting around the British Isles, waiting (impatiently, presumably) to be re-translated.

By chance, in the 1930s, Mildrith's former abbey on Thanet (in private ownership since the Reformation) was put up for sale. The rare opportunity to restore a former sacred space to its original use came to the notice of a clued-up Benedictine monk. He wrote to some monasteries in Germany: then starting to come under pressure from Hitler's Nazi regime. Thanks to the ingenuity and power of the international Benedictine network, the property was purchased on the quiet, and six nuns plus the Jewish-born Mother Superior, Mother Emanuel, were smuggled out of the country from Hamburg to Harwich. The nunnery was refounded in its original location; Mildrith's leg (actually an arm bone, according to the current prioress; actually of an eighth-century abbot, according to recent carbon dating) was restored to its birthplace and, later, Mildrith's now sumptuously pearl-encrusted collarbone was sent over for good measure.

The current prioress of St Mildrith's, Mother Nikola, herself German-born, speaks fervently of both the welcome extended to the new foundation by the people of Thanet and of the importance of recognizing those trans-European links, post-Brexit. Back in the day, women of English royal houses 'were sent to monasteries in Gaul as if to finishing school', she says; today, St Mildrith's houses women of eight different nationalities. Mother Nikola also points out that while Mildrith and her coevals weren't necessarily commemorated in official Anglo-Saxon histories, their names are embedded all over the island in roads and landmarks. The nuns still sing parts of Mildrith's 'big elaborate liturgical office', a thousand years later.

When I visited St Mildrith's Priory (or Minster Abbey, as it is commonly known), the infamous asylum processing centre at Manston, nearby, had recently closed. Mother Nikola spoke fervently about this, too: the chaos that asylum-processing was causing in the local community – not to mention among refugee families themselves; the responsibility the nuns felt for spreading the Christian message that strangers should be seen not as a potential enemy but as guests.

Listening to her speak, I thought anxiously of how the Muslim cultural emphasis on extending welcome to strangers as guests had made my entire first book possible (in Pakistan, particularly); how hard it must be for Muslims coming to this land, by contrast, and not being welcomed. Much easier for presumed-Christian white Ukrainians than for presumed-Muslim headscarf-wearing women from Syria and Afghanistan (worse still for the bearded men of those places). How horrible (how illegal) the government's Illegal Migration Bill; its Rwandan deportation plan ('one of the most atrocious things I have ever heard', said Mother Nikola); its proposed throwbacks such as asylum prison boats off the Isle of Portland.

August. With Sanger's Stage Show we cross into Thanet. Heaving the ponies over the fretful ribbon of the A299, we find ourselves trundling past the acres of glass which is Thanet Earth: stretching away towards the urban conglomeration between us and the sea. The land seems to level off now – not seems, does; we have felt every rise in the road in pony sweat and clatter. Now we are on the island itself, it is easy going. Margate, Broadstairs and Ramsgate tower on the horizon. Today, the Isle of Thanet is mostly houses.

We wind into town, gathering attention like wool around a spindle. 'It's Sanger's.' 'Look, it's Sanger's.' We are passing the Rodney pub and middle-aged ladies in summer attire bring their pints out to the pavement to wave. 'I'll swap you for my house. Actually, you can take it.' 'Fuck off.' At a playpark, kids stop dead wherever they are – slide, roundabout, seesaw – and stare. 'Are you pirates?'

But there is trouble ahead. It is early evening by the time we get to Hartsdown Park, where we are to camp for the night, and the big iron gates are closed. *Fuck!*

'No way it was an accident,' Dave says grimly, 'It's done on purpose.' Finn and Erin hold his horses as he paces up and down the pavement like a demented zoo tiger, shouting at organizers of the carnival through his mobile phone. At last the news comes through: Dane Park is open; we can go there instead.

It is tricky manoeuvring the horses down the hill, but their minders manage it with a minimum of swearing. The park, a big, open green space on the edge of Cliftonville, is perfect. We camp under the trees at the top end and in the last of the evening light the horses crop the grass and the dogs run free. Kids and mums and grandparents wander up to ask questions. Dave won't let them pet the horses, which are tired and hungry. He tells a woman from the stray-dog home to fuck off when she informs him his Jack Russells shouldn't be loose. They're street dogs, he says. An hour later, he shouts at me when he comes out of his caravan again and finds that one of his Jack Russells is missing.

I go into town to get everybody a kebab. Annette writes the order down for me: '3 x Halumi Kebab. + All Salads. Garlic Mayo + Chilli Sauce. 2 x Carlsberg Special Brew.' When I get back, Gary Taylor, recently elected UKIP councillor, has arrived. I recognize his face from the papers. He is upset by local mutterings about Travellers – 'you aren't Romany, you aren't Irish' – the *Showmen* genealogy which distinguishes Dave is important. A kebab is handed in to Dave in his caravan. When he comes out, half an hour later, he apologizes to me for shouting. It was the Pimms – he always thought it was a girls' drink. But it made him rave. Sulkily, he watches the islanders pestering his horses: 'Fucking inbred halfwits.'

Annette says, 'My Danish ancestors came to this exact place.'

The next morning, early, the teenagers and I walk out to the cemetery to see Lord Sanger's grave. It's all in white marble and really grand: a showman on a rearing horse. By the time we get back, the camp has been struck and everybody is ready to move to the far end of Cliftonville, to the field where the carnival is assembling. There are floats from across Thanet adorned with little girls in puffy white wedding dresses and sashes; a proper confection of meringues, princesses and queens from Ramsgate, Sandwich, Minster. At Sanger's, Robyn has dressed up in red ruffles and a blur of Indian mirrors; Annette is in a turquoise bodice and leather riding trousers. Even Dave has changed his hat. Erin gets into Wild Western blue lacy tights and a lacy bodice top, and I, too, am given something to wear: a black-and-white Pierrot's costume with a high ruffled neck and pompoms and billowing limbs. My face is painted white, with glittery green teardrops down my cheeks and a pair of red lips like the bow on a present.

The horses have been brushed and flowers have been dotted all along the harness and the edges of the cart. We are leading the carnival – before even the fire-engine, in second place. The twin showgirls have arrived from London; they ride with Annette. The Irish 'giant' strides along beside, calling out ever more extravagant claims: 'The only solar-powered show in Europe!' 'Over three hundred years of history, and they have walked over three hundred miles from Stonehenge!' 'The longest-running horse-drawn show in the world!' I walk behind him, collecting money in an orange bucket. Kids line the carnival, clutching sticky bags of pennies to give to the floats. 'Go on,' their parents urge, but we are the first float and the children look up fearfully at the giant, hesitant at giving away all they own.

The author Dan Thompson, who lives in Margate, joins the procession, and we walk along together for a bit as the carnival winds down past the Turner Contemporary. Dan says that all showmen are volatile, and moreover that Margate is full of them. Lots of show families settled around Dreamland in the wake of Sanger; they used to run the amusement arcades here and on the nearby Isle of Sheppey; 'now they flog mocked-up vintage furniture to Londoners'. Dan has a theory that Margate has long been associated with the financial emancipation of women – female property-owners. The royal fleet docked in Ramsgate, but Margate was the risqué town of fun and entertainment: specifically, he says, where the mistresses of the admirals and navy top brass lived. I like it as a theory, whether or not it is true; and it fits well with Margate's resurgent reputation as a place of carefree holiday adventure. That identity is still emblazoned all over the town's seafront, in the giant vertical letters Dreamland, in the ice cream parlours, in the shops selling naughty postcards and sticks of rock.

Our procession winds right along the beach; the sun beats down, and the upturned infant faces that line the street look hotter and stickier the further on we go. By the time we reach Dreamland itself, all the performers are thirsty and, in our thick make-up, I feel like sunstroke is beckoning. Some of us need to pee. Predictably, there's a delay getting into Dreamland; we sit for what seems like ages in the stuffy underground car park waiting for the staff to let the horses through. But happily, Dan's flat is just along the road. The 'showgirl' twins, Robyn and I all climb the stairs to his home. I unlace Robyn from her dress; she unhooks me from my Pierrot.

Dreamland has a slightly odd modern history: reacquired recently by a hedge fund and remodelled as Britain's first permanent outdoor festival site. It is absolutely spick and span, an amusement park such as you might expect to find in a more organized country than ours, in Sweden or Switzerland perhaps. It is a world away from FUNLAND, the beachside fairground on Hayling Island in Hampshire, where I took my children, which stank of fags and greasy doughnuts and where the only respite from the heat and the noise was the sight of the sea from the top of the helterskelter.

This evening's show, on DREAMLAND's main stage, is the climax of Dave's pilgrimage: the variety act which SANGER'S STAGE SHOW have come all this way for. The three-person troupe Pyratrix perform their theatrical version of the early life of 'Lord' George; Tarantism Acoustic Disco sing cover versions of techno rave anthems; Crumbs the Magician levitates; and the evening ends with the showbiz twins performing their song about their daddy and his gun. It's a summary of Dave Sanger's life as much as Lord George's, a bringing together of the people he loves from different places, from different points.

I awake in the morning to the sounds of seagulls and the London train. Outside, the dogs are queuing up to pee on my tent. Nobody else is up. I walk down to the wide, endless expanse of the sea, stepping along pavements stained with the detritus of last night's revelry – grey patches of greasy takeaway dinner, squished cigarette ash, the puddle of drink. Here, beyond the Wantsum, that constantly metamorphosing quality of what it means to be English seems to intensify under the all-blinding island sun.

O Thanet, you most English of islands – if by 'English' you understand the sliding, shifting of the immigrant condition. That's what the English were, as Gildas reminds us so well. We rail against newcomers; then we become them, and they us; and then we turn our gaze back across the Channel again, deflecting the new ones with our stare.

NORWEGIAN SEA

6

Shetland

Vikings (ninth century)

They navigate their fast, shallow boats west for two days and meet a land much like their own, in miniature. Long fjords reaching inland, thin agricultural soil, rich fishing, plenty of seals. A scattering of islands collectively shaped like the hilt of a dagger (*hjalt* in old Norse). So they call this – the first place they settle – *hjaltland*. Shetland.

The Shetland Islands were probably not the first British islands to be raided by Vikings. As early as 787, possibly, Northpeople in ships killed an emissary of the king of Wessex, Beorhtric, on the Isle of Portland off the Dorset coast.[1] Thereafter, Lindisfarne was plum-ripe for the picking (793), as was Iona (795, 802, 806) – they used these gold-rich island-churches as casually as cashpoints.[2] The Faroes were taken in 825, the Hebrides in the mid-ninth century, the Isle of Man a century later.[3] Neatly spaced apart islands eased their zeal for expansion. Iceland had never known humans until a band of seafaring brigands from Norway arrived in 870; within twenty years, there was an immigrant population of 24,000.[4] But it was Shetland that was nearest and first to be colonized, Shetland that provided the base for further raiding and expansion.

The islands were the logical place to stop. There they hovered, in the cold northern sea, like a tasty shoal of mackerel, only a day or two's sail from Norway, numerous, easy to snatch. The Vikings of the time were technologically advanced. One of the Icelandic sagas relates how it took only five days to get from Norway to Iceland via Shetland and the Faroes[5] and on to Greenland. The speed is an exaggeration, no doubt, but the route seems sound – islands as motorway service stations.

The Vikings' migration out of Norway was motivated by land hunger, wanderlust, booty, brute strength and brilliant seamanship. 'Never before has such an atrocity been seen in Britain,' wrote Alcuin, a Northumbrian scholar who tutored King Charlemagne's children, of the attack on Lindisfarne, nor was such an incursion from the sea 'thought possible.'[6] His plea of ignorance may well be true. Very likely, Northpeople had come as traders to these islands in the past, but not as plunderers. This changed everything, as Alcuin's Latin poem, 'On the Killing at Lindisfarne' makes clear:

> Ill fortune crowds on good,
> As in the ocean wave succeeds to wave.
> The bright day ends in darkness and dread shadow,
> The buds that flowered in spring are winter-slain.[7]

Monks in remote coastal locations all around Britain grew to expect Viking violence. 'Bitter is the wind tonight,' wrote a monk in Irish, around AD 850, along the top of the Latin manuscript he was copying, 'It tosses the ocean's white hair: / Tonight I fear not the fierce warriors from Norway / Coursing on the Irish Sea.'[8] Fair weather brought bad news.

For a while, the future of Christianity hung in the balance. For a start, the Viking raids put an end to the era of island-bound pilgrim-monks: it was simply too dangerous to live as an ascetic among the sea birds any longer. The ninth-century Irish monk Dicuil, author of *De mensura orbis terra*, described how, off the coast of Britain, were 'other, very small islands, which are almost all separated by narrow straits. On them, hermits who came by ship from our Ireland have lived for nearly a hundred years. But as they were always abandoned from the beginning of the world, thus they are now, because of the Northmen pirates, empty of anchorites, and full of countless sheep and different, excessively many kinds of sea birds.'[9]

The Vikings travelled with their own, robust faith. The Norse religion was not strictly codified, nor, until it encountered Christian literacy, did it have its own texts – but it was forceful, ancient and had once been widespread in northern Europe. The thunder-god traditions that Tacitus encountered in Germany in the first century AD are ancestors of the beliefs that the Anglo-Saxons and Norse exported to Britain, centuries later; so, too, are the Valkyries, 'supernatural warrior-maidens', coevals among the Irish war-goddesses of Celtic times.[10] The Old English word *waelcyrge* seems to be 'the exact equivalent of Old Icelandic *valkyrja* . . . female demons who were connected with war'.[11] That was British culture once. Even after Christianity made Biblical descent from Adam preferable, Anglo-Saxon monarchs continued to list Woden (Odin) as an ancestor, claiming him as a distant hero progenitor ultimately descended from Noah and Adam[12] rather than being (as earlier) an actual god.[13] The ninth-century *Anglo-Saxon Chronicle* is explicit: 'Woden from whose stock sprang the royal houses of many provinces'.[14]

Genetic studies have shown that, whether or not Vikings were related to Woden, Shetland was settled by Norwegian family groups. (In the Hebrides and Iceland, by contrast, Viking men arrived alone and took local wives – Icelanders claim this gene-pool mix as the source of their beauty.) As in twentieth-century Anglesey, the women and children on Shetland spent all year on the colonial farmsteads, tending to the animals and keeping away human predators. But a typical Northern Isles Viking man, as the late twelfth-century *Orkneyinga Saga* explains, spent the winter at home, in Shetland or Orkney, drinking with his friends in his hall and early spring ploughing his fields. The rest of the time he was a pirate. May onwards was for 'plundering in the Hebrides and in Ireland': 'that he called his spring-trip' (*vorviking*). Midsummer was for reaping grain back home. Then it was 'off raiding again until the first month of winter'. 'This he called his autumn cruise' (*haustviking*). It was like this from at least the ninth to the twelfth century.

The sagas are hectic with details of these frenzied plunderers such as Olaf Tryggvason, the Norwegian king, who at the end of the tenth century 'spent four years looting in the British Isles. Then he was baptized in the Scillies and from there sailed to England.'[15] (It was Olaf who forced the Vikings to become Christian.) Olaf's trajectory through the British Isles, dramatic as it was, shows how it was done. Just as it was possible to eradicate wolves and foxes from a small island, so it was possible to eradicate competing people. From one point of strength: proceed to the next place.

The early settlers often carried with them 'earth from a temple in Norway in order to hallow the new land'.[16] The pioneering and persevering Aud (or Unn) the Deep-Minded, in common with other settlers, flung her wooden 'high seat pillars' overboard when she reached Iceland and chose as her colony the place where the pillars washed ashore. ('High seat pillars', which marked the place of the head of the household, were hallowed symbols of home.) Aud's status as a female settler was not uncommon in Norse society; in England, for example, 'a wide range of Scandinavian female names' were preserved in both the *Domesday* book (a small but significant number of female landowners) and in place-names.[17]

Later, in more formal times, when they wished to colonize a piece of mainland, the Norse did so by ritually dragging a boat across it, as if to encircle it with water, to make an island of it. The reason so many places on the west coast of Scotland are named Tarbert may be because it is related to the Norse word for 'portage' (when a boat is carried overland) as well as the Gaelic for isthmus.[18] In 1098, King Magnus Barelegs of Norway came to an agreement with King Edgar of Scotland that any island he could circumnavigate in a ship with a rudder was his. So he had a skiff hauled across Kintyre 'with himself sitting at the helm, and this is how he won the whole peninsula'. As the *Orkneyinga Saga* makes clear, it was both an ancient trick from Norway's legendary past and sometimes the quickest way of getting across an isthmus.[19] *Rex insularum*, 'Island

King', Matthew Paris called the king of Norway in his thirteenth-century *Chronica Maiora*.[20]

Unlike Iceland, virgin land when it was settled, Shetland had a pre-existing population. Among the Shetland locals whom the Vikings killed off, or enslaved, were the Picts. As a people they remain mysterious; the Romans described a painted *Picti* people who were possibly polyandrous; later, Bede insisted that their royalty descended through the female line.[21] It was as a bulwark against the threat of Pictish attack, Bede writes, that as early as the fifth century the southern British king Vortigern invited over from northern Europe the semi-mythical Germanic warlord brothers Hengest and Horsa and gave them the kingdom of Kent. (Hengest means 'stallion' and Horsa 'mare' in Old English; firmly pre-Roman, cultically.)

Whoever the people were who lived in brochs, they produced a most striking, elegant and enduring form of pre-Viking (Iron Age) architecture which still stands in intricate splendour all over the isles and northern coast of Scotland. Brochs have internal spiral staircases built into the walls and may have been communal fortresses. They entranced the Vikings, who used them for romantic liaisons and political meetings, as much as they do us. Amazingly, they have withstood both Norsepeople and transoceanic storms. The broch in Lerwick, Shetland, called Clickimin stands quasi-islanded on the edge of a loch and contains a footprint stone; that on Shetland's eastern island of Mousa, which I visited during the summer sheep shearing, is exquisitely preserved. The sheep farmer Aaron was just going off for his annual three-day holiday in the west of Shetland; less leisure time today than Vikings enjoyed then.

Historians say that land hunger drove the Vikings out of Scandinavia, but there is still academic debate about what they did when they got to the islands they colonized. Was there genocide? Or marriage and love? The big divide in the society of the Norse was between those who were free and those who were enslaved (the *thralls*, hence the English word 'enthrall'); when they got into their boats they were looking for slaves as well as gold. Since there is only the tiniest pinch of pre-Norse place-names in the Northern Isles, it seems likely that in the land of the dagger-hilt the native inhabitants were conquered if not as good as wiped out. As the Frankish *Annals of St Bertin* attested in AD 847

> The Northmen also got control of the islands all around Ireland, and stayed there without encountering any resistance from anyone.[22]

Three hundred years later, when the anonymous twelfth-century author of *Historia Norwegie* wrote about these times, the explanation hadn't changed much:

> In the days of Harald Fairhair, king of Norway, certain pirates set out with a great fleet, and crossed the Solundic sea, and stripped those races of their ancient settlements, destroyed them wholly, and subdued the islands to themselves.[23]

There is no reason to disbelieve either account. Probably the attackers who settled the land were attacked in their turn by new invaders.[24]

From the beginning, as the sagas make clear, Shetland was inhabited by troublesome, rebellious Vikings who left Norway to live as independent pirates rather than submit to the yoke of their king.[25] This annoyed the Norwegian king Harald Fair (or Fine) hair. According to the *Orkneyinga Saga*, he

> sailed west over the North Sea in order to teach a lesson to certain vikings whose plunderings he could no longer tolerate. These vikings used to raid in Norway over summer and had Shetland and Orkney as their winter base.[26]

Even in the twelfth century, by which time the Northern Isles had long been part of a semi-independent earldom, it was men from Shetland who raised the standard of rebellion against Norway. As a result, Shetland was taken under direct rule by the Norwegian crown again and became Scottish only when, in 1469, King Christian of Norway and Denmark pawned the islands to Scotland to pay for his marriage dowry. King Christian always intended to buy the islands back.

Between the ninth and fifteenth centuries, the invading North-people built farms, mined the Shetland islands for soapstone and exported the pottery, 'fishing weights, line sinkers, spindle whorls and beads' they made to Orkney and Faroe.[27] The Norse used their own words to describe the places they settled, and often these are the names that are still in use. Thus, Lerwick means 'bay of clay' in old Norse, 'voe' is a sea-inlet, 'Sandwick' a sandy bay.[28] Old Norse and Old English, after all, were mutually comprehensible tongues. In the late nineteenth century, when the Icelandic philologist Jakob Jakobsen came to Shetland, he documented the Viking Norn language in its dying throes. He claimed that Norn was closer to the Norse mother-tongue than either Icelandic or Faroese, and this he attributed to the very early colonization of Shetland.[29]

The Vikings came to Shetland, dallied in its brochs and changed the history of the islands by treating them as a colony, a distant out-post of Norway. They linked the islands into a Scandinavian world it hadn't known before. Subsequently, they also made them into an independent, pan-island kingdom, the power of which was to endure, in Britain, until the late fifteenth century.

Since the Northpeople were from island/fjord worlds, the island culture and mythology they encountered in Shetland, Orkney and the Hebrides merged with their own beliefs. They continued the islands' crannog tradition, which had roots in the Neolithic, constructing their own new islands in lochs, as was done on Lewis in 3000 BC,[30] and on Orkney in the Iron Age.[31] The Vikings built an island in a loch in Shetland for the purpose of holding their parliament there. The creation of an assembly site (*thing* in old Norse) showed how serious those early settlers were about establishing order and stability in their new land; the creation of the parliament happened centuries before the takeover of the islands by Norwegian kings. These were bold and innovative frontier people, clinging to some traditions and inventing others.[32] Possibly it felt practical and safe to hold the parliament on an island but, maybe, as for the Neolithic Orcadians and the Iron Age Druids of Anglesey, there was some magic afoot.[33] Tingwall is a parish in Shetland the name of which denotes that it was an early Norse assembly site. The Norse chose for their parliament a place of pre-existing sanctity, important to the Iron Age inhabitants and, later, it was next to this loch that the Christians built their church (the 'mother church' of Shetland). Even after Christianity took over, and at least into the late sixteenth century, the island parliament site at Tingwall was where 'judicial actions were announced and witnessed'.[34] Rather like the Odin stone in Orkney's Mainland, which was used for business deals and trysts, at Tingwall, too, the primary purpose endured across the centuries, even without the particular belief system that had fostered it.[35]

The Norse also adapted, or were influenced by, pre-existing Celtic utopias to come up with their own far western paradise islands, some real, some imagined. For centuries, scholars of the Viking age thought Vinland was invented – a 'land of wine' spoken of in two Icelandic sagas, *Saga of the Greenlanders* and *Erik the Red's Saga* – until, in 1960, Norwegian explorers and archaeologists uncovered a Viking settlement from AD 1000, in North America. The final expedition to Vinland was led by Erik the Red's daughter Freydis, one of those fearless women who temper the testosterone-heavy Norse poems and sagas.

But other Norse islands seem to have been imaginary utopias, akin to or directly inspired by earlier Greek and Celtic ones. All the features of Hvitramannaland, or 'Land of White Men', 'have direct counterparts in the Irish voyage tales'.[36] 'Odainsakr', 'field of the not-dead', was the 'Norse Avalon'. The Norse Yggdrasill myth, meanwhile, may have been inspired by Odysseus's island travels.[37] Fridtjof Nansen, who wrote a book in 1911 called *In Northern Mists: Arctic Exploration in Early Times*, even linked the 'Irish ideas of a happy land of women' to the Norwegian belief in the *hulder*, a fairy who 'kidnaps and seduces men, and keeps them with her for a long time'.[38]

The Norse afterlife was a place to which great warriors were taken by the Valkyries – 'beautiful battle-maidens'[39] who picked men off the battlefield and led them away to Odin's feasting hall. But to get there the warriors needed a good send-off from their kith and kin. Often, great Viking leaders – men and women – were buried on ships, within mounds, as if to carry the deceased into the western ocean. Aud the Deep-Minded, from whom the Orkney earls and the nobles of the Faroes were descended, was interred in a ship-burial mound, according to the *Laxdaela Saga*, 'and much treasure with her'.[40] The pre-Viking ship burial in East Anglia at Sutton Hoo has Scandinavian elements: a way of 'bringing the sea to land'.[41] In *Beowulf* – written down in Old English but set in southern Scandinavia and probably originally sung from the seventh to ninth centuries in old Norse – a warrior is laid out in a boat with his treasures around him and sent out to sea. The Norse word for ritualized single combat, *holmganga*, means 'going on an island'. Boats were both how you got around and also an old Norse art form, along with poetry and runes. All three travelled from Sweden and Norway around the islands of Britain, metamorphosing under sail.[42]

Because the Norse interred their important people in great burial mounds, surrounded by jewellery, weapons and great material wealth, to the Viking explorers who encountered Shetland and Orkney for the first time the landscape of the isles, with its Neolithic burial mounds and Iron Age brochs, looked like magic and treasure. (Reverence lingered; Martin Martin writes that when he visited on the cusp of the eighteenth century, the people of South Uist in the Western Isles still retained 'the ancient custom . . . on Sundays and holidays' 'of making a religious tour round' big stone cairns.)[43]

As in Neolithic and Celtic times, the Norse, too, believed that a form of communication was possible with the dead in the mound. Such episodes occur throughout old Norse poetry and sagas. Thus, in

Grógaldr, a poem composed around the time of the Viking migrations (though written down much later), Gróa, a dead *völva* (priestess-prophetess) is raised from her burial mound by her son when he wishes to ask her advice. In the *Orkneyinga Saga* a man called Sveinn Breast-Rope 'sits out' all night on a burial mound near Orphir communing with the dead.[44] In real life, mounds were sometimes broken apart in acts of heroism against a rival clan; or in Christian times, as acts of anti-pagan iconoclasm. In 1153, saga and archaeology met when a band of Vikings, led by Earl Harald, broke into Maeshowe in Orkney. There is a brief description in the *Orkneyinga Saga*:

> During a snowstorm they took shelter in Maeshowe and there two of them went insane, which slowed them down badly.

Those brigands – in the saga and runes they call themselves crusaders: they were on the way to Jerusalem – then made what is the finest collection of Runic graffiti outside Scandinavia. The doodlings include:

> Ingigerth is the most beautiful of all women.

> Thorni fucked. Helgi carved.

> Crusaders broke into Maeshowe.
> Lif the earl's cook carved these runes.[45]

Feminist scholars have noted (with varying degrees of disgust) that the Norse world adored masculinity.[46] Yet a book of essays published by the Swedish History Museum in Stockholm claims that although Viking gender roles were clearly demarcated – in general, women ruled the domestic sphere, while men were farmers and sea-plunderers – there was social equality greater than in later times. Unlike patriarchal Christianity, the ancient Norse religion had important goddesses as well as gods. Their creation story has Ash and Elm, as the first man and woman, in what is possibly an echo of Genesis – but without the weight of censure applied to the woman.

Down on earth, Norse women also performed high-status roles for the community, such as that of *völva*.⁴⁷ Norse literature also reiterates the strong cultural memory from earlier times of ancient female island magic.⁴⁸

The old Norse poems were committed to writing comparatively late, upon codification in the literate Christianized society of Iceland. One of the oldest and most interesting, *Völuspá*, may have been written down in the Western Isles in the tenth century by 'a vigorous believer in the old gods, and yet with an imagination active enough to be touched by the vague tales of a different religion'.⁴⁹ It describes the past and the future and is spoken by a *völva*, who describes how, in the beginning,

> sun knew not
> what temples she had;
> Moon knew not
> what power he possessed;
> stars knew not
> what places they had.

In this Norse world, the supreme being, Sun, was a she (and the Moon a he). Into this time of no-knowledge came 'three maidens, all-powerful', 'much knowing':

> three, from the hall
> under tree stands . . .
> they laws made,
> they life selected;
> all the children
> they destiny say . . .
> Understand ye yet, or what?

Reading these surprising words, with women at the beginning and the end of every thought, I wonder melancholically about the feminist utopia they might have spawned. Instead, what happened?

Somehow (again) other creation myths came to dominate and this one failed to achieve momentum. I had never thought before of the duty we have to honour the women of past ages and the thoughts that once honoured them. It's too easy sometimes to get by in a man's world – not giving these unexamined compromises any thought – until the inevitable crisis happens.

The deepest loch in Shetland, Girlsta, is named after the daughter of one of these early colonizers of Iceland, Flóki, who left western Norway in 868 with his family and overwintered in Shetland. There, he discovered that his daughter Geirhildr was in love with a man of whom he disapproved. Either he enacted an honour killing or she crept out to meet the man, and somehow drowned.[50] Whichever way, Geirhildr's story left a domestic and personal, as well as military and strategic, mark on Shetland. The father had the daughter buried on an island in the middle of the 22-metre-deep loch.[51] A woman I met in Lerwick told me that as a child she was warned never to go near Geirhildr's loch by her grandparents 'because the *swaabies* would attack you to defend her grave'. *Swaabies*, according to the Shetland dictionary, are great black-backed gulls.[52] The tale reminded me of that great Sindhi folk heroine, Sohni, who also drowned for passion: crossing the Indus to meet her lover. (There was sabotage by her sister-in-law.) In that country Sohni's bravery, love and its tragic conclusion have for centuries been depicted in countless songs and paintings and folklore. In this country the commemoration is much quieter.

Today, the Shetland Islands are the most remote inhabited place in the British Isles, almost equidistant between mainland Norway and Scotland. The car ferry takes a good twelve hours from Aberdeen to Lerwick and costs a sweet £600. But that is in the context of the 'mainland'. If you reorient your mind *east–west* rather than *north–south* you will find that the islands sit in the middle of a busy international shipping route, as important now as it was a thousand years ago. The longboat route which led from Scandinavia to Orkney, the Hebrides, Man and Ireland, or up to Faroe and Iceland, remained

Shetland's 'particular maritime niche', as Barbara Crawford, scholar of medieval Shetland, writes, even into modern times.[53] From the twelfth century onwards, after Norway took back control of Shetland – pulling it out of the ambit of the Orkney earldom – 'the Scandinavian imprint on the islands' was strengthened, and even after the islands were pledged to Scotland Shetland remained 'part of the Norwegian world'.[54] This independence became integral to Shetland's national character and meant that by the nineteenth century, when the great whaling ships were adding Antarctica and the island of South Georgia to their trajectories, it was Shetland men they scooped up. When Antarctic whaling stopped in 1963, the Hudson's Bay Company took over, exporting Shetland men to work in the fur trade in the Canadian Arctic. Later, the extraction of North Sea oil and North Sea fish maintained these trans-North Sea links, at the expense of camaraderie with Scotland.

Shetland, with its light summers and dark winters, has a diurnal cycle familiar to any Norseperson. In the summer, Norwegian tourists come in droves to see the land they once ruled. Most arrive on cruise ships. But in June, the brightest point of the year, at the abandoned RAF base on Shetland's northernmost island of Unst, I meet four Norwegians who have just landed after *rowing* over from Bergen. Emotions run high over pints of Shetland beer. 'We can understand local place-names!' the men say, and their faces grow ruddy and shiny, 'We feel more Norse here than we do at home.'

The identification / guilt goes beyond anything an Englishwoman might feel on reaching Calais (lost in 1558) or a French backpacker touring Morocco (independent in 1956). The Vikings made Shetland their own. Never mind that the islands were once a Norwegian colony, one of its *skattlands*. Never mind the intervening centuries of 'Scottification'. While much of the old language has been lost, Shetlanders in general have a pan-Scandinavian lineage of 44 per cent – higher than anywhere else in the British Isles.[55] Even land tenure is still based on Norse Udal law.

Today in Great Britain there are three legal systems: 'English law in England and Wales, Scots law (feudal) in Scotland, and Udal tenure in parts of Orkney and Shetland'.[56] *Udal* (pronounced to rhyme with *noodle*) law was unwritten. The Udal landowner held full rights of possession, acknowledging no superior – neither the monarch nor the state. It was thus the antithesis of Scottish feudalism.

In 1958, during a University of Aberdeen archaeological dig on St Ninian's Isle, off Shetland, a local schoolboy volunteer unearthed a wooden box full of ninth-century silver Pictish treasure. St Ninian's Isle is joined to the west coast of Shetland's Mainland by a shell-sand tombolo. The treasure trove, consisting of intricate silverwork – feasting bowls, a spoon for eating shellfish, decorations from the scabbards of swords, and twelve brooches[57] – probably belonged to a local Pictish family who buried it to keep it from falling into the hands of marauding Vikings. (This was common anti-Viking practice among Scottish islanders, as the *Orkneyinga Saga* attests.)[58]

The Crown immediately claimed the treasure and tried to export it to the mainland. The University of Aberdeen, in association with the local Shetland landowner, objected and took the case to court, claiming that under Udal law the treasure should be divided three ways: between the finder, the Udal landowner and the Crown – and therefore that the treasure ought to be kept largely in Shetland.[59] In 1962, when the case was heard at Edinburgh's Court of Session, the entire history of Orkney and Shetland's Norse past, the mortgaging of the islands to the Scottish Crown, the introduction of Scottish feudalism, was raked over. The defending QC spoke in his summing up of how 'There may yet be laughter in the halls of Valhalla.'[60] But the judge found in favour of the Crown – and the treasure is now in Edinburgh, in pride of place in the Museum of Scotland.

The greatest impact of the clash between Udal and Scottish (feudal) law has been along the foreshore, for that is where the two systems differ. The limit of the foreshore constantly changes, throughout the day, according to the tides. Udal title includes the foreshore, extending 'from the lowest of the ebb to the highest of the hill'.[61] Scottish law defines the foreshore less generously, as the area of the shore between the high and low water mark of ordinary spring tides.[62]

In the 1990s Shetland's Salmon Farmers Association was suddenly inspired to invoke Udal law to argue that it shouldn't have to pay the Crown millions annually in rental of the seabed. This case, too, was lost. 'We were stuffed by the Establishment,' a lawyer I meet in Lerwick tells me, and then shouts at me that I mustn't quote him.

The moot point in the case of Shetland is *who*, and moreover *where*, the 'Establishment' is. After all, it is Edinburgh, not London, that got the St Ninian's Isle treasure, and the UK Treasury which, since 1760, has received the net income of the Crown Estate.[63] One outcome of the 2014 Scottish referendum – when 44.7 per cent of the country voted for independence – was the establishment of an inquiry, the Smith Commission, which recommended that Scotland should finally wrest control of its foreshore and seabed from the Crown estate of the United Kingdom.[64] This happened with the Scotland Act 2016. But in Shetland, this has made little practical difference. The money still goes out of the islands.

Clashes such as these keep the independent spirit of the islands alive and only occasionally result in full-blown calls for independence. In 1967, before oil had begun to enrich the Northern Isles, there was a 'back to Scandinavia' movement in Shetland and Orkney. During a visit to the islands, the Secretary of State for Scotland Willie Ross was stopped by Shetland 'guerrillas' and asked for his passport; in Orkney he was met with demonstrations by 'Vikings' and the appearance of a 'Back to Denmark' slogan.[65]

Then came the oil and the money, and Shetlanders began to feel much more relaxed about their position in the world. Oil, like North Sea fishing, locked them once again into a trans-North Sea community, in association with the Scandinavians.

During the general election of 2017, while I was living in Orkney, I attended a meeting for the 'Shetland Orkney Sovereignty' candidate, Stuart Hill. My four-year-old daughter and I were the only people who showed up. We chatted to Hill and bought his book, *Stolen Isles*, which sets out the case for the Northern Isles' independence – resting again on the fact that all land in Shetland is Udal, and therefore the Crown is not sovereign.[66] Hill is a maverick who deliberately sought to get himself arrested in order that these sovereignty arguments should come before a judge – in 2020, he was 'found guilty of contempt of court and sentenced to two months in prison'.[67] But his point is sound. Orkney and Shetland could have been like the Isle of Man or the Channel Islands: free to set their own laws.[68]

Orkney councillors' majority vote in July 2023 to seek for greater independence, including flirting with the idea of a Nordic connection, shows that economic pressure (the waning of oil money) can cause people to look for solace and example far back in history.

Shetlanders do this too. They vote against the mainstream.[69] They also distinguish themselves from Scotland by giving full vent to their 'atavistic yearning for Norway' (as Dr Ian Tait of the Shetland Museum and Archives described it to me). Since at least Victorian times, Shetland has worn its Viking heart on its sleeve like a soapstone trinket. There is the tourist tat of horned helmets and toy axes which fill the shops of Lerwick; the Shetland flag with its Nordic cross (created in 1969 and hugely popular across the islands); the motto of the Shetland Islands Council, *Með lögum skal land byggja* ('By law shall the land be built up'), a quotation in old Norse from the Icelandic *Njáls Saga*.[70] Above all, there is Up Helly Aa.

Shetland's wintertime Mardi Gras began in Victorian times. As in other parts of Britain, eighteenth-century Romantic poetry and antiquarian discoveries bequeathed to certain British ethnic groups a fascination with their 'indigenous' past. The Welsh dressed up as Druids, the Cornish as Celtic bards, Shetlanders as Vikings. In the Northern Isles, writers began to explore Norse themes in poetry and prose. In 1873, Shetlander Gilbert Goudie translated the *Orkneyinga Saga* (a 'secular scripture' for these northern islanders).[71] The stories of the sagas became so popular that Norse tales began to overlay and displace Scottish ones. Walter Scott, who wrote a Norse-themed novel, *The Pirate*, visited Orkney and Shetland in 1814. He was told that when a minister in North Ronaldsay,

Orkney's most northerly island, read Thomas Gray's 1768 poem 'The Fatal Sisters' – a gruesome depiction of the Valkyries – to his congregation, they interrupted him, telling him 'they knew the song well in the Norse language . . . They called it the Magicians, or the Enchantress.'[72]

There are no native – or even neo-native – speakers of Norn (as there have been, since the 1970s, of Manx on the Isle of Man). Instead, Shetlanders pour all their lost Viking-soul into Up Helly Aa. In Lerwick, the capital, it began as a young lads' festivity, dovetailed over the decades with 'nascent civic pride', until all the components slotted into place – the bonfires, the costumes, the ship, the boat's squad with its male pantomime queen called the Jarl. Because there was no recorded literary reminder of the atrocities perpetuated on the native islanders by Vikings, there is no need for the mind to linger on the horror. Instead, everybody celebrates brute force (from which they are probably descended).

The Viking-themed Jarl Squad is the centre of attention, but many of the lesser squads (in 2020, there were forty-nine) dress up in joke costumes – often as women. There are charming black-and-white photos in the Shetland Museum of squads from the 1920s, costumed as dancers and milkmaids. 'Transvestite Tuesday', some people call Up Helly Aa (it is always held on the last Tuesday in January).

January is not a clement time to visit Shetland, still less to march around town all night, scantily dressed. That is part of the macho show. The hardiest of the fishermen I know described to me what it was like being in the Jarl Squad (a great honour); the year he took part, his costume cost him £2,500, weighed three stone and with his legs in thin hosiery, he got a chest infection.

The Jarl Squad leader of the 2020 Up Helly Aa is dressed like Odin in a pewter helmet cast in Aberdeen with a design of the Norse world-tree. By then the fifty-strong squad will have met all year twice weekly to plan the ceremony in their galley shed. Other parts of Shetland have long celebrated Up Helly Aa in more modern ways, with female participants; there was even a woman Jarl leader in the South Mainland Up Helly Aa in 2015. But in Lerwick, there are some nine hundred participants – and until 2023, not one of them was allowed to be a woman.

In Victorian times, the role of Viking women was less well understood. Nowadays everybody knows about Viking female warriors and goddesses such as Freya.[73] The contemporary sexism of Lerwick's public display of male prowess (endorsed by the council, which hosted the festivities in the town hall) gathered serious amounts of disapprobation. The group called Reclaim the Raven, run by Zara, whom I met over curry in Lerwick, drew attention to women's important position in Viking culture; while 'Up Helly Aa for aa' (for all), a wider, more disparate group active on Facebook, contended that women should be given something more exciting to do than serve sandwiches.[74] I met Lindsey Manson, a young woman who began speaking out after reflecting on what the experience of Up Helly Aa did to her as a child growing up in Shetland. When Lindsey was thirteen, in 2006, her father was Jarl. She describes him as the first blue-collar Guizer Jarl – before that it was middleclass businessmen. So he broke one glass ceiling. But although Lindsey's little brother got to be in the parade and was allowed to attend the meetings in the galley shed, Lindsey was excluded. It made her realize that 'because I'm a woman, I'm respected less.' She was the only member of her family not mentioned in the press coverage, and it hurt. She could see what a great experience it is for the men involved. Boys learn from a young age how to make things, how to talk to each other across families and generations; knowledge is passed down and glory is shared. Women, by contrast, get to 'butter bread and make soup' – to serve the men.

The Vikings were obsessed with their feasting halls; a symbol of true chaos in the *Völuspá* is a river running through the halls. The obsession begins with Valhalla itself and continues into real life.[75] Summer or winter, the same is true in Shetland today, which still organizes its community life around feasting (on sandwiches and cakes rather than mead and stew) in its often remote country halls. In winter, on Up Helly Aa night in Lerwick, the costumed squads carouse, in rotation, from hall to hall – at the ferry terminal, at the British Legion – to be greeted at each one by a team of women who will feed them Shetland hall fare and wait to be asked to dance.

Hostesses at the halls still defend the sexist divide, claiming that it's good family fun, that the women have the best of it, with 'nine hundred men to entertain us' (as one hostess put it to me). But as I watched all those men being cheered and photographed as they moved through the streets of Lerwick carrying burning torches, then throwing them, one by one, into the wooden galley, I couldn't think of an equivalent public celebration of femininity in Shetland's culture – or in many other places either.[76] I did not see a single Valkyrie at Up Helly Aa, nor Freya – nor any of the other plentiful female figures from Norse mythology.[77]

Then, in 2022, following a Covid hiatus, the threat of prolonged protest finally prevailed over macho pride. Despite much resistance from the self-styled traditional majority (thousands of people joined the 'Women for Remain the Same' Facebook page),[78] rules were changed in time for the January 2023 Lerwick Up Helly Aa.[79] The festival I watched was the last of its kind.

As if one change was not enough, in the same summer season Shetland also celebrated its first Pride festival and elected its first Scottish Green Party councillor, Alex Armitage. It can't be easy discussing climate change with islanders whose economy has for decades been flush with oil revenue, who see offshore wind farms as a threat to fish stocks, whose average carbon footprint is sky high on account of the ferries and planes they take in and out. But Alex sees opportunity where others perceive disaster. Take fishing. Mackerel has just been removed from the Good Fish Guide of the Marine Conservation Society,[80] but Alex is adamant that, managed well, this 'abundant marine protein' can be a sustainable choice in an age of climate-change ruin.

By the time I spoke to him, I had already met the most macho of Vikings – the fishers of the island of Whalsay – who broadly speaking scorn marine science, voted for Brexit (a source of subsequent bitterness),[81] and project an invincibility that comes from being bound together by impermeable ties of nature, place and family (plus massive amounts of money).

Tellingly, the island of Whalsay is the only part of Shetland not to run its own Viking fire festival. The majority of working-age men who live on Whalsay are fishers on one of the island's seven supertrawlers. George Anderson, skipper of the *Adenia*, is a man in whose height and self-assurance it would be easy to see his Viking inheritance incarnate. Yet he, too, couldn't care less about the Vikings. 'They were really bad navigators,' he told me flippantly when I went aboard his new mega-trawler; 'they tried to get to America and instead ended up in Shetland.'

Who knows what would have happened to Whalsay, a little outlying hump of moorland, and dirt poor for generations, had it not been for fishing. It became rich almost overnight when the EU fishing quota was allocated.[82] A trawler like the *Adenia* tracks fish with sonar and scoops up entire shoals with a modern purse-seine net. It might lift four to eight thousand tonnes a year. Mackerel travel in like-age groups. As long as you target a correct-age shoal, says George, the operation is drone-neat: no by-catch, no underage fish. The *Adenia* snaffles an entire year's quota in barely five weeks. The rest of the year, George and his crew (of sons and cousins predominantly) tend their crofts, drive their fast cars, or play golf. Whalsay has the most northerly golf course in the British Isles. George sees his grandchildren much more than he saw his own children. His wife, Ruby, told me of the nights she would sit up, feeding the baby, listening to the radio frequency that George and his colleagues used, out at sea in the storms. Now these uber-rich pelagic fishers in their comfy boats are called 'Slipper Skippers' by others.

On the far side of Whalsay, John Arthur Poleson is harvesting grass from his croft, helped by his mother and three young sons. John Arthur is a fisherman; his father was a fisherman too. But while his ancestors spent months of every year scouring the sea in a sixareen (a six-oared wooden boat), John Arthur, like George, floats around in luxury. Both fishing boats have individual cabins en suite, a TV room with Sky – '3D-cinema and leather settees' – a kitchen with a special fryer which pivots with the action of the boat. Automation means that the crew 'barely touch a fish'. John Arthur's young sons, who are making silage by stuffing it into airtight blue plastic chemical barrels discarded by the oil terminal at Sullom Voe, nevertheless declare other ambitions, one to be a doctor, another an engineer.

Instead of Up Helly Aa, Whalsay does 'huge weddings'. When George Anderson's son Michael married his sweetheart, Anne-Marie, the wedding feast was prepared by a team of old men over an open peat fire: mutton stew made from sixteen sheep for seven hundred guests, eaten with bannocks cooked by the women. Michael and Anne-Marie told me that Whalsay, alone of all the islands in Shetland, still uses dialect words from old Norse – 'Whalsay hung on to it longer than the rest of Shetland.'

The distinctive Shetland dialect is a mixture of Norn words, Lowland Scots and English. The 'Unst boat song' is the only living remnant of Norn – sung by quite a few modern folk singers, including the female collective who came together from across Britain to record 'Songs of Separation'. It's ostensibly a song of men in boats – but they call it a 'sea-prayer', poetically.[83]

> *Starka virna vestalie*
> *Obadeea, obadeea . . .*
> *Stala, stoita, stonga raer*
> *Oh, whit says du da bunksha baer . . .*
> *Litra mae vee, drengie.*
> *Saina papa wara,*
> *Obadeea, obadeea.*
>
> Strong wind from the west'ard
> Trouble, trouble . . .
> Put in order, brace up, mast yards
> What do you say . . .

I am pleased with that, boys,
Bless us, our Father,
Trouble trouble . . .[84]

When T. A. Robertson published the Shetland Folk Society's collection of songs in 1973, 'Saina Papa' in the penultimate line was given as 'Father', as in God; but the Norn Saina Papa could easily be one the many saints of these islands; one of the Papar after whom many islands are named. Robertson quotes 'Da Sang O Da Papa Men', sung by fishermen from the now de-inhabited island of Papa, who, in summertime, were drawn back home through the fog by the scent of wild flowers:

Papa some times lies in Simmer,
Veiled wi ask an shooers;
Dan apo da wilsom water
Comes da scent o flooers.[85]

Many of the songs that were collected, from 1945 onwards, when the society was founded, were about the epic travails of fishermen and their families. The one song from Whalsay, 'Da Whalsa Maid's Lament', is also known as 'Shame faa da Laird', ['Shame on the Laird'], from 'the days of the powerful landowners', when many young men were sent to sea to make money for the lairds.

It is very different now. Better for the fishermen; worse for the fish. The big money the fishermen were making didn't prevent their systematic cheating of the quota system. They did it in league with the fish factories in Lerwick (Shetland) and Peterhead (on the Scottish mainland). For at least a decade, skippers falsified their log books. Factories rigged their scales and set up two computer systems, one to declare catch-weights which kept the boats within their quota, another in the loft which logged the true number of fish they landed. Almost all the skippers involved in the 'black-fish' scandal were from Whalsay. George was one of them. The scam came to light in 2005 after accountants noticed that earnings far exceeded declared catch.

(None of them was involved in tax-dodging.) When the case came to trial it was noted in court that the fishermen were 'normally law-abiding'. George himself said in court that he found the practice of dumping by-catch 'repugnant'.

Josie Simpson, three times President of Shetland's Fishermen's Association, spent forty-two years at sea and is now retired on Whalsay. Before the quota, 'we were catching too much', but nor are EU 'restrictions in line with the fish that's in the sea'. He understands why the cheating happened. With the factories involved, it was hard to resist. 'And say if I were landing black fish and you werena, you were going to come home to your family with less money as me.' He didn't like it. But he thinks those times are behind them now. 'That's why the fishing is so important for an island like Whalsay, that you can keep the young people on the island.'[86]

I first met George Anderson in 2014, in Whalsay. He offered to take me on a fishing trip then and there – they were due to leave the following morning, with expected docking in Norway a few days after – but I had an eighteen-month-old baby. I thought I might go mad in the North Sea without her, and she without me.

Over the next five years George and I keep in touch, but it is hard to time it right, because even from Orkney, Shetland is a fair way off, and George and his crew spend so little time at sea. He might text me to say he was out fishing and could I make it to Peterhead by the following afternoon; I couldn't. There was some back and forth for a few years, until one September George said he'd be coming across from Norway and stopping for a few days in Shetland for repairs – and that was my chance. The children were old enough to leave, now, for a bit. I took the train to Aberdeen and got on the night ferry.

Up on the bridge, George hands me a map, 2182C, produced by the hydrographer of the navy. Right-hand side: the Norwegian coast. Mid-left: the Shetland Islands. In the middle: the manically busy waters of the North Sea, dotted with oil fields, at the centre of which is Viking Bank. Mackerel spawn way down west of Spain; their eggs drift north with the Gulf Stream and end up around Norway, where they hatch into little fish. In the spring, these mackerel migrate west across the North Sea, like Vikings on their warm weather raids.[87] Norwegian trawlers follow them through Norwegian waters, as far as the 200-mile mark at the edge of British waters; George and his colleagues pick up the trail at Viking Bank and track them south-west to Orkney and all the way around the Scottish headland. The *Adenia* unloads its catch according to where the price is best: at Ler-wick, at Peterhead, but most often at Måløy in Norway. Every trawler in Whalsay boasts photographs of official Norwegian parties and receptions: fishermen are feted in that mackerel-hungry country. Oil and fish have re-bonded the Norwegians and Shetlanders into a 'North Sea community'.[88]

The boat is huge – but so is the sea, with its vast vistas and waves gigantic like things from myth. Even when the sea is calm, it is an imposing gun-metal grey; the depths seem unfathomable. It becomes obvious, out here, how myths of monsters arise, how saints have visions of paradise, how hungry the Vikings must have been when they finally saw land.

The modern, computer-fuelled dance upon the high seas may not be as dangerous or uncomfortable as it was during Viking times, but it has lost none of its thrill. During the five days we spend at sea, I watch slightly astounded as the crew, salty with sweat and sea, drop gigantic metal doors into the water to fan the nets through the shoal below. The sea churns around us. The fish – silvery-blue-green-black – arrive looking as discombobulated as outraged goddesses. Soon they will be inert and frozen, waiting to be carried over to Norway.

We are almost in Norway when I realize I'm not carrying my passport. But this is a Viking ship; the fishermen aren't bothered by petty regulations. They are in and out of Norway all the time; the maritime agencies almost never come aboard; all the officials know them. For skippers like George, Norway – in the European Economic Area but not part of the European Union – is the model for how a 'coastal nation' such as Britain should interact with the rest of the world. There's even a Lervik here in Norway.

Aboard the *Adenia*, I immediately get seasick, exhausted by the 3 a.m. rises (mackerel are caught at night), and soon tire of deep-fried chips. But adrenaline courses when the boat chases down a shoal. It is easy to see how man eliminated entire species. And it *is* a man's boat; I remember this at every moment. There isn't even a naked-woman poster up in the kitchen, as in other boats; perhaps she was put away politely for my sake. Out in the North Sea, therefore, I am the only woman.

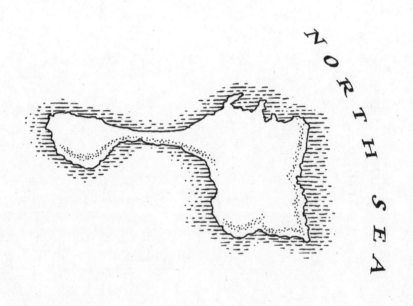

NORTH SEA

7

Lindisfarne / Avalon

Reformations (1296–1537)

December 2018. Six months after leaving Orkney, a couple of months after taking George's trawler to Norway, I am drawn north again. It is the beginning of Advent. Around my neck is an Orcadian scallop shell; in my hand, my Anglesey oak staff; there is a green marble pebble from St Columba's Bay in Iona in my pocket. British medieval pilgrims wore their scallop shells as badges and were buried with their oak staves. In Kirkwall Cathedral, their graves are carved with scallop shells to signify that they had traipsed to holy places – if not Jerusalem, then Santiago de Compostela; if not Spain, then Canterbury or Lindisfarne. Until the Reformation, pilgrims marched up and down the country, touching chips from the true cross, kissing St Aidan's pillar,[1] washing their eyes with the waters of Orcadian virgin Triduana's loch. Southern England's most popular saint was the 'hooly blisful martir' Thomas à Becket, in Canterbury. In the north, there was the island ascetic Cuthbert, whose cult moved back and forth from Lindisfarne to Durham over the course of four hundred years.

I am setting out for Durham some five hundred years after Durham's Cathedral Priory was dissolved by Henry VIII (479 years to the month: December 1539). I plan to walk north out of the city, following in the footsteps of the two servant women from Newcastle, Matilda Burg and Margaret Usher, who in the winter of 1417 were made to perform the penance of walking to Newcastle, dressed in men's clothing, for their crime of trying to reach the shrine of St Cuthbert in drag because female pilgrims were forbidden from approaching it. I will walk on to Lindisfarne, 73 miles as the crow flies, like the *Haliwerfolc* ('people of the saint'), who, in December 1069, sped there in a mere four days – in a hurry not to be harried by William the Conqueror, and that, too, while dragging Cuthbert's coffin to safety.[2] It will not be a straightforward journey – neither in terms of chronology nor geography.

Pilgrim means 'wanderer', 'sojourner'. The first good omen occurs on the train out of London when I sit down next to two men who turn out to be Pakistani. Listening to them talk, I guess that they are from Sindh, my ur-place of pilgrimage. So, I introduce myself. The more talkative of the two claims to have read my first book; by sheer coincidence, I once travelled with his sister, Sassui, then a newly elected politician with the Pakistan People's Party, from Karachi, through rural Sindh, to attend a water-protest rally near Makli, the legendary golden sandstone necropolis of half a million Sindhi saints. Sassui, who has since been Minister for Culture in the Sindh Assembly, is named after a folk heroine sung of by one of Pakistan's most beloved poet-saints.

Britain, like Pakistan today, was once criss-crossed with pilgrimage routes. Often the shrines themselves were in watery places: by lochs, on peninsulas and islands. Many of them honoured female saints. Women such as Triduana from Orkney, or Dwynwen, Anglesey's patron saint of lovers, are Christian avatars of far older spirits of land and water.[3]

In the sixteenth century, when Henry VIII imposed his religious reforms on England and Wales, he changed the outward, spiritual expression of the church for ever. Along with the dissolution of religious houses, his reformers also banned the cult of saints, and while they were at it, pilgrimage. For rural folk, in particular, this put an end to cheap, church-sanctioned holidays. It stands to reason that they minded. Pilgrimage was festival season for rogues and the virtuous alike. In the fourteenth century the poet Geoffrey Chaucer chose pilgrimage as the context for his pan-social storytelling not just because 'folke longen to goon on pilgrimages' but also because this was the *only* way that such 'sondry folk' – men, women, upper and working classes, lay and holy – could 'by aventure yfalle / In felaweshipe'.[4]

I knew a little about Cuthbert before setting off for Durham – that he was born in Scotland in 634, died on the Farne Islands fifty-three years later, was bishop of Lindisfarne – by all accounts a perfectly nice, well-behaved ascetic. During his life he was friends with many women, including his foster-mother and various abbesses; and asked to be buried in a cloth given him by Abbess Verca.[5] Only later (post-Conquest) were stories told of Cuthbert's distaste for women; the same annoying dictum about cows and women regurgitated from Columba to him.[6]

Cuthbert was a recluse. When he died in 687, he was living not on Lindisfarne but on neighbouring Inner Farne – a retreat from a retreat – where he dined on barley and onions in a hut specially designed, like Samuel Beckett's white-wall-facing writing room, so that he couldn't see anything distracting.

He asked that his body be left on Farne. His wish was overruled, and he was moved back to Lindisfarne, thus beginning a tourist trade that sees today around half a million annual visitors to Lindisfarne. (He would have been appalled.)

The process of promoting Cuthbert began eleven years after his death. First, the abbot had him 'enshrined' – an early medieval form of canonization. He was dug up, but – *miracle!* – he was uncorrupted. Bede writes that Cuthbert's body was 'flexible' in death and he looked like he was sleeping. The way in which medieval Christians lovingly venerated the body parts of their ancestors certainly feels like a direct inheritance from the Neolithic; medieval English churches were often consecrated by having relics of saints sealed inside their foundations. (There are parallels with myth here, too: with King Arthur, for example, who is not dead, but sleeping, waiting to be woken.) Abbess Aethelthyrth's enshrinement three years earlier at Ely was probably a spur for Cuthbert's. She, too, was uncorrupted. Because she was a virgin despite two marriages, Bede says.[7]

The Cuthbert cult, in order to outshine Aethelthryth and others, curated a group show, with three different bodies. First there was King Oswald, who gifted Lindisfarne to the monks, and whose head was sent there by his successor, King Oswy.[8] Then there was the founder monk of Lindisfarne, St Aidan, whose bones – at this point, or later when they left the island – were added to Cuthbert's coffin, literally enfolding him in the superior saint's cult.[9]

Cuthbert had feared fame and fuss, but his qualms meant nothing in death. Posthumously, 'he was honoured like an emperor'.[10] The Lindisfarne monks commissioned Bede to write a *Life of St Cuthbert*. Bede wrote two – one in verse, one in prose – working from an earlier biography by a Lindisfarne monk, which was clearly unsatisfactory in some way; or maybe the community just wanted the glamour which Bede's impress would bring. (They were right.)[11]

Around the same time, Eadfrith, Bishop of Lindisfarne to be, began work on the *Gospels* – they were his *magnum opus* and a cornerstone of the Cuthbert cult. Eadfrith, artist-scribe, 'invented the lead pencil and the equivalent of the lightbox' in order to make this masterpiece. He used copper for green, toasted lead for orange, woad for blue, arsenic for yellow and shells for white.[12] He mastered Irish calligraphy, and his intricate decorations evoke the richness of Celtic artistic tradition.[13] The Lindisfarne *Gospels* have been described as 'one of the most complex works of art ever made'.[14]

Inked on the skins of five hundred calves, the *Gospels* were the product of a very rich monastery.[15] They were dedicated (according to an inscription added in the tenth century) to 'God and Saint Cuthbert and all the saints whose relics are in the island'.[16] Between them – dead saint, biography, richly adorned holy book – they became an irresistible draw for pilgrims.

The reason the monks eventually left Lindisfarne with Cuthbert's body in 875 was ostensibly because of the Viking raids – the monastery had received an early hit, in 793. The eighth-century Northumbrian scholar Alcuin, writing with all the smug indignation of the unaffected, viewed the Viking attack on Lindisfarne as godly wrath for the sins of the monks – their love of fine clothes, wine, and pagan music and stories (it seems they listened to *Beowulf* at supper). 'What assurance can the churches of Britain have,' Alcuin demanded of the Bishop of Lindisfarne, 'if Saint Cuthbert and so great a company of saints do not defend their own?' And in another letter: 'What has Ingeld to do with Lindisfarne?' (Ingeld is a minor character in *Beowulf* – suggesting that Alcuin, at least, knew the poem rather well.)[17]

Cuthbert, unable to defend his island from heathens, was taken to the mainland: the typical teleology. From now on, the Haliwerfolc took over the management of his cult. As in the Sufi shrines of Pakistan and India today, this motley band of hereditary families guarded the shrine, controlled visitors – and solicited donations. For one hundred years, the Haliwerfolc toured Cuthbert like a travelling stage show (Sanger's), making an extended circuit 'of the community's estates' in the north,[18] ensuring that everybody came to appreciate his importance. (D. W. Rollason writes that County Durham 'narrowly . . . escaped being called Haliwerfolc' – like Suffolk or Norfolk.)[19]

After much wandering, Durham was chosen as Lindisfarne's ultimate mainland mirror, and with sound topographical basis, too: it was a river island.

Inland islands had long been important, spiritually and strategically.[20] The Fens accommodated a late-seventh-century hermit, a former freebooter called Guthlac, who took up residence with his sister Pega on an ancient burial-mound on Crowland Island, near Cambridge.[21] The nuns of Ely lived on an island, 'surrounded by water and marshes', as Bede attests. The bones of King Oswald were buried in the abbey of Bardney, an island near Lincoln; Bishop Earconwald established a monastery on Cerot's Island in the Thames (modern Chertsey).[22] For a while, even ambitious Bishop Wilfrid and his exiled companions made the most of eighty-seven hides of land 'at Selsey, which means seal's island, a place surrounded by sea on all sides except to the west, where there is an approach about a sling's cast in width.' Until monks drained the levels, Glastonbury Tor was an island (early in the morning, in the mist, it becomes one again), as was Athelney, where King Alfred founded an abbey. (In 877, when Alfred hid from the Danes on Athelney, it was a vision of Northumbrian Cuthbert which fortified him.) And Herbert, Cuthbert's bosom-buddy, Bede says, 'lived the life of a hermit on an island in the great lake which is the source of the river Derwent'.[23]

There is even an early piece of Anglo-Saxon poetry, 'Wulf and Eadwacer', which seems to describe an inter-island tryst as tragic as that of Sohni in Pakistan:

> Wulf is on one island, I on another.
> Fast is that island, surrounded by fens.
> They are bloodthirsty, the people there on the island.
> They wish to oppress him if he comes with a troop.
> We are different.[24]

Just as Lindisfarne drew vicariously on Iona and Thanet's significance, so Durham interlaced itself with other islands and their meanings. Until the Reformation, Cuthbert's shrine was a tidal stream that flowed in both directions.

The Normans – Frenchmen of Viking descent – capitalized on the high emotion that Cuthbert and Lindisfarne evoked. In 1069, when the Conqueror came north, the Haliwerfolc rushed Cuthbert's shrine to Lindisfarne again for safekeeping. But the Normans, keen for Lindisfarne's saline blessing, took Cuthbert back to Durham. There they stamped their conquest on the landscape by building a gigantic edifice high on a hill above the River Wear – in soaring Romanesque fashion, with huge pillars patterned with the Neolithic-pilgrim scallop-chevron. (The masons who worked at Durham then went north to help build Orkney's great Norse red-sandstone cathedral.)

Lindisfarne got a mini version of the cathedral priory, with matching chevron-etched pillars. As the monk Symeon of Durham put it in his early-twelfth-century *Tract on the Origins and Progress of this the Church of Durham*, 'Although for various reasons [the priory] no longer stands in the place where Oswald founded it, nevertheless . . . it is still the very same church.'[25] The Normans did not want to lose the connection to the original holy island of

Lindisfarne any more than the people did. Monks did tours of both houses.

Cuthbert continued to draw pilgrims from both sides of the border into the late Middle Ages.[26] During peaceful times, Scottish kings came to Durham on pilgrimage – Cuthbert, after all, had spent his early life in the abbey at Melrose. King Malcolm III of Scotland attended the foundation-laying ceremony for Durham Priory in 1093 (and was interred at Tynemouth Priory that same year after being killed in battle by the English). Cuthbert was a figure of reconciliation between the Scottish and the English – and thus, of enmity, when it suited. Both sides carried bits of his body, as well as his banner, into battle.

The Normans, meanwhile, enhanced Cuthbert's cult in their own image. Misogyny was the natural first step.[27] The Haliwer-folc were banished, and celibate Benedictine rule was imposed instead – just as, throughout England, the Normans outlawed the double monasteries that had promoted female leadership and learning and put an end to honouring women as saints.[28] Strategically, Durham was the bulwark in the north the Normans needed; they elected bishop-princes, who could not have heirs to bring up as rivals to the English monarchs but, living like kings in palaces, kept the Scottish out.[29]

For the first time, women were banned from Cuthbert's shrine at Durham. A thick dark line of marble marked the point beyond which they were forbidden to go. (It is still there.) The *Rites of Durham* described how, if women inadvertently or otherwise stepped over this 'rowe of blewe marble', they were 'punished to give example to all others'. Women were banned, not only from the church itself, but even from the churchyard, for a time (later they were given the Galilee Chapel, where Bede is buried). It seems likely that they were 'excluded from the conventual church on Lindisfarne' too and 'were certainly not allowed in the chapel of the Inner Farne'.[30]

And so, as I step across the rowe of blewe marble, the disturbing magnitude of the idolatry which bloomed around Cuthbert, post-humously, strikes me like a Thor-thrown thunderbolt. Monarchs and grandees lavished resources on his shrine, making conspicuous pilgrimages (some across borders) to see him, leaving presents of gold and embroidered cloth and expensively illustrated books. Cuthbert, I believe, became the (unwitting) vehicle of a full-blown patriarchal riposte to female religious expression; in death, monarchical putty; channel of male monkish misogyny. Which female saint ever had that amount of resources, attention and time allotted to her? Only Mary. (It is thanks to Cuthbert, largely, that I first dream up my island saint, Cwen, who haunts my eponymous novel. I make her custodian of a fictional island north of Lindisfarne; a gender rebalancing for the less-islanded east coast.)

Upper-class women were allowed to visit the shrine at Durham by special dispensation, but the monks were serious about excluding the riffraff. How very brave, therefore, of Matilda Burg and Margaret Usher, whose protest marks the beginning of my pilgrimage, to have dressed 'in men's clothing', and entered the church in secret, in 1417 – only to be apprehended as they approached 'the shrine of the most holy confessor Cuthbert, knowing this to be forbidden to all women under the penalty of great excommunication'. The monastery punished them with the penance of 'walking in parochial procession to Newcastle . . . dressed in the same male outfits they had worn at Durham'. They were supposed to do this on six feast-days. But after the first, their local chaplain wrote to the Bishop of Durham 'requesting that they be spared further punishment'.[31] (Perhaps, instead of feeling shame, they were being celebrated – for giving other women subversive ideas.) Remembering the secret depositions at Brading Roman villa, and the barren island of women opposite Iona, and the bold land grab of Thanet's Domne Eafe, I approach Cuthbert's shrine with Matilda and Margaret's spirit of defiance in my heart.

The dean of the cathedral gives me a wax taper from Jerusalem and tells me that Cuthbert and Bede's shrines at Durham, and Edward the Confessor's at Westminster, are among the few pre-schism shrines in England. But it is 'more continuous at Durham than Westminster,' he says, cheerfully. 'And more like the old system now, pre-Norman – with non-celibate monastic families as shrine guardians.' He shows me where pilgrims were once able to prostrate themselves beneath Cuthbert's elevated sarcophagus.

Clutching my (unlit) Jerusalem taper, I go to find Cuthbert's coffin, which these days is on display in the cathedral kitchen. When Henry VIII's commissioners opened it in 1537 they found – along with Cuthbert's skeleton, his portable altar, a gold pectoral cross inlaid with garnets and a shell from the Indian Ocean – a small Latin edition of St John's Gospel ('the earliest European book', according to the British Library). It has a cover of tooled red-dyed goatskin, moulded with clay beneath to look as if vines, or hearts – or magic mushrooms, depending whom you speak to – are bursting forth from the book. Mushroom-interlace is a common motif of Anglo-Saxon art. But according to the British Library, it is likely to be a visual reference to the words of John's Gospel: 'I am the vine; you are the branches.'[32]

It is amazing that this book survived the Reformation – most of Britain's sacred medieval scholarship and artistry did not. Even Protestant reformers of Henry's reign, such as the polemicist John Bale, very quickly regretted the scandalous destruction and dispersal of the monastic libraries – which obliterated all the 'lyuelye memoryalles of our nacyon'.[33] Somehow, at some point, Stonyhurst College, a Jesuit-run boarding school in Lancashire, acquired Cuthbert's book. In 2011, they sold it to the British Library for £9 million (and, as an alumnus of the school wrote to me, while I was walking north, 'blew it on an all-weather sports pitch and new catering hall, which he, one of the most athletic and gregarious of the medieval monastics, would surely have wanted').[34]

I remember how funny Chaucer is about the ways in which Norman Christianity changed England:

> In th'olde dayes of the Kyng Arthour,
> Of which that Britons speken greet honour,
> Al was this land fulfiled of fayerye.

The elf-queen, with her jolly company, danced in every green meadow. But all the elves have gone now – for friars have banished them with their constant praying, blessing halls, kitchens, bedrooms; 'As thikke as motes in the sonne-beem' are these holy men – and so there are fairies no more. This is from the opening to the 'Wife of Bath's Tale' – Chaucer's hard-hitting piece of feminist ventriloquism. Chaucer's empathy for women can be uncanny and inspiring. He also understood that Christianity had vanished some local magic. Only since the Enlightenment has Nature has been viewed as something 'passive and mechanical'. Before that, we all took part in a more immanent way of seeing. Since then, as the anthropologist Anna Tsing points out, it has been 'left to fabulists . . . to remind us of the lively activities of all beings, human and non-human'.[35] In his own way, Chaucer, too, was lamenting the fact that humans are slow to perceive soul, spirit or meaningful life in species other than their own.

For the first time in my life, I feel that loss of indigenous magic. How poignant, too, the stories that singled out the specialness of saints such as Cuthbert through their friendship with other species (otters kept him warm after sea bathing). The moment I step outside Durham Cathedral, therefore, I am in another world. I have left the world of male egos and am back with the fairies (having done a volte face since Iona). I circle down towards the river, widdershins, listening to it roaring darkly below me.[36]

Chaucer's mention of King Arthur reminds me that during the very time that Lindisfarne's meaning (and Cuthbert's) was changing under the aegis of the Normans' powerful, patriarchal project to feudalize the court, Church and culture, the legendary feminist island of Avalon was being inscribed like a countercurrent into English literature and thought. The first person we know of who wrote down the name 'Avalon' was Geoffrey of Monmouth, in his *Historia Regum Britanniae, circa* 1139. Whether invented or simply rebirthed – and Geoffrey himself claimed he was merely the Latin translator of an unknown British book – the otherworldly island he describes, ruled by women, has deep roots. It reaches down into the British earth, past the efflorescence of Norman culture, with its French-speaking elite, the reorganization of the family through primogeniture, its misogynistic expelling of women from the Church. It reaches deeper, through the rich soil of Celtic Christianity, with its island-eyrie-bound monks and its pagan voyages to paradise islands; through the substrata of Roman imperialism, where the ghosts of Caesar, Agricola and the Druids still haunt every Roman road, wall and drain. It touches the bedrock of Iron Age sacrificial islands, sacred spaces, crannogs and lake depositions; is washed by the percolating waters of Greek and Phoenician island cults and ports; and even the white-hot core of Neolithic island-based worship of the sun.

Geoffrey of Monmouth, who was likely Welsh, was undoubtedly thinking in ways subconscious and deliberate of all these things when he wrote about *Insula Avalonis* for the first time. He placed upon the island nine sisters (descendants of Pomponius Mela's nine priestesses), the eldest of whom he named Morgan, and made her sister to Arthur, a king who had only recently appeared in British histories – invented or promoted, it seems, out of native desperation for a hero.

It was the ninth-century monk Nennius who, reacting to recent devastation, first drew on his sense of national 'shame', as he put it, 'to deliver down to posterity the few remaining ears of corn about past transactions, that they might not be trodden under foot, seeing that an ample crop has been snatched away already by the hostile reapers of foreign nations'.[37] Nennius makes Arthur fight twelve battles, the majority of which are in the north of England but which also stretch into Scotland: as far north as the Firth of Forth and as far south as Exeter.

Geoffrey of Monmouth, in turn, gives Arthur a court, a queen and Merlin the magician. For Geoffrey, it is Arthur's islands that are the making of him, literally. He is conceived on the Cornish isle of Tintagel, the impregnability of which represents for Britons hopes for their own island, for it is breached only by subterfuge, using Merlin's witchcraft:

For it is situate on the sea, and is on every side encompassed thereby, nor none other entrance is there save such as a narrow rock doth furnish, the which three armed knights could hold against thee, albeit thou wert standing there with the whole realm of Britain beside thee.[38]

Arthur's sword, meanwhile, is forged 'within the Isle of Avalon' – a non-site-specific place of magical female smiths. It is also there, 'wounded deadly', that Arthur is 'borne . . . for the healing of his wounds'.[39]

Some years later, in *Vita Merlini* (*Life of Merlin*), of which he is the presumed author, Geoffrey calls the island where Arthur is taken *Insula pomorum que fortunata uocatur*: 'the isle of apples, called the fortunate isle'. He explicitly evokes the Greek myth of the apples of the Hesperides (in which the apple offered by a man to a woman starts a war),[40] and possibly also the early-medieval Irish text *Voyage of Bran* (in which the hero is offered an apple by a woman, and proceeds to paradise) as well as Genesis (in which the hero takes from the woman an apple and is cast out of heaven).

Geoffrey's island is across the sea from Britain:

This is where, after the Battle of Camlan, we brought the wounded Arthur . . . Morgen greeted us with honour . . . we rejoiced, and left the king in her care, and returned with the sails spread before a following wind.[41]

His mentions of Avalon and the isle of apples seem to have been so persuasive and popular that in 1190, a mere half-century later, the monks of Glastonbury claimed the mythical island as their own, co-opting the entire Arthur corpus – and literally, his corpse – to the Christian cause. Their brazen claim to have uncovered the tomb of King Arthur and Guinevere, his queen, brought together disparate strands of British epic-making under the roof of Glastonbury Abbey itself: Arthur, Avalon, saintly relics, pilgrimage, myths and nationalism.

But Avalon would not be rooted to a Christian master. In 1485, when Sir Thomas Malory, knight, came to write his *Le Morte d'Arthur* for the printer and publisher Caxton, he described the island of Avalon sometimes as a sea island, sometimes as a lake island – but always in terms of the women who rule it. As the medievalist Amy Kaufman has pointed out, while the story of Arthur is totally patriarchal and fairly mainland, running parallel to it is that of the Lady of the Lake, whom Malory calls Nineve. She runs a community of women, uses magic, exercises sexual choice and lives in self-sufficient freedom.[42] It is Nineve's lake island that produces Arthur's magical sword:

> That is the Lady of the Lake, said Merlin; and within that lake is a rock, and therein is as fair a place as any on earth, and richly beseen; and this damosel will come to you anon, and then speak ye fair to her that she will give you that sword.

Malory is both vague and specific with his geography of the British Isles, as suits a man writing from jail about land he may never see again. (He was in and out of prison for twenty years, for political machinations, but was also accused of 'robbery, extortion, and rape'.)[43] The oft-mentioned places, from north to south, are Orkney, Northumberland, Carlisle, Westminster, Canterbury, Sandwich in Kent and Cornwall. The isle of Avilion, Malory says at one point, is beside Castle Perilous; and Castle Perilous, he writes at another, is nigh the coasts of North Wales – making Avalon into Anglesey, perhaps. But Malory does not care to stipulate. The precise location does not matter. What is important is the island's significance in Arthur's life. The last thing Arthur does as he is dying is to command his knight Sir Bedivere to cast his sword Excalibur into the waters of Avalon's lake. Sir Bedivere, loath to cast away so beautiful a sword (and why would he, a Christian, behave in this pagan way?), twice promises the wounded Arthur that he has done as commanded.

What saw thou there? said the king. Sir, he said, I saw nothing but waves and winds.

Arthur calls him a traitor and sends him back. The third time, Bedivere 'threw the sword as far into the water as he might'

and there came an arm and a hand above the water and met it, and caught it, and so shook it thrice and brandished, and then vanished away the hand with the sword in the water.[44]

In this moment, all the sacred depositions of Iron Age Britain find in Christian-Norman England their water goddess. By placing Avalon nowhere in particular, Malory allows it to be all around us – at the edges of civilization, its yet more civilized fringe. And whether consciously or not, Malory suggests that the Lady is controlling it all, from beginning to end. Arthur – one of only twelve great men since time began, and the only one from England, according to Caxton's Preface to *Le Morte d'Arthur* – is intimately associated with that female island magic, even if he does not know it himself.

The Anglo-Saxon name of Lindisfarne was *Farena ealande*, 'island of wanderers', a place of vagrants before it was a place of priests. Or perhaps the name is older than that. The Celtic word *ferann* meant 'land of marshes and quicksand'.[45] When planning this journey, I read in George Skelly's 1888 *Guide to Lindisfarne* that the island 'was named by the ancient Britons, *Inis Mendicante*'.[46] An island of holy beggars. There has long been an association, in Christianity, as in other faiths (the Jains come to mind), between being holy and living on alms. And whatever their undoubted faults, monasteries, in their remote locations, were also once a sanctuary for misfits, for the mentally ill, for people for whom mainstream culture was too conformist and demanding. And so I had the idea of walking this old pilgrimage route to raise money for mendicants, as well as to gain knowledge. Just north of Finchale, a mile south of Chester-le-Street (where Cuthbert's cult rested for a hundred years) is The Fells, a hostel for homeless men. That is where I will sleep tonight.

I walk north along the River Wear, past a women's prison. The air is damp with rain; in every sunbeam dance the once-reverenced fay-eryes of this land. Chaucer is right that the structure of organized religion is oppressively omnipresent: just four miles north of Durham, I come across another priory. Finchale (rhymes with 'winkle') was a holiday home for Durham monks. It was founded by Godric, a reformed pirate, who recanted after visiting Lindisfarne and seeing Cuthbert in a vision. He became the first English person to make the pilgrimage to Santiago de Compostela and the first known English composer. He loved the Virgin, at least. His poem 'A Cry to St Mary' opens my 1963 edition of *Medieval English Lyrics*:

Sainte Marye . . . moderes flur [flower of motherhood],
Dilie min sinne, rix in min mod [blot out my sin, reign in my heart].[47]

After women were banned from visiting Cuthbert's shrine at Durham, they went to other places for their holy amusement – most of Finchale's pilgrims in medieval times were women.[48] Perhaps this accounts for the alacrity with which the prior at the time of the foundation's dissolution, William Bennett, released himself from his monastic vows. His haste to wed, in 1538, gave rise to the local proverb

The Prior of Finkeal hath got a fair wife, and every monk will have one.

I ponder the power and potential of the national church over the days and nights of my pilgrimage. Its resources are vast, its impact now exponentially low. There is a huge opportunity here, if some-body could only find the way to harness it.

That night in the homeless hostel, I cook with Julie in the kitchen for the fifty men having dinner. Julie is cheery, and the men, when they come in, are unfailingly courteous and polite. But not even 25 per cent of these men will get out of the hostel life once they fall into it, a staff member tells me later. Homelessness quickly becomes a way of life once a marriage fails, and a job is lost, and with it a family and home. Or it was a way of life already. 'Often it's people who've been in children's homes all their lives.' I shake at the thought. Even so, 'everyone' prefers working at the men's hostels to the women's. 'Women are so bitchy.' 'They have more belongings.' Intake of breath: 'They get pregnant.' Basically, women's lives are chaos. It is tragic, of course, that women should be seen in this way. Clichéd characterizations have long made it easy to stop women, as a group, from being the authors of their own lives. How strange and disturbing that they (we) had to rely for so long on men such as Geoffrey of Monmouth, Chaucer, Malory, for our textual expression and yet how interesting that, despite this, a subversive strand successfully carries through those representations.

After a restless night sleeping on the floor of the hostel office I walk up the Roman road to the Church of St Mary and St Cuthbert in Chester-le-Street in the drizzle. The church was built from the recycled remains of an old Roman fort. The empire had only recently abandoned Britain, and the power structures of the new Roman religion fitted neatly on top, like pieces of Lego coming together with a satisfying click. At Chester-le-Street, Cuthbert (uncorrupted) was visited by all the important Anglo-Saxon kings and queens, who brought with them costly presents – such as the copy of Bede's *Life of Cuthbert*, presented somewhat meta-textually by King Athelstan, in 934.[49] King Cnut, a Dane, trumped all previous visitors in piety by walking five miles to the shrine, barefoot.[50] Meanwhile, Aldred, monk-bishop, glossed the Latin text of the Lindisfarne *Gospels* at Chester-le-Street, line for line, into Old English, the first such translation.[51]

This was a moment of synchronicity with Europe. Joining the Church of Rome was like belonging to a multinational bank: international, rich, cultured, ideological. Where the cultural influence had been Irish-Saxon, now it was Roman-Mediterranean.[52] The ambitious bishop Benedict Biscop travelled to Rome at least six times, bringing back masons, a cantor from St Peter's and, in particular, glaziers.[53]

Two linked monasteries were at the vanguard of England's early-medieval artistic flourishing: Monkwearmouth ('monks at the mouth of the Wear'), just north of here, and Jarrow (where Bede lived from the age of seven). The Church of St Peter's Monkwearmouth in Sunderland was founded in 674, and it was probably there that the Biblical masterpiece, the *Codex Amiatinus*, was illuminated. One of the outstanding achievements of early-medieval English art – the world's oldest complete Latin Bible – the *Codex Amiatinus* was decorated with a profusion of gold, silver and vermilion; quite different from the *Gospels* produced at Lindisfarne, which made do with local pigments. 'Two thousand and thirty pages!' the warden of the church tells me that evening.

Until recently, nobody could believe that something as accomplished as this came from England, and the *Codex Amiatinus* was thought to be Italian. In fact, Abbot Ceolfrith commissioned it at the mouth of this remote northern river and carried it with him to Rome in his satchel. Unfortunately, he died en route, and later it was easy for an Italian bishop (or his librarian) to paste an Italian name (Peter) and origin over Ceolfrith's.[54] The deception was discovered only in the nineteenth century.

There were at least two other complete Bibles produced at Jarrow-Monkwearmouth. Eleven leaves of one of these were discovered in 1911, being used as covers for sixteenth-century property deeds at Wollaton Hall in Northamptonshire – probably removed from the library of Worcester Cathedral at the Reformation.[55]

Also found was the single surviving copy of a medieval story called *Silence*. Written in French but set in England, this warm and witty story purports to be the biography of a girl who is brought up as a boy in order that she may inherit her parents' estate in Cornwall – in this new age of Norman male-only inheritance. The author's pseudonym, Heldris of Cornwall, conceals their gender and nationality but reveals where their thoughts hie – to rebellious women who refuse to be defined either by gender or the sea-encircled land that spawned them.

It is the text for me: I walk for day after day, in silence, thinking of women and their historical and current oppressions and depressions and regressions. Christianity, which has the potential to help, almost never does; its structural inequality mitigates against it. What does help though? I wonder about those healer women who were so attuned to the taste of water, and the smell of the air, and the rising of sap. What tragedy have we unleashed (through the witch trials) that we no longer speak their language?

The monastery of Jarrow now stands on the edge of an industrial estate – down Monksway, left along Bedesway, right into Abbotsway – south of the Tyne. It has what it claims is the oldest stained-glass window in the world – a reconstructed circle of pieces of blue and green set in an original Saxon window arch – as well as the first inscription of any British church. The refectory drains are older still: made of broken Roman roof tiles. The builders also reused Roman pipe in the sandstone basin and duct. The eastern extent of Hadrian's Wall is just north of here, at Wallsend on the Tyne.

That evening, I catch the ferry across the Tyne. I march west along Hadrian's Wall, built by work gangs of Roman soldiers from all over the empire. The section of wall near Segedunum fort has a modern monument with the names of the work gangs' centurions inscribed upon it: *Antonius Rusticus . . . Valerius Maximus*. The fort the other side of the river from here, in South Shields, was called 'Arbeia', meaning 'place of the Arabs', so named for the multiethnic soldiers brought from far away to police this area. Along wet streets glistening with city lights, I listen to early English music through my headphones. Godric of Finchale wrote the earliest known lyrics – but the earliest melodies may have been composed by the cantor Biscop brought to Jarrow from Rome.

I push on through this throng of male stories, heading for the women's homeless hostel for which this peregrination is raising funds; only a stone's throw from the medieval nunnery of St Bartholomew, the sole traces of which lie in the name of nearby roads: Nun Street, Nuns Lane. It is late by the time I reach Francis House, a 'high-support unit' – which means the women are actively using drugs and alcohol and have what are described as 'complex needs' (they are often involved in survival sex work). The telly is on in the common room downstairs. The women are watching *The X Factor*. Their drug habits have sculpted their faces; like models, there is nothing spare.

The room crackles with their energy and charisma. It is nearly Christmas, the hardest time of year for homeless women with young children in care. All the women in this room have children. One woman has five. They talk over the singing coming from the television of their hopes for family life. One woman has four kids adopted into two different families, who changed their birth names; she is waiting for when they are sixteen and will be able to come looking for her. Another has her child's name tattooed on her wrist; he is twelve, and in foster care, which at least means he gets to keep his birth name. Another woman has just returned from a difficult visit to a former lover and children somewhere south; the children, aged five and sixteen, 'jumped up on to my hips when they saw me'. Someone leans in and whispers to me, 'She's not going for Christmas because there's a man there who is using her for money.'

I listen in horror and sorrow. I cannot imagine a greater destitution than being separated from my children.

Few of these women will escape this life either, Josie tells me the next morning in her office upstairs. Often, women come in clean and leave with a drug habit. She, too, says that it's difficult working in the women's hostels. Men are easy-going and polite. Women really bear a grudge; they're emotional. I understand it suddenly. What they mean is *Women's bodies are vulnerable; hence their lives are hell*.

The women's stories cloud my mind all that day as I walk north out of town, over the remodelled slag heaps of closed coalmines, along the wagonways which Stevenson developed as a way of avoiding the fees charged by the river boats: this was where the railways began. I reach the Lady Chapel of Seaton Delaval that night. The church, which is Saxon in origin, and – a rarity – is still known by its pre-Reformation name (for the Virgin), has an ancient yew tree in the churchyard which is actually two trees, the mother enfolded inside the child. With the Norman Conquest came barons and masons; the church was revamped, by rainbow-shaped windows and scallops for holy water.

I stay that night with a really nice couple who worked for years in the film industry as costumiers. I mend my purse with their gold Admiralty braid and sleep soundly under a huge VOTE LEAVE poster.

From now on I'll be walking along the coast to Lindisfarne and, apart from the nuclear power station and the occasional main road, some mornings, early, I could be in any century, Cuthbert's, Chaucer's, Cwen's. From the little island of St Mary's, with its lighthouse, near Seaton Sluice, I pass Coquet Island, where in 685 Cuthbert had a dynastic meeting with Abbess Aelfflaed – as if they were in an episode of *Succession* and only remote islands might not be bugged. She wanted to know who was to succeed her brother, King Ecgfrith, who had no children; and also whether Cuthbert would do as the king had asked and become bishop of Lindisfarne. Cuthbert's reply was double-island. To the question of royal succession, he answered, 'Look at the sea. It abounds in islands. God could easily provide a ruler for the English from one of them.'[56] (And Aelfflaed knew then that he was talking of Aldfrith, Ecgfrith's illegitimate half-brother, who had been sent away to Ireland to be educated.) As for episcopal succession, he answered that 'the decree of the Supreme Ruler cannot be escaped, no matter where one might flee to. After two years, perhaps, I shall be allowed to go back to my accustomed solitude and peace.' That is, he would get off Farne, and take the job on Lindisfarne. But his virtuous desire for the eremitic life would entirely cloud – or make – his posthumous reputation.

Over the next three days, as I walk north into Lindisfarne's dreamy, other-worldly realm, I become more and more interested in its non-textual meanings, its aesthetic impact on this land and its people. I am also edging towards the border, towards my Scottish grandmother's cultural inheritance. Thus, when I see Lindisfarne,

I also see the Bass Rock, in the Firth of Forth, which had a monk on it once, the power of which is predominantly visual. I realized this when I went to stay with my aunt and saw etchings and paintings of the Bass Rock on her walls. She lived in England, but something in her was deeply attached to that little piece of Scottish rock, within sight of which her elder sister, my mother, was born. I remembered also the iconographic status of Papa Westray's holm, in Orkney: a sacred Neolithic funeral island omnipresent in everybody's vision and thoughts.

I stay with a vicar one night, a devotee of Meher Baba the next. I pass the Warkworth hermitage on the River Coquet (with a fifteenth-century nativity scene carved into rock), then the estate of Earl Grey, the reformist prime minister whose wife's dislike for Northumberland's hard water was apparently the cause of the bergamot-flavoured tea – why it isn't called after her is anybody's guess. I walk with the land at my left, the sea at my right, as if I am an arrow released from a bow, no surrender, privately serenaded by the polyphony of Byrd and Tallis (no female composers here), a musical style which was banned at the Reformation on account of the consequent unintelligibility of the sacred words (and the possibility of lewd texts therefore being interpolated unnoticed).

On one of those long solo days, I think again about Albina. For of course, the Arthurian romances were not the only Anglo-Norman texts to produce counter-cultural female island-dwellers. When epics of origin came to be written under the Norman yoke, the originating ancestor had to be foreign – north-easterly Woden went out and southern scions of Rome took his place. Brutus was favoured, he who gave his name to Britain, apparently. But Britain wasn't the only name for these islands. There was also Albion, as Pliny had attested; and along with male progenitors there were also, perforce, women. Hence Albina.

The thirty sisters of the 'Albina prologue' to the Brut histories are probably drawn from Aeschylus, whose play *The Suppliants* (*c*.450 BC) tells of a group of women – played by the Chorus, the only occasion in Greek tragedy in which it is protagonist – who seek refuge in a neighbouring country, fleeing marital·abuse. In the Anglo-Norman text, the sisters are explicit about the stakes:

> *Mes touz jours en subjection* [Every day in subjection]
> *Ci li tegnez en danger* [Places us in danger].[57]

They observe that their father, by contrast, is free. This is what they want, too: *freedom*. They kill to escape abuse, are exiled, and it is only once they reach the islands of Britain that they become secure in their self-sufficiency. Albina, the only named sister, calls the country after her:

> *Albine est mon propre noun* [Albina is my own name]
> *Dunt serra nomé Albion;* [From which it will be called Albion]
> *Par unt de nous en ceo pais* [And hence this country]
> *Remembrance serra tutdis.* [Will remember us always][58]

That last line always makes me feel a bit melancholic.

The women learn to hunt. Their sexual desire awakens – they sleep with some incubi, evil spirits who sought to copulate with women. In 'the Middle Ages their existence was recognised by law'.[59] As Chaucer hints, nowadays women are safe from incubi – 'Wommen may go saufly up and doun. / In every bussh or under every tree / There is noon oother incubus but he'; it's friars they need to watch out for.[60]

The sisters enjoy themselves, and put on weight. The patriarchal order has been subverted. Into this world of female freedom steps a male leader, Brutus, summoned from Rome to kill their giant progeny, and rename the islands after himself.

As always, the patriarchal response to this story is telling. In the late sixteenth century the influential chronicler Holinshed objected that it was impossible that Albion was named for a woman; the eponymous source must instead be Albion, the fourth son of Neptune. The whole idea of the sisters travelling to these islands, he argued, was stupid:

as the name of their father hath bene mistaken, so likewise that the whole course of the historie in this behalfe . . . And thus much for the ladies, whose strange aduenture of their arriuall here, as it may séeme to manie & (with good cause) incredible.[61]

Others were incensed by the idea of incubi impregnating women – demon sperm was too ethereal. Up to modern times, scholars find the sisters hard going. As somebody put it recently, the 'inadequacy of Albina's dream of a self-sufficient matriarchy is written across her expanding flesh'.[62] Women rulers are hard to stomach, even today. (Hence their paucity.) Across Henry VIII's expanding flesh, by contrast, is written all the success of his self-sufficient patriarchy.

John Hardyng, the fourteenth-century historian, opened both versions of his *Chronicle* of English history with the story of Albina and her sisters, even though he too thought the story 'false in the begynnyng'.[63] Curiously, in the earlier edition of 1457, he describes how Colman of Lindisfarne also wrote about the sisters:

> thay came into this londe and named it Albion of Dame Albyne the eldest sustire (sister), as Seynt Colman, doctour Bisshop of Lyndisfarn, specifieth in hys *Dialoge*.[64]

Yet, mysteriously, no trace of Colman's *Dialoge* has ever been found – nor any reason found why Colman (Lindisfarne's third bishop, four before Cuthbert) might have been thinking or writing of Albina either. Colman is the monk who represented the indigenous case at the Synod of Whitby, and lost; he then retreated to Iona, where the old ways were still being upheld; and then to Ireland, where he fell out with the Irish monks, as they would not work as hard as he and his fellow Englishmen. What can he have had to say about Albina, if anything? The possibility that a connection existed once is tantalizing; another lost text; another recalibrated meaning.

I arrive in Bamburgh, where the Northumbrian king's panopticon-like castle for so long kept an eye on Lindisfarne, and everything around. I stop at the church which incorporates in its ceiling the inflammable forked seventh-century pillar against which Irish St Aidan was leaning when he died. (A pillar which has been understood as a Christian copy of thunder god Thor's sacred staff.)[65]

Aidan learned English as an adult migrant to Northumbria from Iona. And indeed, the DNA of the church's crypt attests to England's hectic history of migration and passage, being crammed with bodies from Anglo-Saxon times, including a North African, a Viking, and a woman whose bone structure indicates 'weaver's bottom'.[66] There's an entire fairy story in that.

Lindisfarne was founded by Aidan, but it was Cuthbert who brought the island to its most fulsome expression within the Christian context – perhaps by articulating exactly that islandness we all have within us – the repulsion/attraction, to be part of the world or to retreat from it, as Cuthbert often did: to islands off islands, and to a cave on the edge of a wood. It is not far off, across some fields, a wall of stone with an overhang. I arrive in the dark. In my sleeping bag I lie against the rock, watching the stars through the trees, missing the sea, which is an hour away, thinking through Cuthbert's life, his female guides and friendships, the guidance he gave and sought from others and his strong antisocial desire to be alone with himself and his thoughts and his immanent God, an island, entire.

The next morning, when I cross the Lindisfarne mudflats, barefoot, I can feel the tide coming in around my ankles. I have been watching Lindisfarne for some days now – surely the most aesthetic of islands, visible from a long stretch of English coastline. Out there on the sand – in the incoming tide – in the open sea, its situation is forever changing. The island is a zoetrope – this and then that, accessible/cut off, earthly but mythical, water and land. Foucault called this state of existing half in myth, half in reality, 'heterotopia' – a slightly unsatisfying name for such a potent concept.

Any visitor to Lindisfarne can see that it is the creation of its constructions – such as the Henrician castle built after the Reformation to shore up the defences. Were it not for the edifice on its rock, this otherwise low-lying island would be inconspicuous, like many other islands are, grey against a wash of grey. To look at its ruined priory is to be reminded that there is violence in Lindisfarne's marrow: proclaimed twice daily by the tides in an invitation to invade, inked by monks in calf-skin parchment, chiselled by masons into gateways for defence. It is palpable in the tense balance between the claim of occupying monks and their sponsorship by monarchs. (Lindisfarne was a naval base from the seventh century.)[67]

Although Durham survived the border wars between England and Scotland – from 1296 as regular as matins – they did Lindisfarne lasting damage. The island's excellence as an unholy fortress was impossible to deny on two counts: the harbour's deep waters,[68] ideal for warring fleets; and its position, the short time it took to reach the Scottish border. A dozen miles, give or take; a few hours' march. (Even less by boat.) The English and Scots traded insults by storming each others' holy islands. The English harried Inchcolm, Inchkeith, Inchgarvie, in the Firth of Forth. The Scots attacked Lindisfarne. The priory was fortified; local people took refuge and battlements were built high up in its walls.[69]

Continual war with Scotland diminished the monks' income. The population of the vaulting, red Romanesque priory – built around 1150 – fell from thirty monks to three. They stopped using the presbytery, paying for servants or minstrels, or buying in exotic commodities such as saffron and almonds. The priory was closed up; the monks retreated to one room, the Warming House.

By 1537, when Henry VIII made his own Viking-style raid on religious houses, Lindisfarne Priory was small fry, dissolved with other houses of an annual income of under £200 (its income was £48). The monks were banished, and the man who Henry sent to transform the island into a military base wrote that there is 'stone plentie and sufficient to make the bulwark that shall defend the Eland' (island). He meant from the Romanesque priory itself. Monastic stone was hauled away to build Henry's new castle. What was left of the priory became a military depot. Soldiers replaced monks, and priory stone was also used to build a new fort to safeguard the harbour. From 1559, until the Civil War, the garrison strength remained at around twenty-four soldiers (zero monks). And so the meaning of an entire millennium, from the time of Columba, came to an end – as it did on countless other islands around the coast of England and Wales, and Scotland in 1560.

On Lindisfarne, the few monks were simply sent packing. Those who had grown up nearby must have feared God's retribution as they saw the priory fall, trembling at the profound religious, cultural, aesthetic changes forced upon them.[70] What would He do in the face of such desecration? Would the island finally be submerged by the sea?

Lindisfarne Priory acquired its picturesque form thanks to centuries of post-Reformation pillage and neglect. The aristocratic owner stripped the roof of lead in 1613. Islanders took more stone for their houses. Between 1780 and 1820, the nave and central tower collapsed; the famous West front fell down in the 1850s. British tourists liked to come and sketch its ruin. They still come. I ask a woman with a beanie, a Scottish religious tourist in the museum, the postman on his morning round, *Do you wish that the priory was still standing? That Henry hadn't done it?* But it is deeply ingrained in the English not to question Dissolution. Nationalism is unattractive, but some states of mind are simply unpatriotic. We are secretly proud of virile, wife-eating Henry. As for Thomas More – he who condensed the best of his islands, and the islands then being discovered beyond Europe's bounds, into an island *Utopia* – allegiance still divides along religious lines. To Catholics, he's a martyr; to others, he's the papal stooge who threatened our independence by siding with the dictates of the Pope in Rome against the king in England. And yet, during the Reformation itself, the two religions took turns at being painted as destabilizing European imports (Roman, German). We have always been adaptable to both sides of the coin of change in these islands. We turn and turn again.[71]

For Renaissance writers, islands were popular emblems of divine power, danger and the boundaries between individuals and their culture. When John Donne wrote that 'No man is an island, entire of itself', he meant that we *are* islands, and as islands we *will* be breached (by collective, political forces beyond our control, even if it is we who have shaped them). It is of once-sacrosanct Lindisfarne – and all the other, defrocked monastic islands around the coast, too – that he is writing.

The lady with the beanie pulls it off to reveal a deep tan mark of long summer days and nights outdoors. She has a dog and a can.

'I am a pilgrim,' she says.

That pilgrims like her still come is testament to the pull of forces more ancient than those they acknowledge at the parish church. It was their Defender of the Faith who dealt the death blow to this ancient island community. But it is the Vikings who have conveniently taken the blame. There is a framed letter in the church, written in 1993 by the Norwegian bishop of Nidaros, apologizing for the Viking raids: 'It is with a deep sense of humility that we address you on behalf of the Church of Norway, 1,200 years after the assault by Vikings on the monastery of Lindisfarne.' But the visible, enduring damage to the island was done by purportedly indigenous kings; the death-blow was dealt from within. There is no missive from the heirs of Henry Tudor, however. Perhaps in another seven hundred years' time.

That night, when the tide is out, I make one further crossing: to Cuddy's Isle, only a few paces from Lindisfarne. This island, cut off from Lindisfarne at high tide, was a place of retreat for Cuthbert, and for subsequent bishops, who came here to fast, pray and repent, during Advent, as I am doing.[72] 'Botte for I am a woman, schulde I therfore leve that I schulde nought telle yowe the goodenes of God?'[73]

In the dark, I lie down in the outline of the medieval chapel and look up at the stars. There are many ways to achieve transcendence. In the centuries following the Reformation, women called 'witches' were feared and burned because of misogyny: for their specialist skill in midwifery and for their knowledge of liberty caps and other milder forms of herbal medicine. Hermits like Cuthbert took the opposite route: access to the divine through starvation and isolation. The pan-species feeling one gets from psilocybin; how dissimilar is it to the ecstatic tenor of the medieval anchorite's mystic poetry?

There is a new moon; the sky is alive and warm with stars. Fasting is one way; plants and meditative practice are others. But two nights sleeping outside also creates, fleetingly, the metaphysical impression of being at peace with the universe. Lying under the stars, lapped by the tides, gazing up at that infinity which seems so near, I shiver to feel time passing. *The same stars Cuthbert gazed on, the same moon, the same water, the same kind earth.*

PART THREE

Female Utopias are Dreamt of

Sister Isles . . . happie Ilands set within the British Seas.

Michael Drayton, *Poly-Olbion*, 1612

8

Islay and the Isles

Rí Innse Gall (*twelfth century*)

In the south of the Hebrides, with nothing but sea between it and Ireland, is an island that was once the capital of this independent, watery world. Today Islay (Île) is the golden egg of Scotland's whisky industry, with nine distilleries[1] and millions generated annually in tax revenue. But for hundreds of years, from at least the twelfth century onwards, it represented something far grander and more potent: clan cohesion, freedom from mainland rule, and the symbolism of islands as self-sufficient political realms.

Stepping along the causeway through the loch, I cross over to Islay's island-in-an-island and enter a vanished world: *Finlaggan*. In the Middle Ages, this place would have rung with the noise of the islands' parliament, of battle preparations, of testosterone production. There were two islands – one natural, one artificial, with a chapel, council chamber and feasting place. There is little to show for it now bar a lithesome carving of a lean island knight who may or may not resemble his presumed illustrious ancestor, the Gael-Norse warlord called Somerled, to whom it all pertained. This was the centre of his island kingdom.

'Somerled' means 'summer traveller' in Norse (Sumarliðr), which is the definition of a Viking; used, for example, by the *Anglo-Saxon Chronicle* in 871, in reference to a Danish fleet.[2] It is a name found throughout the Norse colonies, in Iceland, the Hebrides and Orkney, but not in the homeland. A name for emigrant men on the move, on the rise and the make. Like Norman England, Somerled's kingdom in the Hebrides found strength in its migrant mix.

From Unst in northern Shetland, down to Man in the Irish Sea, island confederacies stretched their influence across the cold northern seas like a skein of *moorit* Shetland wool. At first, for practical expediency, the islands were ruled as two political entities: Orkney and Shetland were *Nordreyjar*, the North Isles; the Hebrides *Sudreyjar*, the South Isles. (The heroes of the early Norse sagas wore Sudreyjar-spun cloth.) Sometimes the earls of Orkney ruled the entire stretch. Sometimes the Norse-born kings of Man controlled all the islands as far north as Lewis.

The islands were multiethnic places. Along with the Norwegians and native Picts, there were also the Irish Gaels and the once Celtic, now Norse Manx. Many languages were spoken, many different habits adopted. Out of this mix arose a new hybrid islander with a dawning political sense. The Latin version of Somerled's title, *dominus Insularum*, 'Lord of the Isles', appeared in a charter from 1336 and is still used by the British monarchy, but the Gaelic name, *Rí Innse Gall*, is older and represents the political apotheosis of all the prior island kingdoms of the Neolithic, Iron Age and monastic Christianity. It means the 'Kingdom of the Islands of Strangers' – 'strangers' denoting both those brave outsiders who arrived and became one with the land and the sea, and possibly also a lingering sense of prior unease.

From around 1100 until the end of his life, Somerled mac Gillebride controlled all the islands of the Inner and Outer Hebrides, a sea-kingdom which stretched from Man up to Skye. Although Islay was his base, his realm was the sea and, within this watery fortress, the islands which stretch like basking seals along Scotland's western seaboard.

Somerled was a Christian, ostensibly.[3] But the world he grew up in was half Norse. By the time Somerled's son Dugall was making an ostentatious pilgrimage to the tomb of St Cuthbert at Durham, there was no equivocating. But in Somerled's day, people were probably still hedging their bets, with a bit of Christ-idolatry and a bit of Thor-obeisance. The Icelandic *Book of Settlements* (compiled by Ari the Learned in the twelfth century) describes the deathbed scene of a man called Thorkel, who in a ceremony reminiscent of Neolithic sun worship 'had himself carried out to a shaft of sunlight, and gave himself to the god who created the sun. He had led a life as blameless as the best of Christians.'[4] 'Holy Bishop Patrick of the Hebrides', meanwhile, was said to have endorsed the Norse pagan practice of using transported Norwegian earth to hallow new land in the frontier.[5]

The nineteenth-century Clan Macdonald historians disputed the idea of Somerled having Norse ancestry[6] – wanting to depict their heroic ancestor as an unambiguously pure Gael. But Somerled's Orcadian mother was definitely Norse – hence her son's Norse name. Somerled married a Norse princess, Ragnhild, daughter of the King of Man, Óláfr Guðrøðarson (Olaf the Black). In 2005, a professor of genetics at Oxford, Bryan Sykes, studied the DNA of the three Highland clans who claim descent from Somerled, concluding that some 500,000 people alive today have a Y-chromosome 'common in Norway but rare in Scotland and Ireland', suggesting descent from a common ancestor 'of Norse Viking paternal origin'.[7] Medieval Irish sources call warriors of what they define as mixed native and Norse parentage *Gall-Gaedhil*, 'foreign Gaels'. Somerled was one such man, a triumphant melding.

There is no portrait of Somerled, but perhaps he looked like one of the walrus-tusk chess pieces found by a crofter, Malcolm MacLeod, only a little further north-west, at Uig, on the island of Lewis. They are exactly contemporary with Somerled; were made in Scandinavia, it is thought, and carried through these Norse frontier islands, probably by people very like those they depict. There is a bearded king with a sword on his knee; a queen, with her hand on her cheek; a warder wearing a conical helmet. All of them are alert, battle-ready, perhaps even apprehensive. The soldiers are biting their shields with their big front teeth. It is believed they are *berserkers*, preparing themselves for slaughter. (Soldiers went 'berserk' – a Norse word – in battle, possibly by ingesting the fly agaric hallucinogenic mushroom.)

Somerled died heroically, hubristically, taking on the young mainland monarch Malcolm at the Battle of Renfrew in 1164. He brought 160 ships to Greenock for the battle, according to the thirteenth-century *Chronicle of Man*. With hindsight, it was absurd to think that an island army, masters of the sea, could defeat the chainmail-wearing Anglo-Norman cavalry of the Scottish king, on land. Somerled's head was carried in triumph through Glasgow as his army 'sought to clamber from the blood-red waves into their ships' – so the victors wrote – 'but were drowned, each and all, in the surging tide'.[8]

Somerled's death was not a defeat for his children, however, who divided his kingdom up between them and found strength in cooperation. Dugall and his descendants ruled Mull, Tiree, Coll and Lorn. Reginald's family controlled Moidart on the mainland and the islands of Rum, Eigg, Barra, the Uists and St Kilda. For Donald and his clan it was Islay, Kintyre, Morvern, Ardnamurchan. Somerled's descendants thus made little pretence of being mainland-Scottish or of looking, as monarchical culture did, south – to England, France – for inspiration and example.[9] The Lords of the Isles continued to make the sea their medium and fulcrum. There is a lovely carving in St Clement's Church, Rodel (Harris), of a *birlinn* – the medieval galley-boat of the type that Somerled and his descendants used.[10] Late one summer night, as my torch passes over the stone, the black schist glitters, as its sculptors surely intended; how magnificent it must have been, lit by candles.[11]

The peacefulness and stability of the Kingdom of the Isles was revealed when Finlaggan on Islay was excavated during the 1990s. The two islands in the loch – the heart of the Lordship – were undefended, meaning this was probably a political entity that had nothing to fear.[12] None of the other castles of the Lordship were fortified either.[13] The Council of the Isles, held on Finlaggan, was attended by 'the Lord of the Isles, the major chiefs of kindred members, the Bishop of the Isles and the Abbot of Iona'.[14] As such, *Rí Innse Gall* had cultural prowess; it drew on the ancient traditions of the land. Finlaggan was the inauguration place of the isles' leaders, with a footprint stone. In 1547, Donald Monro ('Dean of the Isles') described it as the meeting place of the Council of the Isles and noted how well it was run ('In thair time thair was great peace and welth in the Iles throw the ministration of justice').[15] In the late seventeenth century Martin Martin described Finlaggan as a 'place of inauguration of the Lords'.[16] In the eighteenth century Thomas Pennant saw the footprint stone when he visited, but there is no trace of it now.

The mainland monarchs wanted to co-opt this rich island culture. By at least the thirteenth century, the Scottish mainland kings had adopted the islands' investiture. When Alexander III was crowned in 1249, he was 'surrounded by his French speaking court, [as] a Gaelic-speaking Scot knelt before him and read the king's genealogy back through the ninth-century Cinead mac Alpine, and the fifth-century Fergus mac Erca, to Scota, daughter of Pharaoh, the invented eponym of the *Scotti*'.[17]

But the proud sea-kingdoms which washed so nonchalantly against the shores of the mainland were politically irritating. When, in the late fourteenth century, John of Fordun described Hebridean and Highland people as 'a wild and untamed race, primitive and proud, given to plunder and the easy life', he probably spoke for many in the 'establishment'.[18] King James IV made this toxic feeling law in 1493, when he passed an act forfeiting the lordship (presaging the actions of the British against the Isle of Man three hundred years later) and initiating 'the long and complex cycle of violence called the *Linn nan Creach*' [Gaelic for 'Age of Strife']. James IV's forfeiture abolished the 'legal right to the title, Lord of the Isles, and thus the Lord's ancient right to grant lands'. Instead, 'the crown annexed all the Lordship lands', breaking 'the chain of tradition' and depriving 'Highlanders of the Lordship as a focal point of their Gaelic culture'.[19] Finlaggan was suddenly abandoned.[20]

One hundred years later, this aggression intensified when, in 1599, King James VI of Scotland and soon to be I of England wrote *Basilikon Doron*, a treatise on government for his heirs. The people who 'dwelleth in the Iles' James wrote, 'are all-utterly barbares, without any sort or shew of civilitie'.[21] Witchcraft, he thought, was 'most common in wild places of the worlde as . . . in our North Isles of Orkney and Schetland'.[22] Addressed to his son Henry, *Basilikon Doron* was privately circulated in Scots, then republished in English, becoming a bestseller in London. So, in 1609, the king went further, putting his thoughts into law with the *Statutes of Iona*. (There is something especially horrible about naming this brutal attack on the Hebridean way of life after the peoples' holy island.) The statutes, ruled, *Lear*-like, that the chiefs were to cut back the number of their retainers; to stop their 'extraordinary drinking of strong wynis and acquavitie.' Their sons were to be educated as Protestants in lowland Scotland, where they would learn 'to speik, reid and wryte Englische'.[23] Bards 'were expelled the Islands'. Clans that had functioned for centuries as extended family networks in a tradition of hospitality and reciprocity became alienated from each other as landlord–tenant relationships developed in their stead. Anticipating imperial endeavours across the world against the inhabitants of other continents and cultures, the *Statutes of Iona* aimed to culturally impoverish and fragment Gaelic life.

That these efforts did not entirely succeed must be due in large part to geography: the difficulty of imposing a monolithic law code on such remote and set-apart places – as well as to the strength of oral culture. *Rí Innse Gall* still militates against everything which the mainland represents – a divergent model in a deviant geography. Although Somerled's descendants inscribed his tale into Gaelic, Scots and Norse, in poems, clan histories, chronicles and sagas, in language political, genealogical and religious, these testimonies were slow to enter either the national myth-making of Scotland or the story-books of Britain.

The lacuna is geographical: Somerled's kingdom was part earth, part salt, ships his artform and his medium. It is strange how generally this knowledge has vanished. I remember the sailor Ellen MacArthur's description of how, after days and days at sea, land *smells*. I had lived here and there in that watery world in my head. But here was a larger truth: I had never yet *smelled* land.

*

Some people love being out on the water. A teenager I met on Hoy told me about a sailing charity based out of Glasgow which worked with young people and was looking for adult volunteers. The voyage I put myself down for was to begin in Oban and sail south to Greenock, Glasgow's impoverished suburb at the mouth of the Clyde, the place where Somerled moored his ships on the way to fight King Malcolm – via a medley of Hebridean islands. It sounded ideal.

During the seven days I spend at sea, in Somerled's world, there are moments when I feel at ease. I remember my clove hitches and running bowlines from my time as a firefighter in Orkney. I do not fall overboard. I cook and wash up. I manage to sleep in a bunk next to eight other people (that is motherhood for you). Out on the water, with the sails taut in the wind and my hand on the wheel and the rain in my eyes, I sometimes feel, vaguely, piratic.

But the culture is so hierarchical, like the fire service. As Dr Johnson said, during his tour of the Hebrides, 'being in a ship is being in a jail, with the chance of being drowned'.[24] That is indeed how it feels; a bit dicey. Furthermore, I am promoted to bosun. On paper, I am merely in the 'familiarization' berth. But they haven't secured a bosun for this voyage, and so I am granted an unwanted career advancement.

Being bosun, I become intimately reacquainted with the English language. *Bilge*: this is the water that gathers at the bottom of a boat; the bosun has to bail it out. *The bitter end* refers to the very last bit of the anchor chain, as you let it down, and hope to god it reaches the bottom; I crouch in the little compartment at the prow, wearing a large leather glove, with which I bat the anchor chain back and forth, so that it settles in coils, like a Nordic dragon, glistening with seawater drawn up from the depths. *Batten down the hatches*: fastening the windows; I do this every morning, before we set sail. *Man overboard drill*: as I am winched down into freezing seawater to rescue the buoy they have chucked into the sea, our fake drownee, I give extended thought to the generic masculine. The thing I like best about the boat is the gauge which tells us how many fathoms of water we are sailing over. *Full fathom five thy father lies*: this is what he meant: water that falls 9.144 metres (and four hundred years) to the coral and pearls of the seabed.

I have four superiors on the boat, all men. I like the skipper best, partly because he always says please and thank you. The teenagers, all ten of them, are also very polite; five girls and five boys, a mixture of backgrounds, state and private educations, and a young woman, with nails bitten down to the quick, who lives on her own with her cat in a council flat in Largs. But the young people are too young for this, I think, as I see them obediently reporting for duty through the night. None of the young people, however, are as sick as I am.

I am very sick: never have I felt so needlessly exhausted. Late at night, I lie in my bunk listening to the waters flowing intimately around me.

> About myself I can utter a truth-song,
> tell journeys – how I in toil-days
> torment-time often endured
> . . . horrible waves' rolling . . .
> I heard nothing there but the sea's sounding,
> ice-cold wave.

This is *The Seafarer*, a tenth-century Anglo-Saxon poem.

> . . . my mind's thought with mere-flood,
> over the whale's home, wide in its turning,
> over earth's regions comes back to me
> eager and greedy.[25]

I am so sick – vomiting before we even leave the harbour in Oban – that it doesn't feel normal. My literary epiphanies on the way to Lindisfarne are one thing, but this feels offensive: a personal crisis. I conclude that I must be vomiting up bad karma, as in an ayahuasca ritual: some sadness is being brought to the surface.

Certainly, I miss my children; each time I am sick, I see my daughters' faces. I lie in my bunk at night, rocking myself, as if I am in the womb again, or my daughters are, making me puke in some ancient throwback to a time when women used these instinctive superpowers to ward off bad spirits and keep their progeny safe.

When I was pregnant, I became disgusted by the smell of things I thought I loved and now found repulsive. On this trip, aboard the sailing boat, I feel that the sickness has been building for a while: it is in me, all around me. It concerns my life, and my marriage, and my work. It makes me doubt myself: would I have conquered new lands, like an Aud or Freydis, sailing to Iceland and Newfoundland in a fleet of ships? Or am I one of the women they left behind on the homestead, keeping the hall watertight, and sheep and children free of worms, the hunted meat and fish well salted and smoked? Maybe, I think (consolingly) as I pump water into the boat's toilet to slosh my vomit away, I would have been a mead-brewer, rune-carver, song-singer, storyteller. I feel gratitude to the *völva* who told their world that the sun was a woman.

Late one night, as I haul myself up on deck for the watch, I wonder what on earth possessed me to follow the journey of this brutal warrior, Somerled. Cuthbert was bad enough; at least he led to Cwen and her eldritch-islands. But Somerled's story, and that of *Rí Innse Gall*, encodes an almost complete absence of stories about women. How sad that is. The fact that I have so long accepted this status quo makes me wonder again about my acculturation.

The stories that come after Somerled are, if anything, worse: patriarchy tightens its grip. *Basilikon Doron* of (witch-obsessed) King James VI/I emphasizes the importance of *pater familias* and the management of women; this is the Aristotelian social contract, with men in charge of the house, family and country, and women at no point taking part in any 'public political activity'.[26] James advises that a wife should have 'beauty, riches and friendship by alliance' – therefore 'choose your Wife as I advised you to choose your servants: that she be of a whole and clean race, not subject to hereditary sicknesses, either of the soul or the body'. But above all, one must 'suffer her never to meddle with the politick government of the commonweal'. This is the culture of Christianity, of monarchy, of British society: no islands of women here.

Because of its different language, social structure and geography, Gaelic culture maintained certain freedoms, including for women of different classes. Few witches were put on trial or burned here.[27] Around 1500, an extraordinarily ribald and liberated poem was written in Gaelic by Iseabail ní Mheic Cailéin, the Countess of Argyll, and was collected by the dean of the Hebridean island of Lismore as part of a Gaelic compilation he made soon afterwards. The poem, four stanzas long, is a paean to the penis of Iseabail's household priest:

> Although many beautiful tree-like penises
> have been in the time before,
> this man of the religious order
> has a penis so big and rigid.[28]

The unexpectedness catches me; like a Sheela-na-gig, it upends the accepted and anticipated order of things. It is interesting that Iseabail, 'a love poet who belonged to a witty Clan Campbell court circle',[29] was unafraid of censure by her household, society at large, let alone the church. The poem has been interpreted as an anti-clerical satire (*pace* Chaucer); or maybe it was 'ascribed to her through mischief';[30] or perhaps it is simply 'a fairly obscene boast'.[31] Either way, Iseabail's status insulated her.

Possibly the only comparative freedom to be sought at this time in little islands away from the rest of society – atop mountains, in remote valleys, aboard boats.

We are exactly midway through our journey when the first mate mentions the archipelago of St Kilda. A ripple of excitement runs through the sea staff. They stop being stern and capable and become, momentarily, animated; dolphins in the surf. *St Kilda!* I look at the archipelago on one of the charts. It is some hundred nautical miles off course, way out in the Atlantic. St Kilda is made up of the islands of Dùn, Hirta (where people lived until 1930), Boreray (where they went for fowling) and Soay (the sheep from this island are small and wiry, with no herd instinct, and taste delicious – we kept them for a while in Somerset when I was a child).

The islands remained remote up until the point that the people were evacuated. It is extraordinary what a thoroughfare they have become today.

In the last of the phone signal as we leave the Hebrides, I text my friend George in Edinburgh, who worked on St Kilda and wrote a book about it.[32] He texts back with the name and number of the resident archaeologist, Craig, and, by the time I arrive, I am expected.

It feels completely joyous to have a conversation about history on dry land. On Hirta, Craig shows me all over the island, in and out of the little stone houses and on to the famous stones cleits (cupboards) for fridges and larders (they wind-dried their meat) dispersed throughout their fields. St Kilda is the only place in the world with double world heritage status: one for the cleits, two for the wildlife. (The little brown St Kilda wren.) I don't see the bird, but plenty of the Painted Lady butterflies that have flown here all the way from Africa. We discuss the one appearance St Kilda makes in the Icelandic sagas: a bishop stops here in 1202 on his way back to Norway to be consecrated. I ask Craig about Tigh na Banaghais-gich, the so-called 'Amazon's House' which Martin Martin mentioned on his tour here – it has been marked on maps as 'the House of the Female Warrior' since then. But Craig dismisses it as antiquarian romanticism. (By the nineteenth century it was known merely as the 'big sheiling'.)[33]

Martin Martin, at the very end of the seventeenth century, describes a completely illiterate community on St Kilda. He claimed that women, in particular, were 'anciently denied the use of writing in the islands to prevent love-intrigues'. But none of the islanders of St Kilda could read and he attests to the wonder they evinced at this magic:

> writing was the most astonishing to them: they cannot conceive
> how it is possible for any mortal to express the conceptions of his
> mind in such black characters upon white paper. I told them, that

within the compass of two years or less, if they pleased, they might easily be taught to read and write, but they were not of the opinion that either of them could be obtained, at least by them, in any age.

In *Becoming Animal*, David Abram argues that a people who live without the flatness of books and screens are hyper-attuned to the contours of landscape and place in ways that we book-people can never be. What a community it must have been, to have survived out here, so peacefully, adapted to the landscape and climate; how strange the incursions of the outside world, in the form of ministers proselytizing, factors collecting rent, not to mention the occasional abandoned aristocrat (Lady Grange: incarcerated) or hungry sailor. Today the strangeness is compounded by the Ministry of Defence, which has had a base here since 1957, currently run by the subcontractors QinetiQ.[34]

On the way back to Islay we are accompanied by a huge pod of dolphins. I've seen dolphins and whales from afar; killer whales from the deck of the *Adenia* in the North Sea; but never have I seen sea mammals this close. They jump in and out of the ripple that the boat makes, calling to each other. I can hear their high-pitched squeak as they call to their friends, and still more dolphins approach at high speed from the west: thirty-forty-fifty, diving towards us through the water to twist their bodies, again and again, through the waves at the front of the boat. Something about the way the boat moves through the water gives them pleasure. Their joy is palpable. They know how to live. It isn't childish; each one is in control of their own body, their own mind; but they are loving the experience of feeling that joy, together.

Moreover, everything that humankind has done to their species hasn't yet managed to dissuade them from approaching us. (I once saw fishermen in Sicily spearing a dolphin.) For the Romans, dolphins were 'symbolic of good fortune and friendship' but also of 'the journey of the soul after death to the Blessed Isles'.[35] For me, these dolphins signify the ecstasy of wildness, of community, of freedom.

Darkness falls, and the waves churn with phosphorescence. Overhead, the stars seem to be spinning in the sky, but it is an optical illusion caused by their proximity to the boat's moving boom. Under sail, we run at eleven knots, like the Vikings.[36]

The next day, when we come out of the empty Atlantic back into a busy communion of islands, I remember how that was what they were, to Somerled and his family. We are all just searching for communion.

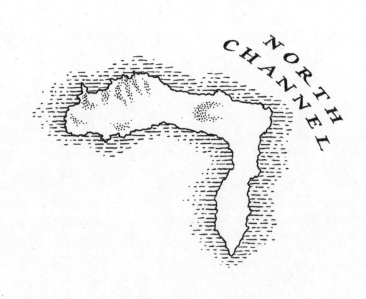

9.
Rathlin
Empire (sixteenth century)

In 1569, a wedding is held on Rathlin, the V-shaped island three miles north of Ireland, twenty miles short of Scotland. It brings together three great Irish and Scottish Catholic clans: the O'Neills of Donegal, the Campbells of Argyll and the MacDonnells of both Irish Antrim and Scottish Islay.

The groom, Tirlogh Luineach O'Neill, is Irish; the bride, Agnes, is a Scot. Born a Campbell, her first marriage was to the recently deceased James MacDonnell. James has been killed in Ireland, fighting the English, and it is his brother Sorley (the name an anglicization of the Gaelic Somhairle or Norse Somerled),[1] who is the wedding host. The ceremony is held on Rathlin because it is a symbolic near-actual bridge between Ireland and Scotland.

For two weeks, hundreds of guests party on Rathlin at Sorley MacDonnell's expense: two hundred or so in the castle, yet more in temporary, withy-built shelters in the castle grounds. There is bull-baiting, dancing, Highland games, horse-racing, jesters and jugglers. The Irish groom has a long black beard and hair half over his face. The Scots wear saffron-dyed shirts, rough fur cloaks, and kilts (so writes Wallace Clark, in his history of the island). The bride, who speaks English, Gaelic and French – 'a very nobell, weyse woman' – has brought along three thousand barefoot Scottish mercenaries as her marriage portion.[2] She is on her second marriage, and so is he. It is a dynastic alliance. Part of the point is to unite the Irish from the north with the Scots of the western islands against the English. As Sorley later says when ransoming a hostage: 'Inglishe men have no ryght to Yrland.'[3]

There is a map in the modern poetry anthology *An leabhar mòr/ The Great Book of Gaelic* which tips everything on its axis slightly so that the Western Isles are at polar north, a protective arm, and little Rathlin shoots out of Northern Ireland towards Scotland like a boomerang, or vulva-V.[4] (The same geology: the Giant's Causeway, extending through the sea to Staffa.)

Unfortunately for Rathlin, its position at the centre of things also put it at the vanguard of English imperialism. In 1557, for example, twelve years before Agnes and Tirlogh's wedding, Queen Mary's man in Ulster, Henry Sidney, massacred every person on the island – deaths that served no purpose other than as an exploratory colonizing gesture. It was too expensive to maintain a permanent garrison on Rathlin and soon the island reverted by default to the Scots.

Island Scots, having long treated Ulster in the north of Ireland as an extension of their kingdom, felt a prior claim and fought the English with the war cry 'Eilean Fraoch' ('heather isle'), this being the name of their island prison in the sound of Jura.[5] For men such as Sorley, who moved freely between the two places, Rathlin was a convenient garrison and fortress. There was no point in settling a permanent population, but the island was the ideal raiding base.

North-east Ireland had for centuries drawn sustenance, soldiers, dynastic and marital alliances from north-western Scotland. There was a natural family, tribal, linguistic, cultural affinity between the islands and highlands of Scotland and that part of Ireland. It was quicker, safer and easier to travel by boat from Glasgow to Ulster than by road down to Carlisle. The early-fourteenth-century Scottish king Robert the Bruce is said to have hidden in a cave on Rathlin, where he famously drew strength from the sight of a doughty spider weaving and reweaving its web. But in earlier times too the chiefs from Ulster in the north used Scottish mercenaries, or *gallowglass*; the scholarly bardic schools of Ireland and the Scottish Highlands strengthened these bonds.[6]

Naturally, Elizabeth I looked to the margins of her territory with an eye to expansion. Her polymathic adviser John Dee wrote a book on the subject called *Brytanici Imperii limites* (*Limits of the British Empire*) in which he argued for the 'existence and recovery of an ancient and vast British empire', a term he seems to have coined; by 1578, he was particularly interested in her 'title Royall to these forene Regions, & Ilands', seeing the domination of Baffin Island, perhaps eccentrically, as key to the conquest of North America.[7]

That was the far-off places. Already in 1566, when Elizabeth had begun to plan a second Pale, or plantation, in north-east Ireland, she had been told by an adviser that islands mattered. As other conquerors had done, 'First for the quietness of Ulster' she must: 'take away the Isle of the Raghlins and there to place 25 soldiers in the castell that one Sorly Boy now keeps.'[8]

The queen didn't act on this advice until 1573, when thirty-four-year-old Walter Devereux, Viscount Hereford, was sent to Ulster on an adventure. His official mission was to rescue the Irish plantation from disaster – for the immigrants there were struggling with the land and weather and unfriendly natives just as badly as those in territories further afield (such as Newfoundland and Virginia) soon would. His personal one was to transform his finances by acquiring Irish land with which to shore up his debts. But to do so he had to finance the plantation and its army himself. His house and land were mortgaged to the queen, which effectively meant he couldn't sell them quickly to anyone else. His rival, Leicester, was making love to his wife, Lettice (or vice versa), and the two of them may have connived to keep Devereux in Ireland, to head him towards death or disgrace.

To sweeten things a bit, the queen made Devereux Earl of Essex, a title once bestowed on his ancestors. She granted him huge tracts of land in Ulster, from the sea west to Lough Neagh and including the island of Rathlin – this was the prototype 'plantation' of the type that the English were soon excelling in across the world.[9]

None of this could deflect the trouble he was in, however, which started the moment his ship left Liverpool. His fleet was blown down the Irish Sea on to the Copeland Islands and the Isle of Man. The military reinforcements he had been promised by the Crown failed to materialize, or when they did proved ineffective – the contingent of Somerset men landed in Ireland armed only with white sticks. The provisions quickly ran out. The gunpowder supplies had been cut with coal dust and dysentery was rife.

The queen made up for these indignities by making Essex (as he was now known) Governor of Ulster. But he remained out of his depth. He tried to convince Tirlogh Luineach – now the major rebel of the north – that 'he had come to free the Irish from the tyranny of the Scots alien',[10] but that was not how the Irish saw it. As if to prove them right, Essex invited a senior scion of the O'Neills to a feast and then had him murdered, without provocation, along with his wife and associates. *Four Masters*, the Irish annals, put it plainly:

> This wicked and treacherous murder of the lord of the race of Hugh Boy O'Neill, the head and senior of the race of Owen, son of Nial of the Nine Hostages, and of all the Gaels, a few only excepted, was sufficient cause of the hatred and disgust of the English to the Irish.[11]

Essex still hadn't achieved anything worthwhile. Perhaps it is a measure of his desperation that the chance for redemption which he seized soon after was so brutal. He had learned that the sailor Francis Drake was at large in Ireland in command of a flagship (having lately seized a Spanish treasure convoy in the Isthmus of Panama, like any common pirate, not yet having circumnavigated the world). Essex hired him at forty-two shillings a month to lead a secret mission to Rathlin.[12] He himself fooled Sorley MacDonnell into leaving Rathlin undefended, then sent in Drake to attack the island with three frigates.

English soldiers swarmed the tiny island. It was harvest time and there were hundreds of people on Rathlin – seasonal labour as well as Sorley's own relatives, his wife and some of his children. The soldiers besieged the castle, which had no well, and when the Scots asked for a truce they slaughtered everyone:

200 slain from the castle . . . and [those] found hidden in caves and in cliffs of the sea to the number of 300 or 400 or more.[13]

Essex wrote to the queen in triumph, describing how 'Sorley stood upon the mainland and saw the taking of the island, and was like to run mad for sorrow, turning and tormenting himself, and saying that he had lost all that he ever had.'[14] It is a horrible image of English cruelty. Elizabeth wrote back, full of praise:

> you advise us of the taking of the island of the Raughlins, the common receipt and harbour of such Scots as do infest that realm of Ireland . . . happy success.[15]

A massacre for each English queen. And yet, like Henry Sidney's massacre in the name of Queen Mary, that which Essex engineered for Elizabeth had no purpose. Sidney himself, dispatched again to Ireland immediately afterwards as Lord Deputy, ordered that Rathlin should be abandoned. It sat in the middle of 'one of the stormiest pieces of sea on our coast'; when the soldiers Norris had left there were brought back to the mainland it was discovered that they had been reduced to eating their horses.

Essex returned to England in despair. As he wrote to the queen, 'why should I sit out my youth in an obscure place without assurance of your good opinion?'[16] The queen replied passionately that though he may think he had unprofitably employed his mind's care, body's toil and 'purse's charge', in fact he should consider himself 'invested . . . with immortal renown, the true mark that every honourable mind ought to shoot at'. She granted him more land in Ireland and made him Earl Marshal of Ireland for life, somewhat forcing his hand. And indeed he did return to Dublin, where he died the following year. It was rumoured that Leicester poisoned him. Essex certainly seems to have known that his days were numbered, for before leaving he wrote letters to the queen and others, attempting to settle his affairs in favour of his children. He begged Philip Sidney, the poet-soldier, and son of Henry, to marry his daughter

Penelope, still a teenager and muse of Sidney's soon-to-be famous sonnet sequence 'Astrophel and Stella'. Sidney hastened over to Ireland, but he arrived just too late at Essex's deathbed.[17]

Two years after Essex succumbed to his dysentery (or poisoning), his widow Lettice married her lover, Leicester, who happened to be Sidney's uncle. His daughter Penelope Devereux (Anne Boleyn's great-niece) never did marry Philip Sidney; instead she was betrothed to a man she didn't like, the well-named Robert Rich, and caused scandal by divorcing him; her brother later married Sidney's widow. Maybe Sorley's family took some comfort from the death of this man who had wronged them, wrought as it was from the incest and intrigue of the English court.[18]

Thus did Henry VIII's Reformation bequeath to his children, and his country, a new strain of religiously tinged conquest, one that flourished particularly well, in particularly nefarious ways, on the country's borders. Hostility to the Catholic Irish and their allies, the island Scots, was a natural consequence of the anxiety that Ireland had long caused the Tudors. The neighbouring island was too separate, too distinct; it was a rallying point for contenders and pretenders to the English throne.[19] The English also liked to sneer at Ireland for never having been colonized by Rome; this was something William Camden emphasized in his popular 1586 history, *Britannia*:

> I can never imagine that this Island was conquered by the Romans. Without question it had been well for it, if it had; and might have civilized them. For wheresoever the Romans were Lords and Masters, they introduced humanity among the conquer'd; and except where they rul'd, there was no such thing as humanity, learning, or neatness in any part of Europe. Their neglect of this Island may be charged upon them as inconsiderateness. For from this quarter Britain was spoil'd and infested with most cruel enemies.[20]

Elizabeth I, the Virgin Queen, was mythologized by her sycophants for her islandness – she was never breached; there was even an attempt to create an etymological link between her name and the Latin word *insulae*.[21] John Dee ascribed imaginary islands to her realms, such as Friseland, which he seems to have invented himself and which was then included in Orelius's atlas, between Ireland and Iceland. Elizabeth was even addressed as 'Sultana of England, France, Ireland, Holland and Friseland' by 'Sultan Ala-uddin of Achin'.[22]

The mythology and topography of Irish lakes and islands in turn inspired the unreliable feminine waterscape of Edmund Spenser's epic poem *The Faerie Queene*, which he wrote while working there as an imperial servant of the queen in the decade after Essex's death. Spenser lived as part of an expatriate English colony at Kilcolman Castle, which stands within its own 'marshy seasonal lake';[23] he also observed the horror of the Ulster famine at first hand, a county with Europe's largest freshwater lake, Lough Neagh. This troubled, troubling, land-and-waterscape enters his poetry. His knight, Guyon, for example, travels into the Idle Lake, past various woman-inhabited wandering isles, to encounter women free of the rule of men.[24]

Irish folklore had long vaunted aquatic maidens.[25] People believed in mermaids for a long time in the British Isles; as late as 1911, a mermaid was seen across from Rathlin, off the Scottish coast.[26] In sixteenth-century England, by contrast, mermaids were a byword for the soulless destruction of men (following Bocaccio).[27] The lake women whom Spenser creates and then condemns – just as Albina and her sisters were condemned, for their independence and sexual freedom – make 'false melodies' or throw 'forth lewd words immodestly' to 'embosome deeper in your mind, / And for your ruine at last awayt.' The Circean witch Acrasia – sexually liberated and free – lives on a paradisical love-nest island in a Bower of Bliss, which is 'melodious', a 'Paradise', 'ioyous', 'Angelicall'. But Spenser's Christian protagonists cannot leave her be. These witch-hunters trap her in a net – as if she is a mermaid, ready to be toured round England – and then – as if they are Drake and Essex on Rathlin – destroy her queendom:

their blisse he turn'd to balefulnesse:
Their groues he feld, their gardins did deface,
Their arbers spoyle, their Cabinets suppresse,
Their banket houses burne, their buildings race,
And of the fairest late, now made the foulest place.[28]

Spenser's long, complicated, highly allusive and erudite poem thus mashes up the rediscovery of Europe's exotic and ancient literature with all the horror and bombast of a nascent colonial project set within Ireland's alien landscape and amidst its hostile, aggrieved and starving population – a horde which, in Spenser's case, succeeded in setting fire to his planter's castle and sending him scurrying back to England.[29] The poem seems to reflect a deep unease with both subjugated peoples and female rulers. Female power is a strained and noxious affair in *The Faerie Queene* – and all the more potent for that. (It cannot have been easy, being a courtier to Elizabeth, brought to heel by a woman unlike any England had encountered in living memory.) While Spenser's female knight, Britomart, lacks 'Antique glory', the Amazon queen, Bellodant, represents a treacherous inversion of the usual order of things, forcing men to wear women's clothes, and to 'spin, to card, to sew, to wash, to wring'. As if there can be no worse fate than that, for a man: labouring as a woman (though fortuitously spared actual labour).

Ireland and its islands challenged the Tudor ruling elite's sense of themselves as conquerors. The Stuart kings' response was to engineer the 'plantation' of Ulster with settlers from Scotland.[30] Thanks to the Union of Crowns, for the first time the combined monarchy was able to do what neither had succeeded in doing independently and divide the Gaelic-speaking tribes of Ireland and Scotland from each other. King James, when advocating the colonial policy of 'plantations', explicitly asked for 'answerable inland subjects' to be sent to these unruly (probably witch-infested) islands.[31]

In 1641, Charles I used Rathlin as a place to garrison the troops which he sent over to put down the Irish Rebellion, and the military commander used it as an excuse to honour a clan vendetta: 'The island was swept bare of any living thing.' Rathlin, which is only seven miles long, still bears the scars in the landscape – *Cnoc na Scriodlaine*, Hill of the Screaming; *Sloc na Cailleach*, Chasm of the Women (they were driven off the cliffs).[32] This little island whispers the larger history of Ulster. As the English meddled in local politics, here, as elsewhere in Ireland, the Scots' independence was bought off as the English made them planters under their own banner. This even happened to Sorley's family: to his own son, who was pacified and made obedient thanks to land grants and titles.

– All this harm inflicted by the mainland; the more I read of Rathlin's history, the more miserable I was expecting to find it. Rathlin's minuscule population of seventy people is predominantly Catholic; the landowning family, the Gages, were once the only Protestants. With Irish land reform, the island was turned over to its inhabitants, and the Gages no longer live there, though they have kept up a connection.[33] As a Catholic enclave, Rathlin is an exception in North Antrim, a constituency which is three quarters Protestant and has returned a Unionist candidate for the past forty years – the same candidate through eleven general elections, the Revd Dr Ian Paisley. (Following his death in 2014, the seat is now held by his son.) Throughout the Troubles, Paisley nevertheless campaigned on Rathlin's behalf for better services, such as a wind turbine, ferry and electricity.[34] Things like these can mean the difference between subsistence and exile for a small island community – as vulnerable now to marginalization by the mainland as it was four hundred years ago to the hostility of rival claimants.

But Rathlin is an ebullient place. It reminded me that islands have their moments, as do nations; peaks and troughs of diffuse community happiness and diffuse community misery. For sure, I fell in with the right family. Somehow, from the mainland, I heard tell of a matriarch kelp entrepreneur, and everything flowed from there. The McFaul family in Rathlin set up the UK and Ireland's first commercial kelp-growing lab. This was irresistible for me. I love seaweed – had come to love it in Orkney where I swam in it, ate it and admired its artistic excrescences along the shore, daily. There is a kelp store on Rathlin, from the time when landlords all along the Atlantic coast of the British Isles forced their tenants to harvest it to obtain the alkaline seaweed extract which was sold for a fortune in Liverpool and Glasgow to manufacturers of soap and glass. The alkali content is highest the further north the kelp is cut and burnt. Landlords made from the kelp almost double what they got from rents. It was family work: women and children would spend all day up to their knees in seawater, cutting, then drying and burning the kelp in kilns which are still visible all along the coasts of these islands. Burning it was worse than wading out to sea and cutting it, even. As the Orkney artist Rebecca Marr told me, the toxic smoke was said to have made women miscarry and limpets fall off rocks.

But on Rathlin, this story of oppression has been transformed into one of entrepreneurial island independence. The McFaul family are a modern island legend. Kate Burns, originally from County Down, came to the island as a birder, but 'fell in love with the place', married a Rathlin man, and had four boys in quick succession, back in the 1970s and '80s, before the shiny pot of EU grant money had been discovered, when things really were dicey for remote islanders. Until the 1990s, there was no electricity, ferry connection or sewage. Kate heated the water with solid fuel, used paraffin lamps, washed terry-towel nappies by hand and cooked on a wood stove. It wasn't quite a starvation diet – they didn't succumb to eating their horses, as Norris and his soldiers had done – nowadays, with hindsight, the family likes to joke that when times were hard they fell back on eating lobster and wild mushroom risotto.

The boys grew up entrepreneurial. Aged seventeen, the eldest, Damien, set up a festival on Rathlin called Jigs and Rigs which ran for the next twelve years. (He now works in renewables.) The second, Benji, is a creel fisherman; Fergus is skipper on the ferry; and the youngest, Philip, does the kelp with Kate.

Kate divorced her island man but stayed put with her boys. I found something inspiring and upbeat about her situation; her hard-earned freedom. She is divinely independent. She set up the kelp lab after working with the Gulf of Maine Research Institute, which she encountered during her work on Northern Ireland's fisheries policy for the EU. Hers is the first private kelp lab in the UK and Ireland and the first place to grow and process kelp for food in Europe. In the summer, the lab propagates wild sugar kelp; in the autumn, it is digitata. Sarah, who runs the lab, takes me with her to gather some digitata from the bay. We wade in up to our navels, dressed in wetsuits, looking for pieces of this long, narrow-leaved seaweed with the little bumps and protrusions which suggest that the plant is ready to mate.

Under the microscope we watch the seaweed spores shimmying around. 'Look!' Sarah says. 'That's it, that's us, that's human evolution's Big Bang.' (I think she means that dexterous seaweed can reproduce both asexually and also, as scientists put it, from 'the carposporophyte, which develops from the fertilized egg cell and depends for its nutrition on the female gametophyte'.)[35]

Sarah's boyfriend, Paddy Bloomer, is an artist-inventor who came up with the spool made from some string, a repurposed electrical drill and a sewing-machine foot pedal, plus a piece of plumbing pipe, with which the seaweed spores are encouraged to reproduce. Kate's son and his girlfriend gather the wild and farmed kelp from the sea, sterilize and package it. Philip is the one who drives the kelp lorry once a month to Belfast. Kate raises the revenue, figures out the branding and represents Islander Kelp at food conferences and fairs all over Europe.

In the kelp lab, Kate sings me a wartime song about seaweed and the Lammas fair:

> At the Ould Lammas Fair, boys were you ever there?
> Were you ever at the Fair in Ballycastle-O?
> Did you treat your Mary Ann to some Dulse and Yellow Man,
> At the ould Lammas fair in Ballycastle-O?

People still gather dulse (a seaweed the colour of red cabbage) on Rathlin, as all over the coasts and islands of Ireland. When I stayed with my friend Declan in Ballina, Co. Mayo, there was a man selling seaweed at the weekly market. I bought some and took it home; I can't remember the variety now, for he had many, and I probably misrecall the claims he made for the one I picked out, an aphrodisiac curing backache and broken hearts. (We also went to the seaweed baths in Sligo, where you broil yourself lightly in a cast-iron tub of seaweed gathered from the shore that morning and then sit in a wooden chair, pull a lever and get steamed like a pudding.)

Kate explains to me that Yellow Man is a type of honeycomb toffee, while Lammas itself is from Lunasa, a pagan goddess – though others say it comes from Lugh, the Sun God; or 'loaf mass' from Christian times, meaning the first bread of the harvest.[36] 'The Fair itself was set up by Sorley Boy MacDonnell,' she adds.

Sláine, who works on the kelp, makes me tea and talks about Irish history and literature and folklore. Mishearing his name, I explain that I've heard it before – also in the context of kelp (and its use as a fertilizer of the soil). When Martin Martin described how

> The inhabitants of this island [Lewis] had an ancient custom to sacrifice to a sea-god called Shony, at Hallow-tide ... one of their number was picked out to wade into the sea up to the middle, and carrying a cup of ale in his hand, standing still in that posture, cried out with a loud voice, 'Shony, I give you this cup of ale, hoping that you'll be so kind as to send us plenty of sea-ware for enriching our ground.'[37]

he is attesting to a pagan libation. But it is not the same word. Sláine means 'good health' in Irish and has nothing to do with kelp.

That afternoon, Sarah, Philip, Eli, Sláine and I get into wetsuits again and take the motorboat out into the bay to cut kelp for the noodles – there's a big order come in from a restaurant in the south.

'Have you got a tide timetable?' I ask Philip as we climb aboard, but he looks at me quizzically, nods to the sky and says, a little crisply, 'The moon's the only chart you need.'

That night in her cabin up on the headland Kate plays me the recordings from the 'No Hard Border' concert they held recently on Rathlin in the wake of the Brexit vote: 'instrumental, medieval, baroque and Irish trad'. The loose coalition of musicians on the island includes Kate's German daughter-in-law Eli Vogel on Baroque flute (she plays for the Irish Baroque Orchestra), Kate on clarinet and various of her boys on violin. They jam together at least once a week in the island pub.

Another night we go to the choir rehearsal which is held weekly in the Protestant church down by the seashore (the two faiths share a graveyard). The choir's influences are diverse too: songs in Irish, Scottish and Rathlin Gaelic. We sing a folksong, 'The Boatman'/'Fear an Bháta':

> *Théid mé suas ar an chn-oc is air-de,*
> *Féach an bhfeic mé fear an bhá-ta.*
> *An dtig thú a-nocht, nó an dtig thúa-már-ach?*

> I went up to the highest hill
> To see if I could see the boatman,
> Will you be coming tonight,
> or will you come tomorrow?

Until the Partition of Ireland in 1921, Irish Gaelic was most islanders' first language. But with the creation of Northern Ireland Gaelic lost its status in the north and today it is barely taught. The last Gaelic speaker on Rathlin died a decade ago. But we sing the song faithfully and, later, in the pub, Kate and her sons play the airs from these old songs.

Rathlin, despite its fiery history and fierce tides, is almost unknown on the British mainland – each time I have to explain to friends or acquaintances where it is I feel the macabre pinprick of history, as if the names of English genocides are being tattooed on my forehead – yet it sent out ripples that reached other islands far away. The other islands whose fates it intersects with had nothing to do with Ireland or Ulster; nothing – except that it was the same nation which came to grab their land, the same nation which massacred their people, the same colonizers who planted a flag that was becoming familiar across the world, on sandy beaches and once-sacred mountaintops. The English took over islands casually – because they were an island people and islands were the resource they knew; but also because it was easy to abuse and oppress these insignificant pieces of land, which nothing protects and nothing holds together – as it was easy to abuse and oppress women, resources to be exploited and dispensed with.

What happened on Rathlin was a portent of events elsewhere. As Shakespeare wrote in *The Tempest*

> SEBASTIAN: I think he will carry this island home in his pocket,
>   and give it his son for an apple.
> ANTONIO: And sowing the kernels of it in the sea, bring forth more islands.[38]

Shakespeare liked islands – five of his plays use island settings: *The Merchant of Venice*, *Othello* (Cyprus and watery Venice), *Much Ado about Nothing* and *A Winter's Tale* (Sicily) and *The Tempest*, ur-island of them all, which draws in influence from everywhere Shakespeare turned his gaze. In the sixteenth century islands were politically as well as spiritually important, for 'navigational technique was a matter of . . . "sailing by the islands" '.[39] Like the theatre, islands are also little worlds of their own. In writing *The Tempest*, Shakespeare seems to have been inspired by the new type of foreign policy then exciting the English: the capture and exploitation of land in seas far away.

Two years before the play was first performed, an English ship, the *Sea Venture*, carrying people and supplies to shore up the struggling colony in Virginia, hit some reefs 400 miles short of America. The ship was wrecked, but everybody on board was saved, and for ten months the passengers in transit made the islands of Bermuda their home. The shipwreck proved to be a god-sent stroke of luck. George Somers (summer traveller) and his crew had chanced upon an oasis of abundance: the Orkney Neolithic come again. Unlike Virginia, where the colonizers were constantly being harried by the native population of Powhatans, this was terra nullius: there were no resident humans on Bermuda (the Spanish had been and gone a century earlier, leaving only the island's name). Birds, mammals and amphibians, never having known such skilled predators as Englishmen, were easy to trap. The colonizers gorged on the native seabird known as a cahow (which almost died out), and so many turtles were eaten, then and later, that as early as 1620 an act was passed 'Against the killinge of over younge Tortoyses'. Surrounded by reef, the warm waters contained such fish that 'if a man steppe into the water, they will come round about him'. The islands also had a good supply of native cedar – an excellent ship-building timber – and two new boats were slowly constructed, *Patience* and *Deliverance*.

The discovery of Bermuda saved England's Virginia colony. When *Patience* and *Deliverance* eventually docked in Jamestown, they found the original colony of four hundred reduced to sixty by disease, starvation and warfare. The only reassuring part of the Virginia colony now was Bermuda's manifest bounty as a supply station. This alone reassured the investors back in London and, as a result, the Virginia Company survived, and the Bermuda (Somers Isles) Company was founded too.

Meanwhile, in 1610, accounts were written by two *Sea Venture* survivors, Silvester Jourdain and William Strachey. They described how, at first, the shipwrecked company was scared and bewitched – for the isle was full of noises, strange, guttural sounds, at first feared to be the voices of devils but which the English soon found to be unfamiliar seabirds calling to each other. Distress was caused by a mysterious disappearing fire; some of the company drank themselves to oblivion, thinking they would never be rescued.

Samuel Purchas, editor of both the Bermuda pamphlets and his famous, bestselling anthology of cusp-of-empire travel-writing, wrote in the margin of the report, 'Were we ourselves made and not born civil in our Progenitors' days? And were not Caesar's Britons as brutish as Virginians? The Roman swords were best teachers of civility to this & other Countries near us.' Thus English imperialists looked to their own experience of being colonized as justification for further conquests.

Shakespeare is said to have had connections in the Virginia Company, and perhaps he drew on these first-hand reports in *The Tempest* – the outlandishness, Ariel's zeitgeist allusion to the 'Bermoothes', a meditation on exile, colonization, submission and creation.[40] Strachey and Jourdain's eyewitness accounts were published along with the *Authorized Report of the Virginia Company*, which admitted that in Virginia, '28 or 30 of the company . . . stole away the Ship . . . made a league amongst themselves to be professed pirates, with dreams of mountains of gold, and happy robberies . . . they created Indians our implacable enemies by some violence they had offered'. If Shakespeare read this too, it became the mutiny of Trinculo, Stephano and Caliban, 'the ocean-going European proletarians' rebelling with the native and 'son of a witch'.[41]

Caliban's mother is Sycorax, a witch, 'and one so strong / That could control the moon, make flows and ebbs'. This doesn't mean that Sycorax actually controls the moon but that, like Philip on Rathlin, she watches it, notices its waxing and waning, and understands what this power will do to the tides. All weather prophets, through history, were people attuned to the other-than-human language of nature: to cloud formation and bird flight, to the taste of the seas and the behaviour of animals and insects; they read this natural language in order to predict storms and droughts before they happened.

In *The Tempest*, Shakespeare, like Edmund Spenser before him, is tantalized by the idea of a powerful European man taking over an island ruled by a woman. As with the story of Albina, it is the conquest of female territory by men which appears to drive these stories, becoming their central meaning and purpose. Unwittingly or not, Shakespeare captured in his play a triple moment of patriarchal dominance: over women, over non-Western cultures, over nature.

And in the wake of these plays and poems about female prophetesses, or weather knotters, or healers, or witches, being subjugated by men, came the real subjugation of this population – witch hunts, trials, hangings, burnings, scorching the seventeenth century with state-endorsed paranoia, murder and distress.

Furthermore, the nascent overseas imperialism Shakespeare dramatized is still playing out today. (Rathlin is part of the United Kingdom; Bermuda, like many British Overseas Territories, functions as a tax haven.) Given the impracticalities (the inequities), it stands to reason that both islands' future independence from the mothership no longer seems that unlikely. But in the five hundred years that have elapsed since Rathlin and Bermuda were breached in the name of the Crown, neither time, nor divisive politics, nor vast bodies of water – the Irish Sea, the Atlantic – have yet extinguished those planter flames.

The unique ecosystems of Bermuda, and other islands, are still far from being preserved in the way that Rachel Carson called for in 1950 when she wrote *The Sea Around Us* – a book that pointed to the sixteenth century, in particular, as a turning point. This was the beginning of the age of species loss, particularly through island colonization:

> In a reasonable world men would have treated these islands as precious possessions, as natural museums filled with beautiful and curious works of creation, valuable beyond price because nowhere in the world are they duplicated.

Instead, we are still in the sixteenth century mindset of discovery, colonization and exploitation. The moment in *The Tempest* when Prospero breaks his staff and drowns his book in an ancient deposition similar to those of the Druids on Anglesey or Celtic Britons in the Thames, is thrilling, historically and mythically. But it also mirrors back to us our contemporary collective attitude to the seas, and how powerfully they may yet rebel.

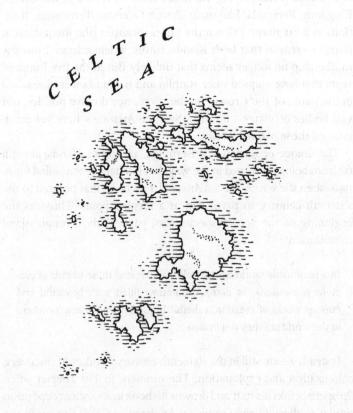

Scilly

Civil War (seventeenth century)

When there's an extreme spring tide in the Isles of Scilly, the waters retreat as if at the touch of Moses' rod and it is possible to walk between the islands of Tresco and Bryher.[1] However much the tide draws back, it will then 'spring' forward, like for like. It can be an excuse for a party, a jaunt – I even went to a Low Tide festival there, and there *was* a certain thrill in eating a burger in the middle of a once-busy sea channel. It is extraordinary to stand on wet sand, rippled by waves, where the waters were flowing an hour before, and will flow once again; weird, breathtaking, a metaphor of the dangerous instability of human endeavour. *Terra in sala*: earth in the sea, Romans called islands.[2] We all live on 'earth in the sea', and yet anywhere other than small islands it is sometimes easy to forget the precarity of our existence.

Stranger still, the insouciant sea walk between Tresco and Bryher is actually the appendix of a real historical event. Whether it happened in fits and starts, or all at once, there was a moment of sea-level rise in recorded history which at some point divided the one large island (known as 'Ennor', even as late as the reign of Edward I in the thirteenth century), into many smaller nuggets of land: St Mary's, Tresco, Bryher and St Martin's. (St Agnes had been separate from prehistoric times.)[3]

In 1612, Michael Drayton called the islands 'half-sunke' in his topographical poem *Poly-Olbion* – but even as late as Victorian times it was possible to walk between all these islands (not just Tresco and Bryher) at spring-tide. In 1961, divers described a submerged 'ancient village' with a standing stone in its centre.[4] Well into the twentieth century, people reported seeing 'a fine regular pavement of large flat stones', underwater by about eight feet, running from St Mary's to St Martin's – 'the boulevards of Lyonesse', in Cornish poet Penelope Shuttle's words.[5]

The legend of the drowned Cornish kingdom of Lyonesse had entered the imagination of Britain at least by the time of Malory, for whom it is a kind of paradise. Tennyson, who read Malory as a boy, believed that 'the rocky Isles of Scilly' were all that remained of Lyonesse and Camelot[6] – and he may be right. Scilly is visible from Land's End, and thousands of years ago it was probably accessible by land. There are believed to be submerged forests in the sea near Scilly.[7] 'That fortie miles now Sea,' Drayton wrote in *Poly-Olbion*, 'sometimes firme fore-land was; / And that a Forrest then, which now with him is Flood.'[8]

Here, once again, are revealed (almost) the civilizations which the oceans drowned. *And this which once happened, will again come to be*: the takeover of our highly schematized lives by cosmic forces far more powerful and inexorable than we are. It is good to remember this sometimes; how tiny we are. Small islands have the ability to act on us like hubris. They make us feel huge and powerful. When actually, if the climate tips, we will be washed away.

Lord knows that deities have manifold uses in the human mind; *wonder* is one of them, and *beauty* another. The historian (and Cornish bard) Charles Thomas argued, in his book *Exploration of a Drowned Landscape: Archaeology and History of the Isles of Scilly* (1985) that Scilly (the etymology is uncertain) probably denotes a female Iron Age deity of water: 'She-who-looks-out; The Watcher'. Waterspouts in the seas 'off Cornwall and Scilly', he wrote, might have been personified in ancient times as 'a hierophany, a revelation of sacred might, by which the aquatic goddess chose to reveal her presence or convey a portent'.[9] Scilly – verdant, jagged, surprising – could easily be Pomponius Mela's island of oracle priestesses; here, under this sky, in this sea, the presence of an ancient goddess cult is immanent.[10] *Sun, sea, sky.* Just as the shrines of Pakistan's Sufi saints are situated on rocky outcrops, around springs or on islands in the Indus

River, so the deity of Scilly and her priestesses would have required pilgrimage to her hallowed place. Pomponius Mela was explicit about this: prophecies are 'not revealed except to sea-voyagers and then only to those travelling to consult them'. Those who wished to be cured or enlightened needed to make the arduous boat journey – and do homage.

I had returned to England from Islay and Rathlin knowing that I needed both things: to be cured and enlightened. And so I went.

I was happy to return to Scilly because of the company I had kept the first time, visiting with my baby daughter, mother and sister. My mother had come to Tresco as a child. We voyaged there, guided by her early memories of chilly beach picnics; me, with my head full of Iron Age goddesses; my baby, content with her three attendant spirits; my sister, another strong branch of our tree.

And yet, again, I was wrong: other than in myth, no island could be further from a matristic society. Since 1337, the land itself (even part of the sea) has been owned by the Prince of Wales, through his lucrative private income generated by the Duchy of Cornwall. Every Prince of Wales benefits, including the present incumbent, bound backwards and forwards in a system of primogeniture, a sexist form of inheritance that traditionally passes landholdings from father to son. The duchy also has the 'right of wreck' in those places, the right to royal fishes (whales and sturgeon), the freehold of most of Cornwall's foreshore; it is the port authority in Scilly and is exempt from direct taxation, leading the campaign group Republic to declare that it functions as the prince's private tax haven. Due to their poverty, Scilly residents were also exempt from income tax until the 1950s (when tourism took off). Both the archipelago and the duchy illustrate how island freedoms lie within Britain's body politic like dazzlingly stalwart fossils.

In the beginning, the Isles of Scilly, some thirty miles from Cornwall, were so insignificant and faraway they were missed off the original grant to the Black Prince, Edward, Duke of Cornwall. Tavistock Abbey controlled the islands through the priory on Tresco, ignoring them mostly, occasionally banishing errant monks there – just as, in Roman times, Emperor Maximus sent the naughty bishops Instantius and Tiberianus to 'insula Sylina, quae ultra Britannias est' ('the island of Sylina, beyond Britain').[11] With the Dissolution, the Crown took the islands back. For most of their history, the islands – very poor[12] – barely registered in the consciousness of the English state. Thomas Seymour (brother of Jane) seems to have been a pioneer of sorts – he leased the islands from the Crown, then dabbled in legalized piracy, as head of the Royal Navy.[13] The 1549 bill of Attainder accused him of having,

> gotten into his hands the strong and dangerous Scilly Isles where he might have a refuge if anything for his demerits should be attempted against him.[14]

But it was only under the Stuarts that Scilly was reckoned to be 'in the possession of the Prince'.

Today, nobody would think of missing Scilly off the duchy's roster. High-class tourism has made Scilly a seasonal cash-cow. Some residents make a year's income in eight summer weeks (not as much as those fisherman in Shetland but with similar rapidity). The island shop on St Agnes is loss-making over the winter; it stays open 'to provide a service', says the postman (whose family has been on the island 'since the Civil War'). Island farms make cultural rather than financial sense. The farmer on St Agnes, with his eleven Jersey cows, does it because it is what his family has always done (also since the time of the Civil War: the same Hicks family as at the post office, mentioned in Parliament's 1652 survey); and because it is encouraged by the terms of the duchy tenancy. But the money is in selling ice creams, tent spaces and sausages to campers during July and August. The subsistence farming of his boyhood is no more, 'thank goodness'.

The affairs of the Duchy of Cornwall illustrate Britain's bizarre and complex constitutional arrangements with its islands, which the state is seemingly unable to clarify or change. In 2005, the duchy's Secretary and Keeper of Records, Bertie Ross, was called before a parliamentary Select Committee and asked to open up the duchy's books to public scrutiny for the first time in history. Its net surplus had just jumped from £6 million to £11 million, and Ross was also asked to explain the duchy's tax regime. But it turned out that much to the real, or mock, horror of the interrogating politicians, the duchy was under no obligation to explain anything. Ross stalled politely ('I think for me to comment on the sums of money is not relevant on this occasion'). Even today, despite everything that happened in the seventeenth century, there are aspects of the monarchy which Parliament cannot touch. For many Scillonians, the Civil War is still the most important historical landmark they know, and yet it left the major mechanisms of power – land and money – untouched. By last reckoning (2022), the duchy provided the then Prince of Wales with an income of £23 million.

In 1646, as his father's realm shrank around him, it was to Scilly that Charles, Prince of Wales, fled. While the king was imprisoned by Parliament on the Isle of Wight, his son retreated through Cornwall, took refuge on St Michael's Mount, the splendid, castle-dominated island off Penzance, and when that became unsafe he had a choice: flee abroad to Ireland or France, or cling like a whelk to the last vestige of his kingdom. His French mother urged the Channel Islands, but he feared the umbrage which they might cause, being 'so near to France'. Instead he went to Scilly. His party spent six weeks there, which passed for the Royals in great discomfort, and for the locals at great expense.

England's civil wars lasted for a decade and changed some aspects of English society and culture for ever. Ann Fanshawe, wife of a Royalist courtier, describes the dramatic escape from Cornwall with Prince Charles in her *Memoirs*. First, the seamen mutinied, and her husband was forced to pay them himself, from his own funds. Then 'they broke open one of our trunks, and took out a bag of 60 pounds and a quantity of gold lace, with our best clothes and linen, with all my combs, gloves and ribbons, which amounted to near 300 pounds or more'. This was all taking place during a sea crossing known for its roughness. Ann, 'extremely sick and big with child', 'was set on shore almost dead in the island of Scilly'. She and her party were put up in quarters near the castle, where the prince was; she describes the house as 'so vile that my footman ever lay in a better'. It 'consisted of four rooms, or rather partitions, two low rooms and two little lofts, with a ladder to go up: in one of these they kept dried fish, which was his trade' – she was staying with a fisherman, many times poorer than she.[15]

There is nothing in the *Memoirs* about the island women Ann Fanshawe encountered, nor those who shared her privations by sharing with her their provisions. A century later, in *A Natural and Historical Account of the Islands of Scilly*, army officer Robert Heath attested that female healers on Scilly treated the sick in the islands; he called them the 'Society of *skilful Aunts*'. (The president, he added, 'is remarkable for her venerable *long Beard*, which some imagine operates miraculously to the Benefit of those who stroke it.')[16] Nothing like this is noted by the Cavaliers, of course.[17]

From Scilly, the Royalists escaped to Jersey – only just evading Parliament's men when a storm drove the approaching boats off course. They fared better in the comfort of the Channel Islands and remained there for some months. Thereafter they moved from place to place, during their seasalt-splashed interregnum: daring to attack the Royal Navy, raising rebels from Britain's fringes, from Ireland, Holland and France, with Britain's offshore islands vulnerable and militarily relevant as never before.

The coastal south-west of England, in particular, saw very bitter fighting, as the Cavaliers were washed south out of England by Parliament, clinging to rocky outposts such as St Michael's Mount and Scilly as they went. Even Lundy, a very small island in the Bristol Channel, assumed new importance, after it was garrisoned for Charles I by Thomas Bushell until 1647. It was to the Isle of Wight that Charles I fled from his house arrest at Hampton Court; there, too, that he was held prisoner. After the navy mutinied, in 1648, from Parliament to the Royalist cause, Prince Rupert sent a ship to the island 'to attempt to rescue the king'.[18] It failed to free him, but thereafter the two princes, Charles and Rupert, exploited Britain's island geography, successfully harrying the king-capturing, king-killing Republicans from various outposts, allowing the Cavalier press to dub Prince Charles 'King at Sea' – even before his father was dead, executed at Whitehall in 1649.[19] Out on these islands, the king and his son the prince metaphorically 'switched roles': the king becoming a prisoner on an island and the prince ruling the waves before he returned to rule the land.[20] In 1645, Charles I himself used a nautical expression for the moment when he gave his teenage son 'the livery of his inheritance' and sent him west to lead the Royalist army: it would, he said, 'unbuoy him'.[21]

Cromwell, too, exploited the islands politically as a Parliamentary commander, during the wars, and interregnum, as Lord Protector. The magnificent red Norse cathedral in Kirkwall still bears the scars of Cromwell's soldiers, who stabled their horses there, deliberately showing their disrespect for the old medieval idea of sacred space.[22] He used Jersey as a place of rendition of political prisoners such as John Lilburne, because the Channel Islands did not recognize habeas corpus and therefore prisoners could be taken away and tortured. Lilburne was broken in the jail on Jersey, in the horribly named castle Mont Orgueil (*Mount Pride*).

Scilly, like the rest of Cornwall, was predominantly Royalist.[23] By 1642, after the Royal Navy had 'defected without firing a shot', the islands became a base for Royalist privateers.[24] Parliament took the islands in 1646, but discontent soon broke out. The Royalists, watching like gannets from Jersey and France, saw their chance, and sent over from Jersey a twenty-year-old friend of the prince, John Grenville.

For the next three years John Grenville ran his own little kingdom in the name of the deposed royal family. It was on Scilly that the prince was first declared King Charles II. Supplies and arms were sent from France, Cornwall and Ireland. Grenville added some reinforcements and began to establish Scilly as a base for privateering – he held 'letters of marque' from the king-in-waiting, making raids on merchant-ships a form of foreign excise, in his eyes. Soon, 'somewhere in the region of twenty or so men-of-war were using Scilly as a base . . . drop[ping] off captured vessels and their crews'.[25] According to Parliament, however, the man was a pirate.

In his 1649 travel-book, *Wandering to See the Wonders of the West*, the writer and poet John Taylor called Scilly 'a second Algiers':

> The main Island is held for the Prince, by one Captain (or as some say, a Knight) called Sir *John Grenville* . . . some do call it a second *Algiers*, for there cannot a ship or vessel pass by it, but they do make out upon them, whereby they have great riches, with all necessaries.[26]

The Dutch, whose ships were being held to ransom, were incensed: they actually waged war on Scilly. Prince Charles, desperate for money, tried to negotiate the islands' sale to Dutch merchants in order to secure a loan of £50,000. Cromwell, wishing to prevent the invasion of England by a foreign force, sent his own men to reconquer the islands instead.

As England's last functioning Royalist commander, Grenville's hand was poor, but he secured safe passage for himself and his officers. Unscathed, he left to join 'King' Charles in France. Several years later Parliament's man, Admiral Blake, received a general letter of thanks from Cromwell, enfolding a bejewelled portrait of the Lord Protector, worth £565, set in gold and crystal amid forty-six diamonds.[27] Upon the Restoration, Grenville was made Baron, Viscount, First Earl of Bath, and also High Steward of the Duchy. The king quickly bejewelled his own portrait by enlarging the burgeoning empire with land (including islands) faraway.

Scilly itself, having been so much in the public eye, seems to have been substantially resettled after the Civil War – probably by Cornish families, though legend likes to suggest by stranded privateers and islomaniac soldiers.[28]

Four hundred years on, time has changed few of these arrangements. John Grenville's descendants include the Duke of Sutherland, Earl of Clarendon and Earl Spencer. The castle on St Michael's Mount is still lived in by the St Aubyn family, whose ancestor, a Roundhead, took it from its Royalist owner by force (eventually paying for it the year before the Restoration).[29] The Dutch remembered to declare peace with Scilly only in 1986. The current Prince of Wales still owns Scilly. And some of the islands colonized during this time, in places as far away as the Caribbean, still form part of Britain's realm.

Today, the duchy's impact on Scilly is as direct as if the prince was encamped there in the fashion of his forebear. 'If you complain the rent's too high, they put it up,' a farmer on St Agnes tells me of his dealings with the duchy's land steward. When the duchy 'went commercial' in 2001, it put up the rent it charged the hotelier of Star Castle by nine times. Elizabeth I ordered Star Castle to be built after the Armada brought the islands to her attention as the Spanish aimed to use them as a liaison point prior to invasion.[30] Ever-stingy, she gave £400 towards its construction, making it the cheapest fortress in British history.[31] The castle was indeed cheap – but robust. Today, for around a quarter of that sum, you can get a room in one of the points of its star, with views out to sea, and Elizabeth's portrait on the wall.

From the island of Bryher, where the female Iron Age warrior was found, I take a dinghy to Samson. Samson is one of those islands only sporadically inhabited; as William Borlase wrote in 1756, in his book on Scilly, 'these Islands, little Colonies (like great Empires) having their sickly times, from which they are sometimes restored, and in which they sometimes expire'.[32] At the time of Parliament's 1652 survey, Samson was quite poorly: 'the whole Iland of Sampsons doth now lye wast and is a mountainos rockie ruggie peece of pasture', but before the war it 'hath been formerlie inhabited by one or two tennants ... but the houses and inclosures are now fallen downe and ruined since the takeing of the Syllies from the enemie'.[33]

By the mid-nineteenth century, however, it again had five families living on it. That was until a Hertfordshire banking heir, Augustus Smith, took over the 'government' of Scilly. Smith was a reforming Victorian who banished all paupers to Penzance, imposed a fee for non-attendance at his island school and required islanders to grow the crops he mandated. Scillonians nicknamed him 'old Caliban' ('old Prospero' would have been more accurate, if too flattering). He was rowed about in a state barge by uniformed crew; he insisted on primogeniture, in order to end the 'practice of subdividing land'.[34] He had the families on Samson cleared off so that he could repopulate the island as a deer park. There are no deer now – they were eaten on the sly, probably by islanders from Bryher – but the abandoned granite houses glint fiercely in the August sun. Veins of white quartz and black tourmaline stretch from Scilly, under the sea and ground, as far as Dartmoor. The duchy's reach: as solid as geology.

Those who managed to stay in Scilly came to the reluctant view that Smith's terrorizing was beneficial in the long run. It was he who saw the potential in the archipelago's geography: a Gulfstream-warmed climate, making it the earliest place in the British Isles for daffodils. This exotic trade took up where kelp production and shipbuilding had died out. His heirs, who still run Tresco, then introduced luxury tourism as the islands' bread and butter, after cheaper flowers from Kenya and Holland catastrophically emptied the islands' fields of daffodils. By rolling out holiday homes across the island, Tresco's owners have erased the unscenic layers of boom and bust which on other islands are still visible in the over-grown hedges and abandoned fields.

I wonder whether, in another context, another country, the duchy's hold on this land would be viewed as a disgrace. No one knows how much the Dorrien-Smith family pays the duchy for their alleged 'thousand-year' freehold of Tresco. But on top of all the islands' rent, the prince also receives a daffodil from the Isles of Scilly Wildlife Trust, nominal tenant of one hundred uninhabited islets. It is a whimsical touch; a gesture from everything the Civil War tried to take away and everything the Restoration returned intact.

In William Strode's play *The Floating Island*, performed in front of Charles I in 1636, an island wanders around until the monarch manages to make it stand still.[35] Now, as then, these islands' fates are determined by the rule of prince and princelings.

*

2019. Late one night on the radio, I hear a piece of music, 'The Meadow 12/04/17 – 5am' by an artist, Full of Noises, who works on St Agnes in the Isles of Scilly. I write to him, explaining that I am coming to Scilly with two artist friends, Rose Gibbs and Léonie Hampton, to make a short film (which Rose later names 'Zenae', after the Gallizenae, priestesses of Sena/Scilly). Would he be interested in collaborating with us? He writes back saying yes, and inviting us to stay.

Piers Lewin moved to St Agnes with his wife, Rachel, when they were twenty-five. As a child, he attended the Royal Academy of Music, later read English at Oxford, and after that trained as a chef in London. By the time he arrived in Scilly he was completely disillusioned with the institutionalized 'insanity' of Western musical education – the hierarchy and lack of spontaneity. For ten years he ran a guesthouse on St Agnes, and never played his oboe again. Then, in 2007, he heard a band playing Cornish tunes. It was a revelation: 'The energy of the music, and the commitment to a culture.' The Isles of Scilly have no surviving indigenous music, perhaps because of being on the trade routes, and being garrisoned, and the Cornish language is thought to have died out here before it faded on the mainland (where it is now resurging. The musician Gwenno has just released her second album in Cornish, *Tresor*).

Piers embarked on a quest to express the essence of the islands in music. His 2018 album, *en plein air*, was improvised and recorded entirely outside (taking inspiration from Impressionist landscape artists), before being finished in the studio. He made a lithophone on his lawn out of stones and roofing slates, and an Aeolian harp – strings over a sound board – designed to fit at the bottom of a sash window, and to be played by the wind during a gale. He created synth pads from field recordings (bird song, wind, waves), to each of which he assigned a pitch on the keyboard so that they could be played like a piano. To make the music for our film, he sat us in his kitchen and had us chant simple phrases from the texts that inspired us; later, in the studio, he layered these vocal fragments harmonically: creating 'a choir in retrospect'.

On St Agnes we set up the camera to make a time lapse of the tide (echoes for me of Orkney, that daily drama). We filmed it on the Gugh, an island joined to St Agnes by a tombolo – as is St Ninian's Isle to Shetland – and daily severed from it by the tide – like Lindisfarne from the mainland. We were thinking about the suppression of female stories but also the imminence of sea-level rise, the tide acting as a diurnal reminder of what is already happening to fragile coastal communities everywhere in the world. Léonie began thinking of islands as emotions – islands of hate, of love. Rose was thinking of care for the world and each other.

St Agnes is an island which no longer allows cottages to be sold as holiday homes (summer migrations create winter bleakness: pricing local residents out). Alone, I walk around the ancient stone labyrinth on the cliffs. Some people think it was put there by Vikings (there are similar mazes on Scandinavian islands). The thirteenth-century Icelandic story which tells of the Norse King Olaf Tryggvason being converted to Christianity in Scilly[36] shows the islands functioning as sites as remote and romantic, in the Norse mind, as other islands had in the Greek, Roman, Celtic and Norman. Some say the labyrinth is a sacred symbol, the descendant of the spiral which Neolithic people carved on their rocks and tombs.[37] In *The Golden Bough*, James Frazer wrote that labyrinths symbolize the sun's movement across the sky, and the dance of Ariadne, invented for her by the engineer Daedalus; that British Morris dances, and the 'old British game of troy', are vestiges of the same tradition.[38] Chaucer is the first author to mention labyrinths in the English language, in 'The Legend of Ariadne'[39] ('for the hous is krynkeled to and fro, And hath so many queynte weyes for to go – For it is shapen as the mase is wrought'). On St Agnes, the nearest settlement to the labyrinth – where the farm is selling ice creams – is called Troy Town.

I loop back and forth, growing dizzy as the roar from the cliffs fills my ears. By this time much of my life has begun to feel like a maze. Whichever way I turn, I seem to run up against the same structural problem. Looking back on that era now, I can see that I found solace in the utopian literature of the Civil War and its aftermath, because it was a time of revolution and constant change, when long-held certainties were dashed away as effortlessly as the sea sculpts land. If it was in the Civil War – the era of wavering kings and princes – that the islands at last took centre stage in mainland English politics, it was also during the Civil War that the boundaries of class, privilege and gender began to dissolve, temporarily eaten away by sea salt.[40] In particular, notions of island freedoms seeped into the literature of the time, as never before, nor since, and frequently – perhaps inadvertently – these freedoms were linked to the status of women.[41]

Even before the war, lavish and out of touch though they were, King Charles and Queen Henrietta Maria had contributed, in their gilded way, to the emancipation of female voices. Female rulers, and islands ruled by women, were a theme of Royalist stagecraft. In 1632, when Henrietta Maria had Aurelian Townshend's masque *Tempe Restored* performed – about an island ruled by tyrannous Circe – she herself took the role of Divine Beauty, dressed 'in a garment of watchet sattine with stars of silver imbrodered and imbost from the ground, and on her head a crowne of stars'.[42] She hired Madame Coniack, a professional actress from France (the French were well ahead of the English in this), to play her opposite in virtue – the island witch Circe deposed at the end of the play.[43] On the very eve of war, the last masque the court would ever stage was *Salmacida Spolia* (1640), by William Davenant and Inigo Jones, in which Henrietta Maria appeared as an Amazon warrior queen; within a year she was calling herself 'Her she-majesty generalissima' and riding at the head of the Royalist troops.[44] *Tempe Restored*'s pointed theme of unstable female leadership – which was only picking up where Homer and *The Faerie Queene* had left off – continued with *The Floating Island*.

The sea, with its own unruly promise of change, seems to have entered these works of artistic expression uninvited. In 1655, during the interregnum, despite the fact that the theatres were closed, *The Floating Island* was printed with a preface which pointed out that, although it was written eighteen years before, 'it must be by Prophesie' that it fits 'these times'.[45] Despite

Cromwell's fearsome army of censors, the new rash of independent printing presses made it hard for his people to control free speech, and in particular the explicitly political newspapers, or mercuries. In 1648, while King Charles I was still alive, imprisoned on the Isle of Wight, another anti-Cromwell island play – or playlet – came off the London presses: *Craftie Cromwell*, the penultimate act of the play set on Wight itself.[46]

Isloanxiety was a theme of the age. In 1658, to get around censorship, Sir William Lower had his pastoral, *The Enchanted Lovers*, printed in The Hague; it too is set on an island, Erithrea, ruled by an unstable woman, Melissa, whose punishments cause the inhabitants such hardship that she is deposed by the goddess Diana.[47] This was all in the manner of a particular vein of 'anti-women satire', epitomized by *The Parliament of Women* (1646), or by the demonization of Pope Joan – the wicked medieval *Femina ex Anglia* (woman from England) who pretended to be a man in order to become Pope – a story popular in medieval Europe and rekindled in England during the Reformation.[48] But possibly this vein of misogyny was caused by the new emancipation of women.[49]

Women were liberated by the Civil War printing presses. They spoke, were heard and published as never before in recorded history – not just aristocratic women but those from humble backgrounds, too, such as Anna Trapnell, the preacher and self-declared prophetess.

With the Restoration, order was restored – and yet it was not; women had found their voices, islands had wandered free. For Ann Fanshawe, the sweetest and greatest glory was in the return itself: a sea crossing which re-enacted, in glorious reverse, the miserable journey that had taken her out of England to Scilly.[50] She was bitterly disillusioned, thereafter, by the venal nature of Charles II's court. Both sides had laid claim to utopia, and when these political arrangements crumbled one after the other, perhaps it was natural to seek for utopia elsewhere – far from England and its wrecked political promises. I am sure that lost paradise is the muse of Andrew Marvell's poem, 'Bermudas' (*c*.1653):

> Where the remote *Bermudas* ride
> In th' Oceans bosome unespy'd,
> From a small Boat, that row'd along,
> The listning Winds receiv'd this Song . . .
> Unto an Isle so long unknown,
> And yet far kinder than our own? . . .

Paradise is elsewhere.[51]

The key image of this age was the Halcyon, borrowed from Ovid, as Dolores Palomo argued in a brilliant essay: that of a bird floating peacefully in its nest in a becalmed sea, used by everyone from Aurelian Townshend in a 1631 *Twelfth Night* masque ('Why should this Ile above the rest, / Be made (Great Gods) the Halcyons nest?') to Marvell in 1654, celebrating the Royal Navy.[52] Everybody, everywhere, of whatever political persuasion, was desperate for peace after the storm.

Britain itself became a meek female warrior once again, as in Roman times. But real women were stormier than ever before.[53]

The Restoration channelled its disappointments into a mania for utopias, many of them based on islands.[54] Margaret Cavendish, the wife of a Royalist courtier, reacted in profligate fashion, by writing three radical plays: *The Female Academy*, set in a women's university; *Bell in Campo*, describing a women's army; and *Convent of Pleasure*, a women's beguine house.[55] This last has a play within a play, in which the two heroines, Lady Happy and the Princess (possibly a man in drag, or possibly a woman pretending to be a man pretending to be a woman), take on the roles of a Sea-Goddess and Sea-God, respectively, and sit together talking on 'a Rock in the Sea'. Lady Happy claims to be the source of the sun's power:

> I feed the Sun, which gives them light,
> And makes them shine in darkest night,
> Moist vapour from my brest I give,
> Which he sucks forth, and makes him live,
> Or else his Fire would soon go out,
> Grow dark, or burn the World throughout.[56]

It is a Maeshowe moment – one which places women's creativity and force at the centre of the play's world. Perhaps, in 1668, it could have sprung only from the bookish mind of a British woman.

The same year, Cavendish published a prose piece, *The Blazing World*, which describes how a shipwrecked woman is taken on a tour of a series of strange islands until she reaches the 'Imperial City, named *Paradise*, which appeared in form like several Islands'. The Lady is brought before the Emperor:

> but he conceived her to be some Goddess, and offered to worship her . . . the Emperor, rejoycing, made her his Wife, and gave her an absolute power to rule and govern all that World as she pleased.[57]

I loved this passage when I first read it – as if Cavendish had read my mind. Why, though? Did I want to rule? Or did it function merely as an electric shock from the past, awakening me from my slumber? I was experiencing my own, internal civil war; wondering whether or not the illness in my marriage had a cure. Representations of radical female freedom made me question how liberated I was – whether I had any power to govern, or whether the agency I had was discrete, isolated and ultimately weak.

Then I discovered another text, a faux travelogue published anonymously in Dublin in 1682, and my surprise deepened. Entitled *A Discovery of Fonseca in a Voyage to Surranam*, it claims to be a description of 'The Island so long sought for in the Western Ocean. Inhabited by Women with the Account of their Habits, Customs and Religion':

> & coming near they saw coming towards them about fifty women armed with bowes and quivers . . . she spake to them but they could not understand each other till at length Mr Greenwood and the rest coming up understood and answering her again in the welsh.

The island is an expatriate colony from ancient Britain. Its political arrangement is dominated by women, for 'our people agreed not to let any men remain above a month on the Isle nor male child above four months'. This 'straight handsom people', with well-ordered houses and neatly embroidered coloured silk garments are moon-worshippers, 'according to the custom of the Ancient *Brittains*'. Although their rivers run with gold, they do not extract these riches but leave them to nature.

This perhaps, is the apotheosis of everything that has gone before. A self-sufficient female community, combining the ancient thinking of Britain before the Romans with the feminist paradise that other texts have hinted of subsequently, plus a counter-Christian ecological awareness – in a place away from Britain. Maybe that was what I longed for.

The importance of these texts does not lie in any reality they purport to represent but in the simple fact of women being *seen*. It is disturbing how easy it has been, throughout all our different societies and cultures and epochs, for women to go unseen, unheard. What texts like *The Blazing World* and *Convent of Pleasure* do, is make sure that it is impossible to turn away one's gaze from women. (She-who-looks-out, The Watcher.)

The disturbing thing for me is that it was only through the process of researching these books that I finally saw myself. Even if I did not want to dominate, nevertheless, in these portraits of independent women, in control of their own worlds, I found solace and example. I saw an example of my possible freedom, the sea-change I longed for.

These texts grew out of the turmoil of the Civil War. They are thought-provoking fantasies, not manifestos. I am still grateful to them. They made me reflect on turmoil's capacity for peace; made me question whether change can stir up the seas into something new and better; forced me to embark on a quest for what feels right – rather than accepting what you know to be wrong – even if the journey is painful and causes sorrow.

PART FOUR

Womanly Forms, Having Been Co-opted, Are Reclaimed

The sea was the giant woman of the planet, fluid and contrary.
All the men shuddered as they gazed at her surface.

Monique Roffey, *The Mermaid of Black Conch*, 2020

I R I S H   S E A

Man

Tax (eighteenth century)

The Isle of Man, Ellan Vannin, sits alone in the sea between Ireland, Scotland, England, too large to miss, yet easy to ignore. Despite the efforts of monks, Vikings, excise men – and money-launderers – it can defy romance. Especially in November: the summer is over; all is grey; as grey as the abandoned concrete buildings, constructed for long-lost tourists (the dance-hall crowds John Betjeman describes in 1951),[1] which deface the island's coastal places. For about a century, from the late 1600s, the island briefly became famous on account of all the money it was making (and taking) from Britain. Then it subsided into quiet respectability again. That, at least, was the impression I had got from reading books about it in British Library. I had arrived – prejudiced by eighteenth-century outrage against this overly independent backwater – but ready to be swayed.

The evidence was there in the archives: excise-evasion changed the island's fortunes. Man once belonged to England, but in 1405, during dinner, Henry IV gave it away to one of his friends. Before that, it was in the possession of Scotland; further back still, it was part of the Viking Kingdom of the Isles. Even after England took it, the Church (which owned a third of the island's arable land) maintained ties to Ireland and Scotland through its benefices.[2] From 1405 to 1765 the island was ruled by the 'Lords of Man' – the Stanleys, from Lancashire, later Earls of Derby, later still Dukes of Atholl, from Scotland, the usual aristocratic titular cornucopia. It is to Old Irish that the Manx owe their Gaelic tongue; from Viking times that they trace their ancient parliamentary assembly, Tynwald;[3] to Britain that they owe their conflicted identity.

Until the late seventeenth century, Man was a poor island, like many others. The non-resident owners, the Stanley family, seemed to have liked the very grand title the island bequeathed them – as 'King' or later 'Lord' of Man – and the 'provisions' such as beef with which it furnished them. During the Middle Ages the island exported cattle and horses in some numbers.[4] But the general population probably didn't eat beef, as a rule; they survived by fishing, and other economic activity 'generally conducted at a level only slightly above that of subsistence'.[5] *Circa* 1643, the Seventh Earl of Derby was supposed to have lamented that 'This Isle will never flourish until some trading be.'[6]

Either the earl was prophetic, or he was already dabbling: for very soon, with the rise in the new global trade in luxury goods from the colonies, 'some trading' came about. Necessity met opportunity: the island was in the perfect position, geographically (at the heart of the four nations), and constitutionally (in theory, free of them all). Man was transformed into a fulcrum of international commerce. Being an independent country, it could set its own customs duties – and it kept them low. Joseph Train, in his 1845 *History of the Isle of Man*, fingered 'a large company of adventurers from Liverpool' who settled at Douglas (the new capital) after 1700.[7] Whoever they were, from wherever, soon the whole island was in on the game. It made complete sense. Dutch-, French- and Spanish-registered ships docked here in preference to Britain (just as multinationals now use Man, Bermuda and Cayman). Because Man was independent, this was not a crime. But the ships did not unload their booty for Manx fishermen to consume. When the tides were right, and the excise men were looking the other way, goods were smuggled across the water.

George Waldron, posted to the Isle of Man for 'near' twenty years, wrote a description of it which was published posthumously in 1731.[8] Waldron was a British patriot.[9] His *Description of the Isle of Man*, written in that not-so-innocent interlude between the smugglers moving in to the island and the British authorities taking back control, is telling for what it includes and what it leaves out. He observes the blatant juxtaposition of underdeveloped Douglas – the main port – and all the 'very rich and eminent Dealers' clustered around '*Dutch, Irish,* and *East India* Vessels'. He notes that although 'his most Excellent Majesty of *Great Britain* is Master of the Seas, yet the *Lord of Man* has the Jurisdiction of so much round the Island', for 'in this Place there is little Danger in infringing on the Rights of the Crown'. He describes the 'stately' entrance into Douglas of a smugglers' ship – which unloads 'Indico, Mastic, Raisins of the Sun, and other very rich Goods' 'without the least Duty paid to his Majesty'[10] – and duly reports the ship to the authorities. He voices little direct criticism of islanders, however. Waldron is more interested in island history, commenting on the plethora of tongues on display in local graveyards, testimony to the 'Diversity of Nations' by which 'this little Spot of Earth has been possess'd'.[11]

But thanks, perhaps, to officials such as Waldron reporting on pirates, the powers that be in Westminster soon became enraged by the island's role in the running trade – and wouldn't let the matter drop. An official report, 'Observations upon the antient state, and rise of the trade of the Isle of Mann', unsigned and undated – but presumed to have been authored between 1721 and 1736 – described how

> When the Crown of England Granted this Isle of Mann to Sir John Stanley and Established the same in his ffamily with the Rights Prerogatives & Privilleges thereof, that particular relating its trade, was then so very inconsiderable, and thought to be so little consequence to the Interest of Brittaine, that it was not possible for human foresight to comprehend, it would ever be carryd to that heigth, to become so obnoxious to that Governmt as now it appeared to the world to be.[12]

Until the eighteenth century, the island modestly bartered 'Exportations of their own product, Growth & Manufacture as Corn, Cattle, Hides, Linnen and Wool Cloath, Herrings, Beeze, Fish, Butter . . . with the English, Irish, Scotts for Timber, Iron,

Coales, Pitch, Salt, Hopps & such the Comoditys as they stood most in need of for their necessary Subsistence . . .' – and (this being the important point), 'whatsoever wines happened to be Imported was wholy for the use & Consumption of this Island itself, and not carryed any where abroad'. But all this changed with the overseas trade in 'Wines, Brandy, Tobbacco's'. As soon as it came to the attention of the government in London that these products were being 'plentifully Imported not for the Consumption of this Island as formerly, but on purpose to be sent off again', two officers were dispatched 'into this Island to detect this fraud'. They found, as Waldron had, that the 'Earle of Derby's Govntmt Officers & others . . . were being unwilling to allow the King any authority at all, in this Isle of Mann', and so a notion began 'gradually' to be 'intertained' 'that the Earl of Derby was King in Mann, and that the King of England had nothing to do with it'. (The points are so similar that maybe Waldron was the author.)

Then, as now, the island asserted its independence from Britain, with the king's revenue officers soon coming to blows with the Earl of Derby (or Duke of Atholl)'s men. There was the occasion of 26 June 1750 – detailed in incensed eighteenth-century handwriting for the benefit of the Commissioners of his Majesty's Customs – when Captain Dow boarded an Irish smuggling wherry and 'after rummaging of him found concealed in a jar of Buttermilk twenty five Guineas English tyed up in a Bagg & also papers showing that the said Moneys were to be laid out in Brandys Teas &cs and that he was then to sojourn with his Cargoe to Ireland'. But the smugglers fought back:

a Tumultuous & riotous Mobb . . . came down upon the Key arm'd with Bludgoons Musquotts Swords and Stones endeavoured to force the said Cruizer on Shore by assaulting the said Cruizers Men with Showers of Stones.

Captain Dow 'desired them in his Majestys Name to disperse themselves but they not minding of him continued to throw Stones'.

They seized some of his crew, carrying them onshore to Castletown Castle, where they locked them up, refusing to release them until the money had been returned. Smugglers, along with the island authorities, were acting as one united front against the English.

On 6 August 1750, Thomas Foley, back in Millbank, wrote to his superiors to complain in exceedingly forceful terms of

> how prejudicial it must be to the Revenues of these Kingdoms to Suffer a small island so conveiniently [*sic*] situated between the three, Inhabited chiefly by Vagrants Rebells to his Majesty & outlawed Smugglers.[13]

In particular, the British authorities feared damage to the 'East India trade' – that is, to the East India Company itself, the hugely profitable business of which was in selling tea and other Indian goods into Europe. Already, on 24 June 1721, an act had been passed in London which specifically targeted the islands off the mainland of Britain. It ruled that

> No Commodity of the Growth of the East Indies shall be Imported or Carried into the Kingdom of Ireland the Island of Jersey Guernsey Alderney Sark or Man &c. – but only such as shall be bona fide & without fraud loaden & Shipt in Great Britain.[14]

But British merchants encouraged smuggling. Since legally acquired tea was 'impossibly expensive', 'England was fast becoming a nation of tea drinkers', only thanks to smugglers who used Shetland, Guernsey and especially the Isle of Man.[15]

Soon, there was uproar on the 'mainland' (as the British call it; 'across', or the 'other island' is how it is known in Man).[16] *Gentleman's Magazine* termed Man a 'great STOREHOUSE or MAGAZINE for the French'. *London Magazine* shrieked that 'this Island may be looked upon as a fortress in the hands of our enemies'.[17] The rumour in London was that the loss to the Exchequer was £700,000 per annum. A general notion began to establish itself – English tabloid indignation – that the insular treasonous Manx were a 'nest of smugglers', sheltering 'bankrupts, thieves, rebels and murderers outlawed from three kingdoms'.[18]

Buoyed by public feeling, MPs in Westminster drew up the Revestment Act (or 'Manx Mischief', as it was colloquially known). In 1765, the Lord of Man relinquished his rights to the island to the Crown for £70,000 – in what amounted to a forced sale, though some say Westminster was ripped off, for the Atholls got to keep their landed estates, manorial rights, ecclesiastical patronage, and received an annuity of what would be £200,000 today (plus the one-off seventy grand, which equates to a neat £7 million).[19] The British monarch became, and still is, 'Lord of Mann'.[20] (Queen Victoria, unlike Elizabeth II, chose to be 'Lady of Man'.)[21]

Like it or not, the island never really shook off its disreputable reputation. Edmund Burke called it 'the very citadel of smuggling' in 1774.[22] When Walter Scott came to write his second novel, *Guy Mannering* (1815), he placed the Isle of Man at the centre of a web of wrongdoing:

> Smuggling, for which the Isle of Man then afforded peculiar facilities, was general, or rather universal, all along the southwestern coast of Scotland. Almost all the common people were engaged in these practices; the gentry connived at them.[23]

For most British people, Man's Revestment meant the end to a cheap drink (and thrill). In his 1798 *A Tour through the Isle of Man*, John Feltham quoted a laconic song:

> All the babes unborn will rue the day
> That the Isle of Man was sold away;
> For there's ne'er an old wife that loves a dram
> But what will lament for the Isle of Man.[24]

In the island itself, the 'running trade' had been a way of life. The 'comeover' bishop, Thomas Wilson, wrote anxiously in 1742 that the

Manx were enlarging the harbours at Peel, Ramsay and Douglas, and feared that 'the iniquitous trade carried on, to the injury and damage of the Crown, will hinder the blessing of God from falling upon us'.[25] But it had benefitted most Manx, allowing them to make enough money to change their prospects. A Manx fisherman could buy his wife a new dress; businessmen could buy respectability; a shipping merchant from Liverpool might purchase an estate and his daughter's marriage to someone titled.

Still, it is rare to hear islanders embracing this aspect of their history today. The Isle of Man plays up its status as an independent country ('the nation's station', goes the jingle on Manx Radio), and when Britain was part of the EU it had a 'special relationship' via 'Protocol 3',[26] allowing free trade even though it wasn't a member: the very small number of Isle of Man passports claimed by true-born Manx were stamped 'not permitted to work in the EU'.[27] So it is perhaps strange that the defiant, independent part of their eighteenth-century history has not become a point of pride, as in Cornwall or the Isle of Wight. Instead, there is amnesia, or embarrassment. A culturally defining history of tax-dodging is perhaps too close to the bone.

For example, the eighteenth-century financier George Quayle is celebrated for having established the island's first bank. He sat as a respected, influential member of the House of Keys – the island's parliament of 'twenty-four good men' ('keys' is said to be an English garbling of *kiare as feed*, the Manx word for twenty-four). But the source of Quayle's wealth lay tucked away in another house, on the coast, at a discreet distance from the capital. The house was built pre-Revestment and still stands on a narrow wooded hill, unfrequented but for the ravens overhead. There are anti-trespassing signs up on the gate and a miniature railway in the formal gardens. The glen leads down to the secluded harbour at Port Soderick, where, for safety, Quayle had his boat fitted with a set of cannon. His fortune was kept under lock and key in the house itself. Here were the sumptuous goods which made him rich: Spanish lace, American tobacco, Indian silk, Jamaican rum, Chinese tea.

Today you can visit the house in Castletown where Quayle lived with his family and see the remains of his boat, *Peggy*. You can walk past the house that he used as a bank. You can visit the ancient institution which, like that of Sweden and New Zealand, claims to have been the first in the world to allow women the right to vote, in 1880; and was also the last in Western Europe to legalize homosexuality, in 1992 (though it recently won praise from Peter Tatchell of Stonewall for its progressive equal marriage laws); only abolished the death sentence in 1993; and was also the place which birthed the man, Abdullah Quilliam, who established Britain's first mosque, in Liverpool (in that brief nineteenth-century epoch when it was fashionable to convert to Islam).[28] But as far as smuggling goes, there is nothing to direct you to the more significant part of Quayle's history out in the glen.

As Waldron and others pointed out, Douglas grew in stature because its harbour was better than Castletown's for large cargo boats. As late as 1880, Brown's *Directory* records that 'narrow winding streets . . . innumerable openings and passages, and the great rambling houses with their vast storage spaces . . . were all constructed to facilitate the landing and storing of goods'. Very little of the old town is left. Down on the quay is a tall building which was once owned by the firm of Black, Ross and Christian, 'who traded pre-Revestment' (that is, they were smugglers). The building had a huge hidden space at the back for smuggled goods. It too is covered in scaffolding and crawls with men in hard hats, being renovated for offices.

At the Isle of Man Antiquarian Society I was told that smuggling was mostly done by 'comeovers' (Liverpudlians are the ones they blame). Or that families who made money from smuggling 'sold up and left to become landed gentry elsewhere'. (George Quayle went to the south of England.) In 1860, when J. F. Campbell (who published *Popular Tales of the West Highlands*) tried to collect some Manx Gaelic tales, he found that 'The Manxman would not trust the foreigner with his secrets; his eye twinkled suspiciously, and his hand seemed unconsciously to grasp his mouth, as if to keep all fast.'[29] Why should they trust him, or any foreigner? Or me?

But somebody at the Antiquarian Society introduces me to Peter Farrant, a venerable and voluble old widower with a smuggling history which he is happy to share. We meet at his home out in the countryside, where he tells me about his great-great-great-great grandfather, William Farrant, who was a carpenter and cooper. Pre-Revestment, William was employed by the Lords of Man to repair their ships and residence at Castle Rushen. But he also made the metal-bound barrels which were sent out empty with the slave ships to Virginia and Jamaica and returned full of rum. As a skilled craftsman, Farrant's services were increasingly in demand from smugglers like Quayle; soon he was flush enough to dabble in land. Wealthy by the time of Revestment, he married well, wooing the daughter of the island's archdeacon. A good marriage needs a good home: in the mid-1750s Farrant paid £92 for Bagnio House, a fine dwelling with gardens which stretched as far as the moat of Castle Rushen. The 'bath-house' was once the castle brothel. But it, like the cooper and his island, experienced a moment of transition. Farrant made his money by working with smugglers; his son Robert became Collector of Customs and married an heiress.

For the Farrants, smuggling-money bought respectability. But after smuggling was banned and did a midnight flit elsewhere, there was poverty anew on the island – or emigration. The Channel Islands picked up a lot of Man's former smuggling trade;[30] according to Frances Wilkins, who has written numerous books on the subject, smugglers into the coast of Galway, for example, merely took greater risks, in bigger boats, with more violent crews.[31]

A letter of March 1788 from the Collector of Customs in Liverpool to the Board reveals the frustration of officials at the continuation of smuggling: 'a great part of the tobacco which is exported from this kingdom to the Isle of Man, after being manufactured there is fraudulently re-landed'.[32] For those who could emigrate, smuggling was a transferable skill, and there were success stories elsewhere – such as that of 'François Thurot, one of the most famous Manx smugglers', who 'rose to command [a] French naval squadron', or John Paul Jones, 'who had learned his skills among the local smugglers, [and] went on to help found the American Navy'.[33]

There are also more horrible legacies. Wilkins examined the Manx role in the slave trade out of Africa, post-Revestment, and concluded that 'slaving subsidized smuggling'. She estimates that there were up to fifty Manx captains of slave ships.[34] At Liverpool and other places in England, ships were loaded up with goods such as cowries and brass pans and gunpowder, and, with a crew of Manx sailors, set off for West Africa, where the shells were traded for people. After selling their human cargo into Jamaica and South Carolina, the ships returned to the Isle of Man, stocked high with rum for selling into Britain. The Manx captain Ambrose Lace made eight such journeys, between 1754 and 1768, transporting around three hundred slaves from West Africa each time.[35]

Captain Hugh Crow, born in the island's northern town of Ramsey in the year of Revestment, 1765, justified his life as a slave-ship captain in his memoirs, which were published (according to instructions in his will) after his death, in 1830. He writes of the natural 'inclination for a sea-faring life', growing up in a seaport town;[36] and then, quite explicitly, of overcoming his 'abhorrence' for – thus partaking in – the slave trade from the coast of Africa. He made thirteen slave-ship voyages, seven as captain, from 1790 to 1807 (when the Slave Trade Act was passed in Britain).[37] He writes of the practical measures he undertook with regard to sanitation and over-crowding – in order to produce saleable cargo at the end of the voyage. The horrific nature of the trade he was part of runs through every sentence:

> We frequently bought from the natives considerable quantities of dried shrimp to make broth . . . I am thus particular in describing the ingredients which composed the food of the blacks, to show that no attention to their health was spared in this respect . . . About eleven, if the day was fine, they washed their bodies all over, and wiping themselves dry, were allowed to use palm oil, their favourite

cosmetic . . . I considered that on keeping the ship clean and orderly, which was always my hobby, the success of our voyage mainly depended.[38]

For most Manx, the era post-Revestment merely brought economic depression. Only from the mid-nineteenth century did the Isle of Man recover by becoming 'a playground for holiday makers from the industrial North' – and later, a centre of tax evasion.[39]

The effect of Revestment wasn't just economic. 'Colonization by Britain made us into a secretive people,' Annie Kissack, who set up Bunscoill Ghaelgagh, the island's first Manx-medium primary school, told me. 'We are ashamed of who we are. That's how the language died out. Our grandparents thought speaking English was better.' Annie and her husband, Phil Gawne, who, when I first met him, was the Isle of Man's Environment Minister, have become some of the island's more successful 'neo-native' Manx speakers. They set out to reintroduce the Manx language following the death of the last native speaker in 1974. Gawne believes that here, as elsewhere (in the Western Isles, for example), British rule has resulted in cultural schizophrenia: 'Language death alone is enough to screw up the generations.'

As on other small islands, one man must wear many hats, and Gawne worked as a farmer, accountant and teacher before going into politics. It was his accountancy work which made him a militant Manx nationalist. By the 1960s, the Isle of Man was so desperate for revenue that it had become a low-tax jurisdiction. Immediately, the island was flooded – not with smugglers this time – but with British millionaires, retirees from empire and other 'people who brought their money over and lived off it without taking part in island life'. In 1988, aged twenty-three, in an act of nationalist fervour, Gawne set fire to an 'ugly' new development built by a tax-avoider and was sent to jail for sixteen months. His own tastes run to the traditional (and ecological): he helped set up the Manx Model Farm and ploughs the lovely fields around his house with the aid of a horse.

It must indeed be galling to live and work like this, as a Manx person, and to see the lawyers and, even worse, money-hiding come-overs, living in their luxurious bubbles. Some of the island's real estate is no joke. There have been properties on the market in the Isle of Man for £30 million – the type with heli-pads and panic rooms, alongside jacuzzis and bathrooms lined top to toe with marble.

Gawne's popularity with the Manx may have been due to his early militancy; for although the island depends on its low-tax status for income, some Manx seem to consider it dishonourable, even tragic. Westminster sporadically makes flashy gestures, putting pressure on Tynwald to conform to its rules on tax avoidance – in 2013, the *Financial Times* was reporting that 'Britons hiding money in the Isle of Man have three years to come clean or face penalties of up to 200 per cent of unpaid tax.'[40] But the island still functions as a tax haven. The people who ardently defend tax avoidance are the comeovers from Britain. At the Manx National Museum, I had a lunch of queenies (a small local scallop) with an English-woman who has avoided tax all her working life. 'The Channels, Cayman Islands, we islands stick together as tax-avoidance jurisdictions. These aren't dirty words; it is something to celebrate,' she said. 'My business is registered in Jersey. I pay no tax and never have. On the day London forced Man to stop being a tax haven my daughter stayed up seventy-two hours to reroute her clients' money. She works with doctors and dentists mostly; lawyers and accountants know how to manage these things themselves. Now no money touches Isle of Man banks. But the paperwork goes through here.'

A retired couple at the neighbouring table, he in a tweed blazer, she with a bouffant hair-do and pearls, leaned over and said, 'She's right. Barclays and all the other big banks take part in tax avoidance. Tax avoidance is our right.'

2022. Eight years pass before I return to the Isle of Man. I am so glad I went back.

The first time I visited I was married, with only one child; I hadn't yet moved to Orkney and felt the beauty and rhythms of the islands change me. Between that first visit and this, almost everything had changed (for worse, for better). The necessary crisis in my life had occurred. My husband and I had had a conversation of truth, and now we were no longer married.

And in the meantime the island had lodged itself like a flint in my mind, adamantine, stubborn, the trickiest of islands – secretive, perplexing, contradictory.

Coming back to the island, I see only beauty – the huge dark hills, the glittering sea, the bright bursts of golden gorse (Spanish and Manx). I return to the Viking crosses in the north, some carved, bethedgingly, with Odin and the wolf at the Battle of Ragnorok on one side, and on the other with the Bible and a cross. Others are signed in runes by Norsemen and women who hailed from all over the place, including, of course, the Hebrides ('son of Bjorn from Coll').[41]

Up at the very northern edge of the island, where the closeness of land to sea gives the sensation of being a meniscus, one drop from overflowing, I walk with a Manxman, Dave Martin, across his farmland. The expanse of ocean stretches away before us, as he demonstrates the island's ancient and complex interaction of faiths and cultures by showing me, first, the site of a *keeil* (chapel), with its very early (AD 450) bilingual dedication stone, in Ogham and Latin, and then, up on the highest point, the site of a Viking boat from half a millennium later. The boat burial was excavated, in 1927, by the legendary Manx archaeologist P. M. C. Kermode: a working boat, thirty feet long, with a horse under the bow, and a bowl containing blood, and a dog, and a body wrapped in a cloak. The boat's exact outline was denoted by its three hundred iron rivets (a complete set), one of which the family was allowed to keep. They were also given a replica of the bronze Viking cloak pin, with a very faint Celtic cross on each side of the head, which Dave's granddad had picked up from his field only 'to save the sheep from stomach ache'.

I drive right down to the south of the island, to see Annie and Phil again. Since my last trip to the island, Annie's poetry has made her the island's fifth Manx Bard and Phil has stopped being Environment Minister and is spending time singing with his Manx band, and in

Annie's Manx Gaelic choir. I listen one night in the Arbory parish hall as Annie rehearses the choir, Caarjyn Cooidjagh ('Friends Together'). They practise old folk songs and new compositions. I ache to hear their singing; Manx has a soft mellifluousness to it that I am not expecting. And then, there is everything I can't understand, linguistically, and the beauty that registers at some other level entirely.

There is a lot of emphasis, in Manx culture, on singing. Earlier in the day, Annie showed me *Skeealyn Vannin / Stories of Mann*, a transcription of the 1948 recordings by the Irish Folklore Commission – in an act of pan-Celtic camaraderie – just as Manx was dying out in the island. This linguistic salvation was the result of an unscheduled visit to Man by the then Irish Taoiseach Éamon de Valera, during a boat holiday in 1947. While there, he met and conversed with Ned Maddrell, 'De Valera speaking Irish and Ned speaking Manx' – the two tongues are mutually comprehensible.[42] De Valera subsequently sent over his state-of-the-art recording van to help 'in the rounding up of the stragglers of the Manx oral tradition'. The compilation is interlaced with funeral dirges, rhymes and stories unique to different parts of the island, and also includes recordings of the twenty remaining speakers of Manx, most of whom had deliberately failed to pass their language on to their children and grandchildren.

As with many non-mainstream British cultures, the attempt to record, save and preserve Manx happened when it was almost too late. A purely oral language until the seventeenth century, it was written down for the very first time only in 1610, when the Welsh bishop John Phillips translated the *Book of Common Prayer* into Manx, but this wasn't printed for another century. Bishop Wilson came up with the orthography in the eighteenth century. Because there were very few other published works in Manx, the religious ones took on undue weight.[43] In 1896, T. E. Brown, a poet of Anglo-Manx who became the island's first unofficial laureate, wrote that 'It is impossible to overestimate the baleful effects upon our song literature of the Church discipline as maintained by Bishops Barrow and Wilson.'[44]

Then there was the contemptuous attitude of outsiders – particularly the English, who didn't understand the language and tended to be customarily rude about it in the usual arrogant way. John Feltham, visiting in 1797, commented that 'The enlightened Manksman, if he is fond of his native language, must lament the barrenness of its literary field, and the almost daily disuse of his mother tongue.' Samuel Johnson called Manx 'the speech of a people who have few thoughts to express'.[45] As neither had Manx, it is a wonder they thought to express themselves thus.

Somehow, the Manx kept their language alive – folk songs were their Bible. Annie herself began singing with the legendary Manx song collector Mona Douglas when she was a teenager; she shows me a picture of Mona aged seventy and she aged seventeen, outside Mona's cottage in the island. Before coming to the island for the second time, I had listened to Annie's rendition of the 'The Smuggler's Lullaby' in the British Library sound archive (a song, which, she tells me, is largely Mona's creation):

See! the Excise men are coming (Sleep, my little hero!)
They'll be seeking wine and whisky (Sleep my little hero!) . . .
Daddy's late, and we must warn him (Sleep my little hero!)
This run, he'll have naught illegal (Sleep my little hero!)
O, the English-men may board us (Sleep my little hero!) . . .
Nothings in the hold but herrings.[46]

Mona based her rendition of 'The Smuggler's Lullaby' on the historian A. W. Moore's 1896 *Manx Ballads and Music* – for he, she wrote, was 'one of our pioneer folk-song enthusiasts'. Her publications of Manx folk songs allude freely to the island's pagan past – with songs such as 'Geay Jeh'n Aer' ('The Sea Invocation) calling upon 'the sea-deity known in the Hebrides' as 'Shony', and as 'Shonest' in the Isle of Man. (If not Sláine in Rathlin.) There is a song, 'Tappagyn Jiargey' ('Red Top-knots'), about the battle between the King and Queen of Winter and Summer, and another, 'Berrey Dhone' ('Brown Berrey'), about a famous witch – Annie has a version of this one too.

The Manx have a musical form called carvals – redemption songs based on Old Testament sources – as well as 'Carval Drogh Vraane' ('Carol of the Bad Women'), which Mona and others published:

> And let no woman rule you
> For Woman is accursed . . .
> The Scriptures tell how women
> Are wild as beasts of prey –
> How like a fiery dragon
> They take their wicked way.[47]

The misogyny reminded me of George Waldron's surprisingly frank and widespread discussion of the treatment of women in the island in his 1731 book. Waldron described several tragic stories, beginning with Eleanor, wife of the Duke of Gloucester (heir presumptive to the throne), who was imprisoned in the island after having been tried in Westminster for necromancy. In 1441 she was accused 'of associating with Wizards and Witches' – specifically with Margery Jourdemayne, the Witch of Eye, from whom she admitted to obtaining potions (to get pregnant). Margery was later burned at the stake for witchcraft; Shakespeare mentions her in *Henry VI Part 2*. Eleanor was carried to the island by Sir John Stanley, Lord of Man. Because she 'appeared so impatient and turbulent under this Confinement', Waldron writes (that is, she tried to escape), she was locked up in Peel Castle, the chapel-dungeon of which was, 'one of the most dreadful Places that Imagination can form, the Sea runs under it thro' the Hollows of the Rock with such a continual Roar, that you would think it were every Moment breaking in upon you, and over it are the Vaults for burying the Dead'.[48] Later she was conveyed to the island of Anglesey, where she died in 1452.

Waldron can't have known this – since his work was published posthumously in 1731[49] – but Eleanor's fate was meted out to a contemporary of his, Rachel Chiesley, Lady Grange, who was kidnapped and transported to Hirta, St Kilda, by her adulterous husband. She spoke no Gaelic, the islanders no English; she wandered the shore, drinking whisky. Like Eleanor, she was moved from island to island, dying in Skye, after some fifteen years of captivity.

In his book Waldron also told the story of the nunnery (now a wedding venue) which later provided refuge for Cartesmunda, fleeing the violence of King John. Waldron was unusually alert to the sinister and cruel aspect of these stories. Perhaps he was a good husband; certainly, his own widow's preface to his collected works is very tender. He tells of the unique island punishment meted out to transgressive nuns, who were 'brought to the Foot of this Rock, when the Sea was out, and obliged to climb to the first Chair, where she sat until the tide had twice ebbed and flowed'; and again to a second level; and a third. 'In my Opinion,', Waldron writes

> besides the Danger of climbing the ragged and steep Rock (which now very few Men can do above thirty or forty Paces) the extreme Cold when you come to any Height, the Horror of being exposed to all the Fury of the Elements, and the horrid Prospect of the Sea, roaring thro' a thousand Cavities, and foaming round you on every side, is enough to stagger the firmest Resolution and Courage.

Although this now seems unlikely, there were other similar punishments for women at the time. In his book on Manx prisons, N. D. Quilliam writes that 'The sentence of death of a woman other than for witchcraft was to be put into a sack and cast into the sea', and only in 1733 was 'Dragging behind a boat in Castletown harbour' abolished.[50]

Mermaid-mania was at its height in Britain at the time, and Waldron duly describes the capture of a mermaid, reprising the same language that he used to describe the confinement of Eleanor. The mermaid, despite being 'used very tenderly, nothing but Liberty being denied' refuses to speak. Her captors know she can talk; the silent protest works. They let her go.

He also notes that during the interregnum:

few or no ships resorted to this Island, and that Uninterruption and Solitude of the Sea, gave the Mermen and Mermaids (who are Enemies to any Company but those of their own Species) frequent Opportunities of visiting the Shore, where, in moonlight Nights, they have been to sit, combing their Heads, and playing with each other.

This poignant description of a sea free from human interference is prescient of the peace experienced by dolphins and other sea mammals during the recent lockdown – and their distress when it ended. In July 2020, after shipping returned to the Bay of Gibraltar, orcas began butting the boats which passed through that stretch of water. They have continued doing so. Noise pollution in the seas is a known cause of cetacean disturbance; whales that live around the busy waters of the British Isles are said to experience less reproductive success because of the difficulties of communicating with each other.[51] One scientist described the noise of the seas (big game fishing, whale watching, fast ferries) as a form of trauma, with whales and dolphins having to communicate with each other by shouting at the top of their voices.[52] Shamefully, these waters are no longer the 'whale-burdened' seas of Horace's description.

Waldron's surprising book ends with a reflection on the very 'little Complaisance' paid to 'the Weaker Sex' in the Isle of Man – for example, men commonly ride to market in comfort and ease, whereas women make the same journey barefoot through bogs and rough terrain. 'I wonder that these Creatures can ever taste any Felicity in Love . . . in a Climate so Uncourteous to their Sex,' he writes; and yes, it is a wonder, not just here, but everywhere that women are and have been so ill used.

Waldron puts the mistreatment down to the story of an Enchantress, who came to the island and 'by her diabolical Arts, made herself appear so lovely in the Eyes of Men, that she ensnared the Hearts of as many as beheld her'. The result was a kind of love-fuelled re-wilding of the island:

they entirely neglected their usual Occupations . . . their Gardens were all overgrown with Weeds, and their once fertile Fields were covered with Stones; their Cattle died for want of Pasture, their Turf lay in the Bowels of the Earth undug for.

The Enchantress, riding on her milk-white Palfrey, led six hundred men of the island into the middle of a river, where she drowned them all. She then flew off as a bat, while the palfrey dived into the sea, becoming a porpoise. This story seems to be a misogynist reprisal of the *Voyage of Bran*, giving vent to the deep and violent fear of female domination which has haunted our culture for so long.

Perhaps these misogynist stories are a given on an island with a name (in English) like Man. While staying on the island, one night at supper in the north, I enquire of my hosts as to the etymology of the island's name.[53] In 1798, when John Feltham published his *Tour through the Island of Mann*, he described how the word 'Man' came 'from the Saxon word *Mang*, signifying among [the surrounding kingdoms]' but that,

> others suppose the word to originate from Maune, the name of
> St Patrick, the apostle of the island, before he assumed that of
> Patricius. By Caesar it is called Mona; by the inhabitants, Man-
> ning; and by people in general Man.[54]

At the dinner table is a former curator at the Manx Museum archives; the next day in the library, she kindly pulls up an article for me from *Manx Miscellanies*, published by J. M. Jeffcott in 1880, 'Mann, Its Names and their Origin'. Jeffcott speculates that '*môn* = isolated'; that Mann (Mona) may 'denote a mountainous, heathy, or peaty expanse'; or 'originated in mean = middle . . . middle island'; or 'may have been derived from Mannus, the Teutonic deity'. He quotes Revd Cummings – it says a lot about the Victorian arrangement of the Anglican Church that vicars so often double up as antiquarians – who first speculated that the name derived 'from *maen*, a pile of stones or rocks'; then that it

> had to do with the reputed holy character of the isle, as the *Sedes Druidarum*, the abode of the holy wise men, and that it has the same connection with the Sanskrit root *Mân*, in reference to *religious knowledge*, as our word *monk*.'[55]

The reverend tried out various analogous words from Sanskrit and other languages – *Moonshee, Manu, Menu, Minos, Menes* – but for Jeffcott a Britannic dialect was more tempting; the island's name must, he thought, have something to do with the 'fabled enchanter' Mannann beg Mac y Leah, 'who could hide the little island in a disguise of magic fog'.

None of these vicars, doctors or antiquarians quote the theory which – luckily for me – I had already come across in Barbara Walker's *Women's Encyclopaedia of Myths and Secrets*. Her entry for MAN made me laugh out loud:

> In the original old Norse, *man* meant 'woman'.[56]

I had brought the book with me to the island, and looked at it now and again for reassurance:

> The Isle of Man was formerly sacred to the Moon-goddess, who was sometimes a mermaid or an androgynous Aphrodite . . . Apparently the Isle of Man used to be a sacred Isle of the Dead . . . The Goddess or God Mana-Anna, or Mananan, was masculinized as a "Son of Lir" . . . the same as Shakespeare's *King Lear*.[57]

King Lear was first published in 1608, only three years before the first Manx *Book of Common Prayer*. I had long been turning it over in my head – Shakespeare's choice of this ancient, patriarchal leader of Britain as the subject of his play – and it was for this reason that I took refuge in it, late one night after a dinner party in the west of the island with some very rich comeovers (one claimed to be descended from the Dukes of Atholl) whose relentless conversation about their money and this island and the world outside shocked and depressed me. Just the rhythm of those sentences helped, their familiarity, their always-anarchic beauty:

> Meantime we will express our darker purposes.
> The map there.
> Know we have divided
> In three our kingdom . . .
> Tell me, my daughters,
> Which of you shall we say doth love us most.

It is exactly from Lear's arrogant objection to Cordelia's inability to express her thoughts in speech that the tragedy of the play unfolds. And yet *King Lear* is written in the language of oppression and colonization which is English.

Walker is right that the Isle of Man has since ancient times been associated with the mythical islands of women to which Bran sailed, meeting Manannán son of Ler on the way. Manannán, as the academic Matthias Egeler writes, recites 'a poem to Bran' in which the 'Land of Women is given the name *Emnae . . . Emain*.[58] Thus, the Isle of Man was 'established as an otherworld island at a very early time'; 'right from the beginning', it was associated with Manannán, and the Land of the Women.

In later mythological texts, such as *Baile suthach síth Emhna*, a twelfth-century panegyric about Raghnall, King of Man, the island is again twinned with Emain:

A fertile settlement is the fairy mound of Emain . . .
A fresh apple-d Emain, it takes on the bright colour of summer . . .
Emain of the yew trees; the tips of its (sacred) trees shine . . .
Emain of the aromatic apple-trees, the honest Tara of the Isle of
   Man . . .
. . . what god from Newgrange conceived you with her secretly?[59]

This description is so evocative and potent: with its apples from the *Voyage of Bran*, and with Newgrange, the Neolithic chambered cairn at the ancient heart of Ireland, sacred still.

Later there are other texts which associate the island with female sanctity. One of the medieval Welsh *Peniarth Manuscripts*, for example, describes how 'there used to be women making wind for sailors, which wind they confined within three knots made on a thread. And when they had need of wind they would undo a knot of this thread.' Even at the end of the nineteenth century, James Frazer attests to wind-making in the isles of Man, Lewis and Shetland:

> The art of tying the wind up in three knots, so that the more knots are loosed the stronger will blow the wind, has been attributed to . . . witches in Shetland, Lewis, and the Isle of Man. Shetland seamen still buy winds in the shape of knotted handkerchiefs or threads from old women who claim to rule the storms.[60]

As late as 1901, in *Celtic Folklore: Welsh and Manx*, John Rhys asserted that the 'practice of wind making goes on to this day'. Later still, in *Folksongs and Folklore of South Uist*, first published in 1955, Margaret Fay Shaw described how, in those islands, 'Witches were said to have the power of raising storms by knots.'[61]

It seems to me that these writers are describing a belief in island-women's attunedness to nature that harks back at least to the Roman-era women on the island of Sena, if not earlier – to the women of Maeshowe and other places, marking the passing of the months with their bodily calendars.[62]

Everything about these poems and beliefs points to the Isle of Man as a site associated with female power. It is sad, is it not, that few speak of this now? Maybe, one day, this amnesia will come to seem a scandal. It is not surprising, of course. Deliberately or not, our culture lost sight of female wisdom, just as it closed its eyes to the beauty and wisdom of nature. But everything depends on how we see. These texts (lost, suppressed, ignored) abound with possibility. They show that it is always within our power to transcend how we were, and to see, and be, differently.

In 1935, Mona Douglas put on a one-act play, *Teeval*, which was performed in Douglas and published eight years later in her compilation *The Secret Island: Poems and Plays in Verse*. Based on an old Manx legend, its Chorus is the waves, played by eight women, and its protagonist, Teeval, daughter of the former 'Queen of the land'. The 'old Powers of the Sea Put enchantment on' Teeval's mother (they dethroned her: that old island story), but she is freed at the end of the play, disappearing back into the sea, her final journey spoken by the Chorus:

> She returns to the deep of the sea . . .
> the wondering island-folk
> Shall see her image sometimes . . .
> When pale lights dance on the waters far away
> Or hear a strange song drifting on the air.[63]

It is a lovely description of the ineffable. I feel a swell of admiration: yes, Mona did it. She evoked female freedom, island legend, and Manx discreteness, all encircled by a greater and more mysterious power: the sea.

12

Western Isles

Exodus (nineteenth century)

> The long isle,
> the Western Isles,
> the Outer Hebrides,
> *Na h-Eileanan an Iar,*
> the Wyld Ilis – are some of the names by which Scotland's west-

ernmost chain of islands have been known.[1] They stretch north for
130 miles, through pagan Catholicism (Barra to Benbecula), Scottish
Presbyterianism (North Uist to Lewis), mountains (Harris), ancient
stone circles (Lewis), and everywhere long white beaches, crannogs,
brochs, tragically cleared islands, and a redoubtable modern tourist
industry sustained by a self-sufficient society that has no need of
anything from outsiders (so it seems, to outsiders). All lit by the sun
and the wind and the pounding, merciless Atlantic.

For me, they will for ever after spell freedom.

1. Coll to Tiree

For over a year, in Orkney, I listened out for the female acoustic of
the Neolithic without being sure what I was hearing. On the eve of
my journey to the Western Isles one last rumour reaches my ears.

Summertime. I am travelling with my daughters through the
Inner Hebrides. On a hilltop on the island of Coll, I wriggle like a
fiend under the 'Rocking Stone' (an *erratic*, balanced on two pebbles).[2] Coll's erratic is also called the 'Queen Stone', for it is said that
island women would pass beneath it to ensure fertility (or prove

virginity; you couldn't do this with child). I look out at the long, luminous lines of Tiree, the flat neighbouring island.

There is someone there, waiting for me. (From now on, I am waiting for him too.) He has told me about the Ringing Stone, a huge boulder on the seashore which is played like an instrument, he says, with pebbles. Since I have never heard tell of it before, I half don't believe him.

But on a sunny day near midsummer, I take my children over to Tiree. Our journey is at the children's pace; we play in the broch and walk down to the sea. We cross a little sandy bay. Then, as we make our way along the strand, still a good way from the musical boulder, one of my children picks up a cowrie shell – and another – and another. *Look, Mum! Look!* There are cowries everywhere – here, there and – *over here!* Even my five-year-old is gathering them. The sea has offered them to us like a charm. I have been looking for cowries in the Hebrides all my life and never seen anything like it. We don't reach the Ringing Stone, my girls and I, that day. The cowries bewitch us.

Back in Coll, the girls asleep beside me in the hostel's bunks, I read the archaeologist's report from the 1970s. The Ringing Stone of Tiree is described as breast-shaped. The archaeologist counted fifty-three 'circular or oval depressions', probably 'prehistoric in origin'. With its careful carvings, the stone created a sound like that of a metal bell when struck with a pebble – what an unearthly noise it must have been, for people who didn't have metal. The boulder and its acoustic were at the centre of some form of female worship. During 'very high tides' on Tiree, when 'the sea floods the bay . . . the area on which the panel sits becomes a peninsula, almost totally surrounded by water'.[3] *An island of women.*

After my daughters go south with their uncle I return to Tiree. Somehow I progress beyond the cowrie beach and there it is, an island of its own on the seashore. When we play it with pebbles, it sings, just as he told me it would. We spend all afternoon there, worshipping at this site of ancient female reverence.

This is what I have learned on my travels through these islands:

you think the world is designed around male bodies and male thoughts,
and then an exception jumps out. Albeit a very old one.

2. Tiree to Barra

Tiree was once the breadbasket of the Hebrides. But in 1886 there
were agrarian riots. The bard wrote a song, 'Oran nam Priosanach':

> Before a Duke came or any of his people,
> Or a kingly George from Hanover's realm,
> The low-lying isle, with its many sheilings,
> Belonged as a dwelling to the Children of the Gael.[4]

Something about these remote, self-sufficient islands has long
made outsiders yearn to interfere.[5] For hundreds of years, the Hebrides bore the brunt of a mainland attack on island life that killed
people, reconfigured landscapes and struck at the roots of language
itself. First the Scottish monarchy undermined the clan system of
Somerled and his descendants. British rule saw the suppression of the
Jacobite rebellions and private clan armies.[6] Finally, landlords took up
the baton, moving people off the fertile runrig land they had farmed
for centuries to unprofitable crofts along the seashore, thus forcing
them to take on work as virtually indentured kelp labourers.[7]

Life was so hard for those who didn't own land – whole families
cutting kelp – that in the eighteenth century people began fleeing
their native lands in what they saw as an Exodus from the Egypt of
landlord exploitation. Gaelic-speaking bards urged people to 'flee
the rents' to this 'isle of contentment' (*Eilean an àigh*) in the British
colonies of North America. In 1801, Father Austin MacDonald, a
Catholic missionary priest in the Western Isles, wrote, 'We begin
now to look upon America as but one of our Islands on the Coast
and on the Sea that Intervenes as but a little brook.'[8]

Emigration led to cultural annihilation. As Murchadh Mac a'
Ghobhainn sang in the late nineteenth century,

The sweet mother-tongue dies,
The deer in the wilderness do not speak
And the white sheep has no language.[9]

Landlords became so concerned about losing their workers that they campaigned for legislation to make it prohibitively expensive for their tenants to emigrate, and the government complied, passing the Passenger Vessels Act in 1803, turning the islands into virtual prisons.[10] But after British victory in the Napoleonic Wars led to a fall in the price of kelp, the financial interests of landlords swung around by 180 degrees. The favoured trade was now in wool, which required large amounts of land but barely any people.[11]

Castle-dwelling Lord MacDonald of Sleat (descendant of eleventh-century Somerled) evicted hundreds of people from Skye to make way for sheep. Even in the nineteenth century, people in Edinburgh and London regarded the population of northern Scotland as outlandish and illiterate; 'the aborigines of Britain', as the Countess of Sutherland's ruthless land agent put it, 'shut out from any general stream of knowledge . . . in common with the brutes'. The ensuing 'Clearances' were portrayed by the government and establishment as part of the inevitable march of progress – the desolation of an entire society part of 'the peace'. Yet again, the intransigent islands needed to be brought into line; a process which culminated in modern times with the evacuation of the St Kilda islanders in 1930 (at their request, apparently).

Almost nowhere in England compares in scale with the ghostly scenes and empty landscapes of post-Clearance Scotland: whole abandoned islands, entire songs that tell of once-bustling communities, the tragic interplay of architecture and emptiness. England's abbeys, maybe.[12] Its nature. 'Bare ruin'd choirs where late the sweet birds sang': Shakespeare would lament the actual birds today.

And yet these islands in Scotland freed themselves from oppression. It was slow and hard – but it was done.

The once-a-week ferry from Tiree to Barra comes into the south of the island, past the islanded-castle, Kisimul, in the bay. At the other end, to Barra's north, is Traigh Mhòr, which means 'Big Beach' in English. In 1549, Donald Monro, High Dean of the Islands, wrote of these 'grate sands of Barray . . . all full of grate Cokills . . . Ther is na fairer and more profitable sands for cokills in all the world'.[13] Since 1937, this long strand has also doubled up as the world's only beach-runway. But there are still regular cockle pickers (warned off the sand by an orange windsock when planes are expected). Barratlantic, a fish processing company, now exports cockles and other shellfish all across Europe. I go out there in the rain, with my spade, to see what I can find; and find a Romanian man, Cornel Simionof. Over tea in his house, he tells me that the first place he worked in Britain was Ramsgate – the Isle of Thanet – with the fishing fleet. He came to Barra with eleven other Romanians. He is the only one left now – the weather is 'so hard, windy, so windy'. And 'you need a strong back'. In good weather he can get fifty kilos of cockles. Half that in the winter.

Until 1840, Barra, along with the neighbouring islands of Vatersay and Mingulay, was owned by the chief of the clan Macneil, a general who fought in the Napoleonic Wars. With the subsequent collapse of the kelp industry upon which Barra's fortunes, and the large island population, depended, Macneil tried to shore up his estate by forcing tenants to become crofters or to take up fishing. In 1836, he wrote a threatening letter to the parish priest: 'if I don't on my arrival find them heart and hand engaged in fishing, I pledge you my honour they shall tramp, and the Land shall be this ensuing spring occupied by strangers'. But his tenants were reluctant to turn to deep-sea fishing. Macneil's creditors grew increasingly aggressive and eventually seized the entire estate. Barra was sold for a knockdown price to one of the people to whom Macneil was indebted, a mainland man called Colonel Gordon.

Already by 1827, the island's parish priest had described in a letter how 'people were actually starving, fainting away in different parts of the island. Had it not been for the cockles of Traigh Mhòr there would have been hundreds dead this day in Barra'.[14] Twenty years later, with Barra under new ownership, another clergyman visited the island, and his report attests that nothing had changed for the island's poor. Just as Mesolithic hunter-gatherers explored Britain outside-in, island-hopping as they combed the beaches for reserves of protein, so Victorian inhabitants of Barra were reduced to falling back on the last remaining reserve of nature's bounty: 'on the beach the whole population of the country seemed to be met, gathering the precious cockles', he wrote; there was 'starvation on many faces'. Colonel Gordon grew impatient with his hungry tenants. In 1851, he had the inhabitants hunted down. One eyewitness described it being like 'Gambia on the Slave Coast of Africa'.[15] The islanders were shipped off to Quebec.

From Barra we who are now the we cross the modern causeway to camp on the neighbouring island of Vatersay. With its mirror-image beaches, back to back, and a road down the middle as a spine, everything on this island reflects everything else: the water of the high hill lochans the sky, the beaches each other, the population exchange in and out from islands nearby. The people of Vatersay live on land 'reclaimed' between 1907 and 1912 from the absentee landowner Lady Cathcart by landless fishermen from the islands of Mingulay and Sandray. At first they merely squatted in protest, then they began building huts and planting potatoes.[16]

In 2016, with my four-month-old baby strapped to my chest, I visited Mingulay, the island self-cleared a century earlier. We walked up through the heather to the steep sea cliffs, dazzled by the wind and sun. On the way down we passed through the abandoned village on the bay. I laid my baby on the beach and watched her watch me as I swam. She who watches. I loved my baby's gaze.

Later, hearing Hugh Roberton's 'Mingulay Boat Song', set to an old Gaelic tune, I think of the animated emptiness through which we briefly stepped:

> Wives are waiting on the bank, or
> Looking seaward from the heather;
> Pull her round, boys! And we'll anchor,
> Ere the sun sets at Mingulay.[17]

The island was always barren, difficult to farm; one resident had never seen corn before she came to Vatersay.[18] But there was a happy ending. Unlike the population of St Kilda, dispersed to Glasgow and other places on the mainland, the Mingulay islanders found new land for themselves, nearby, on islands of their choice. Ten of the fishermen who 'invaded' Vatersay in 1906 were served notice by Lady Cathcart in 1907 and in 1908 travelled to Edinburgh to represent themselves, in Gaelic, during a celebrated court case pitting the landless against the landed. They were sentenced to two months' imprisonment, but as they left the court the crowd waiting for them outside raised 'a cheer' exhorting them 'to keep up their courage'.[19] When they returned home to Vatersay it was to find 172 islanders from Mingulay, Barra, Eriskay and Pabbay living there in thirty-two huts.[20] (The creel fisherman next door to the house where I stayed in Vatersay was living on the exact spot his Mingulay grandfather had claimed, and ploughed, in 1906.)

The Secretary of State for Scotland eventually intervened to purchase the island from Lady Cathcart, a move which was widely criticized outside the islands – the *Scotsman* described him as 'being in the tightest grip of his Highland delinquencies' and evoked 'a fiery cross of licence' 'passing from district to district'.[21]

In a way, the *Scotsman* was right. Everything was changing in the islands, the beginning of the end of the long cycle of grief unleashed on them by outsiders. It was the agitation for land reform by crofters on Skye that led in 1883 to a public inquiry, and in turn to the Crofters Act of 1886. Throughout the early twentieth century, from Vatersay north to Lewis, 'land raiders' protested and campaigned and fought to get their land – often from absentee landowners. In 1997, campaigning resulted in the community buy-out of the island of Eigg: 'the first known case in which Scottish tenants cleared a laird from his own estate'.[22] There have been other community purchases on Harris, Lewis, Skye, Mull and the Uists – all islands once devastated by landlords in the Clearances. It is said that 'feudalism is at the heart of Scotland's land law still'. But out on the islands everything is changing.

3. Barra to Benbecula

The islands from Barra north to Benbecula remain Catholic. Near
to Traigh Mhòr on Barra is a little chapel dedicated to an early Irish
saint, Finbarr, with a modern-day shrine to Bride, that ancient goddess, Mary's companion in Christianity, adorned with seashells.
Mingulay had a chapel dedicated to Mary, the neighbouring island
of Sandray to Bride.[23] In the pairing of Mary and Bride lies all the
strange magic of Gaelic Catholic-pagan culture.

My mother, whose uncle was a Scottish priest, remembers a
trip to these islands in the early 1960s. Her uncle, grandmother
and she stayed in a hotel in South Uist and toured the island par-
ishes, visiting priests that her uncle had trained in a seminary in
Fife. Quite different then from the travails in 1638 of the Catholic
priest who complained to his bishop that 'The labour of the mission in these remote and barbarous spots is almost indescribable . . .
Sometimes the same missionary has been there in different years
for six months together without tasting any kind of drink except
water and milk . . . there is no city, no town, no school, no civilization, no one can read except a few who have been educated at a
great distance from home.'[24]

My mother and great-grandmother called on the monthly nurse
who had looked after their cousin and granddaughter, born posthumously after her mother died of polio. The nurse had been
summoned back to the islands soon after, to make an arranged marriage with the scion of the local ferry company (later conglomerated
into Cal-Mac). She didn't speak to or acknowledge any neighbours
who weren't Catholic.

My mother gave me a copy of Alexander Carmichael's *Carmina
Gadelica*, first published in 1900. That these islands retain a great reverence for female saints such as Mary and Bride is thanks in part to
this, Carmichael's work of cultural exegesis, a potent, resonant
document of an age that has now almost completely vanished but
of which Carmichael was a witness. Born on the Inner Hebridean

island of Lismore, Carmichael put the songs he had collected from the islands into *Charms of the Gaels: Hymns and Incantations with illustrative notes on words, rites and customs, dying and obsolete, orally collected in the Highlands and Islands by Scotland* – or *Ortha nan Gaidheal* in Gaelic – and *Carmina Gadelica* in Latin. Gathered predominantly from 'the Western Isles, variously called "Eileana Bride", Hebrid Isles, Outer Hebrides, Outer Isles, "Eilean Fada", "Innis Fada", Long Island, and anciently "Iniscead", "Innis Cat", Isle of the Cat, Isle of the Catey',[25] there are prayers to the sun and moon; fairy songs; plant songs; songs for harvesting, birth and travel; and charms of protection ('an island thou art in the sea').

Some forms of magic endure. While the fairy culture in the Isle of Man only lasted into the early twentieth century[26] in Scotland belief in magic, and fairies, and second sight, endured longer than that, regardless of what the priests and ministers and politicians said. A forester I met on the train to Oban told me that plenty of his colleagues, young and old, would never cut the rowan, 'because it is the fairy tree'.

Magic meant little to me until recently. But since travelling to Lindisfarne, I think about it in the context of the repression and silencing of women. I remember how I cycled round and round the courtyard of the house where I stayed in Bannu, Pakistan, forbidden to leave the compound for days on end, on account of my gender; of how hard it has been, even in twenty-first-century Britain, to bestir myself against manifestations of male dominance, overt and subtle. I begin to wonder: what would I have done, as an oppressed woman, in the colonial culture of Iron Age Britain; on a remote, eighteenth-century island? Something secretive and subversive; a ritual deposition; a secret ritual. The turning point for me in the English house I was trying to leave came after four female friends arrived and, responding to my desperation, adorned the place with their plant and body magic: depositions of menstrual blood around the perimeter of the garden, singing, talking, the burning of sacred plants throughout the house. We walked in darkness up to the attic, carrying candles, to sing over my two

daughters, asleep in my bed. We looked at their little naked, inter-
twined bodies, and all five of us were moved by the sight; that
sisterhood, and our role in protecting it. Afterwards I was surprised by how much the entire, secret, home-made ritual meant to
me, unspiritual as I thought I was. The solidarity gave me the
strength I needed.

One of my favourite incantations in *Carmina Gadelica* is that for
'kindling a fire' – 'Togail an Teine' – something that always fills me
with a twinge of anxiety, so important is this task, so key the basic
components, so tremendous the alchemy between spark and wood:

> I will raise the hearth-fire
> As Mary would
> The encirclement of Bride and Mary
> On the fire, and on the floor,
> And on the household all.

Women's voices from this time are nowhere else but in the prayers,
spells and songs; that is why guarding them became so vital. There is
something mystical about singing; vibrating with other people,
bodily. Also, it was always free, and often about freedom. On a Gaelic
song course at Sabhal Mòr Ostaig, the Gaelic college in Skye, with
the Lewis singer Christine Primrose, I learn Exodus songs, Sheiling
songs, sung by pastoral daughters during the long summers spent up
on the hillsides with the sheep, and Satire songs: for the word-fighting
which kept Hebridean tunes and traditions alive after 1745, once
Highland musical instruments had been banned by the English. It
was the Waulk songs in particular – women's rhythmic work songs,
sung during the shrinking of the famous island cloth – that produced
a people with voices naturally trained, by exercise, for opera-like
feats of breathwork.[27]

Each island seemed to produce its own rebellious singing female,
or female singing tradition.[28] Marjory Kennedy-Fraser collected a
song about a rebellious female from Benbecula, 'the isle of a thousand lochs', fifty miles due north of Barra:

> The Queen of Lochlin of the brown shields
> Deep love gave, that all endureth,
> At Aillte, the young, of the keen-edged blades,
> And secretly with him fled she.[29]

She heard it from 'an old Ossianic singer, of a type supposed to have long since passed away':

He chanted tales of such length that you would go every day for a week to listen to one long tale, and he would begin tomorrow exactly where he left off today, and his tales were all in verse and traditional, for he could neither write nor read. At eighty-seven, still bright and active, he was to be seen daily out on the machar [coastal grasslands] herding his cattle. And in the clean white sanded kitchen of his thatched cottage he sang, but not before he had set everything in perfect order for the ceremony – these old pagan tales are sacred to the Isleman.[30]

By 'Ossianic singer' she meant the legendary mythical figure who had become a contentious firebrand of Scotland's precious indigenous Gaelic revival after James MacPherson published *Fragments of Ancient Poetry* in 1760. MacPherson hailed from the Highlands; he spoke some Gaelic and was no fake. He came to believe that he was excavating from the semi-literate highlands and islands of Scotland the remnants of ancient oral epic poetry, verse of a Celtic Homer whom he called Ossian. That he was transported by his material does not surprise me. Literary and cultural exegesis is as thrilling as any Hebridean storm. I know its seductions well. I have often been whirled around in the vortex of discovery, searching for a glancing fragmented reflection of the rich vein of literary culture about women that throve, once, and was distorted or lost. In the mid-eighteenth century, travelling through the Western Isles must have been epic – no hotels or campsites, cars, regular ferries, imported food or central heating. How thrilling to record, transcribe and translate Gaelic voices that no book had yet captured in their integrity, alchemizing those trowel-scrapings into the grandeur of lost epics.

For MacPherson, Gaelic was a language, 'pure and original'. He was undoubtedly inspired by the Romantic trend of looking back into the past and beyond mainland English consciousness to the repressed parts of British cultural life. But his own background was also at one with his subject matter. He 'lived in a country where mountains, streams and caves were named after the Celtic heroes' – and heroines too. During his travels, he came to the conclusion that there was something ancient and undefiled in the linguistic heritage of Gaelic; as he gathered songs and stories, and saw the repetition of themes, tropes and storylines, he became convinced that he would be able to identify, for Scotland, an author to embody this creative effulgence.[31]

Writing is a comparatively recent phenomenon, for almost the entire course of human evolution a redundant invention of the future. It seems that on the periphery of Scotland, in the islands particularly, an unscripted Gaelic literature survived largely in the memories of its people.[32]

Until MacPherson, this culture had no comprehensive scribe. It is not surprising that he was impatient to get it all down before it was lost. It was also brave of him. Wearing of tartan had been banned only fourteen years before he published *Fragments of Ancient Poetry*, following the Jacobite rebellions and the brutal Battle of Culloden. The collection was an immediate hit, and MacPherson was strongly encouraged by his friends, and members of the Edinburgh literati, to collect and publish more material. He became inspired, ecstatic. His next publication was titled *Fingal, an Ancient Epic Poem in Six Books, together with Several Other Poems composed by Ossian, the Son of Fingal, translated from the Gaelic Language*. Naturally, some of the oral material he received needed tweaking; it is hard to say how much. Everything needs an edit, even this; but MacPherson's southern detractors cried foul, howled with derision, shrieked that the Gael had cheated. From England, in particular, came a deluge of hate. Samuel Johnson said MacPherson was a phony. Detractors in

Edinburgh materialized soon enough. Irish scholars didn't praise him either; they questioned his Gaelic and his grasp of history.

In England, the level of disapprobation about Scotland had long been racist – and would long remain so. In 1699, the anonymous author of *The Character of Scotland* expressed an English aversion to the very topography of Scotland, in particular its islands, by comparing it to a louse:

> those nitty Islands called the Orcades, and the Shetland (quasi Shite-Land) islands . . . the country is fill of Lakes and Loughs, and they well stockt with Islands, so that a map thereof looks like a pillory coat, bespattered all over with dirt and rotten eggs.[33]

Nowadays, to many in the English-speaking world, the name Ossian is a byword for fraud. But in the world of Gaelic revival, it is a lifeline.[34] The bards of the clan houses had been employed to sing of the heroes and heroines of the past and to keep the ancestors alive in the minds of their descendants. It was an ancient impulse, going back at least as far as the ancestral bone curation of the Neolithic. The idea of Ossian emerged from that connection and transmitted something vital to literate cultures all across Europe – that there was so much they had lost, or were missing, but which it was possible to save, if only they could look and listen.

Carmichael came in MacPherson's wake, as did Kennedy-Fraser, who dedicated the first volume of *Songs of the Hebrides* (1909) to 'the women of the Hebrides' – thus underlining, as neither MacPherson nor Carmichael had, quite, the predominant role of women in the transmission of this ancient culture into modern times. As Kennedy-Fraser wrote, 'I had sailed, I felt, out of the twentieth century and back into the 1600s.'[35]

Kennedy-Fraser's English recitals of Gaelic songs inspired a young woman from Pennsylvania, Margaret Fay Shaw, to move to South Uist in 1929. Margaret lived with two sisters, Peigi and Màiri Campbell, in a small thatched house in South Uist, learning Gaelic and songs: 'Everybody sang, it was their melody of life . . . You sang on the croft, you sang while you were working, it made your life easier . . . It was the people's way of putting pen to paper'.[36] Later, with her folklorist husband, John Lorne Campbell, she would make the first ever recordings of this oral culture. The archive is still extant, in their house on the island of Canna, where they lived until he was ninety, and she 101.

4. Benbecula to Berneray

Thus did the song collectors of the eighteenth, nineteenth and twentieth centuries show that many traces of female reverence remained in Gaelic culture. It is not just the plethora of churches dedicated to Mary, Mother of God, and to Brigid. Those who observe and tend the Gaelic language point to the naming of hills and lochs and stone outcrops after women: often the *cailleach* ('old woman') who embodied the spirit of the landscape and whose form is traced across islands and hills.[37] J. F. Campbell even believed that the *gruagach* (a female fairy) 'may have some connection with the groac'h or grac'h, a name given to the sacred women who dwelt in the Isle of Sein'.[38] Those ancient prophetesses again. Silvia Federici pointed out that 'women were safe during the witch burning times' in the Celtic lands of Wales, Ireland and Western Scotland.

Hebridean belief in second sight – in Gaelic *an da shealladh*, 'two sights' – is strongly connected to place.[39] It is not gender-determined (as on the island of Sena); men have it as much as women. Likewise, even though the bardic tradition was traditionally male, there were female bards. Mary MacLeod, known as Màiri nighean Alasdair Ruaidh in Gaelic was born at Rodel, Harris, in 1615, and spent her childhood on Skye, where she worked as bard for the laird of Dunvegan Castle, and also on the island of Berneray. She was banished to Mull, after she composed an acidic song that burned the laird's pride, and also to the island of Pabbay, off Harris. Pabbay is now owned by an English horse-racing family whom I met when the island manager gave me a lift over in his boat to collect them at the end of the summer. Màiri's world was one on the cusp of change, of lingering traditions and foreign incursions. Possibly she was a witch, or a healer, or a shaman. Berneray, where I camped one night by her house, also has an ancient footprint stone up on the hill: a remnant from the island kingdoms of Columba's day. I imagine her standing there, looking out over the neighbouring islands as she composed her sharp-edged lines:

In my father's house were found venison and the bones of the deer
In thy father's house bree [soup] and bones of the fish were your fare.

(There it is again, coastal Britain's snobbery about its own geographical diet.)

Màiri is buried, it is said, *beul nam breug a chur foidhpe* – 'with her lying mouth down' – to stop her reciting verses, perhaps. Were she St Cuthbert, they would have unearthed her numerous times to check.

5. Berneray to Harris

North of Rodel is the fishing village of Leverburgh. It used to be called Obbe, until Lord Leverhulme, the Lancashire soap magnate who started the globally dominating firm, Unilever (the Lever Brothers) with a soap called Sunlight, bought the islands of Lewis and Harris in 1918. (The renaming of places by the English – one of the things that fester in Scotland.)[40]

Kenny Campbell, now in his eighties, spent his life as the shepherd on Pabbay, the very island to which Màiri was once deported. Kenny remembers Leverhulme, and the nigh million quid he sunk into infrastructure in the islands. Tempted north by the prospect of transforming Hebridean society for the better, Leverhulme got grandiose ideas. He was greatly exercised by fishing and tried to persuade the fishermen to adopt more efficient methods. But his time in Harris and Lewis coincided with the land raiders' protests, and islanders were in no mood for listening to paternalistic outsiders. Leverhulme left; Kenny stayed.

I sleep one night at a sheiling under the stars – as women were once wont to do, guarding the animals from mishap and theft. In the morning, I leave the path of cars and walk up into the hills, where there is a loch and an island within it, Eilean na Caillach, which had been a nunnery, according to the writer Alastair McIntosh.[41] Far above that is a place called 'The Sanctuary', so I was told the day before, by Ruari, owner of the Leverburgh bunkhouse. He explained to me, in some excitement, that up there in the hills, a good two hours' walk, was an extended line of stone cairns. He had walked these hills all his life and had only just now come across them.

Hills without motorable roads transmit secrets better than any bard. Ruari marks on my map where he saw these cairns, and I follow his directions with impressive determination. I walk for hours that day, just as, in 2005, I walked for hours in the hills near Gilgit, Pakistan, after a man at a roadside teashop described an ancient carving he had seen, 'like the war between India and Pakistan'. In Pakistan there was no GPS coordinate; to follow the man's directions I had to be carried forward simply by the momentum of his excitement. In Harris, I am trying to speak the language of contours and streams and outcrops. By the time I am high above the sea, at the 150-metre contour mark, the island is humming with insect- and birdlife. Probably nowhere else in Britain is as redolent of past centuries as this – a place beyond the reach of vehicle fumes, and farmers' chemicals, and plastic pollution borne by littering car drivers, or sewage outlets, or fishing-boat tackle. Perhaps *this* is how it felt, one, two, three hundred years ago, to the bards and shepherds, a place of heather and gorse and the chirruping of water as it streams over bare rock.

I wander for a while more, suddenly disconsolate. *Where are they?* I stare at my Ordnance Survey map. *Have I misunderstood everything?*

And then I turn my head. All along the hillside, for two hundred metres or so, stretches a line of more than ninety structures (sculptures) made from piled-up stones. They are so delicate and mysterious, individual yet conjoined, with no apparent purpose other than aesthetic joy – and the satisfaction of building something up from the ground.

When I send him the photographs, my quizzical archaeologist friend George thinks that the cairns look modern rather than pre-historic (as the Canmore archaeologist speculated they might be in her report).[42] Maybe they're an installation by Julie Brook, who lived on Jura, Mingulay, in Orkney and on Skye, and makes 'Fire-stacks', cairns in the sea which she sets alight. It's more likely that *her* work was inspired by both this landscape and the artistic flair of a shepherd girl from a time when we lived differently with our surroundings, fearing and treasuring them equally.

I touch the rocks as I move between them, thinking again how I had never expected this intensity of love emanating out of these islands; the dizzying and exuberant sense that history is concertina-ing in on itself – maybe, even, of how these invisible lines which pass through this earth and these waters leave their trace in the placement of stones, in the purity of a waterbody, in the light falling out of the sky over Luskentyre, in the stones of a church – carved into a Sheela-na-gig, or a birlinn, or placed over the body of a rebellious female with a wickedly clever tongue.

6. Harris to Lewis

Again and again I go north between these islands, with my babies, alone, with friends, with my lover. Three times I hear this singing, haunting and unearthly: of the waves at Uig, and the sea mist that curls around the throat at Tholastaidh (Tolsta), and the perfect arrow-drop of a bird into the Minch as you approach Steòrnabhagh (Stornoway) by boat. Each time, the minister calls first, to be echoed by the congregation, and soon some beautiful complex improvisation is underway; the singing swells and lifts, swirling around the still air of the church, voices of women and men borne upwards, intermingling, lower resonances and higher meeting and parting and meeting again.

I shut my eyes and listen, understanding nothing. I have already looked through the words of the English translation of the psalm ('I will extol the Lord at all times; his praise will always be on my lips') and maybe because I always feel deeply nostalgic for this country, and yet so foreign – upbringing betrayed by accent – I savour for a moment the alienation of these Hebrew sacred songs from some three thousand years ago, being chanted in Gaelic, in an island on the edge of Britain. *What a world.* But very soon the pews where we are sitting dissolve in the sea mist. In the warm blackness of my eyelids we are away across the moor which is the body of the island, skimming our fingers through the peaty orange waters of Loch Langabhat, with its Neolithic crannog,[43] curling up like smoke around the staircase of the broch at Càrlabhagh (Carloway), brushing our noses across the warp of a brown tweed jerkin, tasting salt on our tongues at Beàrnaraigh (Bernera). I see the wind forcing the waves backwards, against the tide; I see the sunlight on these abundant waters, which speckle this land like stars; I see the mountains of Na Hearadh (Harris), blue in the distance, a body of rock which gave me such a thrill when I first drove across it late one Saturday night – as if I had at last reached a place in Britain that approached something of the epic grandeur of Pakistan's Karakoram mountains, whose heft and history I once knew much better than these.

The Gaelic psalm-singing reminds me that as an English speaker I move through these islands ineptly mispronouncing most place-names; failing to hear the naming of hill and sea; wanting to understand but failing.

The psalm-singing is taking place in the seminary in Stornoway in Lewis, an island possibly named from the old Norse, 'song house'.[44] The special collection today, as at all Stornoway's Free Church services, Gaelic and English, is for 'Day One Ministries', 'formerly the *Lord's Day Observance Society*' – so the service sheet explains – which 'campaigns for Sunday to be a day of worship and rest, particularly as its importance as a Creation ordinance is increasingly under threat from retail businesses, sports events, and entertainment'. Children's playgrounds here are still locked up on Sundays, with signs forbidding entry on the Lord's day; and why did nobody warn me, when I first visited Lewis – alone that Saturday night with my baby and toddler in the car – that there was only *one* shop in the entire island open on a Sunday: a garage in Stornoway, sixty minutes' drive across the moor from where we were staying, selling sausage rolls and Ginger Snaps for our breakfast, lunch and tea. Lewis still maintains an eerie silence on Sundays; it stretches over the island as tremulous as a spider's web – and please let it not be I who blunders through. (Later, I feel retrospectively self-conscious for going out into the garden in my jeans, and – conspicuously, as it turns out – hanging up a wash.)

The church is even plainer, on the inside, than a mosque; on these blank blue walls not a curl of calligraphy; certainly no Virgin Mary, infant Jesus, altar, or formal rigmarole. Instead, all the focus is on listening and thinking: there are three sung psalms, a reading from the New Testament, and a forty-five-minute sermon in Gaelic.

It was in this same church with my baby (vocal), and three-year old (fidgety), that I first heard Gaelic psalm-singing, five years earlier, and it had haunted me since then, bodily and mentally.

Later I took my friend George to church in Harris, where, though the service is in English, they were singing psalms in Gaelic. Again, the singing seemed to articulate better than any book how the collective acoustic of a people can keep alive their connection to a language and landscape and history; a reincarnation. I was listening to something which was spiritual in ways that transcended the words being uttered.

The sermon, also quite long, was based on that day's reading from Matthew (9.20), about the woman 'with a twelve-year flow of blood', which ceased after meeting Jesus. (Clearly, she had polyps, fibroids, or endometriosis.) 'And behold, a woman who was diseased with an issue of blood twelve years, came behind him, and touched the hem of his garment.'[45]

The young minister, whose wife gave birth a few days earlier, spoke (in what seemed to me horribly eugenicist terms) about heaven: how in the afterlife there will be no genetic 'impurities'. In the church hall afterwards, he told me that for a Gaelic congregation one assumes great Biblical knowledge; not so in English.

The chat among the congregation was of the gannet harvest, which had just happened out on the uninhabited, waterless island of

Sùla Sgeir: 'We keep the gannet in the freezer and eat it all year.' (Fledging gannets, called gugas, are gutted and salted and preserved in brine in a historical-cultural get-out clause of the UK's Wildlife and Countryside Act 1981: 'Section 1 and orders under section 3 do not apply to anything done for the purpose of providing food for human consumption in relation to – (a) a gannet on the island of Sula Sgeir.')[46]

Sùla Sgeir once had a woman living on it, Brenhilda – not the Valkyrie, but the saintly sister of St Ronan. They lived together on the island of North Rona, until he developed a passion for her lovely legs (it is said that he became inhabited by devils). She left – not he – making a new home on Sùla Sgeir. The island with running water, where they had both lived, took his name, not hers.

7. Lewis to Handa

In 1845, a minister sent to check up on the small community of Handa, an island in Sutherland, due east across the Minch from Lewis, reported that it had elected its own queen:

> The island of Handa is tenanted by twelve families . . . It is curious enough, that they have established nothing less than Royalty amongst them, in the person of the eldest widow on the island, who is designed Queen; and her prerogative is recognized not only by the islanders, but by visitors from the mainland.[47]

It is of course easy to be cynical about the wider significance of this. The island had been cleared in the 1800s and resettled by fishing folk in 1828. But the fact that this remote island community, completely at the mercy of mainland landlords, chose a 'queen' rather than a 'king' to organize themselves as a society and keep them safe in the face of the wind and the weather and political forces beyond their control, suggests something potent: that an idea had carried over from the ancient past. The idea was preserved so carefully, in stones, and songs, and shapes in the landscape, and legends at sea – that the natural reaction to the terror and trauma of the Clear-ances, on a small island in 1845, was for a woman to be leader.

That is why I want to go there.

I almost don't manage it. From Lewis we take the boat to Ullapool, then wind for hours through the moonscape which is Sutherland, towards the place where the Handa ferry docks. An hour short of my destination, I get a call from the ferryman's son, cancelling my booking. The boat's steering has gone and they are awaiting a part from south; they don't know if it will arrive on Friday, or maybe Monday, or even Wednesday – or maybe never. It is the end of the season and they have better things to do, such as hauling in the creels from their other, better boat. And definitely they can't take me over, well they *can*, because they are obliged to go over and get the other tourists off, but it would be entirely at my own risk, and there is no water on the island, and there is definitely no chance of being picked up again before the end of next month, there is no way that I can get a ride from any local fishermen – now they begin to get angry – that would militate against their ferry trade, and anyway, as it turns out, they *are* the local fishermen. It would be an act of provo-cation. So, they won't rescue me even if I beg.

We go anyway.

The rangers who meet us off the boat as everybody else is leav-ing suggest – urge, instruct – that we camp on a shelf of land above a south-facing beach, a little tranquil bay of turquoise water. We have supplies for about three days, if we are careful. We had been expecting to stay just one night, and there had been no time or place to buy any more.

I am not alone, I have loving, careful company – but in hindsight it is interesting how unreasonably terrified I was, that first day, at being stranded on this island. Finally, it had happened to me: a glimpse of the existential state in which almost every islander of the eighteenth and nineteenth centuries must have lived: that of not knowing, not controlling, being at the whim of forces beyond one's ken, being self-reliant.

We walk around the island that night, he and I, past the abandoned village with its eight or so houses (cleared to Nova Scotia in 1848, following the potato famine),[48] and up around the headland. The fog comes down, and the cliffs are high, and there are fierce skuas nesting. I begin to wonder out loud at how strange and perplexing it is, all the feelings it evokes – hunger, despair, elation, trepidation.

Now, finally, I have the chance to experience for myself, in microcosm, the self-sufficiency of islanders; their domination by the mainland; to dream of what it took to elect a woman leader, in this remote world, a law unto itself. This is the landscape of Ringing Stones and chambered cairns, of weather prophetesses and lake healers, of women who once held counsel.

The water of the bay is glimmering with phosphorescence. We take off our clothes and swim in the moonlight.

The next day the island is lovely; as sunny as Greece. I climb the cliff that stretches up as shelter for our tent, perched as it is like a seabird's nest, and stretch out on the rocks, listening to the island. I wonder what Handa sounded, smelled and looked like in the era of its queen; before electricity and phones, in that time of proper noticing of nature.

At the tent, we sip our water parsimoniously. I think of Bermuda, where the early settlers limed the rocks, because there was no fresh water; the roofs are still limed for that reason, the technology unchanged. Maybe we should lime something. But there is no rain. The sun extends its journey through the sky. It is paradise island here in northern Scotland.

That night, I have strange, portentous dreams. I dream that I am telling the story of my quest, my process, to a friend, in a damp basement flat, like the London one I lived in once. I look up to see sunshine streaming in from the world outside. There is a lovely garden. I walk outside. Above me, somebody pushes open a casement window and leans out to listen to the musician in the garden, who is playing the cornet.

There's a cornet at the beginning of *King Lear*. I wake to feel sunshine streaming through the walls of our tiny tent. There is sand in every orifice, every crevice. For days, sand has added a mild crunch to every meal. I unzip the door and look out over the bay. Down below us, moored at peace, is the most thrilling sight: a boat.

I dress in haste; there is a dinghy on the beach. Whoever they are, they have rowed across and are now walking around the island, as we had. There is not more than an hour's entertainment here to detain them. Who could they be? A family of eight, unable even to fit in one tiny hitchhiker, let alone two with laptops, a tent, basket of supplies, ungainly mattress? I pace up and down on the beach.

After an hour, by which time the sand hoppers are as anxious as I am, two bodies appear on the horizon. It is *them.*

They are two very nice men from down the coast. They can't believe the ferrymen have abandoned us. Don't believe it. But they give us a moment to pack, and we run up the cliff to our tent shelf. As I throw everything into our bags, I see a fishing boat, zigzagging between lobster pots that loop around this part of the island like a shoelace. We fold away our tent, pack up the wicker basket, haul our mattress down to the beach.

We are waiting when they come back for us in the dinghy. It takes four trips, and it is only once we are stowed with our belongings and the boat is on its way out of the bay again that our sea-path takes us directly across that of the creel boat I had seen from the clifftop. It is the ferryman and his son.

I laugh, amazed. And then I realize why this place is so important. Through being here I have come to recognize and be grateful to those men and women who, out of their own initiative, gave women a leadership role. The task now is to take that appreciation back to the mainland, and into my life.

Already, these islands which freed themselves have taught me something.

to every mind, I keep the door and look out over the bay. Down below, in some of places, the most thrilling sight a beach...

I mean, these they feeling, of the beach. Whatever they are they hurried along and to now walking around the island, as we had. What is not those than all note concentration here to death there. Who while they be. A family of eight mother and by in her fifty inadvisable fur those saw, with laptops, or any of her every one unnaturally invented I peered past down on the beach. As each look by which time the sun stops, are as an ocean in two bodies appear in the same that they...

They are now very nice and around to the close. They can't to have the horizon near, should be there is near a time to give us a clearer so I can see where the horizon may well. A I think everything into these. I was being a flat sharping lever in happen tons that bound around they peer away and like a singular. We told may out into peer in my peer behind they stood the distance down, to the front line...

We sit waiting when they come but come until the thought that were hurried away, and it was only once we are so much about belongings and the back of all by three, or all of the back are much taken directly away, that if all this be ambition from the calling, it is the territory and to it...

I laughed, amazed, and then I realise with this piece so an her small. They hanging how I have come to recognise and be graceful in these much and when some all of their own fantasy, gives a woman a capable of... how a to take this apparition, back to be tangled and untied...

Maybe, the truth, a woman is married the attacks have ring on the something.

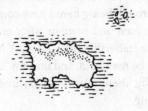

ENGLISH CHANNEL

13

Channel Islands

Inselwahn (*twentieth century*)

Freedom, once acquired, is not a given. It is best to be wary. It is best to be prudent. Even so, sometimes the effort is too much. Freedom becomes impossible to guard and hold in the face of violence.

Over time, islands come and go; as do rivers, and rulers, and species of human. Before *Homo sapiens* reaches Britain, before Britain is surrounded by sea, before the riverbed becomes a channel and its passing is impossible, Neanderthals venture to the far north of Europe's landmass. What will in time become the islands of Britain is now the outer extremity of Europe's hominid habitat. Sometimes lions roam the grasslands, as elephants push down the deciduous trees; at others, ice caps descend from the north, rendering unviable any vegetation taller than moss. For many millennia these future isles are the frontier between frozen desert and human life.

Around 200,000 years ago, a river separates Britain out as an island and becomes the sea. Neanderthals make their home across the water, on the coast of northern Europe. They sit in a granite cave, watching mammoths on the plain below. They hunt their prey by geological trickery: driving them off cliffs, or (the newer theory) by ambush in narrow valleys.[1] They stack the bones they have chewed against the cave wall and place two rhino skulls on top. Somebody drives a mammoth rib through a mammoth skull. These people are the first human inhabitants of the Channel Islands – a people before the people we are, in a land before the islands we now know.

An ice age comes and goes. The climate warms, sea-level rises, creating a series of small offshore islands around both Britain and the northern coast of Europe. On the island which eventually comes to be called Jersey, the Neanderthal's hunting cave is lapped by the tide; mammoth bones and ribs are sealed inside by a protective layer of sedimentary loess.

New human groups move out to the islands. Neanderthals find themselves in competition with a taller, more perspicacious version of themselves who live in larger social groups and hunt in ways which nourish art and a frighteningly powerful degree of social organization. *Sapiens* prevail; Neanderthals die out, but not before sexual encounters with our species leave their DNA locked within our own.

By 1066, *Homo sapiens* at St Brelade (a parish in the south of Jersey), where Neanderthals once planned mammoth murders, speak Norman French, a language heavily inflected with Norse.[2] When William the Conqueror crosses the Channel to claim the English crown, stopping en route at the islands to enlist soldiers for the invasion, his actions pit Norsemen against Norsemen. The DNA of Norse, Norman, Saxon interlock in their turn.

One of the most significant dates in Channel Islands' history is 1204, when Normandy became part of France again but the Channel Islands remained with England. It was not part of the kingdom, though they shared a king; no longer part of Normandy – though, to them, the king was Duke of Normandy.[3] King John had tempted them with the promise of autonomy and governance by their own law and customs. So it is still. The islands are a crown dependency, but not in the United Kingdom.

The separate states (or bailiwicks) of Jersey and Guernsey (which includes Alderney and Sark) control their own domestic affairs, including tax; there is no dole, handguns have never been outlawed, property prices are similar to London. Half of Jersey's residents work in financial services for like the Isle of Man, the island functions as a low-tax jurisdiction. Preferential immigration status is allocated to the very rich, known in Jersey as '1(1)(K)s', who negotiate their own tax rate (a privilege unique in the world, I was told). The flat tax rate is 20 per cent on the first million, and up to 10 per

cent on the rest. It is said that some early millionaire-settlers nego-
tiated a set rate of £3,000 per annum, which some still pay, forty
years later.

The Channel Islands remained Norman in law, culture and language at least until the Second World War. Even now, the islands'
statute books contain criminal and property laws written in French;
speakers of Jèrriais (Jersey), Guernésiais (Guernsey) and Sercquais
(Sark) number in the low thousands, but as late as the Second World
War, for example, my godmother's family's gardener spoke Jèrriais
as his first language. Auregnais (Alderney) has been gone for a century or more.

And yet, linguistic difference, which elsewhere functions as a
marker of ethnic difference, never quite translated into longing for
France. Instead, the Channel Islands lived for centuries with the
threat of French aggression. Jersey, for example, which is only fifteen miles from France, ringed itself with twenty-three coastal
towers and eight Martello towers and throughout centuries of war
with France managed to resist invasion.

In 1939, therefore, when war with Germany was declared, hardly
anyone in the Channel Islands imagined that they were at risk.
Jersey's tourist office even produced posters advertising it as 'the
ideal resort for wartime holidays this summer'.[4] But everything
changed in May 1940, when the Belgian, French and British armies
collapsed and 338,000 Allied troops retreated to England; Britain
faced the prospect of invasion by a militarily superior enemy. In
his famous speech of 4 June 1940, Churchill alluded to the vulner-
ability of 'our Island' (by which he meant Britain), observing that
'there has never been . . . an absolute guarantee against invasion'.[5]
He ended the speech declaring, 'we shall prove ourselves once
again able to defend our Island home, to ride out the storm of
war, and to outlive the menace of tyranny, if necessary for years,
if necessary alone':[6]

> we shall never surrender . . . even if, which I do not for a moment
> believe, this Island or a large part of it were subjugated and starving.

Historical, heroic isolation was one thing for Britain – which escaped occupation – but soon after Churchill made this speech, those in Westminster decided that, for the first time since 1066, more or less, the Channel Islands would no longer be defended. Small and weak and too near France, they alone were left to discover for themselves whether Churchill was right – that it was possible to be subjugated and starving, but not surrender in spirit.

By the end of June 1940, 25,000 people were evacuated from Jersey, Guernsey and Alderney, along with all the British troops and the island militia. Many more decided to stay, however. As the Guernésiais saying goes, 'Chatchun bat sa maraïe' ('Each chooses their own tide').[7] The Germans sent over planes on a bombing raid and quickly realized the truth – there were no defences. On 30 June, the islands formally surrendered.

The first thing the Germans did upon arriving in the islands was to cut the telephone lines to Britain. Then they declared that all schools must teach German, and cars drive on the right; tarmac was repainted with instructions in German. Officers took over the best island houses, and marching bands filled the villages with German music and the cinemas with German films. Thanks to a quirk of geography and history, a symbolic piece of the British realm came under Nazi control.

Certainly, the Nazis wouldn't have bothered with any of these details had the islands still belonged to France. But the Channel Islands stood for Britain. Hitler's ambition was that they should function for the German empire as Gibraltar did for the British overseas – a strategic outpost. After the war, they 'were to remain in perpetuity under German rule'; 'there was no question of handing the Islands back to the British Crown'.[8] The Germans governed the islands by 'indirect administration' – 'a principle borrowed from British Imperial administration', as Paul Sanders, Anglo-German official historian of the Occupation, points out.[9] What they were meting out to other cultures across the world was now being done to them within the British Isles.

The islands, in Hitler's mind, would dominate sea approaches from the Atlantic. He ordered their fortification as *Festung* (fortress) *Jersey*, *Festung Guernsey* and *Festung Alderney*. In the summer of 1942, thousands of bags of cement arrived, 800 tons of barbed wire, along with hundreds of artillery pieces, howitzers, aircraft flak guns, infantry support weapons, mortars, machineguns and rocket launchers. Six thousand slave labourers were brought in from Europe (mostly Russians and Ukrainians, but also French Jews and Spanish Republicans) to build a series of new defences along the coast. The number of German troops throughout the islands was doubled to 25,000: 'three German soldiers for each inhabitant';[10] this calculation includes the slave labourers – or almost one German to every islander in Guernsey, while 'in Jersey there were more Germans per square mile than were to be found in Germany'.[11] It was the most intense occupation in Europe; insanely intense. In the same year, the Germans deported all British-born residents of the islands to internment camps in Europe, on Hitler's personal orders.

Soon, Germans posted to the Channel Islands began to talk of the Führer's *Inselwahn*: island madness. The islands, as Churchill pointed out, had no strategic value, in military terms, whatsoever; as the Elizabethans had found centuries before on Rathlin, it made no more sense for Britain to defend them than it did for Hitler to occupy them. But the Führer would not be overruled. He rejected the plans he was shown for the fortifications for the islands, insisting on greater resources, and for twice-weekly updates thereafter.[12]

Among the occupying Germans, 'paranoia thrived'.[13] The 'occupier-occupied ratio was higher than in any other part of occupied Europe', and 'magnified . . . island siege syndrome'.[14] In 1945, Hitler replaced the high command in the Channel Islands with a fervent and paranoid Nazi, Vice-Admiral Hüffmeier, who banished Lieutenant Colonel von Helldorf (aide-de-camp to the previous Island Commander, von Schmettow), to the tiny island of Herm,[15] a couple of miles from Guernsey, in case he tried to stage a coup. (Today, Herm is a bit of a party island.)[16]

In December 1945, von Helldorf testified that Hüffmeier 'was determined "to hold the island[s] in a state of siege until 1947, whatsoever might befall the civilian population" '.[17] There had been shortages of food in the Channel Islands from early on in the war – 'Starvation has never been far off since the Germans came,' wrote one islander to her friend; some children grew up not knowing what sweets were[18] – and in 1944, after the D-Day landings, the islands were cut off from German supply lines in France. The price of butter increased by twenty times as food stocks ran low. Islanders survived on Red Cross parcels. The Germans, like so many before them, foraged on the seashore for limpets (the coastline, a salvation). They stole islanders' pets. There are photographs of emaciated German soldiers holding up decapitated cats for dinner. The island fortress had become an island trap: Britain's war shortages, accentuated in miniature.

Those who were children at the time remember the shortages. At Pomme d'Or, a hotel in St Helier which was home to the Hafenkommandant during the occupation, I meet Jo Tirel, who was ten at the beginning of the war. His father was a farm worker whose fields were in the middle of the German lines, so Jo would come and go, and every now and then he would steal some loaves of bread or bottles of German beer ('I tasted that beer and it was lovely, thank you'), or an armful of kindling.

'Everyone was stealing,' says Jo's wife, Jean. She remembers her brother nicking some of the Germans' 'horrible dark bread'. It was pouring with rain when the Gestapo knocked on the door. Her brother had run inside, moments before, soaked to the skin. The Gestapo came in with their guns and searched the house. 'We children were terrified. They went into my brother's room. He was in bed, fully clothed. They didn't realize it was he who had been stealing, thank God.'

There are many such stories of islanders' humour and bravery in the face of an impossible situation. By geographical definition, there could be no grand resistance on islands barely a few miles wide, with no mountains to hide in, or *maquis*, as in France. It was almost impossible to escape beyond the heavily mined shoreline. The islanders were trapped.

For fifty years this narrative of quiet heroism was accepted, even celebrated. But in 1995 the journalist Madeleine Bunting published a book, *The Model Occupation*, which argued that there was fairly widespread collaboration with the Germans. This, as a friend of mine from Jersey put it, 'devastated the many wonderful islanders who kept their integrity'. Undoubtedly, the book contained a lot of truth. Presumably it is possible for both narratives to coexist. But it makes conversations around the war very difficult, especially for outsiders.

In Pomme d'Or, Jo and Jean's friend Marie-Antoinette, who is Corsican (where the name is commonplace) and married a Jersey doctor, tells me that 'Some families in Jersey made money from the black market.' She lowers her voice to a whisper. 'My husband's family did that. They didn't suffer, because my father-in-law was a *charcutier*. We in Corsica knew the Germans were the enemy, but here in Jersey they were impressed by their singing and order and superior culture.'

I heard that comment a lot: that the 'local grandees got too friendly with those aristocratic German army officers' – men like Prince von Oettingen, whom the Dame of Sark, Sibyl Hathaway, hosted at the Seigneurie. Indeed, she makes much of an aristocratic meeting of minds in her *Autobiography*:

> my name and status were included in the Almanac de Gotha,[19] which in those days could be guaranteed to make clear my rights and authority when dealing with upper-class Germans; and if the lower classes made any attempt to bully me or my people I knew full well that neither they nor I would show any signs of cringing.[20]

Until the high command was replaced by diehard Nazis in 1945, it seems that the occupying Germans were, at the elite level, polite and courteous. Sibyl Hathaway writes that she never had to endure a Heil Hitler salute.[21]

With most British men of fighting age away from the islands, the German soldiers also filled a sexual void, and Bunting points out that some island women could not resist the glamour and comfort offered by those young and handsome German soldiers, that Teutonic culture, with its emphasis on physical beauty (the Germans liked sunbathing and swimming nude) was a very pleasurable shock. (Not all the soldiers were young and handsome; some were hoary First World War veterans.) Soldiers also had access to resources: they brought back nylon stockings, champagne and lipstick from Paris for their girlfriends. There were some genuine love affairs. Bunting interviewed one island woman, Mary McCarthy, seventeen when war broke out, who said that 'Jerseymen were horrible to their women. Women had to do heavy work in the fields . . . There was also a lot of incest. Then along came the Germans; many of them had never known such kindness.'[22] A few of these love affairs resulted, after the war, in marriage.

As always, how women behave comes under a particular kind of scrutiny. The matter of 'local women prostituting themselves with the Germans in the most shameless manner'[23] was brought to the attention of the authorities in Britain during the occupation itself.[24] It was estimated by MI19, and duly reported in the press, that there were eight hundred illegitimate births on Jersey during the war[25] – it was presumed, babies fathered by Germans. The Jersey Superintendent Registrar thought the number was much lower, at 176.[26] According to a report by MI19, 'Abortions have been innumerable at a now standardised rate of £5.5.0 for a German father and £3.0.0 for a local man'.[27] Venereal disease, it was reported, was rampant, among the troops, and the Germans repatriated some of the French prostitutes they had brought over on this account.

Very few islanders experienced an occupation of aristocratic connections, sex and champagne, however. This was a conservative society, of 'Church and chapel', where premarital sex was not the norm. For most of the population, malnourished as they were, life under German rule was unpredictable and frightening, with sometimes deadly results.[28] In the Pomme d'Or, Jo says, 'Mothers had a terrible time, scared of starvation.' We were 'hungry all the time. It was frightening. But for myself I think they were the most educational days of my life. I learned so much. How to survive and how not to waste.'

Still, the bitterness lingers – in the minds of both those who experienced it and those who observe it from afar. Marie-Antoinette says, 'A lot of people reported on each other during the war.' A shocking number of letters were sent, anonymously, to German High Command: islanders denouncing neighbours for crimes such as possessing a radio – 'the only place in Europe where wirelesses were banned altogether'.[29] Then again, many of these letters were opened, read and bravely discarded by now-anonymous post office clerks – sometimes warning those who had been informed on.

Impossible as it had been to live through those years, as those who weren't there will probably never fully understand, from the moment of liberation, the dominant narrative became that managed from London: Churchill's original message of stoicism. British authorities investigated whether there had been collaboration. Jewish shops, such as Krichefski's on Hilgrove Street in St Helier's, had been made to put up signs in their windows reading JUEDIS-CHES GESCHAEFT ('Jewish Business'), and it appears that some Jews in the islands – instead of being sheltered by island officials or lawyers – were denounced to the German authorities and deported. Some, such as June Sinclair – sent to Ravensbrück for slapping the German soldier who molested her – are presumed to have died there; others disappeared 'into the abyss of the Third Reich's camps and prisons without a trace'.[30] These deaths are a stain on Britain. But it was more convenient for Britain, and the Channel Islands, to make the official history one of heroism – to make Britain different from France, which had fallen so quickly to the Nazis.[31] Thus, when the Home Office duly investigated whether the island authorities had collaborated or merely cooperated for the greater common good, they found a mixed picture. Ultimately, after the investigations of 1945, the decision was to silence further inquiry – *Our Man in Havana*-style – by knighting the Bailiffs of Jersey and Guernsey and refusing to give in to calls, by left-wing groups such as the Jersey Loyalists, for a proper process of legal and social reckoning.[32]

Jo remembers the 'very bad feeling, especially afterwards. Some of the women who went out with German soldiers got tarred and feathered, black bitumen swastikas were painted on their houses.' There are no official reports of tarring and feathering. Churchill was determined to avoid the awful scenes that had occurred in liberated France in 1944, when women had their heads shaved and were paraded in the streets. Plans had been made by groups in the Channel Islands with names such as 'The Underground Barbers', to punish women in this way, and when the British liberation forces arrived (with 'the arms of the Duke of Normandy gallantly emblazoned on their shoulders'),[33] they saved at least one woman from being lynched by other islanders. The British army had to evacuate Ginger Lou, the most notorious 'Jerry-bag' (as girlfriends of Germans were known), for her own safety.

Bob Le Sueur, who when I meet him is about to celebrate his 101st birthday, was nineteen when the war broke out. He considered leaving in 1940, but the queue for the boat was so long that in the end he stayed on, becoming boss at his insurance broker's office. He remembers Ginger Lou – Mrs Baudains, nicknamed Jersey's number-one collaborator by the local paper.[34] 'She was recognized on the boat out and her young son George tried to defend her.'

He knew other women who went with Germans, too. One of the 'Jerry-bags' was a 'card-carrying member of the British Union of Fascists'. Bob remembers her telling him about visiting Berlin during the Olympics in 1936; 'she returned enthused with Hitler. Pearl Vardon. She got a German boyfriend during the war and afterwards managed to go and join him in Germany, where they were married.'

A third woman he mentions got pregnant by a German soldier and after the war went to live in England. 'I know the name, but I won't say.'

Bob is the sprightliest 101-year-old you will ever meet; he looks like he's been doing yoga and living on Himalayan apricots his entire life. I visit him in his home by the sea, where, as he explains, he is sitting on a goldmine – the smaller house next door recently sold for £1.7 million – but day to day he subsists on his tiny pension. It is he, not I, who makes the analogy between the Jerry-bags and Jersey's current status as a low-tax regime: 'Some people say that our low tax regime is territorial prostitution.'

'A few of the Jerry-bags were, yes, physically mistreated,' but he didn't see it himself. All he knows is that the people threatening them were 'fine young Jerseymen who had not lifted a finger at any time during the occupation'.

In these small island communities, all kinds of blatant and subtle disapprobation must have cut through homes and hearts. It is said that those who left for England in 1940 were booed at the docks when they returned – but there are also stories of returnees being welcomed back and helped. Women who had got close to Germans – fairly innocently, perhaps, in the way that Irène Némirovsky, the Jewish French writer deported to Auschwitz in 1942, describes so tenderly in her posthumously published novel *Suite Française* – were sometimes treated cruelly. I heard a spectrum of stories. Women who committed suicide from the shame; but also local men who married women who had got themselves with child by Germans, thus protecting them.

The official consensus indeed seems to have been one of gentle oblivion: to commission an official report (General Snow, the commander of the liberation of forces in 1945, delegated this to policemen assigned to the army), but then to classify it, never publicising its findings, and eventually making it 'unfindable'.[35] In the Channel Islands, Reichsmarks were handed in and exchanged for sterling – thus allowing those who had profiteered to get away with their crimes. Nor was any 'Island official or lawyer . . . ever prosecuted or otherwise sanctioned for their participation in the imposition and implementation of the series of legal measures aimed at the Islands' Jewish population.'[36] The impression is that the men in power got away with serious crimes, and that the women became the visible marks of disgrace.

The gendered disparity in how stories of the war are told has become one of the most notable aspects of the occupation histories. In his Foreword to Paul Sanders' official history of the occupation, Philip Bailhache, Bailiff of Jersey from 1994 to 2009, describes the islands as 'small communities largely bereft of their menfolk of fighting age, and swamped by superior force'.[37] (Notably, there has not yet been a female bailiff, since the first appointment in 1302.)[38] Jersey and Guernsey suffered, in Sanders' words, because the population was 'depleted of its combative members – the men serving in the British armed forces'[39] – leaving the islands in the hands of women and old folk. Both men are making the same point: that things went wrong in the absence of men. That the islands became overly feminized.

Sark, officially feudal until 2006, had a female leader at the time of the outbreak of war – the 'Dame', Sybil Hathaway. She seemed to manage pretty well, and certainly no worse than the male bailiffs on Jersey and Guernsey. Unlike the men in charge, she made a point of never signing any order issued by the Germans; whereas the Guernsey Bailiff Victor Carey aided the Germans in their search for those of Jewish heritage.[40] Likewise, the Jersey Bailiff Coutanche, Bunting writes, showed 'complete indifference' to the fate of the island's Jews.[41]

There was one island which provided a test case (should one require it) of what can happen when an island is entirely dominated by men. Being only seven or eight miles from the Cotentin peninsula, the islanders of Alderney could hear the German advance through Normandy in 1940; it spooked them enough that they voted to leave, and on 23 June the church bells rang out at six in the morning, summoning everybody to the harbour, where six ships had arrived to take them to Weymouth.[42] On 2 July the Luftwaffe arrived to find the island almost deserted.

The war still haunts the islands, with the German fortifications among the many ghosts. On Guernsey, I saw a fortification tower that had been bought up as part of a private residence: giving these well-heeled locations a bit of Bauhaus glamour, perhaps. But Alderney is a much smaller island; with no resident population, the

Germans had almost complete carte blanche, and there Hitler's *Inselwahn* took on new levels of insanity – and it still shows.

At first, the posting was a glorious one for Germans. For a start, it was distinguished by being the first bit of occupied British soil. Secondly, it was an island which, like the rest of the Channel Islands, never saw armed combat – a holiday island for soldiers at war (as Wight was for the occupying Romans, arguably). A handbook, *Die Insel Alderney*, was issued to the occupying forces, detailing Alderney's flora, fauna and important buildings. French women were brought in as cooks, washerwomen and prostitutes. A large dance hall was constructed. The Germans set to work trying to make Alderney productive: they removed the boundary stones that had separated family plots and ploughed large areas of the island as big fields. They used the grand Victorian Gilbert Scott-designed church as a storehouse, put in new roads, drains, mains water, introduced a telephone system and two new electricity generators.

For the islands to shape up as Hitler's ideal war trophy, fortifications were apparently not enough. After the war he planned to use them as a holiday camp for the Nazi ideology of 'Strength through Joy'. But during the war itself, Alderney became an outpost of the SS, a lab of experimental German racialist oppression. Sixteen thousand prisoners were brought to the Channel Islands in total by the Germans, with at least five thousand labourers on Alderney. They were given the task of fortifying the island, but there was a more sinister objective, seemingly that of extermination of human life, so ill clothed were the prisoner-workers (in ragged summer garments), fed once a day, on thin soup and bread. They were housed in camps named nostalgically after German North Sea Islands: Helgoland, Norderney, Sylt and Borkum. Prisoners reported the existence of a fifth camp, Citadella, which housed Moroccan prisoners of war (but the SS destroyed their own archives at the end of the war, so its existence is hearsay). How the labourers were treated depended on their ethnicity, with French and other northern Europeans faring the best, Spanish Republicans further down the pecking order, and the worst treatment seemingly meted out to those from Stalin's Soviet Union. Some labourers were treated like slaves, set to work for twelve hours a day, seven days a week. An unknown number died from ill treatment.

In March 1943, Sylt camp was transferred from being run by Organisation Todt, which managed the forced labour force all over the German empire, to being controlled by the SS stormtroopers, with their strict and secretive culture and code. At this point, Sylt became an extermination camp. It used starvation and overwork as its modus operandi. The workers were known only by the numbers pinned to their backs.

The existence of Sylt within the SS was a secret; according to Solomon H. Steckoll, the Israeli archaeologist and journalist who, in 1982, wrote an extraordinary book about Alderney's Nazi era, Sylt 'became the highest security penal colony established by the Third Reich'. Himmler, head of the SS and the Gestapo, 'issued special orders that the existence of this one camp on Alderney was to be kept as a most closely guarded secret'.[43] Steckoll speculates that the reason for this was the 120 'Wehrmacht prisoners' – prisoners from within the Nazi armed forces – who were sent to Alderney to keep them away from civilians; a 'hermetically sealed island' was the perfect place.[44]

There were also, according to testimony that Steckoll collected, 'special' civilian experts of some kind on the island; one of the men who worked as a cook on Alderney – Norbert Beernaert, a Belgian – described suddenly being given superior ingredients to cook with after these special visitors arrived: 'I had better food there than I ever had in my life. Real coffee; at this moment, I was making chips every day and cakes. We had live geese brought from Cherbourg.' He was told after the war that these 'important men' were 'specialists in "buzz bombs"'.[45]

Whatever was going on in Alderney was unusual, even for the time. The Germans themselves soon began to call the island *das Arschloch der Welt* ('the arsehole of the world'), and also 'Adolf'.[46] A French woman who worked as a cook on Alderney for the Nazis described Alderney as '*île du silence, du cauchemar et de l'épouvante*' ('isle of silence, nightmares and horror'). French Jews called it *le rocher maudit* ('the cursed rock').[47] Francisco Font, imprisoned on Alderney after having fought in the Spanish Civil War, termed it 'a kind of Devil's Island, even worse than Devil's Island'.[48]

To this day, there remains uncertainty over the total number of dead. Some survivors described seeing bodies pushed off the cliffs into the sea, dead and alive.[49] The Alderney Museum states that it is 'impossible to calculate' but suggests that there were four hundred buried in the cemeteries (in 1961, the German War Graves Commission exhumed the 'Russian cemetery' on Longis Common and reburied the bodies in France). But a Spanish forced labourer, John Dalmau, wrote that the number of slave workers who perished 'must run into the many thousands'. He calculated that of the four thousand Spaniards in the Channel Islands, only fifty-nine survived. Steckoll, too, estimated around four thousand deaths, most of them concealed by the bodies being dumped into the sea.[50] (That old taboo again, about the disposal of the dead at sea.) Dalmau's twenty-four-page booklet, *Slave Worker in the Channel Islands*, written a decade after the war, described how 'Throwing men over the cliff became the standard way of getting rid of exhausted workers.' One day he was sent down below the water to untangle an anti-submarine boom and saw a scene that 'haunted' him for years:

a fantastic picture presented itself. Among the rocks and seaweed there were skeletons all over the place. Crabs and lobsters were having a feast on the bodies which remained intact. I wanted to be sick. I thought I must be dreaming . . . but the sight of the fresher bodies standing, blown with internal gases, showed that I was not.[51]

It is thought that there were at least two mass graves; that some graves in the cemetery contained more than one body; that bodies were buried on the common; and that at least one emaciated worker was drowned in a concrete mixer and cemented under one of the fortifications. Major Theodore Pantcheff, who in 1945 was deputed to investigate the crimes committed on Alderney, made clear in the book he published later that the occupying army practised obfuscation:

> the German records on Alderney were so confusing that one cannot but doubt whether those traditionally so renowned for meticulous and efficient administration were in this instance really aiming at clarity. There are death certificates, sometimes manifestly misleading; there are executive reports, which do not always tally with the certificates; there are the names on the crosses, out of chronological sequence, in nine cases bearing two different names on the same grave with one body, and in 22 cases marking two graves in different places with the same names and dates of birth.[52]

Much evidence was destroyed by the Germans themselves when they evacuated the camps in 1944. The SS burned all their files from Sylt before leaving, and the dossiers from Organisation Todt were repatriated to Germany.[53]

These crimes – 'committed on British soil – have never yet been subject to British public inquiry or legal process. While the French investigated the matter during a military tribunal in 1949, in the absence of British presence, only two Nazi officers were brought to trial.[54] According to Steckoll, the British government 'officially stated' that that 'the former Commandant of Alderney, Carl Hoffmann . . . had been executed by the Russians for war crimes'. But this was untrue: 'The documentary evidence shows, indeed, that he was released from a British POW camp in April 1948 and that he died in his bed in Hamelin, West Germany, on 8 March 1974.'[55]

Missing documents, presumed destroyed, include the reports of investigations ordered by British Military Intelligence, Channel Islands high command, the Anglo-Soviet Mission of Inquiry and 'hundreds of investigation reports on German war criminals'.[56]

A copy of Major Pantcheff's British Military Intelligence report was, however, sent to the Soviets, and thus Bunting was able to read it, by going to Moscow after it was declassified in 1993.[57] Pantcheff himself had retired to Alderney by then, where his papers were stored in the museum; and according to Trevor Davenport, President of the Alderney Society, whom I spoke to on the island, Pantcheff's 'wife kept them [her husband's war papers] until MI6 asked for them about ten years ago.' The papers were duly sent. Apparently, MI6 'promised to send copies but never did'.[58] According to Davenport, the museum did not make copies of the papers before handing them over either.

While Davenport believes that Steckoll and others exaggerated the extent of both SS atrocities on Alderney and the British cover-up, Steckoll writes that he found in the Yad Vashem archives in Jerusalem 'a thick file of original documents from Guernsey so incriminating that they had been secreted away'.[59] He published a photograph of Guernsey's promulgation into law of the 'Order relating to Measures against the Jews' on 27 September 1940 and witnessed by ten named Guernsey officials, including the bailiff Victor Carey:

la Cour . . . a ordonné que le dit ordre sera enregistré sur les Records de cette Ile
    (the Court commands that the said order be registered in the records of this island).

Eighty years on, now that the UK government has finally announced an inquiry into the Nazi era on Alderney, undoubtedly much will be uncovered. The process will likely prove traumatic, divisive and, hopefully, ultimately cathartic for islanders, as well as for the families of those killed there.[60] The forensic archaeologist Caroline Sturdy Colls had this to say about Alderney:

[N]one of the sites on Alderney are scheduled monuments and, consequently, they are not protected by law. Sylt now lies in wasteland next to the airport; the gate posts of Helgoland have been incorporated into the gateway of a private property. Borkum now stands in the island's refuse depot; Norderney is now a holiday campsite.[61]

In 1945, before the British let the Alderney islanders return, there was a mass clear-up of Alderney by the British Army, aided by

German prisoners of war. Nevertheless – unsurprisingly – Alderney still bears the visible scars of this traumatic history. I visited the island in December 2015, just as it was celebrating seventy years since its liberation. I heard birdsong – one of the absences that islanders reported when they returned that Christmas. Six months pregnant, I visited all the German fortifications with a young historian of the island, Alex Snowdon, who had become convinced that there was more to Alderney's grim outlines than meets the eye, and was taken on a tour of various island houses by Graham McKinley, a jovial chain-smoking member of the island's states, whom I met by chance after sitting next to him on the plane in from Guernsey. Both Graham and Alex believed that their island's heritage is a British cover-up of mass deaths.

Some of the houses I visited with Graham were still crammed with Nazi memorabilia – china, knives, cigarette lighters, stamped with the SS insignia. Graham's friend Louis Jean was born, in 1954, into post-war Alderney, but his family, who owned a lot of property on the island, also accumulated a hellish number of Nazi relics – china tea sets, bottle openers, cutlery. Each corner of his long drawing room proffered something shocking. He told me that after the war farmers converted those huge cooking vats used to feed the slave labourers into water troughs for cattle.

It was traumatic for those islanders who left – more traumatic returning than leaving, possibly. In the words of the St John Ambulance man who, in 1940, went to Alderney to try and persuade the one remaining family to leave: ' "There were cows roaming the streets with udders bursting and an old gentleman was trying to chloroform them to kill them" '.[62] By the end of the war, these cows, symbol of Alderney's bucolic fame, were no more. Guernsey people had come over in 1940 and taken what they could from the nigh-deserted island before the Germans arrived, and during the occupation the Germans ate the rest.

In 1945, British troops arrived on Alderney a week after arriving on the other islands. Most of the islanders' houses were in a terrible state, having been lived in by starving Germans who ate or burned anything they could. The Home Office considered abandoning Alderney and resettling the population elsewhere, but a Committee of Inquiry decided it was possible to move back. The German prisoners of war lifted 37,000 mines.[63] The 'German jetty' was destroyed only in 1978. The German substation is still in use.

Conrad Gries, a German soldier, had been ordered to destroy the detailed drawings he had done of the minefields, but he left a second copy for the Allies to find, which they did. (He also painted landscapes of Alderney.) Prisoners were set to work doing repairs and running the electricity plant. Louis Jean told me that his house was used by officers, so it was 'fairly intact', but others were in 'a dreadful state'. A neighbour's home 'had been used by the Germans to house prostitutes'; 'they had started dismantling the stairs to the attic' (to burn as firewood).[64]

The first boat brought islanders home on 15 December. From then on there was a hierarchy of return: the boats were filled up in order of importance, with those deemed to have useful skills coming on the first boat, and the less important people (such was the perception) arriving thereafter.

Since they weren't sure who owned what, the British authorities collected all the furniture and linen and tableware from all the island houses and placed it on the Butes, the island's common.[65] Islanders were summoned in the morning to look and see what was rightfully theirs. Then, at midday, the whistle blew, and there was a 'scrum'. Inevitably, accusations of theft and appropriation abounded. That morning became known as 'the Battle of the Butes'. Old friendships ceased as treasured heirlooms fell into a neighbour's hands.

Because all the field boundaries had gone and there were no trees (they had been burned), the island was converted into a giant communal farm and for some years it functioned as Britain's only government-sponsored communist agricultural experiment. Men were paid £3 a week, women £2. They used German agricultural implements. But in the end it split the island and the experiment stopped.

When I visited, it was a waxing crescent moon, still the dark side, rain, December. My pregnancy was no longer making me sick, but it was strange having to get up and leave the room where I was interviewing people, until they finished their cigarette. The island was ostensibly celebrating the seventieth anniversary of its post-war homecoming with a church service, a musical play ('An Island Story') and a documentary by Charlie Gauvain, whose family hailed from the island. Even in the daytime – especially during the day – the historical, climatic darkness felt like too much, for one small island; that extreme Nazification.

I talked to Eileen Sykes, who was thirteen when she was evacuated. By then her father, a soldier, had already left. Each islander was allowed to take one suitcase. When they arrived at Weymouth, all the remaining men of military age were taken away. Eileen looked on aghast at the filthy refugees from France and Belgium, 'popping with fleas'. The train north left late in the morning, stopping in tunnels during air raids – an invasion of southern England was expected after Dunkirk. All the station signs had been removed so they didn't know where the train was going. Eventually it stopped, and they were taken by bus through Edinburgh – although in fact, it turned out to be Glasgow. Immediately, a lot of the children went down with measles; 'they weren't that used to germs'.

Eileen loved Scotland; she would have stayed there happily. But soon after the war ended a man knocked on the door. When she opened it, he said, 'Hello, you must be Eileen.' She looked at him. 'You must be my father.' She hadn't seen him since she was ten years old.

It was shocking, returning to Alderney. Her grandparents' house was a shell; not even the flooring was left. 'News about Alderney's use during the war never really got out.' She pauses. 'On the Longis Common there were graves when I got back.'

Like Eileen, Joyce Buckland, twelve when she left Alderney, remembers seeing dead bodies. She is convinced that the long German-built wall around Longis Bay 'is full of skeletons'. 'Lots and lots of people died here on this island,' she says. Afterwards, Sylt, the concentration camp, was knocked down; she remembers that workers were sent in to pick up the pieces without gloves. 'Just the word "Sylt" was left.' (On the gatepost.)

Like Eileen, for years and years – seven decades, in fact – Joyce didn't speak about what she saw on Alderney when she returned after the war. 'You didn't learn anything from the British. They didn't want to admit that there had been a concentration camp. We got more information from the [German] POWs.'

Joyce's house, where we are speaking, was the German headquarters – the local armistice was signed here. The garden had been dug up and turned into barracks. She says, 'For seventy years I've tried to forget all this. I've never even talked about it with my own children.' When she came back to Alderney, 'everything was black'. The Germans had burned almost all they could during the previous winter. Then they had begun to starve. 'I lived in Glasgow,' she says. 'I'd go back tomorrow. I miss the buses. There are no buses here.'

It wasn't the fact that the island was poor after the war, which made it hard; everybody was poor before the war, the island was a poor place; indeed, post-war rationing wasn't a hardship, Joyce explained, because it meant they had more than before. She, too, mentions the bodies on Longis Common. 'You could see their boots sticking out of the ground, where they hadn't buried them properly. It still makes me feel –' She shudders. 'It was taboo. Nobody asked questions, and nobody talked about it.'

There wasn't a winkle or a limpet left all along the seashore. The starving Germans had eaten everything. 'The only thing left was ormers [sea snails], which you found under rocks. You got sick of them. Picking a hundred, two hundred, at a time; shell, gut, clean, beat them and beat them. But beautiful when simmered in a casserole.'

The Alderney returnee children played in the German tunnels. 'All we youngsters wanted for our birthdays was a five-cell torch' – a long one, she explains – 'and a ball of string.' They would go for miles, like Ariadne guiding Theseus towards the minotaur at the heart of the mountain. Then an island man went for a walk in the tunnels and was never seen again. After that, they blew up the entrances to all the tunnels.

'We weren't easily scared,' Joyce says, 'We'd lived through the Blitz in Glasgow. But coming back was worse than the Blitz. I don't know why I am still here, actually.'

Along with the concrete and the mines, the Germans left behind many murals – some pornographic, some of their loved ones and children; they, too, were homesick and starving and ill treated by their high command. The German prisoners stayed on the island until 1948 and, after the islanders returned, friendships developed, even love. Doris was sixteen when she married Karl Curth, aged twenty. He was an electrician. The Greffier (Alderney court registrar) married them at her mother's house, then returned the fee of 7 shillings sixpence as a wedding present. 'Most POWs left in 1948,' she tells me, 'But we got married in May.' They stayed in the island, Karl working as an electrician. That was one of the happier stories.

Even within Jersey and Guernsey, it took many many years for the bravery of those who resisted the German high command to be recognized. Those who went against the dictate of their own island government by keeping radios to listen to the BBC, or helping foreign slave labourers, were seen as 'rocking the boat'. Louisa Gould, deported to Ravensbrück by the German authorities for sheltering escaped Russian slave workers, was murdered there in a 'makeshift gas chamber' in 1945.[66] Afterwards, her family felt 'they had done something wrong'.

In 1966, the USSR decided to honour those islanders who had helped or saved Russian citizens from Nazi mistreatment during the war with the present of a gold watch. But when the call went out, only twenty people – all men – came forward. The reasons were perhaps to do with fear of communism – and British islanders' dislike of boasting, their dread of hubris.[67]

The bravery of Claude Cahun and Marcel Moore, too, was almost confined to the dustbin of history, as was their entire artistic œuvre. Cahun was a surrealist artist who moved to Jersey from

Nantes in France, with Marcel, her stepsister and lover (their birth names were Lucy Schwob and Suzanne Malherbe, respectively). The women were in their forties when war broke out, living in the south of Jersey at St Brelade (where there is a beautifully frescoed church). It appears that they came to Jersey to escape sexual censure: in this island between nations, they were free to behave as they choose. Cahun chose androgyny.

During the war, the women launched a covert anti-Nazi campaign, producing anonymous pamphlets, written in German (Moore had been taught German as a child), which they placed on café tables and in the coat pockets of German soldiers during church, designed to look as if they were the work 'of an international organisation'.[68]

In 1944, they were eventually caught, imprisoned, tried and sentenced to six years in prison (the radio) and to death (the pamphlets). The bailiff appealed their sentence, which was stayed, and the women were saved by the liberation. But while in prison, thinking they were about to be deported to concentration camps in Europe, they took barbiturates and almost died. Cahun was very ill thereafter, and the poison probably hastened the end of her life.

The Germans believed that Cahun was part of a wider network of resistance and were convinced that their work must be 'the brainchild of a man, or men'. Later, Cahun spoke about how the society of Jersey militated against organized resistance – politically, too old-fashioned; socially, too stratified; with women afforded little domestic and personal autonomy, let alone political representation.[69]

The women's resistance work wasn't just heroic – it did have an effect. During their incarceration they met German soldiers 'imprisoned for desertion or insurrection, and many claimed the tracts to have been the impetus behind their actions'.[70]

By the time war broke out, both women had produced a large body of artistic work. Cahun, in particular, excelled in self-portraits and, decades later, her work would be cited as an influence by artists such as Cindy Sherman. There is one especially powerful self-portrait of Cahun standing in the doorway of her home, post-imprisonment, with a Nazi eagle badge that a fellow prisoner had given her between her teeth.

Cahun died in 1954; Moore lived on until 1972. But despite the fact that their 'resistance activities . . . were unique within the Island', '[p]ostwar life passed for both women without incident or acknowledgement from the Island authorities'.[71] Moore died, there was a house sale, and a local book collector bid for some books, packaged in tea chests, which he acquired for £21. When he went to collect his purchase, he 'had to retrieve several items that had fallen onto the floor and . . . had already been swept up . . . ready for the bin'.[72] It was this collection of garbage that later became the women's posthumously celebrated artwork.

How many other such stories have gone, and may still go, missing.

It took many years for islanders to begin to examine the shame and humiliation with which they had lived during the war and, even worse, how they were treated afterwards. In 1946, German guns were pushed off the high cliffs at Les Landes in Jersey, and bunkers closed up and grassed over. Half a century would pass before people would begin to speak, before the archive of notes and letters and records was opened and examined, before the guns were dragged back up the cliffs from the seabed and placed on the headland as memorials to that time. Many guns are still out there, visible at low tide, hulking evidence of Hitler's *Atlantikwall*.

Any examination by outsiders into this troubled history still provokes extreme reactions. Bunting, a journalist and a woman, got the worst of it. *The Model Occupation* reads as a brave, thought-provoking examination of an incredibly difficult subject – but is widely seen locally as inflammatory and blundering. Bob Le Sueur began his interview with me by talking about how Bunting, whom he drove around Jersey, helping her with her research, 'was only wanting material to really illustrate that the islanders had all got on very nicely with the Germans and that we'd all collaborated, which of course was grossly untrue'.

Undoubtedly, like Steckoll, Bunting cracked open the door and let some more light flood in. But it is hard not to feel sorry for the Channel Islanders, who have had to turn and turn again as their five years under the Germans have been appraised and reappraised. Bunting quoted Rollo Sherwill, 'son of Ambrose Sherwill, the President of the Guernsey Controlling Committee, [who] said: "We had no alternative, we had to stick to the laws of war. Since the war, we have felt like a woman must feel in a rape trial. People accuse her of having led the rapist on. But just as a woman might cooperate for fear of not surviving, so did we. If we hadn't cooperated, we would have been harshly treated" '.[73]

At around the time that Channel Islanders began to re-examine their Nazi past, another light was shone, quite literally, into their ancient history. In the east of Jersey is an area of high ground, constructed during Neolithic times. It is called La Hougue Bie. As at Maeshowe, the name 'hougue' or 'howe' is derived from the Norse word for mound. The Neolithic builders designed the temple so that during the spring and autumn equinox the rising sun would shine down the entrance passage and light up the inner chamber. But the tunnel was blocked off at the end of the Neolithic, and it wasn't until the spring equinox of 20 March 1996, after a modern concrete structure was removed from the entrance, that the chamber was flooded with light again, for the first time in five thousand years.

Although the temple had been sealed off, the mound dominated the landscape, intriguing and obsessing subsequent inhabitants. Early Christians built a chapel on top. During the French wars a Gothic folly was constructed over the chapel by the Royal Navy's commander in the Channel Islands. There was a bowling alley; the site was used as pleasure gardens, according to the eighteenth-century fashion. When the Germans controlled the islands, they burrowed into the opposite site of the mound from the Neolithic passage, and made their own subterranean bunker from which to control the east coast defences. An island astrologer whom I met there on the autumn equinox believed that Hitler ordered La Hougue Bie to be occupied on account of its esoteric energies.

From the time of its construction, La Hougue Bie has been a place of accretion. It is an icon of the British islands' collective mongrel history, of the fertile union of past eras and peoples; of the islands' long history together; of all we have destroyed and of the traces we still manage to preserve.

Neighbouring Guernsey, too, preserves unique relics from the past. By chance, my first visit to Guernsey was in September 2021, just a month after being shown the Ringing Stone in Tiree. If I hadn't stood throwing pebbles at that rock on its high-tide island for half a day, I probably wouldn't have noticed the reference in Guernsey's Museum to *La Roche Qui Sonne*.[74] Instead my mouth opened wide with wonder. Two Ringing Stones, in islands in the far north, and far south, of Britain. (Ancient mega-versions of the lithophone Piers made on Scilly).

If Guernsey's *La Roche Qui Sonne* was also a site of female reverence, like Tiree's, it is impossible to say now. As with Orkney's Odin stone, it survived for millennia – only to be destroyed by a landowner in the eighteenth century.[75] Edgar MacCulloch wrote about it in *Guernsey Folk Lore* in 1903:

> it is said that when struck it emitted a clear ringing sound. It was looked upon in the neighbourhood as something supernatural, and great was the astonishment and consternation of the good people of the Clos du Valle, when Mr. Hocart, of Belval, the proprietor of the field in which it stood, announced his intention of breaking it up in order to make doorposts and lintels for the new house he was on the point of building ... Every stroke of the hammer on the stone was heard as distinctly at the Church of St. Michel du Valle, distant nearly a mile.[76]

Some of the rock was sold and transported out of the island, bringing Mr Hocart bad luck. Some was preserved, in pieces, in the middle of a nearby primary school playground, where it still stands.

It is impossible to tell now what the Ringing and Singing Stones of Tiree and Guernsey meant to the people who lived beside them in the past. But I later heard tell of the *sinmedwe'ek* ('bell rocks' or 'sounding stones'), quartzite boulders regarded as 'more-than-human grandfathers' by the 'Ojibwa/Nishnaabeg people of Wiigwaaskingaa', Whitefish River First Nation, in north-central Ontario. Such was the music of these stones that French fur traders named the area 'La Cloche' (the Bell), a name still in use. The Sinmedwe'ek, in an area which had 'a pre-historic and historic occupancy by the ancestors', were said to 'symbolically "speak" of the historical experience' of the people. They were rung to announce a meeting or ceremony. This account of how a people elsewhere in the world rooted themselves and their history through an acoustic connection with the landscape helps us to free our imaginations as we dream about the past and the future.[77]

Clos du Valle, was, like Tiree's Ringing Stone, a tidal island (until at least 1806),[78] a sacred site during the Neolithic and possibly long prior and after. There is a large passage grave, from 4000 BC. We (he and I) spend the night there, sleeping on sheets of cardboard in our sleeping bags beneath the capstone, which is even older than the tomb itself: a recycled statue menhir carved with the image of a male warrior: 'a unique occurrence within the Neolithic of north-western Europe'.[79] The warrior's face, long and lean and bearded, has a 'dark, melancholic and enigmatic stare'. At dawn, I lie watching the ivy which overhangs the entrance; I say to him, 'Look, it's a map of the islands.'

Rare though this menhir statue is, it is not the islands' only one. Guernsey has two others: unique anthropomorphic carvings of women carved on to standing stones. Nowadays, they stand guard in – or are guarded by – churches. La Gran'mère du Chimquière, at St Martin's Parish Church, is garlanded during weddings; the Câtel menhir wears a lunula necklace;[80] and both, with their round bosoms, 'are incorporated into folklore traditions that involve fertility and prosperity'.[81]

At sunset, I stand before the Câtel menhir, looking into her face, admiring the set of her jib, thinking how quickly events can turn – in the chip of stone, in the outline of a bosom. In the existence and disappearance of those war stories, the women's stories of heroism and desire, the way narratives are written, through what is preserved and what is lost, we can see so clearly the tragic fragility and durability of human history and culture.

PART FIVE

And So She Returns

And the end of all our exploring
Will be to arrive where we started
And know the place for the first time.

T. S. Eliot, 'Little Gidding', *Four Quartets*, 1943

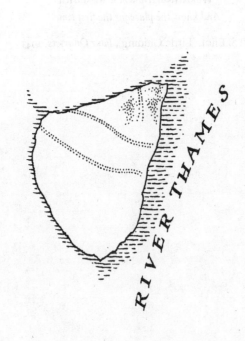

14.

Westminster

Estuary to Elsewhere (twenty-first century)

1. Estuary, 2016

Out on an Essex mudflat, in the 'gutway' between Two Tree and Canvey islands, a man is digging up lugworms. The tools of his trade are a squeegy broom, a fork and a bucket. Bill has been a bait collector his entire working life. 'Thirty-odd years. Trust me, what we see on the mud, people would give their eye teeth. We see everything.' I stand barefoot, ankle deep in sticky mud, watching and listening. Does he mean treasure? Gold bracelets lost from cruise ships? Plastic-wrapped heroin? No, he doesn't mean that. 'All the birdlife. The sunrise, the sunsets. I go inland, look up, start to see the change of wind; and my family'll be like, "Will you leave it alone?" But I can't help it. We're all alone, out there on the mud.'

From October to May, Bill and other Essex bait-collectors gather lugworms, the thick, reddish, wriggling winter bait for seabass, from the entire northern stretch of the Thames Estuary: Canvey to Thorpe Bay at Southend-on-Sea. These little creatures are the cause of the perfect sand squiggles which I've prodded with my toes my entire life on various British beaches. But I've never dug one up before. The summer bait, Bill says, is Southend peeler crab (from under the seaweed) and ragworm (from under the sand). He sells it to sea-fishermen, who in turn supply the family-run cockle sheds near Two Tree, the oyster cafés on Mersea Island, or fish restaurants into London. Here in the Thames Estuary, people have eaten the same diet for millennia, and the evidence is out there on the mudflats:

rippling oyster shells, translucent crab casings, murderous-looking skate skeletons, all piled up among the seaweed. We're thirty miles from Westminster, yet the islands are hemmed with wilderness.

Almost all these islands are an intriguing amphibious mix of the degraded and pristine. During the twentieth century, the islands at the mouth of the Thames seemed the perfect place for large industry to site oil refineries. The oil terminal now evocatively called Oikos (formerly known as Texaco, Regent Oil and London Coastal Oil Wharves Ltd, in reverse order)[1] has been on Canvey since 1936. Since the 1950s, there has been a gas terminal. The IRA tried to blow up the oil terminal (then Texaco) on Canvey in 1979, and the unfinished jetty of Occidental's refinery still looms over West Canvey marshes, beautiful, eerie, outlandish. Canvey now boasts the greatest biodiversity in Western Europe. Foulness, meanwhile, is MOD land, 'the mud full of unexploded armament', as the man who keeps horses there tells me; and there hasn't been any development in decades, 'the island's unchanged, a time-warp'. Two Tree Island, a nature reserve with dog roses, wild cherry trees and cuckoos, is a haven for turtle doves – sub-Saharan migrants and long-time inhabitants of Britain's landscape and literature, now ten years from extinction in Britain because the wild, weedy places they need for food are disappearing.

Canvey was almost wiped out by the infamous east coast flood of 1953, which wreaked devastation on the coast and islands of Essex. The flood was caused by a fatal combination of high tide, hurricane winds, fall in barometric pressure 'and the displacement of an estimated four billion cubic metres of water from the North Atlantic into the North Sea'. This may be Britain's future. In a way, it always has been. This land was formed by how it interacts with cosmically controlled water. As William Camden described, in 1586

> That vast and wide Ocean that surrounds Britain on all sides but the South, ebbs and flows with so strong a tide, that . . . sometimes it overflows the fields adjoyning, and then retreats and leaves them: to speak with Pliny, it lyes so wide and open, that the force and pressure

of the Moon does considerably affect it; and it flows with such an Impetus, that it not only drives back the rivers that run into it, but either surprizes the beasts upon the shore, it advances so fast; or leaves sea-monsters behind upon the banks, it returns so quickly.[2]

Another more recent William, Thomson, wrote in his *Book of Tides* of the epic forces that went into the creation of London:

As the earth rotates on its axis, the changing gravitational pull from the moon powers two giant waves flowing around the coast of Britain . . . The two waves begin their adventure at Land's End. One travels north up the west coast, around the tip of Scotland, then down the east coast. The other flows up the English Channel and the two converge off the Thames Estuary.[3]

I stand at Tilbury Fort, watching river meet sea, making myself understand how insulated we are from the elements in our modern lives. We forget that the sea is one of our organizing principles; that society is the art-form of its force; that it makes islands of us all.[4] *This is why we are here, in this place.* It has everything to do with the moon and the tides; kings and commerce are its children.

2. Eyots, 2017

The River Thames has some 190 islands altogether, and in the capital, too, they inject its veins with wildness. The Thames calls its islands eyots and aits. Some have been reclaimed by the mainland over the centuries, such as the island in Rotherhithe where the Plantagenet king Edward III had a riverine manor, the remnants of which now sit in the middle of a housing estate; or Folly Ditch in Bermondsey, where *Oliver Twist* is partly set. Other islands were shored up by human activity. Rubble was dumped on the tidal islands during the rebuilding of London following the Great Fire, and again in the nineteenth century when London's Underground and sewage systems were constructed. The uninhabited islands that survive, being free of humans and thus of cats, allow wildfowl and woodland birds to thrive in places unexpected.

Despite the modern miasma of glass and steel there is even some greenery left in the Isle of Dogs. Mudchute Farm has Victorian allotments made from dock-dredgings; Island Gardens was paid for by Greenwich Hospital to the south, to somehow absorb some of the brick kiln fumes which blew there across the river. The original 'Ile of Dogges', an actual island in the river, was tiny, a mere nipple on the breast to which it gave its name. It was last seen on a map in 1588. Soon afterwards, it was absorbed into the entire peninsula created by the river's meander. This, east London's rich pastureland, became an island proper in 1800, when construction began on the City Canal and West India Docks. The recent development of Canary Wharf for bankers' offices made a feature of the docks, and water still slices the island off from the rest of London to the north.

There was real riverine life here until the 1980s. Tall, bald, Keith Henney, an island man, worked on a tug from the age of fifteen, reporting for work at Babcock Wharf (now a block of luxury flats), going out to Tilbury in Essex and towing back barges of tea, or petrol from the refinery at Canvey, all the way upstream to Hammersmith. Keith's grandfather came to the island as a seaman from Belfast. *He* worked on a Tate & Lyle sugar boat, going back and forth between London and the West Indies. In one of those weird loops that British history makes, this trajectory has once again become crucial to the British economy. Nowadays, of course, it is men in suits from Canary Wharf, rather than able seamen, who are sent out to look after business in Tortola.

3. Overseas, 2014, 2015

Canary Wharf banks and law firms do plentiful business in offshore jurisdictions. Tortola in the British Virgin Islands is one; Cayman, Bermuda and Jersey are some of the others. Many tax havens are islands; many of the island tax havens belong to Britain. Jersey, Guernsey and Man are all a short flight from London; Bermuda, Cayman and the British Virgin Islands lie further off, for more exotic types of business. The connection to Britain, and in particular its legal system, is integral to the small-island business model. In 2010, the IMF calculated that small-island centres housed one third of the world's GDP.

Twelve of Britain's fourteen Overseas Territories are islands or island groups: they are a motley crowd, widely dispersed between the Mediterranean, Atlantic, Pacific and Indian Ocean. They form a historic miscellany; outlandish evidence of an archipelago's former power, of its still-innate habits and patterns; 'remnants of empire', as the Americans put it in the 2009 US Embassy cable published online by Wikileaks. They remain vivid parts of Britain's *Realpolitik*: integral to its financial system, key to its relationship with its allies, to the geographical reach of its armed forces. Diego Garcia is loaned to the USA as a military base; Ascension is used by the RAF and US air force; as is the British part of Cyprus. Most of the rest function as 'secrecy jurisdictions'. Caribbean islands which (in living memory) had economies based on fishing now host international banks. Cayman is the fifth-largest banking centre in the world. The British Virgin Islands has thirty-two companies per inhabitant.

The more I read about these faraway islands, the more I wanted to visit them, to witness for myself their ongoing connection to Britain.

I started with Bermuda, the richest of them all, a banking playground for millionaires. The reef islands, now conjoined by roads and reclamation, are lush and pretty. Geographically, Bermuda is extraordinarily isolated – as far from the Caribbean as it is from the States. Beneath the waves, coral's purple branches and yellow brains teem with stripy banner fish; a little further out, the annual commute of migrating whales. But Bermuda has become one of the most densely populated places on earth. Its GDP is higher than that of Britain, the motherland to which it is still tenuously attached (unlike all other OTs, it is self-funding). Its people produce twice as much waste as the average US resident. Nothing is made here; little is grown. Everything must be imported, and Bermudians, with their high salaries, want to own everything.

Bermudians are mostly descended from the African slaves brought here by the British to work on the plantations, but the islands' businesses and political class were for centuries controlled by a white minority, a group which, during the Civil Rights era, became known as the 'Forty Thieves'.[5]

The first person I meet is Walton Brown Jnr, then Bermuda's shadow immigration minister. We lunch together on Front Street, the white bastion of Hamilton, Bermuda's capital. As we eat lobster penne Mr Brown tells me that he is currently campaigning against elite white immigration (as are some Caribbean tax havens). The problem is the exact reverse of British islands such as Thanet, where the fear is that foreigners are coming in to claim state benefits and steal low-paid jobs – but the same, perhaps, as on the Isle of Dogs, where the working-class community of dock workers and river tugmen has been outpriced by Canary Wharf. In Bermuda, the fear is that the government is encouraging a racist policy of preferential immigration by rich white people to work in the financial services industry.[6]

We discuss Eva Hodgson, whose book, *Second-class Citizens; First-class Men*, has as its epigraph a poem, 'Protest and Warning from the Negro', by Ernest Mair:

> Hear me, white brethren! Your souls are sick
> With an hypocrisy so deeply engrained
> You do not even know you practice it.[7]

Later, I meet Dr Hodgson in the national library, set back from Front Street. Everybody knows her: she has campaigned for decades to bring Bermudians' attention to their 'two-tiered society'. She is ninety when we meet yet could be twenty years younger – neat, severe and sprightly. A librarian shows us to a room on the ground floor where we can speak without being interrupted (Tennyson-like) by her fans. She begins by explaining that Britain, which had granted universal suffrage to all male voters (and some women) by 1918, did not intervene to make Bermuda a fairer place. Segregation in schools, buses and hotels, lasted until the 1960s – tourists from the southern United States wouldn't have tolerated a holiday here, otherwise; nor was universal franchise extended to non-landowners until then, which effectively meant that only white people could vote.[8] It was the American Civil Rights Movement which put pressure on Bermuda through example. But Dr Hodgson described very little having changed from the state of affairs she wrote about in 1974, of her island's 'very deep and intensely racist heritage', which was still impacting on black lives.[9]

Today, black and white Bermudians 'work well together but play separate', says Gavin Smith, a Bermudian who runs Chewstick, a charity promoting social integration through music and events. Chewstick started out in Back-O'Town, traditionally a run-down, black residential area, with a reputation for skulduggery (or rather, a place associated with the struggle for workers' rights; Bermuda Industrial Union is based there). But it recently moved to Front Street. Despite this symbolic real-estate shift, it is difficult to get white and black Bermudians to mix. Black people celebrate Good Friday and Bermuda Day with parades, kite-flying and parties on the beach; 'white folks leave town during national holidays'. White culture's centuries-old obsession with boats, Smith says, is 'a way of escaping the black Bermudian on the street': the yacht as ultimate island stronghold.

Early one morning at the pier, I buy a spiky guinea chick, a small and tasty local lobster, for $5 from Monty, a Seventh Day Adventist who, on account of religious dietary scruples, has never eaten this or indeed any of his hard-shelled harvest. The lobster season ends at Easter, at which point Bermuda's six-month-long summer starts. Monty's fishing boat has been chartered for the entire summer: from July onwards, it will become a pleasure craft-for-rent, used by rich men (mostly) for champagne-fuelled deep-sea fishing.

Although black Bermudians have some contact with the Caribbean, they were traditionally educated to look down on West Indians, as Eva Hodgson points out.[10] In the British Virgin Islands, by contrast, the British plantation owners had abandoned the islands by the time of emancipation, and former slaves took over the estates. Hence, black families dominate the island politically and, because of the financial services industry, these islands haven't had to rely on selling the colonial dream to tourists. As somebody I spoke to put it, 'we aren't yet reduced to flogging genocide by reconstructing plantations as hotels'.

I went to Tortola because a lawyer friend who had been there for ten years was on the point of leaving – 'It's now or never,' he wrote. He loved the place; defended all its eccentricities. Almost everyone I met in Tortola, incomers or locals, was irritated, angry or affronted by how they were seen by outsiders. 'People come here with their banana republic glasses on,' said Richard Georges, BVI's first poet laureate and president of its college. 'What about Switzerland, Luxembourg, the City of London, the Crown Dependencies?' British expat staff in the governor's office (sipping champagne at three o'clock on a Friday afternoon) expressed frustration at the way 'journalists from the *Guardian*, BBC and other places turn up and demand interviews, then write pieces which callously misrepresent us, illustrated with a photo of a palm tree and beach hut'. (A *Guardian* photo-portrait of tax havens had just been published when I was in Tortola, including a picture of the 'poor Premier's wife', at home, 'shoe-horned into tight lycra'.)

When I visited Tortola in 2015, 'belongers', as natives call themselves, were outnumbered twice over by expats: highly paid Europeans, and working classes from all over the Caribbean. The island was both dismal – financial services; and lovely – steep volcanic hillsides that bloom with bougainvillea, flamboyant and oleander, with chickens browsing the verge at Wickham's Cay 2, where yachts are moored and law firms based, and the grass outside the Sugar Works Museum (a sugar mill until the 1940s), cockerels waking trust-company managers and offshore lawyers alike.

The dangers of relying on rich non-belongers to keep the economy afloat – in an age of climate heating-induced shifting weather patterns – was revealed in 2017, when Hurricane Irma, 'the most powerful Atlantic hurricane in recorded history', hit; 85 per cent of homes were damaged or destroyed. There was an immediate clear-out by law firms, resorts and hotels; the population dropped by a quarter.[11] Lawyers and hospitality staff from Europe left for calmer waters – Jersey and Guernsey were popular choices.

It is easy for rich white folk to travel between British tax havens; less so for belongers. It is only in the past decade – thanks to stubborn demands from the governments of those places – that inhabitants of Overseas Territories became British citizens rather than subjects. When Britain's vast empire broke apart in the twentieth century, only some of the places it had conquered claimed full independence. This was occasionally inconvenient for Britain; or rather, according to John Duncan, Governor of the British Virgin Islands from 2014 to 2017, Westminster has not yet caught up with the reality – that not all of its former colonies want to go it alone. Modern Britain is a multicultural place; the legacy of empire. Yet unlike France, the United States of America, or the Netherlands, all of which treat their offshore territories as part of the mothership, Britain grants 'autonomy', a policy which gives freedom – but can also, Duncan says, become a form of neglect.

The damage that such remoteness can do was tragically illustrated on Pitcairn in 2004 when most of the adult male population of this tiny, remote island halfway between New Zealand and Peru tried to deny the connection to Britain as their key line of defence in a child sexual abuse trial. (It was the habit of Pitcairn men to treat all the island's women, however young, as sexual prey.) Pitcairn islanders number barely fifty people, and live alone in the Pacific. They are descended from Tahitians and HMS *Bounty* mutineers who beached there in 1790. The defendants' lawyer argued that because of the mutiny Britain never formally claimed the island, and therefore legislation such as Britain's Sexual Offences Act did not apply. At the time, the Pitcairn case was depicted as disgusting and bizarre – impossible to imagine in mainstream society; but in the wake of Britain's own paedophile-ring exposés, it now seems like a terrible foreshadowing of all that was about to be uncovered elsewhere. The case was referred to the Judicial Committee of the Privy Council (JCPC) in London. In their final judgement, the judges expressed grave concern about 'the rule of law in remote communities'. The case magnified Britain's absence of policy with regard to its islands, and its own island identity.

The Privy Council (as lawyers refer to it for short), where the Pitcairn case was heard, dates from the Norman Conquest. Appeals from the Channel Islands provided the first regular business, and this was followed by appeals from countries in the empire. It is now used by all Britain's Overseas Territories, Crown Dependencies and military sovereign base areas. To add a strange twist, even those islands which gained independence long ago, such as Jamaica (a Commonwealth realm) and Mauritius (an independent republic), are still tied to the imperial apron strings. Even though Trinidad and Tobago now house the alternative Caribbean Court of Justice, between 2009 and 2012 almost a third of the British court's caseload was referred from there. Occasionally, this results in a ruling from London which changes the constitution of a foreign independent state – this happened to Jamaica when the Privy Council ruled that death sentences have to be commuted if a prisoner spends more than five years on death row. Occasionally, a Privy Council ruling changes English law (as happened with a case of premeditated murder from Jersey).[12]

The Privy Council is convened in an early-twentieth-century building designed by James Gibson in a style that Pevsner called 'art nouveau Gothic'. It stands on Parliament Square, facing the Palace of Westminster, on the site once occupied by Westminster Abbey's Sanctuary Tower, where 'fugitives could seek refuge from their pursuers'. Nowadays, because small-island jurisdictions are heavily embroiled in financial services, two thirds of the cases heard by the Privy Council are civil law. Many are of global concern, involving famous names or business malpractice – such as the fate of a mutual fund of Bernard Madoff's in the British Virgin Islands or the attempt by Lakshmi Mittal's steel company to curb the Steel Workers Union of Trinidad and Tobago (after it tried to enforce stronger collective agreements for the workforce). When the judges deliver their judgements they sometimes invoke cases from imperial times (the Madoff judgement referred to a case from 1874, concerning the collapse of the Indus Valley's Oriental Inland Steam Company). British law lords also hire themselves out to other countries (Lord Neuberger, President of the Supreme Court, spends his long vacation as a judge in Hong Kong). Nothing demonstrates better than the Privy Council how effectively Britain fashioned the political architecture of both new nations and old dependencies, or how successfully it embedded itself into their political futures.

In Britain, appeal cases are referred to the Supreme Court only if they can prove public interest. Overseas jurisdictions which use the Privy Council, however, have an automatic right to appeal enshrined in their constitutions. As a result – as several British lawyers working in Tortola admitted to me – 'there is no vetting of the merits'. Any case can be sent to London, however trivial, and there is nothing the JCPC can do about it. Indeed, it is precisely this legal guarantee that 'creates investor confidence'. A billion-dollar business based in Pakistan, China or Russia and registered for tax reasons in the British Virgin Islands needs to know that the jurisdiction is sound, politically and legally – that if its assets are subject to dispute, the case will be dealt with by the world's best judges. Britain provides this guarantee. Without Britain, islands like Bermuda might become places to launder money – as Cyprus is said to be.[13] Thanks to the monarch, they are meta-colonial outposts.

Imperialism spread the English common law system across the world, and nowadays it is often British law firms which benefit from tax havens. It's a professional gamble for a barrister, moving out to a cowboy island such as Tortola (they lose the right to practise at the Bar in London, for example). But the compensations are magnificent. Work responsibilities soar ('from double-glazing disputes in London to feuds between Saudi princes'); as do bank balances (in Tortola, salaries are taxed at 8 per cent above $38,000). Clients tend to be the world's richest business families; the details of their lives often baroque, sometimes lurid. Lawyers live in colonial-style country houses with temper-soothing sea-views; and since there are few outlets for their money (no Chanel boutiques – 'the climate would make the bags go mouldy'), their stint in the sticks allows them to save and put down a deposit on a house in London. As during imperial times, there are still ways of making money from Britain's historic dalliances overseas.

Lord Phillips, former head of the Supreme Court, made headlines abroad when he criticized the Privy Council's workload from overseas. He is now retired and talks openly of the peculiarity which is the Privy Council when I visit him at his home in north London. Most judges, he says, regard Privy Council cases as 'light relief'. Many of the cases are 'a waste of Privy Council time'. But in his opinion, the system endures because Britain views its ongoing involvement in the countries it once governed as part of its post-colonial 'responsibility' (the JCPC is part-funded by the FCO).

Whether it is from conscientious duty, pragmatism, paternalism or neglect, Britain continues to rule over islands far away; with taxes it continues to support the infrastructure of islands from Lindisfarne to the Caribbean – and sometimes of island tax havens. And with dazzlingly circular symmetry, Westminster, which lies at the heart of this island web, was itself once an island.

4. Thorney Island, 2018

The river Tyburn, which flows south 'from the Hampstead hills', divides under Buckingham Palace. One arm flows southish towards Vauxhall Bridge. The other flows east down Tothill Street, where it divides again to fall into the river at Millbank, south of the Abbey, and at Whitehall, near Downing Street.[14] After the Great Stink of 1858, Sir Joseph Bazalgette's Victorian sewage system completely subsumed the Tyburn (which had already been diverted by medieval monks to flush their toilets). That the river's rising sewage scandal was so rapidly addressed was largely because the problem was particularly potent at Westminster. The Thames, being tidal, washed the entire city's shit back and forth in front of politicians' eyes, and under their noses. They found themselves fainting from the smell, in their rooms in the Palace of Westminster. Sewage volumes had increased exponentially in part through the middle-class adoption of the flush toilet, but also because of the importation of guano from Peru as a fertilizer, which put nightsoil families in the city out of a job.[15] I wonder when there will be a clean, swimmable, drinkable river again. Is that just for the past? Or will we one day do something useful with our own excrement?

Nowadays, apart from the Thames' slosh and intermittent blaze, there is little about modern Westminster to tell you it was once an island. Perhaps the fact that it is London's richest borough, with one in ten of its properties owned by offshore holdings – by anonymous people in island tax havens. Arguably the medley of architectural styles suggests the intensity of islands, built and rebuilt on the same small bit of land. Certainly the Palace of Westminster's many narrow windows refract the glow of the Thames in green and yellow glimpses. But stop any of the tourists, or government wonks, hurrying through Parliament Square, and few of them could show you where the streams of the Tyburn once flowed. And yet, until at least the seventeenth century, maps and pictures show that all the principal places of the English state and Church were surrounded by water, set apart from the rabble.

The Anglo-Saxons, who made Westminster famous, called it Thorn Ey – Bramble Island. Although this name was gradually superseded, Thorn Ey lives on in the name of a Westminster street, and the Anglo-Saxon names of other, sister islands in London: Chels-ea, Batters-ea, Bermonds-ey.

The sand and gravel island of Thorn Ey had the Thames on one side and the streams of the River Tyburn on the other. It was inhabited from the late Neolithic; it was possibly this site that Julius Caesar was referring to when he mentioned that there was a place where the Thames was 'fordable high up'. Thorn Ey's history is first properly attested, by archaeology and literature, in the early seventh century, when, in the time-honoured way which is practically a 'how to' guide to British power, it acquired a monk and a church, settled there post-Augustine.

It was St Dunstan who founded the abbey, in 959 (having already founded another quasi-island abbey at Glastonbury in Somerset). The abbey – and hence the island – acquired the popular name 'Minster in the West', to distinguish it from the rival minster in the east (the Church of St Paul's, built over the site of the deserted Roman city). Around this time, a strange island legend evolved out of these murky waters. It concerned a fisherman called Edric who gave a ride in his river-taxi to St Peter, the church's founding saint. Even now, every feast day, the abbey celebrates its island origins with a re-enactment of this legend. Each 29 June the Worshipful Company of Fishmongers arrives at the abbey with their biggest salmon and, in a performance 'that's more am than dram' (as the abbey's precentor told me), the tithe of fish is redeemed by the church with beer, bread and candles.

London is still inhabited by the sea, and when the tide is in, these sea islands are circulated by sea-fish, even whales, on occasion.

Cnut was the first king to live on Thorn Ey. It was possibly here that the argument with his nobles about holding back the tide took place, in 1035, for the Thames is tidal this high up. The story was written down by Henry of Huntingdon to prove Cnut's piety (not his hubris) – that he alone of his courtiers understood that a monarch's rule was temporal, while the forces of nature would never be bidden:

> at the summit of his power, he ordered a seat to be placed for
> him on the sea-shore when the tide was coming in; thus seated, he
> shouted to the flowing sea . . . 'I command you, then, not to flow
> over my land' . . . The tide, however, continuing to rise as usual,
> dashed over his feet and legs without respect to his royal person.
> Then the king leapt backwards, saying: 'Let all men know how
> empty and worthless is the power of kings.'[16]

It was Edward the Confessor, however, who made Westminster England's primary seat of power. He built a royal palace and a Romanesque abbey with eighty monks; both buildings are depicted in the Bayeux Tapestry. In 1066, first Harold II, then William I, held their coronations in the abbey, keen to ingratiate themselves with Edward's nobles and the tradition he established. It, too, is an isle tradition that continues to this day.

In 1540, when the abbey was dissolved (it being the second-richest religious establishment in the land after Glastonbury), even Henry VIII could not bring himself to deconsecrate the land where his father and ancestors were crowned and buried. The abbey was saved from destruction; and though the palace in Westminster was eventually destroyed by fire, and Henry moved to Whitehall, the island maintained its primordial status in the state. During the seventeenth century, with the rise in importance of Parliament, the island's position as foremost power centre in the land was assured. Today, the House of Commons, House of Lords, Supreme Court and ceremonial places of the British monarch still occupy this quasi-island in the Thames, with Buckingham Palace and Downing Street on the periphery. Thorney Street, just to the south of the Palace of Westminster, encloses the security service MI5 on two sides.

As you pass through the House of Lords (which could well be renamed the House of Lords and Ladies, since a third of the chamber is now women), the river flickers in the distance, across rooms, beyond peers' chatter. I meet Baroness Kathy Willis, professor of biodiversity at Oxford University, whose current book is about humans' therapeutic interaction with plants. She cites studies which prove that environmental microbiome has a direct impact on health; for example the experiment that took soil from the forest floor and put it in an inner-city playground, changing toddlers' gut flora after three months (inevitably, I think of Norse colonizers, bringing soil from home to hallow their colonies). Or the effect of horizons on brainwave activity – a hillside with a few trees is more calming than a jagged cityscape or coniferous plantation (maybe this explains why the sight of distant islands is so calming). Kathy points out that

Buddhist meditation traditionally took place in shady groves, where human thought was eased by interaction with the trees. I mention the groves the Druids were said to worship under in Anglesey, such as the wooded Iron Age village I visited near Moelfre, with its neat, beehive-like arrangement of stone-built altars, thrones and temples, by the sea.[17] I wonder out loud what Westminster will look like in the future; will we live among plants again, in beds made like Odysseus's, from living trees; in giant greenhouses? Will vines and creepers wind through the debating chambers?

5. Mother-Father Thames, 2022

These thoughts fit into a long-held literary interest in Westminster's ruin.[18] William Morris's dystopian novel *News from Nowhere* (1890), for example, imagines the Houses of Parliament as 'a storage place for manure'.[19]

By now I am living back in London again with my daughters, in our very own three-way gynocracy. Soon after we get to town, the queen dies, and it is exactly here, in Westminster Hall, at the Palace of Westminster, that she lies in state.

In 1953, during her coronation, the queen was stripped off to a white robe and anointed by the archbishop of Canterbury, as if he was Columba and she the new ruler of Dalriada. (The same happens to Charles, naturally.) The queue to glimpse her in death snakes back along the river, over Lambeth Bridge, and down along the Southbank – for the Thames, like all rivers, lends itself to pilgrimages.

I walk all the way up the queue, from Southwark where it began, to its ending on Thorney Island.[20] In the afternoon, I take my daughters back into Westminster to witness these scenes of the present for themselves. I find to my surprise (maybe to my sorrow) that I want them to acknowledge the passing of the *femaleness* of the queen's rule, retrograde as it was. (As some witty person wrote on Twitter in September 2022, 'Can't believe they are going to make a

MAN queen.')[21] English, after all, is the only Indo-European language in which the word for a female ruler, 'queen' (*cwen* in Old English), is etymologically distinct from the word for a male ruler, 'king'. But my daughters know this already; I have told them so, tiresomely, many times. We stand looking up at the statue of Boudica opposite the Houses of Parliament; she and her two daughters. The Iceni lost their battle with forces greater than them; their people were wiped out. But Boudica's bravery is still remembered.

My girls and I watch the mourners as they emerge from Westminster Hall. I think of Cuthbert's pilgrims to Lindisfarne; of Shah Abdul Latif's *urs* in Sindh, Pakistan. I point out to my daughters the Houses of Parliament – the stone of this building, lit from the sky and the river, has warmth and even agency – and the House of Lords – a name that sounds so silly, and redundant, and repressive, out loud. To cheer them up, I say, 'I was born on this island.'

I realized this belatedly. After moving down from Orkney and feeling homesick for island life, I joined the Thorney Island Society. Over drinks at the annual AGM, I got talking to a smart Westminster lady. She told me that all her children were born in Westminster Hospital.

'Oh, that's where I was born,' I said. (My father was working for a homeless charity at the time, and my newly married parents lived in the flat above the charity's shop; I made it into the local paper, snapped in the window of the shop in my Moses basket.)

'Well then,' she replied, 'You, too, are an islander.'

The children and I wander with the crowds through St James's Park, marvelling at the bouquet mounds laid out at the foot of each tree, wondering about composting and the plastic, and who is going to deal with it. Just as we pass the palace, where the Tyburn trifurcates, it begins to get dark, and we find that we are being kettled (ever so politely) by the police, into immobility, in front of the gates. The new king is about to make an appearance. As we stand there, waiting, the children laughing at the guards in their tall hats and red coats walking to and fro – 'Is he making fun of himself, Mummy?' – I get talking to one of the legion of temporary-hire South Asian security guards. He turns out to hail from Lahore; his name is Mohammed Etihsan. I tell him in my rusty Urdu about the book I wrote about his river. He says to the children, 'It's your mother, who is queen.' But they are entranced by the marching soldiers.

Just then, the king comes out in his car – and even I am shocked by the way my blood runs cold at the sight. There is something truly oppressive in being ruled over by a *man*, in this day and age, by a toxic fusion of patriarchy and heredity. It feels wrong. What have we been talking about, fighting for, figuring out, all this time, through these islands, if not to move on from *this*? I remember what Kathy Willis said – that maybe the new king will encourage an era of strong environmental legislation. He can't really; but still, I hope he does, somehow. He was once ridiculed for speaking to plants, but now it is well known that when a pollinator comes near a flower, the flower vibrates, to increase its sugar concentration. Maybe there is something about the vibration of the human voice, or body, that benefits plants.

Of all the power we distill into this island, it is perhaps the massive capacity humans have for metamorphosis that is most potent. Just because something has always been done like that doesn't mean that it will be this way for ever.

Three years before the queen died, I joined the XR water pilgrimage from Tower Bridge to Westminster. It wound along the opposite side of the river, starting at the Tower of London (where Brân's head is buried), as the group sang a water song and poured the sacred waters we had brought – I had a vial from a spring on Iona – into a bowl, which was then poured into the river. We walked into Westminster westwards, visiting hidden springs in the City, sacred trees near St Paul's, the solemn and sacred-seeming Roman baths in King's College (apparently not really Roman, a nineteenth-century exaggeration, but very old anyway, and as nice to imagine the Romans bathing there as Charles Dickens, and his creation David Copperfield). By the river near Temple, women from four different continents of the world offered their menstrual blood to the river. I remembered the majestic personifications of the Thames which the

Romans carved – statues were found in the Temple of Mithras near St Paul's.[22] (The cult of Mithras admitted only men.) We sang a closing song outside the abbey on Thorney Island itself. I visited the little chapel of St Faith's, cold and dark and enclosed in stone, like Maeshowe. Later, during the XR protest, I walked through Parliament Square and camped for a night in Marble Arch, relishing birdsong, where once traffic flowed. How we acculturate ourselves – how and what we see around us – is everything.

One of the few MPs to speak at XR is also the youngest member of the House. Nadia Whittome (twenty-three when first elected), a socialist, woman of colour, queer, even gives some of her MP's salary to local causes in Nottingham. We meet in her office at 1 Parliament Street (backbench MPs are housed in a converted hotel, which, with its stripy wallpaper and green patterned carpet, resembles a shabbier version of the place where I worked in Orkney). We walk over (under the road) to the Palace of Westminster as she speaks of the 'alienating experience' which this institution incarnates – the sexism, outdated atmosphere and terminology (members of staff calling you Ma'am and holding open doors; officials in tights; the unnatural way in which politicians must address each other indirectly in the chamber); the 'dazzle and pomp' that is carefully tended from one generation to the next, to create reverence and deference for politicians, to mystify and make opaque, and encourage the political class to expect this as their right. She has survived thanks to the 'collective solidarity of my all-female team and the wider movement'.

We speak the day after the House of Commons has passed the Illegal Migration Bill, which has been internationally condemned. Nadia calls the Bill 'particularly barbaric'. She points out that 'nobody fleeing Ukraine has come to the UK on a small boat' – it is possible to create safe routes. One reason that refugees want to come to these small islands in particular is due to the imperial history of the English language: 'The British colonized a large amount of the world,' and with climate change accelerating, migration is likely to increase exponentially. 'Our history brings with it a responsibility to do something.' To avoid complete disaster, she says, 'we will need to completely reimagine what work looks like.' Care jobs, for example, 'are currently disproportionately done by working-class migrant women of colour on poverty wages' – yet are also eight times less carbon intensive than other professions. 'It's exciting. Imagine – a care economy which contributes to reaching net zero.'

Such language may be rare in the House of Commons, but it is becoming more common outside these gilded rooms. On an evening of monsoon downpours I meet the environmental lawyer Farhana Yamin to discuss modern-day weather prophecies for our planet. We sit in the Westminster pub where I bought hot chocolate for my children three weeks earlier, as the rain tips on to the pavement. Farhana has just been in Egypt for a meeting with the COP presidency team – she has worked for decades representing small-island states at international negotiations – and I was expecting her prognosis to be grim. But she is full of optimism. She speaks of how lucky we are to have born at this moment of paradigm shift; of the disintegration and joyous-harsh realignment that is happening all around us. 'It's going to be like childbirth,' she says, 'painful but ecstatic . . . The old DNA was based on control and mastery of the world. What we need now is mystery.'

We talk about how weather patterns are changing with accelerated, tragic speed in Pakistan, where Farhana was born; and that Britain and other rich countries are in denial or doing the bare minimum. 'The planet will outlast us another billion years,' she says, 'It's us, as a species, who are under threat.' Farhana and others like her are working to create an economy based on 'care rather than profit'. How radical the concept of care is, she says; entire humanitarian disasters, such as those in Pakistan, could be *taken care of* with the profits of a few companies. People fail to challenge the elites' vast concentrations of wealth largely because the scale is beyond our comprehension and also we are being misled.

'As for Westminster,' she says, 'it should probably sink back into the ocean. Politically, it's a bit of a distraction.' In the last few years, Farhana has been constructing citizens' assemblies, councils of all beings, 'culture COPs' and local climate justice hubs of different kinds, to change and reinvent the idea that it is politicians and the titans of industry who can solve the crisis we are in.

'Just as we are all birthed into bodies we didn't choose,' she says, 'so our past is fundamental, but we didn't choose it. We can reach some kind of grace and peace with white patriarchy and other oppressions that still shape our world and exclude so many.'

The thunderstorm abates, and we walk outside, into this new, glistening world, where the river rushes past and the lights of this powerful piece of the planet blur and soften in the rain. Here she is: one of the modern climate prophetesses from the ancient island of Sena, forming a citizens' assembly to show us how the world is non-binary, how the myths we choose to live by and 'the names we give things are all up for grabs'. We stand on Westminster Bridge, looking down at the waters of the Thames. 'All the borders that separated us into hierarchies are dissolving. All the traditional ways that we defined ourselves are changing. It's happening anyway, whether we like it or not.' I think of how my work has been focused on rescuing and re-understanding the female role as we knew it from the past; and that now the work is in respecting bodies as they are.

A few days later, Farhana speaks at the council and ritual of thanksgiving to the River Thames that the Chilean artist-poet Cecilia Vicuña holds as she installs her Turbine Hall commission at the Tate Modern – Farhana celebrating somewhat ironically the movement from oil-fired turbines to detritus-honed artwork. For Cecilia's installation, 'Brain Forest Quipu', is delicate and deathly, bleached white like the mourning clothes of Indian funeral-goers, made with wool and rope and little pieces of white Victorian smoking pipe, mussel shells and pottery gathered from the river – an artwork physically wrought from loss and devastation. Quipu is an alphabet of knots and threads, made by the Quechua people in the Andes and destroyed by the Spanish conquest of the sixteenth century. And yet, even as she brings this work of creation and extinction from the other side of the world to the part of the hemisphere from which its destruction hailed, she also thanks 'every scrap the River Thames gave us':

> I thank above all the River Thames that gave life to this London town. We owe everything to those early settlers who found shelter and sustenance on its banks. They are the foundation of this Universe we now call London.[23]

Early one morning, before sunrise, I cycle back into Westminster, following the half-moon, leading me all the way back to Boudica. I am speaking with Cecilia on the phone this afternoon, and I want our words to be island-to-island (she is now in Manhattan). From the riverbank below the Tate, I pick up a piece of wet rope and knot it twenty-two times, for him and me, remembering the women of Shetland, Orkney, the Hebrides and Man who made their own Quipu to create wind and clement weather for fisherfolk (as well as the witches of *Macbeth*). I cycle on to the garden below the Palace of Westminster, by the statue of Emmeline Pankhurst (born the year of the Great Stink), where the river glows orange with the rising sun, a light reflected in the hundreds of windows of Westminster Palace. Cecilia tells me that she was born by a sacred river in Chile – 'sacred long before colonization'. Through ritual and art she began letting this memory which is not-memory grow into something that addresses 'these aspects of hatred within us.' Chile 'will soon be left without water; hundreds of fires are burning, and rivers are dying. We have to manage these concepts, turning hate into love, and rage into love.' In 2022, 'the Thames also began to make its death apparent': one of its sources dried up and shifted five miles downstream.[24] 'We have released the forces of nature in a manner that is completely different from before; it is completely out of control. We imagine that we can recover control through hatred but it is just a cover-up of fear and despair, a force of obscuration.'

Here on the banks of London's river, she decided to make an offering that honoured the confluence of river and sea, salt water and sweet: 'These are the most fertile places . . . The symbolism of this was completely apparent to ancient people'.[25] I look down at the river, thinking of its environmental degradation – and that of all our rivers, seas, soil and forests. As Cecilia says, recently we have successfully blocked the instinctive empathy we evinced for other species for most of our historical existence. But we have that inheritance in us. To awaken it, we need to see differently – to go back to the same places and love them anew. 'We must acknowledge and care for the sacredness of land and water, sense the beauty and pain there. To me there is nothing more beautiful than that.' It's never too late for new understanding.

The world might do it for us. As before, the seas are likely to rise and make islands of our mainlands, forcing the shift to a new way of thinking and being. I think of my daughters – of their future here, or elsewhere. I want to take them across the world to other places where there is still some wildness left; more and more, I feel sadness rising in me at the thought of that diminishment. Then I think of everything that this long pilgrimage through the islands associated with Britain, from Shetland to Scilly, Orkney to Thanet, has taught me; of this small island called Thorn Ey, which has generated vast amounts of discord since humans first settled here in the Neolithic, or before (a Mesolithic flint axe was found at New Scotland Yard).[26]

Even in the most patriarchal of times, people knew what to do. They created an island in the imagination, a creative country from which women could be seen and heard. So, in the present, new islands of rampant love, and effervescent ecology, and bold equality, can be made. We could yet found an archipelago which lives up to the dreams of its descendants. That is the hope.

Acknowledgements

Thank you to everybody mentioned in this book, to the people and places I wasn't able to name, and to the more than human entities, rainbows and storms, birds and shells, whom I accompanied on island wanders, walks, swims and adventures. Thank you to the livelihoods, voices, species and places, marginalised or overlooked, which alert us to other ways, and to the work that has been done of listening and helping them be seen and heard. Thank you to the tunes and words, songs and calls which have travelled such long distances, often carried out of the past by people whose names we no longer know.

Thank you to island people of living memory for everything you shared. My onetime Orkney neighbours at large, the late Kristin Linklater, Rebecca Marr, all those at the Ness of Brodgar, Yali Zhu, Reebs & Josh, and now, as then, Max & Jill Collop. In the Isle of Wight, Charity Garnett and the Stone House. For help and company on the journey to Lindisfarne, David Potts and Guy Hayward. In the Isle of Man, Fenella Bazin and also Fenella Edwards and family. En route to and from the Hebrides, Roselle & John Boyd-Brent, and also the Findlay family (descendants of Orcadian writer Ann Scott-Moncrieff, whose book *Auntie Robbo* formed my first literary peregrination through the Highlands and onwards to the islands). In Jersey, Peter Roberts and colleagues at La Hougue Bie, and also Bobby & Traci, Katy & clan. In Guernsey, Philip de Jersey – his great knowledge and also his sleeping bags.

I wrote parts of this book in Chloe Dewe Mathews' studio in St Leonards-on-Sea, and other parts in Catherine de Zegher's castle in Coll during an Embrace Space residency. Thank you very much to both. Some of the words from the introduction come from an article I wrote for the art magazine *See All This*, and some sentences in chapter 1 from my blog for the Ness of Brodgar (anybody wishing to donate to this very interesting archaeological project may do so here: https://www.nessofbrodgar.co.uk/donate/). Thank you to the librarians at the Orkney Library & Archive in Kirkwall, the Manx National Heritage Library and Archives in Douglas, and the British Library in London. Thank you to all the people contributing to online libraries and resources, especially the transcribers of Latin and Old English texts.

Much changed during the long writing of this book, including my agent and editor. Thank you to those original stalwarts, Sarah Chalfant and Helen Conford. Many thanks for the excellent editing, guidance and patience of people at Penguin – my editor, Simon Winder, Eva Hodgkin, Sarah Day, Pen Vogler, Dahmicca Wright and Rebecca Lee (thank goodness for Rebecca Lee) – and at W.W. Norton, Jill Bialosky and Drew Weitman. Thank you also for the editorial witchery of Hannah Dawson, Rowan Boyson and Shan Vahidy (she an actual witch, as well as an actual editor). Thanks likewise to Nick Card, Anne Mitchell, George Geddes, James Meek, Duncan McLean, Ffion Reynolds, Anthony King, Stephanie Hollis, Nikola Proksch, Alex Armitage, Kate Burns, Piers Lewin, Annie Kissack, Peter Davey, Philip de Jersey and Jacky King, who read individual chapters. The *Macbeth* witches and their wind are Neil Bennun's. Martin Heslop gave me the article on 'bell rocks'. Any mishearings, mistakes, misconstruals, are all mine, obviously, for which I apologise in advance.

I am so grateful for friendship, for sisterhoods, for brothers. Thank you to my actual sister Immy, and to my brothers Ralph, Simon and Jack. For the sometime conversation, counsel and camaraderie of Aika Esenalieva, Amy Cooper, Chrystal Genesis, Clare Carlisle, Flora Pethybridge, Gemma Mortensen, Laura Yates, Leyla Nazli, Naomi Goulder, Niki Sitara, Rosanna Lowe, Rose Gibbs, Ruby Hamid, Taran Khan – gracias amigas.

I do not know how I would have managed without Rebecca Carter (editor-friend-agent).

Nor without Léonie Hampton's inspiration and example.

And Tito – grace for and to you – first reader of this book and (at time of writing) of me.

I dedicate these pages to the ovumvirate of my mother, who travelled to some of these islands with me and gave me solidarity as I made the literary and emotional journeys recounted here; my beautiful-hearted daughters, Aphra and Adi, fellow travellers through time and space; and to the memory of my cherished grandmother, Elsie, who loved these islands too.

Notes

Introduction

1 As Mark Edmonds writes, Orcadians prefer to live 'in' rather than 'on' Orkney, just as people live 'in' rather than 'on' Britain. Many islanders prefer 'in'; however, when I showed a draft of this book to somebody who lived on St Agnes in the Isles of Scilly, he turned all my 'in's to 'on'. So it entirely depends: *Orcadia: Land, Sea and Stone in Neolithic Orkney*, London: Head of Zeus, 2019, p. xi.

2 The Ordnance Survey of Great Britain estimates '5000 or so smaller islands scattered around' the coasts of the British-Irish Isles, https://www.ordnancesurvey.co.uk/blog/whats-the-difference-between-uk-britain-and-british-isles. Figures from the separate mapping agencies of Great Britain, Northern Ireland, Republic of Ireland, Isle of Man, Guernsey and Jersey are quoted here: http://www.sovereignty.org.uk/features/articles/uk6.html.

3 'The term "St Kilda Parliament" was first used by George Clayton Atkinson in 1838', https://www.ambaile.org.uk/asset/38917/. Enlli/Bardsey, 'King of Enlli': https://www.bardsey.org/kingofbardsey

4 George Monbiot, Prize Lecture, Orwell Society, London, 14 July 2022.

5 Indeed, the mainland, with its tax breaks for non-doms, has arguably begun to imitate the islands. Meanwhile, the island of Anglesey has just acquired freeport status.

6 https://www.bbc.co.uk/news/uk-scotland-north-east-orkney-shetland-66090102. In 1724, following the Union, Daniel Defoe began publishing his *Tour thro' the Whole Island of Great Britain*. In 1852, Tennyson wrote of 'our rough' and 'fair island-story'. In 1905, H. E. Marshall

published *Our Island Story: A History of Britain for Boys and Girls* – a text which was republished, unabridged, by the pro-Union think tank Civitas in 2005.

7 II, 264.

8 This looked silly from afar; hence Eustache Deschamps' fourteenth-century ditty, 'Sur les divers noms de l'Angleterre': MCLIV in *Oeuvres*, https://archive.org/stream/oeuvrescomplteo6descuoft/oeuvrescom plteo6descuoft_djvu.txt.

9 Such as: Plato on Atlantis; Strabo on the arrival of new islands; Viking sagas on the disappearance of Gunnbjørn skerries; Camden on Alderney being overcome by sands; Raleigh on Eden as an island drifting in the Tigris. See Lisa Hopkins, *Shakespeare on the Edge: Border-crossing in the Tragedies and the Henriad*, Aldershot: Ashgate, 2005, p. 88.

10 Lynn Staley, *The Island Garden: England's Language of Nation from Gildas to Marvell*, Notre Dame, Ind: University of Notre Dame, 2012.

11 Kenneth Jackson, *A Celtic Miscellany: Translations from the Celtic Literatures*, Harmondsworth: Penguin, 1971, p. 173.

12 Marina Warner, *Monuments & Maidens: The Allegory of the Female Form*, London: Weidenfeld and Nicolson, 1985, p.45: 'an acute irony, that the allegory of Britannia was first developed to characterise a conquered country.'

1. *Orkney*

1 Orkneyjar.com, quoting Dr Berit Sanders, of Lund University: orkneyjar.com/history/maeshowe/placename.htm

2 Dr Ragnhild Ljosland, 'The men in Maeshowe: John D. Mackay Memorial Lecture', Orkney Science Festival Lecture, Kirkwall, 2017.

3 Chambered cairns vary in their internal shape. As for their exterior form, some may have been stone-covered by design, others intended to be turfy, as most now are.

4 A counterexample is given in Anne Teather's interesting article on how the presence of phallic Neolithic objects is 'sidelined' in current archaeological discussions due to 'a meshing of embarrassment and

identification', in her 'Neolithic phallacies: a discussion of some south-
ern British artefacts', in Mats Larsson and Mike Parker Pearson (eds.),
*From Stonehenge to the Baltic: Living with Cultural Diversity in the Third
Millennium BC*, Oxford: Archaeopress, 2007, pp. 205–11.

5 Caroline Wickham-Jones, *Orkney: A Historical Guide*, Edinburgh: Birlinn, 2015, p. 16.

6 Mark Edmonds, *Orcadia: Land, Sea and Stone in Neolithic Orkney*,
   London: Head of Zeus, 2019, p. 207.

7 According to the guides at Maeshowe.

8 https://www.metmuseum.org/toah/hd/lasc/hd_lasc.htm.

9 Alexandra Shepherd, 'Skara Brae', in Anna Richie (ed.), *Neolithic Orkney
   in Its European Context*, McDonald Institute for Archaeological Research,
   2000, Cambridge, p. 155.

10 Wickham-Jones, p. 14.

11 See the photo on Orkneyjar.com.

12 'Colonization of the Scottish islands via long-distance deer (*Cervus elaphus*)', David W. G. Stanton, Jacqueline A. Mulville and Michael W.
   Bruford, *Proceedings of the Royal Society B: Biological Sciences*, London, 2016.

13 J. G. Frazer saw the worship of solstices as a newbie innovation by farmers, moving away from the old pastoral division of the year at May and
   November; Frazer, *The Golden Bough* (1922; reprint 1971), p. 829.

14 J. L. Davidson and A. S. Henshall, *The Chambered Cairns of Orkney*,
   Edinburgh: Edinburgh University Press, 1989, p. 63.

15 Wickham-Jones, pp. 42, 92. See also Michael Balter, 'From this remote,
   520-square-kilometre island, these innovations swept nearly every
   corner of Britain and Ireland, culminating in the famous monuments
   of Stonehenge and Avebury in southern England', 'Monumental
   Roots', in *Science*, 343, 3 Jan. 2014, p. 19. There is some doubt or dispute
   about the origins of animals as coming from Orkney.

16 Miranda and Stephen Aldhouse-Green, *The Quest for the Shaman: Shape-
   shifters, Sorcerers and Spirit-healers of Ancient Europe*, London: Thames &
   Hudson, 2005, p. 79.

17 The agricultural Wheel of Life, according to Julian Cope, *The Modern
   Antiquarian: A Pre-millennial Odyssey through Megalithic Britain*, London:
   Thorsons, 1998, p. 15.

18 'FERRY-LOUPER, n. comb. Also -looper, -lupper (Ork.). An inhabitant of Orkney who is not a native but has come from the mainland,
i.e. across the Pentland Ferry (Ork. 1822 A. Peterkin Notes on Ork. and
Zet. 21; Ork. 1951)': *Dictionaries of the Scots Language SCIO*, https://
www.dsl.ac.uk/entry/snd/ferrylouper.

19 Possibly they are from Transcarparthia: https://www.britannica.com/
place/Ukraine/Transcarpathia-in-Czechoslovakia; https://en.wikipedia.
org/wiki/Hungarians_in_Ukraine.

20 Julie Gibson, 'Tourism and archaeology in Orkney: the Ness Effect',
Archaeologist, 91, Spring 2014: 'More than half of the visitors to Orkney
make it their destination based on interest in our archaeological sites', p. 14.

21 http://www.orkneyjar.com/history/skarabrae/skarab1.htm.

22 Jo Grimond, *Memoirs*, London: Heinemann, 1979, p. 146.

23 Nick Card, 'Neolithic temples of the Northern Isles: stunning new
discoveries in Orkney', *Current Archaeology*, April 2010, p. 19.

24 M. and S. Aldhouse-Green, p. 87.

25 Davidson and Henshall, p. 60.

26 Julian Thomas, 'Identity of place in Neolithic Britain', in *Neolithic
Orkney in Its European Context*, Anna Ritchie (ed.), Cambridge: McDonald Institute for Archaeological Research, 2000, p. 80.

27 Nick Card, 'we are looking at a population of 10,000 or more', quoted
in Balter, p. 23.

28 https://www.ed.ac.uk/news/2023/orkney-cancer-gene-link-revealed.

29 Vicki Cummings and Amelia Pannett, 'Island views: the settings of
the chambered cairns of southern Orkney', in Cummings and Pannett
(eds.), *Set in Stone: New Approaches to Neolithic Monuments in Scotland*,
Oxford: Oxbow, 2005, p. 16.

30 George Mackay Brown, *An Orkney Tapestry: Drawings by Sylvia Wishart*,
London: Gollancz, 1969, p. 33.

31 https://www.royalnavy.mod.uk/news-and-latest-activity/
news/2022/june/27/20220627-scapa-flow-naval-museum-set-to-
reopen-after-4m-revamp.

32 St Columba is said to have been buried with his stone pillow. See
https://electricscotland.com/history/iona/chapter07.htm.

33 There is controversy about the spelling of the word 'stone' in this context: *stane* is Orcadian dialect, but local people in Hoy objected to the use of a dialect word when the display boards in the local museum were put up, and there, the word used is 'stone'. The folk tales about the dwarf who lived there, meanwhile, describe a person as vain and ambitious as any tyrant; the Orkneyjar version is at http://www.orkneyjar.com/folklore/snorro2.htm.

34 Mark Edmonds writes that this shouldn't be exaggerated, however; they did eat some fish. 2019, p. 45.

35 Aaron Watson and David Keating, 'The architecture of sound in Neolithic Orkney', in Ritchie (ed.), p. 261.

36 The nineteenth century also bequeathed to the island the now-abandoned laird's estate: the wealth and power of that age, expressed in a great house and kitchen garden, the stone walls splashed graffiti-bright with yellow lichen.

37 'Hoy, Lyness, Royal Naval oil terminal', https://canmore.org.uk/site/98128/hoy-lyness-royal-naval-oil-terminal.

38 Nick Card and Antonia Thomas, 'Painting a picture of Neolithic Orkney: decorated stonework from the Ness of Brodgar', in Andrew Cochrane and Andrew Meirion Jones (eds.), *Visualising the Neolithic: Abstraction, Figuration, Performance, Representation*, Oxford: Oxbow, 2012, p. 118.

39 It happens only in January, towards the end of Maeshowe's six or so sun-filled weeks.

40 Orkney has so much turbulence in its seas and skies it is said now to produce 120 per cent of its electricity needs from renewables: Orkney Renewable Energy Forum, https://www.oref.co.uk/orkneys-energy/.

41 It was used to make fires, polish leather, colour houses, pottery and temples. (I read a lovely description by a local archaeologist of being shown where to find haematite by the island's schoolchildren.)

42 Ora Maritima: https://topostext.org/work/751.

43 Wickham Jones, p. 12.

44 They stared at us inquisitively all spring with their large dark eyes but do not linger. Too many of them have been clubbed to death rather than sung to submission. Most of them have plastic in the gut.

45 https://hoyheritage.wordpress.com/natural-history/eagles/#:~: text=White%2Dtailed%20eagles%2C%20or%20sea,And%20it's%20 a%20family%20thing.

46 Later that same summer, on an islet off Sicily, I will lie in an almost identical white-rock Neolithic seaside chamber – same carved bed, even more proximate sea view – as if one of them, Sicilian or Orcadian, had texted the other a picture of their clever new construction.

Epigraph

1 Pliny the Elder, *Natural History*, XXX. 13, quoted in Mary Beard, John Norton and Simon Price, *Religions of Rome: Volume 2, A Sourcebook*, Cambridge: Cambridge University Press, 2001, p.264.

2. Anglesey

1 Plutarch, *Moralia*, quoted by Anthony King and Grahame Soffe in *A Sacred Island: Iron Age, Roman and Saxon Temples and Ritual on Hayling Island, Winchester: Hayling Island Excavation Project*, Winchester: Winchester University Press, 2013, p. 1.

2 Graham Robb, *The Ancient Paths: Discovering the Lost Map of Celtic Europe*, London: Picador, 2013, pp. 31–2.

3 Alfred Watkins, *The Old Straight Track: Its Mounds, Beacons, Moats, Sites and Mark Stones*, London: Abacus, 1925 (reprint 1974), p. 215.

4 Barry Cunliffe, *Druids: A Very Short Introduction*, Oxford: Oxford University Press, 2010, pp. 49, 4.

5 Ibid., p. 65.

6 National Assembly for Wales, *Key Statistics of the Isle of Anglesey*, April 2008, p. 5; https://senedd.wales/NAfW%20Documents/anglesey. pdf%20-%2018042008/anglesey-English.pdf. Arguably, that has eased a

bit in the decade since. Welsh Government, *Welsh Index of Multiple Deprivation, 2019: Results report*, 2019, p. 25: https://gov.wales/sites/default/files/statistics-and-research/2019-11/welsh-index-multiple-deprivation-2019-results-report-024.pdf.

7   D. E. Jenkins, *Bedd Gelert: its facts, fairies, & folk-lore*, 1899, Portmadoc, Llewellyn Jenkins, (facsimile edition 1999), pp. 204ff.

8   H. N. Savory, 'Excavations at Dinas Emrys, Beddgelert (Caern.), 1954–6', in *Archaeologia Cambrensis*, 109, Cardiff, Cambrian Archaeological Association, 1961.

9   *The Mabinogion*, Charlotte Guest (trans.), 1849, transcribed 2004, https://www.gutenberg.org/files/5160/5160-h/5160-h.htm

10   Quoted in Barry Cunliffe, *The Extraordinary Voyage of Pytheas the Greek*, London: Penguin, 2001, p. 33.

11   According to Barry Cunliffe, ibid., p. 93.

12   Virgil, *Eclogues*, I.66.

13   Plutarch, *Life of Julius Caesar*, 23.2; Vol. VII of the Loeb Classical Library edition, 1919: http://penelope.uchicago.edu/Thayer/E/Roman/Texts/Plutarch/Lives/Caesar*.html.

14   Quoted in Miranda Aldhouse-Green, *Boudica Britannia: Rebel, War-leader and Queen*, Harlow: Pearson Education Limited, 2006, p. xv.

15   Caesar, *The Gallic War*, H. J. Edwards (trans.), London: William Heinemann, 1919, Book IV.

16   Richard Hobbs and Ralph Jackson, *Roman Britain*, London: British Museum Press, 2010, p. 20.

17   Cassius Dio, *Roman History*, LIX.25, https://penelope.uchicago.edu/Thayer/e/roman/texts/cassius_dio/59*.html; see also David Braund, *Ruling Roman Britain: Kings, Queens, Governors and Emperors from Julius Caesar to Agricola*, London: Routledge, 1996, p. 95.

18   Ovid, Metamorphoses, XV.752; quoted in David Braund, *Ruling Roman Britain : Kings, Queens, Governors and Emperors from Julius Caesar to Agricola*, London : Routledge, 1996, p. 78.

19   F. E. Romer, *Pomponius Mela's Description of the World*, Ann Arbor: University of Michigan Press, 1998, p. 3.

20   Horace, Odes, IV.14, quoted in Miranda Aldhouse-Green, Boudica Britannia, 2006, p. 12.

21 Cassius Dio, *Roman History*, LX.19.

22 Ibid., LX.22; Greg Woolf, 'A distant mirror: Britain and Rome in the representation of empire', in Juan Santos Yanguas and Elena Torregaray Pagola (eds), *Laudes Provinciarum. Retórica y política en la representación del imperio romano*, Vitoria: Universidad del País Vasco, 2007, pp.135–147, p. 140.

23 Aldhouse-Green, p. 42.

24 Miranda J. Green, *Exploring the World of the Druids*, London: Thames & Hudson, 1997, p. 53.

25 Tacitus, *Agricola*, 14, http://www.perseus.tufts.edu/hopper/text?doc =Perseus%3Atext%3A1999.02.0081%3Achapter%3D16.

26 Also spelt Divitiacus. Cicero, *On Divination*, Book 1.41: 'Nor is the practice of divination disregarded even among uncivilized tribes, if indeed there are Druids in Gaul – and there are, for I knew one of them myself, Divitiacus, the Aeduan, your guest and eulogist. He claims to have that knowledge of nature which the Greeks call physiologia, and he used to make predictions, sometimes by means of augury and sometimes by means of conjecture'; I.41; http://penelope.uchicago. edu/Thayer/e/roman/texts/cicero/de_divinatione/1*.html.

27 Tacitus, *Annals: Books 13-16*, John Jackson (trans.), Loeb Classical Library, London, 1937.

28 Tacitus, *Agricola*, 16.

29 Aldhouse-Green, p. 62.

30 Ibid., p. 18.

31 Aldhouse-Green, pp. 52, 197.

32 Nora Chadwick, *The Celts*, Harmondsworth: Penguin, 1970, p. 45: 'The eloquence of the Gauls impressed the Romans deeply throughout their history.'

33 And all the more glory, then, for Agricola, who, when Tacitus gives him his turn to speak, evokes Alexander the Great – like Caesar, Caligula and Claudius before him – substituting the forests of Caledonia for Alexander's monsoon Indus: 'you and I have passed beyond the limits reached by former armies or by former governors, and we now occupy the last confines of Britain . . . Britain has been both discovered and subdued . . . it would be no inglorious end to perish on the extreme confines of earth and of nature'.

34 Where the rivers Rhône and Saône meet; Cunliffe, *Druids*, p. 79.

35 The 'god visits the island every nineteen years, the period in which the return of the stars to the same place in the heavens is accomplished'. The modern archaeoastronomer Aubrey Burl believes that Diodorus is writing of the Neolithic stone circle of Callanish on the Outer Hebridean island of Lewis; and that the nineteen-year visits of the god reflects the 18.61-year lunar cycle which (according to Caesar) was also the approximate length of a Druid education in Britain.

36 The Celts sacked Delphi in 279 BC; the geographer and historian Strabo testifies that the infamous gold in the southern French lakes came from there.

37 For example by Anne Ross: 'Boudicca's fierce human sacrifices in honour of her goddess Andraste . . . in the series of Romano-British temples found at Springhead in Kent, the remains of six-months old babies, several of them decapitated and placed carefully in the corners of buildings, together with a decapitated seagull, hint at the sacrifice of children at the foundation of the buildings, and are reminiscent of the child whose head was torn off by his mother in the Irish tale of Inber n-Ailbine': Anne Ross, 'The divine hag of the pagan celts' in *The Witch Figure*, Venetia Newall (ed.), London and Boston: Routledge & Kegan Paul, 1973, p.158. The dedication of infant children could be read differently in the light of Eleanor Scott's work (1991).

38 Strabo, *Geography*. He also writes about an island in the Loire estuary inhabited by a cult of Dionysiac women. Men are forbidden to go there, the women come to the mainland for sex, and once a year one of them is torn to pieces by the rest as they unroof their sacred structure – possibly an ancient stone circle; a story reminiscent of Dionysius's maenads, disporting themselves near Delphi, with Pentheus's mutilated body.

39 Samothrace, ruled over by a Sibyl, or prophetess, also had a tholos (as Delphi does). Tholoi, circular stone structures, are viewed as something of an anomaly in the classical world, but coming from Orkney, Callanish or Stonehenge, they look like sophisticated versions of a Neolithic stone circle; like the roofed stone structure of Strabo's

description, perhaps; or the circular stone sun-temple which Diodorus situated on a northern British island.

40 Strabo, *Geography*, II, 5, 15 and III, 5, 11.

41 The Romans inherited from the Greeks a belief in islands as places of the dead, most particularly the islands of Britain. John Rhys, *Studies in the Arthurian Legend*, Oxford: Clarendon Press, 1891, Chapter 15, 'Isles of the dead', p. 359.

42 Quotation from Pomponius Mela adapted from F. E. Romer (trans.), *Pomponius Mela's Description of the World*, Ann Arbor: University of Michigan [III.48].

43 The idea of sacrosanct islands continues even into the fifth century, when Avienius, in his *Ora maritima*, describes 'a two-day voyage to the Sacred Isle . . . thickly populated by Hierni [Irish]. / Nearby lies the island of the Albiones.' A sacred island populated by the 'Irish', near England, could be Anglesey, or any of the islands in the Irish Sea – even Ireland. Quoted in Philip Freeman, *Ireland and the Classical World*, Austin: University of Texas Press, 2001, p. 30.

44 See J. L. Lightfoot, *Dionysius Periegetes: Description of the Known World with Introduction, Text, and Commentary*, Oxford: Oxford University Press, 2014.

45 Procopius, 'Thule', *History of the Wars*, taken from H. B. Dewing, *Procopius with an English Translation*, in seven volumes: *History of the Wars*, Books VII (continued) and VIII, Vol. 5, London / New York, 1928.

46 Robert Briffault, *The Mothers: A Study of the Origins of Sentiment and Intentions*, New York, Macmillan, 1928, p. 417.

47 See Eleanor Scott, from the Introduction to *Invisible People and Processes: Writing Gender and Childhood into European Archaeology*, Jenny Moore and Eleanor Scott (eds.), Leicester: Leicester University Press, 1997, p. 11.

48 Aldhouse-Green, p. 94.

49 *Caesar's Gallic Wars*, V.14.

50 Today, in Tibetan Buddhist communities in both Tibet and northern India, polyandry is explicitly linked to greater female autonomy and power.

51 Caesar, meanwhile, makes the revealing comment that as Roman civilization advances through Gaul it corrupts the Celts with luxury – specifically
making them 'effeminate', by which he means, like Roman women.

52 Tacitus explained that normally a woman wouldn't be sitting in front
of Roman standards: 'It was indeed a novelty, quite alien to how things
used to be.' Tacitus, *Annals*, 12.37.

53 Tacitus, *Agricola*, 16.

54 Tacitus, *Annals*, V.14.35.

55 Tacitus mentions warrior women during the attack on Anglesey, and
again during Boudica's sack of Roman Colchester. It is possible that
Romans were simply not accustomed to seeing women outside the
home, certainly not on the battlefield. Pliny writes that British women
dye their skin blue for religious purposes – maybe British female warriors looked frightening. Or perhaps, as with modern-day photographs
of Kurdish all-female militias, the sight of martial women is innately
disconcerting because unusual.

56 *Roman History*, LXII.1, http://penelope.uchicago.edu/Thayer/E/
Roman/Texts/Cassius_Dio/62*.html.

57 Aldhouse-Green, p. 45. See also 'Sebasteion reliefs', www.aphrodisias.
classics.ox.ac.uk/.

58 Nicholas Orme, *Medieval Children*, Yale: Yale University Press 2001,
p. 133.

59 The archaeologist Richard Bradley writes of his epiphany about what
it means to leave no impression on the landscape in *An Archaeology of
Natural Places*, London: Routledge, 2000.

60 David Abram, *Becoming Animal*, Vintage: London, 2011, p. 3.

61 Alastair McIntosh, *Poacher's Pilgrimage: An Island Journey*, Edinburgh:
Birlinn, 2016, p. xxii.

62 Miranda and Stephen Aldhouse-Green write of islands as 'powerful
metaphors of liminality' in the shamanic context in their *The Quest for
the Shaman: Shape-shifters, Sorcerers and Spirit-healers of Ancient Europe*,
London: Thames & Hudson, 2005, p. 200.

63 The *Macbeth* witches added some human ingredients. David Lewis-
Williams and David Pearce, *Inside the Neolithic Mind: Consciousness,*

Cosmos and the Realm of the Gods, London: Thames & Hudson, 2005, pp. 189–192.

64 Richard Hobbs and Ralph Jackson, *Roman Britain*, London: British Museum Press, 2010, p. 125.

65 Anne Ross and Don Robins, *The Life and Death of a Druid Prince: The Story of an Archaeological Sensation*, London: Rider, 1989.

66 Melanie Giles, 'Iron Age bog bodies of North-western Europe: representing the dead', *Archaeological Dialogues*, 16: 1, 2009, pp. 75–101. 2009; also Aldhouse-Green, p. 29.

67 https://philipcarr-gomm.com/.

68 At the foot of the mountain is a cluster of prehistoric hut circles (about twenty are extant); on the summit, covering 17 acres, was a huge Iron Age settlement. https://cadw.gov.wales/visit/places-to-visit/caer-y-twr.

69 Recently, new archaeological sites have been discovered in Anglesey which prove the very close cultural links between this island and Ireland, and Orkney, as far back as the early Neolithic. They have Orcadian pottery at Bryn Celli Ddu and Irish stone axes at the newly discovered site at Llanfaethu. The axe they found recently had been kept for one thousand years as a family heirloom before it was buried in the Iron Age. Dr Ffion Reynolds, Cadw archaeologist, lecture on Bryn Celli Ddu, Societies Pavilion, Anglesey Eisteddfod, 9 Sept. 2017; also https://archaeology.co.uk/articles/features/wales-earliest-village.htm.

70 David Hopewell, 'Tai Cochion Roman settlement, Anglesey 2011–12 (G1632), Summary Report, April 2011–March 2012', http://www.heneb.co.uk/cadwprojs/cadwreview2011-12/taicochion11-12.html.

71 https://peterfinnemore.com/About.

72 https://www.sacred-texts.com/neu/celt/bim1/bim1005.htm.

73 https://warwick.ac.uk/fac/arts/classics/warwickclassicsnetwork/romancoventry/resources/xx/britain.

3. Wight

1 For example, by the fourth-century Roman theologian, Orosius: 'et quoniam oceanus habet insulas, quas Britanniam et Hiberniam vocant . . . haec propior Britanniae', quoted in Philip Freeman, *Ireland and the Classical World*, Austin: University of Texas Press, 2001, p. 111: i.e. together, Britain and Ireland were known as the 'Britannias'. Orosius, *Historiae adversum paganos*, Book I, 75–80, http://www.attalus. org/latin/orosius1.html.

2 Miranda Aldhouse-Green, *Boudica Britannia: Rebel, War-leader and Queen*, Harlow: Pearson Education Limited, 2006, p. 25.

3 *Caesar's Gallic Wars*, V.12.

4 Aldhouse-Green, p. 41.

5 Barry Cunliffe, *The Roman Villa at Brading, Isle of Wight: The Excavations of 2008–10*, Oxford: Oxford School of Archaeology, 2013, p. 272.

6 See Malcolm Lyne, 'Roman Wight', Isle of Wight History Centre, 2006, p. 5: 'This and the presence of a ?wine press base in front of what appears to be a two story [*sic*] stone building with undercroft rooms suggests that we are dealing with a winery with storage facilities. The situation of the site beneath the south facing slope of the chalk ridge running across the centre of the Island would also be ideal for the cultivation of the vine. It has also been suggested that the terraces on the south side of Mersley Down further to the east indicate the presence of another Roman vineyard', https://oxfordarchaeology.com/images/ pdfs/Solent_Thames/County_resource_assessments/Roman_IOW. pdf.

7 The island's tourism website proposes varying theories, such as the Beaker people calling the island *wiht* (weight), meaning raised above the sea; the Romans turning this into Latin *veho*, lifting; or Iron Age Celts naming it 'division', 'because it is between the two arms of the Solent'; see https://www.visitisleofwight.co.uk/information/frequently-asked-questions#:~:text=Around%201900%20BC%20the%20 Beaker,Latin%20veho%20meaning%20%22lifting%22.

8 https://farringford.co.uk/history/tennyson/tennyson-on-the-isle-of-wight.

9 William Spickernell, *The Roman Villa, Carisbrooke, Isle of Wight, with ground plan &c.*, Newport, Isle of Wight, 1860, p. 7: 'The plastering on the western side of this apartment still remained, but has since yielded to frost, &c. It was painted in panels of a red, green, and white colour. Many pieces were found among the rubbish on the floor, with leaves, flowers, and other figures on them. The colours red, white, yellow, blue, green, &c. were very bright at first, but have somewhat faded since.'

10 The Roman discoveries caused a stir. 'At Shanklin, coins of Arcadius and Honorius have been found, and recently coins of Claudius and Vespasian were met with on land belonging to the Poet Laureate at Freshwater': John E. Price and F. G. Hilton Price, *A Guide to the Roman Villa Recently Discovered at Morton, between Sandown and Brading, on the Isle of Wight*, Ventnor, Isle of Wight, 1887 [12th edition], p. 8.

11 Cecil Aspinall-Oglander, *The Roman Villa at Brading*, Newport, Isle of Wight: J. Arthur Dixon, *c.*1950, p. 19.

12 Jane Timby in Cunliffe, 2013: 'Some of the Central Gaulish beakers show the use of phallic designs similar to that at Brading suggesting the products of one potter or workshop', p. 191.

13 https://www.theguardian.com/uk-news/2016/aug/05/ofsted-chair-david-hoare-isle-of-wight-poor-ghetto. See also 'Island mentality: bad schools and low aspirations used to be inner-city problems', *Economist*, 27 Jan. 2014.

14 'For the nineteenth year, the Isle of Wight is above the national average for suicides according to the Office for National Statistics': Iona Stewart-Richardson, Isle of Wight Radio, 10 Sept. 2020, https://www.iwradio.co.uk/news/isle-of-wight-news/island-suicide-numbers-are-worrying-says-charity-on-prevention-day/.

15 https://onthewight.com/ofsted-chairman-says-isle-of-wight-inbred-poor-white-ghetto/.

16 See www.gov.uk/guidance/wreck-and-salvage-law#responsibilities-of-the-receiver-of-wreck.

17 Martin Carruthers, 'The life and death of a broch', Kirkwall, Orkney, 2017.

18 Barbara Flower and Elisabeth Rosenbaum, *The Roman Cookery Book: A Critical Translation of 'The Art of Cooking' by Apicius for Use in the Study and the Kitchen*, Edinburgh: Harrap, 1958: 'the cookery book shows very clearly that the Romans abhorred the taste of any meat, fish, or vegetable in its pure form. There is hardly a single recipe which does not add a sauce to the main ingredient, a sauce which changes the taste radically', p. 19.

19 Richard Hobbs and Ralph Jackson, *Roman Britain*, London: British Museum Press, 2010, p. 89.

20 Aspinall-Oglander, p. 26.

21 Cunliffe, p. 4.

22 Aspinall-Oglander.

23 Christopher Grocock and Sally Grainger, *Apicius: A Critical Edition with an Introduction and English Translation of the Latin Recipe Text Apicius*, Totnes: Prospect, 2006, p. 40.

24 Archaeologists found beans, peas, onion, leeks, carrots, parsnip, cucumber, radish and cabbage, parsley, thyme, marjoram, garlic and mint. Many still grow wild in the hedgerows and fields around Brading.

25 Jane Timby, 'Material culture: pottery and fired clay', in Cunliffe, p. 189.

26 Rabbits, meanwhile, were first imported to Britain by the Romans, and this has been proved recently at Fishbourne Roman Palace, a luxurious villa on the south coast of England built from Wight Bembridge limestone that dates from the time of the Claudian invasion, https://archaeology.co.uk/articles/news/roman-rabbit-discovered-at-fishbourne.htm; see also *Romans on the Wight*, Isle of Wight Cultural Services Department, Isle of Wight County Council, 1992, p. 5.

27 Strabo describes grain, cattle, gold, silver, iron, as well as 'hides and slaves, and dogs that are by nature suited to the chase'; *Geography*, IV, 5, 2.

28 Tacitus, *Agricola*, 12.

29 Barry Cunliffe, *The Extraordinary Voyage of Pytheas the Greek*, London: Penguin, 2001, p. 79.

30 *Mesolithic Occupation at Bouldnor Cliff and the Submerged Prehistoric Landscapes of the Solent*, Garry Momber et al. (eds.), York: Council for British Archaeology, 2011, p. 13.

31 Ibid., p. 6.

32 'All this evidence gives support to a relatively recent breach of the western entrance to the Solent': Garry Momber in ibid., p. 135.

33 Diodorus Siculus, *Library*, V.22.

34 David Tomalin in Tomalin et al. (eds.), *Coastal Archaeology in a Dynamic Environment: A Solent Case Study*, Oxford: Archaeopress, 2012, p. 489.

35 'Among the ancient southern civilizations with their written documents, all individual experience, whether practical or intellectual, could quickly be pooled so as to become the common property of the community, whereas among the illiterate Celtic peoples, experience was exchanged orally.' Nora Chadwick, *The Celts*, Harmondsworth: Penguin, 1970, p. 43.

36 Caesar's *Gallic Wars*, VI.24: 'their proximity to the Province and knowledge of commodities from countries beyond the sea supplies to the Gauls many things tending to luxury as well as civilization'.

37 John Creighton, *Coins and Power in Late Iron Age Britain*, Cambridge: Cambridge University Press, 2000, p. 117.

38 '[F]or example, Fawler in Oxfordshire, which derives from "fagan floran", or variegated pavement': David S. Neal and Stephen R. Cosh, *Roman Mosaics of Britain*, London: Illuminata, 2002, Vol. 1: Northern Britain, p. 7.

39 Martin Henig, 'The mosaic pavements: their meaning and context', in Cunliffe, p. 263.

40 https://www.britishmuseum.org/collection/object/H_1899-0614-1.

41 Aldhouse-Green, p. 19, quoting Creighton, p. 131.

42 This 'small villa on an offshore island may have been a thriving centre of late Roman pagan culture'; Henig, p. 261. Meanwhile Tomalin's new interpretation examines the relationship between the Greek philosopher Aratus's study of the effect of the night sky on Earth and how this was picked up by Roman authors such as Virgil and subsequently represented in mosaics such as those at Brading. David Tomalin, *Roman Vectis: Archaeology and Identity in the Isle of Wight*, Vectensica Publishing, 2022, pp. 184ff.

43 David Neal and Stephen Cosh, *Roman Mosaics of Britain: Volume III: South-East Britain: Part I*, London: Society of Antiquaries of London, 2009, p. 266.

44 https://www.granger.com/results.asp?image=0018869.

45 A subject which is also depicted in a mosaic in Pitney, Somerset.

46 There is lots of literature on this, but see for example Susan R. Bowers, 'Medusa and the female gaze', *NWSA Journal*, 2 (2), 1990, pp. 217–35.

47 Miranda and Stephen Aldhouse-Green, *The Quest for the Shaman: Shape-shifters, Sorcerers and Spirit-healers of Ancient Europe*, London: Thames & Hudson, 2005, pp. 86–7.

48 Aldhouse-Green, p. 28.

49 Eleanor Scott, 'Animal and infant burials in Romano-British villas: a revitalization movement', in P. Garwood et al. (eds.), *Sacred and Profane: Proceedings of a Conference on Archaeology, Ritual and Religion*, Oxford: Oxford University School of Archaeology, 1991, pp. 115–21.

50 The well was found 'within the twin apse bath house in a position which shows that it must pre-date this structure': David Tomalin, *Roman Wight: A Guide Catalogue*, Isle of Wight: Isle of Wight County Council, 1997, p. 27.

51 Ibid., p. 28. Cunliffe, 2013, p.31.

52 Interview with Catherine de Zegher, 14 October 2022. See also https://www.bl.uk/russian-revolution/articles/women-and-the-russian-revolution#:~:text=During%20the%20October%20Revolution%2C%20women,men%20into%20joining%20the%20army.

53 Quoted by Aldhouse-Green, p. 108.

54 Aldhouse-Green: 'he says of Britain . . . the sexes were accorded equal treatment', p. 110.

55 As Eleanor Scott writes, 'A people who have been subjugated by an occupying force and administration start to bring back and rework old myths.' Clandestine activities and rites 'may be held to be a response by women to fundamental changes in their world . . . to strengthen their female domain', p. 120.

56 Ronald Hutton, *Pagan Britain*, Yale: Yale University Press, 2013, p. 367.

57 See Jessica Hemming, 'Reflections on Rhiannon and the Horse Episodes in "Pwyll"', Western Folklore, Vol. 57, No. 1 (Winter, 1998), pp. 19–40, p.20.

58 Talk by Professor Anthony King (University of Winchester), 'Reviewing recent findings in Hayling Island and Meonstoke, Hampshire, which have given new insights into Roman sacred landscapes', University of Sussex, 2 May 2019.

59 Professor Anthony King, personal communication.

60 Tomalin, p. 12.

61 Eleanor Scott, *A Gazetteer of Roman Villas in Britain*, University of Leicester School of Archaeological Studies, Leicester, 1993, pp. 101–2.

62 https://www2.bgs.ac.uk/mineralsuk/download/EHCountyAtlases/Isle_Of_White_Building_Stone_Atlas.pdf.

63 https://www.pba-consulting.co.uk/the-quarr-abbey-oak-shortlisted-for-tree-of-the-year-2018-they-need-your-votes.html.

4. Iona

1 Or quills. It is the same paradigm shift that occurred in India with the upsurge of Buddhism – also a caste-free religion. Until Buddhism, India's Vedic Hindu priests had, like the Druids, retained religious knowledge within their sacred caste by transmitting knowledge orally. Buddhist monks changed that by writing down sacred texts about their founder. There is an argument that Jesus, or the authors of his cult, absorbed key ideas from Buddhism. Just as Alexander the Great's incursion into India changed monumental art there, introducing new ideas and techniques that inaugurated the rich vein of Buddhist Gandharan sculpture, so ideas flowed back west with soldiers, merchants and other travellers.

2 Michelle P. Brown, *The Lindisfarne Gospels and the Early Medieval World*, London: The British Library, 2011, p. 35.

3 All quotes from *Vita Columbae* are taken from Adomnán of Iona, *Life of St Columba*, Richard Sharpe (trans.), Harmondsworth: Penguin, 1995.

Notes

4 Text at http://research.ucc.ie/celt/document/T201090.

5 Making this rock-cut 'sepulchral bed' sound like the Dwarfie stone in Hoy.

6 Quoted in Philip Freeman, *Ireland and the Classical World*, Austin: University of Texas Press, 2001, p. 99.

7 https://canmore.org.uk/site/9560/south-ronaldsay-st-marys-church.

8 Fiona Macleod quoted in F. M. MacNeill, *Iona: A History of the Island*, London: Blackie and Son, 1920, p. 58.

9 Charles Plummer, *Bethada Náem n Érenn: Lives of Irish Saints. Edited from the original MSS. with introduction, translations, notes, glossary and indexes*, Oxford: Clarendon Press, 1922, Vol. i, p. xvii.

10 *The Age of Bede*, introduction by D. H. Farmer, Harmondsworth: Penguin, 1965 (reprint 1985), p. 11.

11 Irish hermits certainly seem to have lived in Iceland – so the Norse discovered when they arrived there in the ninth century. There is a theory that Quetzalcoatl, the Aztec serpent deity, is based on a wandering Christian monk. (And a competing theory that he is really a Buddhist bhikku. See Duncan Scott Craig, *Quetzalcoatl Rising: A Buddhist Monk in Fifth Century Mexico*, Createspace Independent Publishing Platform, 2012.) It seems possible, if not likely, that Brendan and his crew even got as far as Newfoundland. In 1976, the daring British explorer Tim Severin proved that such a journey would have been feasible by sailing there, in a replica sixth-century currach made only of ash planks and ox-hide. He island-hopped from Ireland to the Hebrides, up to Faroe, across to Greenland, and down to Newfoundland. It took him a year. Tim Severin, *The Brendan Voyage*, London: Hutchinson, 1978.

12 Seamus Mac Mathuna, *Immram Brain: Bran's Journey to the Land of the Women*, Tübingen: M. Niemeyer, 1985, p. 285.

13 David N. Dumville, 'Echtrae and Immram: some problems of definition', in *Ériu*, Dublin: Royal Irish Academy, Vol. 27, 1976, pp. 73–94, at p. 73.

14 See also 'The adventures of Art Son of Conn', a story in which both father and son travel separately to apple-paradise islands to find pure-hearted people to bring back to Ireland.

15 Denis O'Donaghue, *Brendaniana: St Brendan the Voyager in Story and Legend*, Dublin, 1893 (reprinted by Forgotten Books, 2018), pp. 71–2.

16 'Adomnan managed to get the law guaranteed by a list of over fifty Irish kings, the king of Dal Riata, and the king of the Picts', Ewan Campbell, *Saints and Sea-Kings: The First Kingdom of the Scots*, Edinburgh: Birlinn, 1999, p. 36.

17 Miranda Aldhouse-Green, *Celtic Goddesses: Warriors, Virgins, Mothers*, London: British Museum Press, 1995, pp. 26, 30. The Irish hero Cú Chulainn was trained by Scáthach, a prophetess, and fathered a child on the warrior queen Áife. In the Welsh story tradition Peredur is trained by nine island witches. The northern Picts had matrilineal succession until the ninth century (until their conversion).

18 The 'Kells *Madonna and Child* picture is without precedent in early medieval Latin illumination', Martin Werner, 'The *Madonna and Child* Miniature in the "Book of Kells"', *Art Bulletin*, 54 (2), 1972, pp. 129–39, at p. 136.

19 Barbara G. Walker, *The Woman's Encyclopaedia of Myths and Secrets*, New York: HarperCollins, 1983, pp. 180–82.

20 Sharpe, endnote 280, p. 332.

21 Canmore ID 21621.

22 In Steve Callaghan and Bryce Wilson (eds.), *The Unknown Cathedral: Lesser-known Aspects of St Magnus Cathedral in Orkney*, Kirkwall: Orkney Islands Council, 2001, p. 60.

23 Marija Gimbutas, *The Living Goddesses*, Miriam Robbins Dexter (ed.), Berkeley: University of California Press, 2001, p.30. See for example Anne Ross, 'The divine hag of the pagan celts' in *The Witch Figure*, Venetia Newhall (ed.), London and Boston: Routledge and Kegan Paul, 1973, pp. 139–64.

24 See Ronald Hutton: 'many echoes of British prehistory can be found in the cultural forms of the British Middle Ages. The enclosure of monasteries in the north and west of the island echoed promontory forts . . . Stone crosses, or pillars with inscribed crosses, might have been inspired by standing stones. The quintessential instruments of the new religion were books, but their decorations were based on Iron Age art, and the cult of saints' relics mirrored the special ritual treatment given to parts

of the human body at many times since the Neolithic.' Hutton, *Pagan Britain*, Yale: Yale University Press, 2013 (reprint 2014), p. 335.

25 As the anthropologist Jeffrey Mark Golliher puts it pithily, ley lines, in particular, bring together the 'competing worldviews' of different spiritual movements, in 'rejection of official interpretations of reality as offered by academics, religions, and government institutions'. Jeffrey Mark Golliher, 'Leylines in modern Britain: the sacred geography of a pilgrimage site as an expression of folk protest', *New York Folklore*, 13 (3), p. 73.

26 Kenneth Jackson, *A Celtic Miscellany*, Harmondsworth: Penguin, 1951 (reprint 1971), p. 279.

27 http://www.welcometoiona.com/.

28 Interview with John Maclean, who formerly ran the Iona hostel and sat on the island council, 14 Aug. 2014.

29 https://www.crofting.scotland.gov.uk/what-is-crofting.

5. Thanet

1 Damian Le Bas, *The Stopping Places*, London: Chatto & Windus, 2018, p. 233.

2 Orosius, *Seven Books of History against the Pagans: The Apology of Paulus Orosius*, Irving W. Raymond (ed.), New York: Columbia University Press, 2002, Book I, Chs. 1–2, section 76, p. 43.

3 There *is* something inescapably comic about the importance this island assumed in English history, as Walter Carruthers Sellar and Robert Julian Yeatman made clear in *1066 and All That: A Memorable History of England, Comprising All the Parts You Can Remember, Including 103 Good Things, 5 Bad Kings and 2 Genuine Dates*, London: Methuen and Co., 1930, pp. 1–11.

4 Quotations from Seamus Heaney's translation of *Beowulf*, London: Faber & Faber, 1999.

5 J. R. Green, *A Short History of the English People*, London: Macmillan, 1874, p. 7.

Notes

6 *The Earliest Life of Gregory the Great, by an anonymous monk of Whitby,* Bertram Colgrave (trans.), Lawrence: University of Kansas Press, 1968 [Cambridge, 1985], p. 91.

7 Celia Chazelle, 'The power of oratory: rereading the Whitby *Liber Beati Gregorii*', published online by Cambridge University Press, 2 Nov. 2021, *Traditio*, Vol. LXXVI, 2021, 29–77, p. 31, https://doi.org/10.1017/tdo.2021.3.

8 Pope Gregory I, *The Book of Pastoral Rule and Selected Epistles of St Gregory the Great, Bishop of Rome,* James Barmby (trans.), Vol. XII, Book VIII, Ep. 30, Buffalo, NY: Christian Literature Publishing Co., 1895.

9 Quoted in *The Earliest Life of Gregory the Great,* p. 145.

10 Isidore of Seville, *Etymologies,* XIV.vi.3. Latin text: 'Tanatos insula Oceani freto Gallico, a Brittania aestuario tenui separata, frumentariis campis et gleba uberi. Dicta autem Tanatos a morte serpentum, quos dum ipsa nesciat, asportata inde terra quoquo gentium vecta sit, angues ilico perimit.' https://penelope.uchicago.edu/Thayer/L/Roman/Texts/Isidore/14*.html.

11 A. R. Burns, 'Procopius and the Island of Ghosts', *English Historical Review,* Vol. LXX (275), Oxford, 1 April 1955, pp. 258–61.

12 Theo Vennemann, 'The name of the Isle of Thanet', in *Language and Text: Current Perspectives on English and Germanic Historical Linguistics and Philology,* Andrew James Johnston, Ferdinand Von Mengden and Stefan Thim (eds.), Winter 2006, Heidelberg: Universitätsverlag, pp. 345–74, pp. 356, 370.

13 Stephanie Hollis, *Anglo-Saxon Women and the Church: Sharing a Common Fate,* Martlesham, Woodbridge: Boydell Press, 1992, p. 26.

14 *The Earliest Life of Gregory the Great,* p. 145. For the Victorian Anglican church, Augustine's labours with the pagan Angles were an inspiration for theirs elsewhere in the world. At the Lambeth Conference of 1878, the Archbishop spoke of how 'Augustine's work is full of encouragement for you in your missionary labours. What difficulties greater than his can stand in your way wherever you go?' (*The Pan-Anglican Synod before 'St. Augustine's Chair',* London: Hardwicke & Bogue, 1878).

15 John Henry Newman, *The Lives of the English Saints,* London: S. T. Freemantle, 1901, Vol. III, pp. 176–7.

16 *Bede: The Reckoning of Time*, translated, with introduction notes and commentary by Faith Walls, Liverpool: Liverpool University Press, 1999.

17 Barbara G. Walker, *The Woman's Encyclopaedia of Myths and Secrets*, New York: HarperCollins, 1983, p. 645. As she points out: 'The church's so-called moveable feasts were movable because they were determined by lunar cycles, not solar ones. Christian holy days were copied from pagan ones, displaced by 12 hours in their solar reckoning; therefore the older, heathen version of each festival was celebrated on the "eve" of its Christian counterpart', p. 648. For Easter etymology, see also India Rakusen, 'Witch', BBC Radio 4, 2023.

18 https://www.martinpaul.org/thestoryofstmartins.htm.

19 Graham Phillips, *The Marian Conspiracy: The Hidden Truth about the Holy Grail, the Real Father of Christ and the Tomb of the Virgin Mary*, London: Sidgwick and Jackson, 2000.

20 Bede, *History of the English Church and People*, Leo Sherley-Price (trans.), R. E. Latham (ed.), London: Penguin, 1968, pp. 101–2. This work by Bede is also known as *Ecclesiastical History of the English People* (or variations thereon) including in later editions of this translation.

21 In what has been called one of the 'earliest ecclesiastical attempts to regulate women and marriage in Anglo-Saxon society', Hollis, p. 11.

22 Leo Sherley-Price, Introduction to Bede, 1968, p. 23. As early as 428, the Pope protested 'against the election of wanderers and strangers [*peregrini et extrani*] to episcopal seats' – referring to wandering monk mystics but also possibly an early expression of distaste for 'Travellers': Myles Dillon and Nora Chadwick, *The Celtic Realms*, London: Cardinal, 1973, p. 211.

23 One Catholic author calls the writing of Bede 'Augustine's greatest achievement': Anthony Marett-Crosby, *The Foundations of Christian England: Augustine of Canterbury and His Impact*, Ampleforth: Ampleforth Abbey Press, 1997, p. 47.

24 When Bede was writing his history of the English Church, it was to Abbot Albinus, 'an eminent scholar educated at Canterbury by Archbishop Theodore and Abbot Hadrian, both of them respected and learned men', that he turned: 'He carefully transmitted to me verbally and in writing . . . anything he considered worthy of mention that has

been done by disciples of the blessed Pope Gregory in the province of Kent or surrounding regions.'

25 https://www.electoralcommission.org.uk/who-we-are-and-what-we-do/elections-and-referendums/past-elections-and-referendums/eu-referendum/results-and-turnout-eu-referendum/eu-referendum-results-region-south-east.

26 https://www.thanet.gov.uk/margate-charter-trustees-confer-freewoman-of-margate-honour-on-tracey-emin/.

27 Damian Le Bas, *The Stopping Places*, London: Chatto & Windus, 2018, p. 10, p. 296.

28 Asser was quoting Nennius, who, around 829, wrote in his *Historia Brittonum*, 'insulam quae in lingua eorum vocatur Tenet, britannico sermone Ruoihm'. J.A. Giles translates this as: 'the island which is in their language called Thanet, and, by the Britons, Ruym.' https://www.gutenberg.org/files/1972/1972-h/1972-h.htm.

29 See Ronald Williams, *The Lords of the Isles: The Clan Donald and the Early Kingdom of the Scots*, London: Chatto & Windus, 1984, p. 38. Of nature itself, Gildas writes, damningly, 'I will not call upon the mountains, fountains or hills, or upon the rivers, which now are subservient to the use of man, but once were an abomination and destruction to them.' (Quoted by Gwen Benwell and Arthur Waugh, *Sea Enchantress: The Tale of the Mermaid and Her Kin*, London: Hutchinson, 1961, p. 59.)

30 'Bede's revision of the *Anonymous Life of Cuthbert* . . . reflects hostility to the eminence of abbesses . . . despite Bede's knowledge of at least one papal letter urging an Anglo-Saxon queen to take an active part in the conversion of her husband, reigning queens barely figure': Hollis, p. 13. See also Clare A. Less and Gillian R. Overing's analysis of Bede's underplaying of the role of royal mothers and abbesses in Kent and Northumbria in *Double Agents: Women and Clerical Culture in Anglo-Saxon England*, Cardiff: University of Wales Press, 2009; for example of Hild: 'What we witness in Bede's account of Hild's role is an appropriation and a rewriting of mothering, a reinscription of the feminine within the parameters of patriarchy', p. 43.

31 Stephanie Hollis, 'Minister-in-Thanet foundation story', *Anglo-Saxon England* 27, Michael Lapidge (ed.), Cambridge: Cambridge University Press, 1998, p. 58. See also Hollis, *Anglo-Saxon Women & the Church*, p. 12.

32 D. W. Rollason, *The Mildrith Legend: A Study in Early Medieval Hagiography in England*, Leicester: Leicester University Press, 1982, p. 11.

33 Hollis, 'Minister-in-Thanet', p. 58.

34 'Thanet's power as a sacred and royal place' and 'monastic home for a remarkable dynasty of Anglo-Saxon royal saints . . . persists well after Bede. This island, yet another of those islands so important to the history of the Christian mission in England, would later become a monastic home for a remarkable dynasty of Anglo-Saxon royal female saints': Clare A. Lees and Gillian Overing, *A Place to Believe In: Locating Medieval Landscapes*, Pennsylvania: Pennsylvania State Press, 2006, p. 16. See also their article on Bede in their *Double Agents: Women and Clerical Culture in Anglo-Saxon England*, Cardiff: University of Wales Press, 2009, p. 40.

35 D. W. Rollason, 1992, p. 13.

36 Hilary Powell, 'Following in the Footsteps of Christ: Text and Context in the *Vita Mildrethae*', *Medium Ævum*, vol. 82, no. 1, Oxford: The Society for the Study of Medieval Languages and Literature, 2013, pp. 23–43. JSTOR, https://doi.org/10.2307/43632968.

37 *History of St Augustine's Abbey of Canterbury* (MS 1): https://cudl.lib.cam.ac.uk/view/MS-TRINITYHALL-00001/159.

38 Stephanie Hollis, personal communication.

39 Hollis describes 'a direct decline in the education of female monastics in the late Anglo-Saxon period as the replacement of double monasteries by segregated and more strictly enclosed female communities diminished both their opportunities to participate in the learned culture of their male counterparts and the respect they were accorded by clerics', in 'Wilton as a centre of learning' in Stephanie Hollis (ed.), *Writing the Wilton Women: Goscelin's Legend of Edith and Liber confortatorius*, Turnhout: Brepols, 2004, p. 309.

40 'The whole trend of medieval thought was against learned women', Eileen Power, *Medieval English Nunneries, c.1275–1535*, Cambridge: Cambridge University Press, 1922, p. 238. See also Ann M. Hutchinson,

'in England there is very little evidence concerning the literacy and learning of girls and women, even less for that of nuns', in *Nuns' Literacies in Medieval Europe: The Antwerp Dialogue*, Virginia Blanton, Veronica O'Mara and Patricia Stoop (eds.), Turnhout: Brepols, 2017, p. 81.

41 Powell: 'In 1723, the Thanet historian and antiquarian John Lewis wrote that '. . . but a few years ago there was a little rock at Ebbs Fleet called St Mildred's rock'.

42 Sue Harrington, 'Stirring women, weapons, and weaving: aspects of gender identity and symbols of power in early Anglo-Saxon England', in *Archaeology and Women: Ancient and Modern Issues*, Sue Hamilton, Ruth D. Whitehouse and Katherine I. Wright (eds.), Walnut Creek, California: Left Coast Press, 2007, p. 343.

43 'Such a female / life: male / death separation may well have generated a potent symbolism for the early Anglo-Saxon and southern Scandinavian peoples': Harrington, pp. 343, 350–51.

6. Shetland

1 Janet Montgomery et al., 'Finding Vikings with isotope analysis: the view from wet and windy islands', *Journal of the North Atlantic*, Special Vol. 7, 2014, pp. 54–70; Derek Gore, 'A Review of Viking Attacks in Western England to the Early Tenth Century: Their Motives and Responses' in Ryan Lavelle and Simon Roffey (eds.), *Danes in Wessex*, Oxford: Oxbow Books, 2015, p. 56.

2 'All the Islands of Brittaine were wasted & much troubled by the Danes; this was theire first footing in England', entry made in 791: *The Annals of Clonmacnoise being Annals of Ireland from the Earliest Period to AD 1408*, Conell Mageoghagan (trans.)(1627), Denis Murphy (ed.), Dublin, 1896 (facsimile reprint 1993 by Llanerch Publishers, Somerset), p. 127. 'Vastatio omnium insularum Britanniae a gentilibus' ['devastation of all the islands of Britain by heathens], *Annals of Ulster*, entry made in AD 794.

3 T. D. Price, 'Introduction: new approaches to the study of the Viking Age settlement across the North Atlantic', *Journal of the North Atlantic*, 7, 2018, p. ii.

4 Ibid., p. vi.

5 Gunnar Andersson (ed.), *We Call Them Vikings*, Stockholm: Statens historiska museer, 2016, p. 183.

6 See Nicholas Howe, *Migration and Mythmaking in Anglo-Saxon England*, New Haven/London: Yale University Press, 1989, p. 24.

7 Felicitas Corrigan (ed.), *More Latin Lyrics: From Virgil to Milton*, Helen Waddell (trans.), London: Victor Gollancz, 1985, p. 161.

8 http://irisharchaeology.ie/2015/01/tonight-i-fear-not-the-vikings-an-early-irish-poem/; also http://www.e-codices.unifr.ch/en/list/one/csg/0904#details.

9 Matthias Egeler, *Islands in the West: Classical Myth and the Medieval Norse and Irish Geographical Imagination*, Turnhout: Brepols, 2017, p. 43.

10 Charles Donahue, 'The Valkyries and the Irish war-goddesses', *DMLA*,. 56 (1), March 1941, pp. 1–12.

11 Ibid., p. 3.

12 John Creighton, *Coins and Power in Late Iron Age Britain*, Cambridge: Cambridge University Press, 2000, p. 134.

13 Craig R. Davis, 'Cultural assimilation in the Anglo-Saxon royal genealogies', *Anglo-Saxon England*, Vol 21., 1992, pp. 23–36.

14 Geoffrey Hindley, *A Brief History of the Anglo-Saxons: The Beginnings of the English Nation*, London: Robinson, 2006, p. 28.

15 *Orkneyinga Saga*, trans. Hermann Pálsson and Paul Edwards, London: Hogarth Press, 1978 (this edition Penguin, 1981), p. 37.

16 Hermann Pálsson and Paul Edwards, 'Narrative Elements in the Icelandic *Book of Settlements*', in *Mosaic: An Interdisciplinary Critical Journal*, 4 (2), 1970, 1–11, at p. 3.

17 Judith Jesch, *Women in the Viking Age*, Boydell: Woodbridge, 1991, p. 78.

18 C. Blackie, *A Dictionary of Place-Names Giving Their Derivations*, London: John Murray, 1887, p. 187. Truly a 'North Sea Empire', as Perry Anderson described it in his *Passages from Antiquity to Feudalism*, London: Verso, 1974, p. 158.

19 Pálsson and Edwards, p. 12. 'Gor ruled the islands . . . He had one of his ships hauled over . . . with Gor sitting aft, his hand on the tiller. So he laid claim to all the land lying to port', Ch. 3, p. 26. Also: 'the

isthmus connecting it [Kintyre] to the mainland is so narrow that ships are regularly hauled across', Ch. 41, p. 86. He also 'sent his men into the Scottish sea-lochs. He got them to row in hugging the shore on one side, and out hugging it on the other, and thus he claimed as his own all the islands down the west of Scotland', *The Orkneyinga Saga*, Alexander Burt Taylor (trans.), Edinburgh: Oliver and Boyd, 1938, p. 201.

20 Steinar Imsen, 'Introduction', in *The Norwegian Domination and the Norse World c.1100–c.1400*, Steinar Imsen (ed.), Trondheim: Rostra Books / Tapir Academic Press, 2010, pp. 13–14.

21 See also Hyde Clarke et al. 'The Picts and Pre-Celtic Britain', *Transactions of the Royal Historical Society*, 3, 1886, pp. 243–80. 'In examining the lists of some forty or more Pictish kings, Dr. Skene found . . . The names of the fathers of the kings did not fall into the lists of kings, and the names of the kings did not fit into the lists of fathers . . . he adopted a theory . . . as to the institution of matriarchy . . . that polyandry existed among the Picts.'

22 *The Annals of St-Bertin*, Janet L. Nelson (trans.), Manchester: Manchester University Press, 1991, p. 65. See also Montgomery et al., pp. 54–70.

23 The 'Solundic sea' is a term apparently coined by the *Historia Norwegie* to describe the sea around the Solund islands, off the coast of Norway; *Historia Norwegie*, Peter Fisher (trans.), Inger Ekrem and Lars Boje Mortensen (eds.), København: Museum Tusculanum Press, University of Copenhagen, 2003, p. 185.

24 Pálsson and Edwards, p. 12.

25 Ronald Williams, *The Lords of the Isles: The Clan Donald and the Early Kingdom of the Scots*, London: Chatto & Windus, 1984, p. 74.

26 *Orkneyinga Saga*, p. 26. Also, 'Vikings would raid the [Orkney] islands, as well as Caithness, looting and killing, but when the farmers complained of their losses to Earl Hallad [earl of Orkney and Shetland], it seemed to him beyond his power to right matters for them: so, tiring of his rule, he gave up his earldom and went back to Norway . . . a laughing-stock', p. 28. https://www.britannica.com/biography/Harald-I-king-of-Norway.

27 Esther Renwick, 'In depth: steatite in Shetland', *Shetland Archaeology*, 16 Jan. 2016, https://www.archaeologyshetland.org/post/2016-1-16-in-depth-steatite-in-shetland.

28 Doreen Waugh in *Viking Unst*, Val E. Turner, Julie M Bond and Anne-Christian Larsen (eds.), Lerwick: Shetland Amenity Trust, 2013, p. 9.

29 Jakob Jakobsen, *The Place-names of Shetland*, London, 1936, p. 1.

30 Duncan Garrow and Fraser Sturt, 'Neolithic crannogs: rethinking settlement, monumentality, and deposition in the Outer Hebrides and beyond', *Antiquity*, 93 (369), June 2019, pp. 664–84.

31 'New project to investigate crannogs in Orkney launched', 2022: https://archaeologyorkney.com/2022/08/05/new-project-to-investigate-crannogs-in-orkney-launches-next-week/.

32 Alexandra Sanmark, 'Patterns of assembly: Norse *thing* sites in Shetland', in *Debating the* Thing *in the North: Introduction, Journal of the North Atlantic*, Oct. 2013.

33 Small islands and isthmuses were popular locations for Norse *thing* sites; 'the entering of a *thing* site may have involved the ritual crossing of "holy waters", 'as suggested by the eddaic poem *Grimnir's Sayings*', Sanmark, p. 104.

34 Sanmark, p. 98.

35 Ibid., p. 98.

36 Egeler, p. 71.

37 See Matthias Egeler's essay in Aisling Byrne and Victoria Flood, *Crossing Borders in the Insular Middle Ages*, Turnhout: Brepols, 2019. Also Mark-Kevin Deavin 'Ulysses in the north? The Yggdrasill myth re-considered', *Rivista di cultura classica e medioevale*, 55 (2), 2013, pp. 517–38.

38 Fridtjof Nansen, *In Northern Mists: Arctic Exploration in Early Times*, London: William Heinemann, 1911, Vol. 1, p. 355: footnote 2.

39 Neil Gaiman, *Norse Mythology*, London: Bloomsbury Publishing, 2017, p. 3.

40 https://sagadb.org/laxdaela_saga.en.

41 Clare A. Lees and Gillian R. Overing, *A Place to Believe in: Locating Medieval Landscapes*, Pennsylvania: Pennsylvania State University, 2006, p. 103.

42 Perhaps the many Selkie myths which swirl through the cold seas around north-west Britain were inspired by these peripatetic Viking

habits – those men who came and went from the islands 'wearing cloaks of finest seal-skin . . . [they] vanish into the sea, to come again to claim their sons, and reward with a bag of gold a woman who has raised a strong boy'. 'Manx law ordained that a son inherited his mother's cloak', Catherine Smith-Mason, *The Stones of Laxey*, Dunblane: DOICA Ltd, 2001, p. 5.

43 Martin Martin, *A Description of the Western Islands of Scotland circa 1695 and a Late Voyage to St Kilda*, Edinburgh: Birlinn, 1999, p. 66.

44 Ragnhild Ljosland, Orkney Science Festival, 'John D. Mackay Memorial Lecture', 11 September 2017. See also her blog with Chris Gee: https://brodgar.co.uk/2016/02/24/a-rouge-viking-at-swanbister-orphir/.

45 Sigurd Towrie, http://www.orkneyjar.com/history/maeshowe/maeshrunes.htm.

46 See for example: 'The most positively valorized gender is the idealized masculinity', Kathleen M. Self, 'The Valkyrie's gender: Old Norse shield-maidens and Valkyries as a third gender', *Feminist Formations*, Baltimore: John Hopkins University Press, 26 (1), spring 2014, pp. 143–72, at p. 145.

47 Miranda and Stephen Aldhouse-Green, *The Quest for the Shaman: Shape-shifters, Sorcerers and Spirit-healers of Ancient Europe*, London: Thames & Hudson, 2005: 'in early medieval Norse practice it was considered effeminate for men to enter a trance state and thus communion with the spirit world was reserved for female ritualists', p. 162.

48 'It is noteworthy that later Norse lays retain memories of such cults in the Channel Islands, allusions being made in the Helgi lays to the existence of sibyls or hags such as Mela mentions, in Guernsey and other adjoining insular localities', Lewis Spence, *The History and Origins of Druidism*, London: Rider, 1949, p. 63.

49 Henry Adams Bellows, *The Poetic Edda, Volume 1: Lays of the Gods: Voluspo*, New York: American-Scandinavian Foundation, 1936. Völuspá is also spelt Voluspo.

50 Lawrence Tulloch, *Shetland Folktales*, Cheltenham: The History Press, 2014, pp. 76–8.

51 Ibid., p. 76. https://eip.ceh.ac.uk/apps/lakes/detail.html#wbid=1271.

52 https://www.shetlanddialect.org.uk/john-j-grahams-shetland-dictionary.php?word=2464.

53 Barbara Crawford, 2000, review of Brian Smith and John Ballantyne (eds.), *Shetland Documents 1195–1579*, Lerwick: Shetlands Islands Council and The Shetland Times, 1999, https://www.euppublishing.com/doi/pdfplus/10.3366/nor.2000.0012.

54 Crawford writes about the impact of 'Lubeck and Hamburg merchants on the life and society of the islands' and of the resistance this 'self-sufficient and self-governing Norse community' evinced towards its new Scottish overlords.

55 S. Goodacre et al., 'Genetic evidence for a family-based Scandinavian settlement of Shetland and Orkney during the Viking periods', *Heredity*, Glasgow: Springer Nature, Vol. 95, 2005, pp. 129–35.

56 Derek J. McGlashan, Robert W. Duck and Colin T. Reid, 'The foreshore: geographical implications of the three legal systems in Great Britain', *Area*, 36 (4), Dec. 2004, pp. 338–47.

57 National Museum of Scotland, 'St Ninian's Isle treasure', https://www.nms.ac.uk/explore-our-collections/stories/scottish-history-and-archaeology/st-ninians-isle-treasure/.

58 'The Hebrideans were so scared of them, they hid whatever they could carry either in among the rocks or underground'; *Orkneyinga Saga*, Pálsson and Edwards (trans.), Ch. 106, p. 215.

59 Eileen Linklater, 'Udal law: past, present and future?', University of Strathclyde (LLB Hons. Dissertation, 2002), p. 17.

60 T. B. Smith, 'The law relating to the treasure', in *St Ninian's Isle and Its Treasure*, A. Small, C. Thomas and D. M. Wilson (eds.), Oxford: Oxford University Press, Vol 1, 1973, p. 165.

61 See Lord Kinnear in ibid. at p. 693.

62 According to Fisherrow Harbour Commissioners *v* Musselburgh Real Estate Co Ltd (1903) 5F 387 per Lord Low, at 393–4.

63 'Our history', https://www.thecrownestate.co.uk/en-gb/our-business/our-history/.

64 https://webarchive.nationalarchives.gov.uk/ukgwa/20151202171017/http://www.smith-commission.scot/wp-content/uploads/2014/11/The_Smith_Commission_Report-1.pdf.

65 Allan Macartney, 1983, 'Routes to island autonomy?', Open University Scotland, http://www.scottishgovernmentyearbooks.ed.ac.uk/record/22892/1/1983_10_Routestoislandautonomy.pdf.

66 Hill points out that when King Christian of Denmark pawned the islands to Scotland in 1469, only 10 per cent of the land was his to give away. 'The other 90% was owned by the Lords of Norway.' http://www.sovereignshetland.com/.

67 https://www.orcadian.co.uk/jailed-hill-goes-on-hunger-strike/.

68 It was only in 1615 that James VI abolished the earldom on account of its rogue tyrant Earl Patrick Stewart and in doing so abolished the islands' powers.

69 Since 1859, apart from the elections of 1935 and 1945, the Northern islands have voted Liberal, subsequently Lib-Dem. This has meant that, ever since the creation of the Labour Party (in 1909) and Scottish National Party (1934), the Northern Isles have pitted themselves against mainstream politics in both Scotland and England. https://en.m.wikipedia.org/wiki/Orkney_and_Shetland_(UK_Parliament_constituency).

70 https://www.heraldry-wiki.com/heraldrywiki/index.php/Shetland_Islands.

71 Pálsson and Edwards, p. 9.

72 Thomas Edward Spray, 'Patterns of nationalist discourse in the early reception of the Icelandic sagas in Britain', Durham University Ph.D. thesis, 2019, p. 117, http://etheses.dur.ac.uk/12964/.

73 Certain warrior burials, such as that in Birka, Sweden, excavated in the 1880s, were assumed, from their lavish wealth and weaponry, to be those of men. Only in later, more enlightened, times did they turn out to belong to women – and even so, as Caroline Criado Perez points out, people *still* argued that the Birka skeleton might have been a man – until the full gamut of DNA analysis in 2017 proved conclusively that the skeleton was that of a female, in her *Invisible Women: Exposing Data Bias in a World Designed for Men*, London: Vintage, 2020, p. 3. 'A female Viking warrior confirmed by genomics' is on open access here: https://onlinelibrary.wiley.com/doi/full/10.1002/ajpa.23308.

74 https://en-gb.facebook.com/S4UHAE/.

75 Along with their *thing* sites, the surest architectural hallmark of a Viking settlement in the skattlands is a long rectangular hall built for feasting. I have seen them in Shetland, in Orkney, in Iceland. Noel Fajut: 'Shetlanders can, at least, claim an unchallenged Norse pedigree for their homes: in shape, layout and location, the dwellings of rural folk changed only in minor detail from the arrival of the Vikings to the mid 20th century,' in his *Prehistoric and Viking Shetland*, Lerwick: Shetland Times Ltd, 2006, p. 100.

76 Susan Bowie is a GP in Shetland who moved up from Glasgow in the 1970s. She said it was 'like the Wild West', back then, pre-oil. She loved it – found it more egalitarian than the mainland, where she was always 'the lady doctor' and given gynae-jobs. And yet: 'there was Up Helly Aa, an anomaly'. So, for a bit of fun, at the Up Helly Aa of 1986, she persuaded some friends who were in one of the minor squads to let her dress up in a white lounge suit and don a hat and tie, and she became the fiddlebox carrier. 'I made a good man – and only got found out in the very last hall; apparently the squad got in terrible trouble later, were hauled before the Up Helly Aa committee.' What she remembers most is what fun it was, on the male side, at the centre of things, feted wherever she went. By contrast, being a hostess in one of the halls was simply 'tedious'. She did it once only: 'waiting all night for the men to come and go, waiting for them to invite you to dance, and then, desperately tired and bored, expected to do the dishes at 5am'. (She once saw a man dressed as 'Bertie Bassett' shagging a hostess; sometimes, obviously, there was the thrill of random sex.) She thought things would change in Shetland thereafter – but nothing did.

77 Self, pp. 147–50.

78 https://www.facebook.com/LerwickUHA/.

79 https://www.shetlandtimes.co.uk/2022/06/22/lerwick-up-helly-a-to-allow-women-in-squads-for-first-time?fbclid=IwAR3HSMh PtuOiibXZJ1sHjIsncKZ_m8ftgkkBKe6pZpRTXkyiL66ytmfQkTw&f s=e&s=cl.

80 https://www.theguardian.com/environment/2023/apr/05/mackerel-loses-sustainable-status-as-overfishing-puts-species-at-risk.

81 As one Shetlander told me, 'They have been sold out massively by the government, are not free from the constraints of the common fisheries policy, still have to share fishing grounds with EU boats, yet now have more problems exporting fish to their principal market – the EU!'

82 George and five other shareholders bought their boat, *Adenia*, eleven years ago for £11 million, and when I met them for the first time in 2014 they had 'almost made the money back'. In 2019, they bought another *Adenia*, custom-made in Spain, for £23 million.

83 https://sos-music.bandcamp.com/track/unst-boat-song.

84 The fourth line, Robertson writes, 'is plain, modern Shetlandic'. *Da Sangs at A'll Sing ta Dee: A Book of Shetland Songs*, T. A. Robertson (ed.), Lerwick: Shetland Folk Society, 1973 (reprint 2013), p. 32.

85 'Da Sang O Da Papa Men', Robertson, pp. 72–3, at p. 105.

86 Interview on Whalsay, 1 Aug. 2014.

87 Interview with Shetland pelagic fisherman Alastair Inkster, 30 Jan. 2020.

88 Barbara Crawford: 'development of North Sea oil has indeed done something to recreate the atmosphere of a North Sea community among the Norwegians, Orcadians and Shetlanders', book review in *Scottish Historical Review*, 60 (170), Oct. 1981, pp. 205–8.

7. Lindisfarne/Avalon

1 Different man, same name, different spelling, here in Northumberland: the anglicized version of the Irish name Aodhán: https://en.wikipedia.org/wiki/Aidan#:~:text=Aidan%20is%20the%20anglicised%20version%20of%20the%20Irish%20male%20given%20name%20Aodh%C3%A1m.

2 George Skelly, *A Guide to Lindisfarne, Bamburgh, Farne Islands, Dunstanburgh Castle Etc.*, Alnwick: C. E. Moore, 1888, p. 23.

3 Wikipedia has an article about St Teneu, or Thaney, or Thenaw, co-founder of Glasgow with her son Kentigern. She is said to have been cast adrift in an oarless coracle in deep waters beyond the Isle of May

by her father, King Leudonus, after being raped and becoming pregnant; her sea journey resulted in an abundance of fish in the seas nearby: https://en.wikipedia.org/wiki/Teneu.

4 *The Riverside Chaucer*, Larry D. Benson (ed.), Oxford: Oxford University Press, 1987, p. 23.

5 Alan Thacker, 'Lindisfarne and the origins of the cult of St Cuthbert', in *St Cuthbert, His Cult and His Community to AD 1200*, Gerald Bonner, David W. Rollason and Clare Stancliffe (eds.), Woodbridge: Boydell Press, 1989, p. 105.

6 Skelly, p. 18.

7 Aethelthyrth [also Etheldreda] was enshrined by her sister Sexburg, who sent some brethren out in a boat from Ely to find stone for a coffin. They came back from the ruined city of Grantchester – a Roman settlement – with 'a white marble sarcophagus of very beautiful workmanship which fitted her body exactly.' Bede, *History of the English Church and People*, Leo Sherley-Price (trans.), Harmondsworth: Penguin, 1968, p. 239.

8 Ibid., p. 150. King Oswald's hand and arm, Bede writes, 'remain uncorrupted to this day. They are preserved as venerated relics in a silver casket at the church of St Peter in the royal city, which is called after a former queen named Bebba [Bamburgh]'. The arm was later stolen by a monk and taken to Peterborough to be venerated there.

9 Aidan was venerated after his death through the medium of a wooden post against which he had been leaning when he died. As Henry Mayr-Harting writes, 'It was constantly incumbent on the Christian saints to show that they were in all essentials the equals of Thor's priests . . . Aidan's pillar succeeded Thor's.' *The Coming of Christianity to Anglo-Saxon England*, Pennsylvania: Penn State University Press, 1972, p.30. In the end, however, the rise of Cuthbert's cult meant 'the complete eclipse' of the cult of St Aidan: Thacker, p. 113.

10 Ibid., p. 105.

11 At the end of his *History of the English Church and People*, Bede lists at least eighty-five books of which he was the author.

12 Michelle P. Brown, *The Lindisfarne Gospels: The British Library Treasures in Focus*, London: The British Library, 2006, pp. 6–7.

13 They suggested to one scholar simultaneously 'the whole grand repertory of Celtic curvilinear ornament, which stretches back in a tradition of Irish metal-work to the La Tène civilization of the first century' – plus Coptic book-binding, Kentish cloisonné brooches, Sutton Hoo birds' heads, Irish enamelled escutcheons and Armenian manuscripts: Henry Mayr-Harting, p. 160–61.

14 Brown, p. 6.

15 Thacker, p. 105. Lindisfarne was rich: an important 'landed proprietor' with a series of 'dependent monasteries'. See David W. Rollason in *Cuthbert: Saint and Patron: Lectures Given in the Prior's Hall, Durham, February 1987*, Rollason (ed.), Durham: Dean and Chapter of Durham, 1987, p. 15.

16 Joanna Story, *Lindisfarne Priory*, London: English Heritage, 2005, p. 28.

17 Early medieval monasteries were 'a special kind of noblemen's club'; the origins of Anglo-Saxon poetry (such as *Beowulf*) may have been 'monastic entertainment', J. Campbell, 'Elements in the background to the life of St Cuthbert and his early cult,' in Bonner, Rollason and Stancliffe (eds.), p. 12.

18 Rollason in Rollason (ed.), p. 50.

19 Ibid., p. 56.

20 Miranda Aldhouse-Green, *Boudica Britannia: Rebel, War-leader and Queen*, Harlow: Pearson Education Ltd, 2006, p. 160.

21 His biography was written by Felix, an East Anglian monk: Mayr-Harting, p. 230. Crowland was not offshore but also not onshore, being surrounded by incoming seawater. The burial mound was Bronze Age, and subsequently there was a Roman temple at the same place. Guthlac's sister Pega left the island after the devil appeared to Guthlac in her form, persuading him to break his daylight fast. As he was dying, Pega sailed back downriver to prepare his body and help promote his cult. A year after burial, he, too, was found to be uncorrupted (with a smile on his face). Thank you to David Searle at Crowland Abbey for this information, 26 Feb. 2023.

22 The Scottish monk Dicul had a monastery near Chichester, encircled, Bede says, 'by woods and the sea'.

23 Bede, 1968: Selsey: p. 229; Ely: p. 241; Bardney: III.12. p. 161; Chertsey: IV.6, p. 218; Dicul: p. 228; Wilfrid: p. 229; Herbert: p. 264.

24 Richard Hamer, *A Choice of Anglo-Saxon Verse*, London: Faber & Faber, 1970 p. 84.

25 David Rollason in David Brown (ed.), *Durham Cathedral: History, Fabric and Culture*, New Haven: Yale University Press, 2014, p. 35.

26 Lindisfarne, and the hermitage on Inner Farne, remained 'the main foci for devotees of St Cuthbert north of the Tyne': Lynda Rollason in Brown (ed.), p. 75.

27 The 'position of women in England underwent a radical change for the worse in the period immediately following the Norman Conquest': Dorothy Stenton, *The English Women in History*, London: Routledge, 1957, quoted in Stephanie Hollis, *Anglo-Saxon Women and the Church: Sharing a Common Fate*, Woodbridge: Boydell Press, 1992, p. 2.

28 Lina Eckenstein writes that 'no woman living during Anglo-Norman times has been thus honoured, for the desire to raise women to saintship was essentially Anglo-Saxon and was strongest in the times which immediately followed the acceptance of Christianity': *Woman under Monasticism: Chapters on Saint-Lore and Convent Life between AD 500 and AD 1500*, Cambridge: Cambridge University Press, 1896, p. 80.

29 Durham's Norman bishop-princes thus continued the early-medieval relationship between spiritual and temporal power; some early archbishops in Northumbria had coins struck in their names; see J. Campbell in Bonner, Rollason and Stancliffe (eds.), p. 16.

30 Victoria Tudor, 'The cult of St Cuthbert in the twelfth century: the evidence of Reginald of Durham', in ibid., p. 457.

31 Martin Heale, 'The late Middle Ages, 1380–1539', in Brown (ed.), pp. 64, 521–2: fn 76.

32 Bernard Meehan and Claire Breay, *The St Cuthbert Gospel* in *Anglo-Saxon Kingdoms: Art, Word, War*, Claire Breay and Joanna Story (eds.), London: the British Library, 2018, p. 122.

33 Craig M. Rustici, *The Afterlife of Pope Joan*, Michigan: University of Michigan Press, 2006, p. 39.

34 See https://www.medieval.eu/s-cuthbert-gospel/. Cuthbert's coffin was opened up again in 1104, when it was moved into the new Norman cathedral. First the monks had a look, then the bishop, and finally the public. The miracle witnessed – of his un-corruption (which, it has been argued, may have been a real phenomenon caused by self-mummification through mortification of the flesh, his onion diet) – solidified Durham Cathedral Priory's reputation as 'heir of Lindisfarne'. By placing Cuthbert's cult at the centre of their brand-new church, the Normans were emphasizing that they got it – they understood and did homage to the island zeitgeist (time-ghost) of the north. See David Rollason, in Brown (ed.), p. 37.

35 Anna Lowenhaupt Tsing, *The Mushroom at the End of the World: On the Possibility of Life in Capitalist Ruins*, Princeton: Princeton University Press, 2015, p. vii.

36 That day I walked with Sam Slatcher, a local folk musician who had just set up the Songs of Sanctuary project, which trains refugees in choral singing and was inspired by the great green copper knocker on the northern door of the cathedral. Until the reign of James VI and I, anyone who clanged it was given thirty-seven days' sanctuary and a black robe to wear with 'St Cuthbert's Cross sewn on the left shoulder': www.durhamworldheritagesite.com/architecture/cathedral/intro/sanctuary-knocker. Sam released an album of Syrian and British folksongs which he wrote and performed with Raghad Haddad, a viola player from the Syrian National Symphony Orchestra.

37 Nennius, The History of the Britons, J.A. Giles (trans.), London: James Bohn, 1841, pp. 1–2.

38 Geoffrey of Monmouth, *Historia Regum Britanniae*, VIII.19, Sebastian Evans (trans.), London: J. M. Dent, 1912 [1928], p. 148.

39 Ibid., IX.4; XI.2.

40 'The Hesperides are said to have a vigilant dragon who guards golden apples beneath the leaves', Geoffrey of Monmouth, *The Life of Merlin*, Paul White (trans.), Launceston: Bossiney Books, 2004, pp. 1–2.

41 *The Life of Merlin*, p. 22.

42 Amy Kaufman, 'The law of the lake: Malory's sovereign lady', *Arthuriana*, 17 (3), 2007, pp. 56–73: 'one wonders whether Malory's women use magic because he considers both women and magic inferior, or

whether critics consider magic inferior because Malory's women are the ones who use it.'

43 Joshua J. Mark, 'Thomas Malory', *World History Encyclopedia*, https://www.worldhistory.org/Thomas_Malory/.

44 As with Geoffrey, it is this same island that Arthur is taken to when he is wounded to death: 'for I will unto the vale of Avilion to heal me of my grievous wound . . . thus was he led away in a ship wherein were three queens; that one was King Arthur's sister, Queen Morgan le Fay; the other was the Queen of Northgalis; the third was the Queen of the Waste Lands. Also there was Nimue, the chief lady of the lake'. Malory, Book 21, Ch. 6; https://www.gutenberg.org/cache/epub/1252/pg1252-images.html#chap257.

45 Charles Cromarty, *The Lindisfarne Story: A Saga of Island Folk*, Newcastle upon Tyne: Graham, 1971.

46 Skelly, p. 9.

47 R. T. Davies (ed.), *Medieval English Lyrics: A Critical Anthology*, London: Faber & Faber, 1963, p. 51.

48 Tudor, p. 457.

49 Sarah Foot, in Brown (ed.), p. 23.

50 Victoria Tudor in Bonner, Rollason and Stancliffe (eds.), p. 450.

51 In Durham there is a sixteenth-century English Bible which shows Henry VIII handing out copies of the Bible.

52 Gareth W. Dunleavy, *Colum's Other Island: The Irish at Lindisfarne*, Madison: University of Wisconsin Press, 1960, p. 95.

53 The River Wear produced the best sand for glazing, and Sunderland's glass industry, which peaked in the nineteenth century, was the glorious result. According to Victorian commentators, the Romans may have made glass on the Isle of Wight, for glass was found there during excavations and 'the sands of Alum Bay and Whitecliffe Bay would be suitable for the purpose', John Edward Price and Frederick Hilton Price, *A Guide to the Roman Villa Recently Discovered at Morton*, Ventnor: Briddon Bros, 1887, p. 36.

54 Claire Breay and Joanna Story (eds.), *Anglo-Saxon Kingdoms: Art, Word, War*, London: British Library, 2018, p. 125.

55 Another was found in 1982, at Kingston Lacy, also used as covering for another document. A canon at Durham Cathedral used three more leaves as cushioning for the binding in a medieval manuscript. Jarrow Hall displays, notes taken 1 Dec. 2018. Stephanie Hollis notes that John Aubrey recalled how, in his early-seventeenth-century childhood, 'old manuscripts "flew about like butterflies", and were variously used for covering new books, stopping bungholes, cleaning guns, and as wrapping paper by glovers'. Quotation from *John Aubrey: Brief Lives*, Richard Barber (ed.), London: Folio Society, 1975, p. 26 in Hollis, 2004, p. 318.

56 Bede, *Life of Cuthbert*, Ch. 24 in *The Age of Bede*, J. F. Webb (trans.), Harmondsworth: Penguin, 1965, p. 74.

57 Text quoted by Lisa M. Ruch, *Albina and Her Sisters: The Foundation of Albion*, Amherst, New York: Cambria Press, 2013, p. 63; my own adaptation of her translation.

58 Quoted in Lesley Johnson, 'Return to Albion, in *Arthurian Literature*, James P. Carley and Felicity Riddy (eds.), Cambridge: D. S. Brewer, 1995, pp. 19–40, at p. 31. Johnson translates the last line quoted here as 'by this we shall always be commemorated in this country'. The full Anglo-Norman text and its variations were edited by Georgine E. Brereton, *Des Grantz Geanz: An Anglo-Norman Poem*, Oxford: Society for the Study of Medieval Languages and Literature, 1937.

59 *The Shorter Oxford English Dictionary*, Oxford: Oxford University Press, 1973, Vol. 1, p. 1051.

60 Wife of Bath's Tale, *Riverside Chaucer*, p. 117.

61 Quoted in Ruch, pp. 2–3.

62 Jeffery Jerome Cohen, *Of Giants: Sex, Monsters and the Middle Ages*, Minneapolis, Minn.: University of Minnesota Press, 1999, p. 48ff.

63 John Hardyng, *The Chronicle of Iohn Hardyng*, London: F. C. & J. Rivington, 1812 (New York: AMS Press, 1974), p. 27.

64 John Hardyng, *Chronicle: edited from British Library MS Lansdowne 204*, James Simpson and Sarah Peverley (eds.), Vol 1, Kalamazoo: Medieval Institute Publications, 2015, p. 33.

65 Mayr-Harting, p. 30.

66 https://www.northumberlandgazette.co.uk/news/fascinating-stories-unearthed-at-crypt-415814.

67 D. W. Rollason, in D. W. Rollason (ed.), *Cuthbert: Saint and Patron*, Durham: Dean and Chapter of Durham, 1987, p. 17: 'from the beginning the Northumbrian kings used it as a naval base . . . That the early North-umbrian kings possessed a considerable fleet is clear from Bede's accounts of their successful conquests of Anglesey and the Isle of Man and of King Ecgfrith's apparently successful invasion of Ireland in 684. It is just possible, although we cannot prove it, that the seventh-century visitor to Lindisfarne would have seen not only the monks at their work and prayers but also the Northumbrian war-fleet riding at anchor.'

68 Mayr-Harting, p. 98.

69 Lynda Rollason, in Brown (ed.), p. 75.

70 As Peter Ackroyd writes, 'There has always been an organic need among the English to connect the present and the past, and the forced disassociation from a thousand years of Catholic history provoked in some a profound unease': *Albion: The Origins of the English Imagination*, London: Chatto & Windus, 2002, p. 246.

71 As Bede wrote of Britain in the context of the Arian heresy, 'This poi-sonous error after corrupting the whole world, at length crossed the sea and infected even this remote island; and, once the doorway had been opened, every sort of pestilential heresy at once poured into this island, whose people are ready to listen to anything novel, and never hold firmly to anything': Bede, *History of the English Church and People*, Leo Sherley-Price (trans.), Harmondsworth: Penguin, 1968, p. 48.

72 Ibid., p. 266.

73 The mystic fourteenth-century poet Julian of Norwich imagined Jesus as Mother; this is from *Revelations of Divine Love*.

8. Islay and the Isles

1 See https://islay.com/about-islay/islay-distilleries/.

2 John Marsden, *Somerled and the Emergence of Gaelic Scotland*, East Linton: Tuckwell Press, 2000, p. 23.

3 His council island was Islay, his religious base was Iona; Clan Donald historians claim that he is buried at the abbey on Kintyre, which his son

Ranald endowed (along with the new Benedictine foundation on Iona). His daughter, Bethoc, was the founding prioress of the Iona nunnery, according to the seventeenth-century traveller Martin Martin, who read an inscription at Iona to that effect. See Marsden, pp. 84, 120.

4 Quoted in Hermann Pálsson and Paul Edwards, 'Narrative elements in the Icelandic *Book of Settlements'*, in *Mosaic: An Interdisciplinary Critical Journal*, 4 (2), 1970, pp. 1–11, at p. 9.

5 Pálsson and Edwards, p. 3.

6 Kathleen MacPhee, *Somerled: Hammer of the Norse*, Glasgow: Neil Wilson, 2004, p. 53.

7 'DNA shows Celtic hero Somerled's Viking roots', 26 April 2005, http://www.scotsman.com/news/sci-tech/dna-shows-celtic-hero-somerled-s-viking-roots-1-709181.

8 St Mungo, patron saint of Glasgow, called Kentigern in the twelfth-century Latin poem about Somerled's death ('Carmen de Morte Sumerledi'), was roundly rebuked by clerics for failing to protect the city from Somerled's first attack, in 1153, when 'Gardens, fields and ploughlands were laid waste and destroyed: the gentle, menaced by barbarian hands, were overwhelmed'. See Alex Woolf, 'The song of the death of Somerled and the destruction of Glasgow in 1153', *Sydney Society for Scottish History Journal*, 14, 2013, pp. 1–11, at p. 7.

9 Marsden, p. 94.

10 The 'descendants of Viking longships': David H. Caldwell and Gordon Ewart, 'Finlaggan and the Lordship of the Isles: an archaeological approach', *Scottish Historical Review*, 72 (194), 1993, pp. 146–66.

11 Martin Martin writes that in the sea near Rodel, '3 fathoms under water, and about two stories high' is a 'circle of stone'. He says that he 'saw it perfectly on one side'. But 'the season then being windy, hindered me from a full view of it. The natives say that there is such another circle of less compass in the Pool Borodil, on the other side of the bay'. Martin Martin, *A Description of the Western Islands of Scotland circa 1695 and a Late Voyage to St Kilda*, Edinburgh: Birlinn, 1999, p. 38.

12 Indeed, throughout the fifteenth century, the lordship fielded 'large armies in opposition to the royal forces'; Caldwell and Ewart, p. 146.

13 James A. Stewart Jnr, 'War and peace in the Hebrides: the origin and settlement of the "Linn Nan Creach" ', *Proceedings of the Harvard Celtic Colloquium*, 16/17, 1996, pp. 116–56, at p. 119.

14 The Finlaggan excavations showed that the lordship was clearly more than merely a 'powerful chiefdom'. Although there was a lack of the 'burghs, money, new people' which you would expect at the site of an incipient state with its 'strong central government, hierarchical society and distinctive culture'; Caldwell and Ewart, p. 158.

15 Donald Monro, *Monro's Western Isles of Scotland and Genealogies of the Clans*, 1549.

16 Caldwell and Ewart, pp. 240–41.

17 Scota 'had brought from Egypt a stone of black marble whereon strange runes were carved'. The story told of their ancestors wandering from Scythia all the way to Britain and Ireland 'in search of an Island of Destiny in the west which had been promised them in the elder time'. John Creighton, *Coins and Power in Late Iron Age Britain*, Cambridge: Cambridge University Press, 2000, p. 134, drawing on Dumville 1977:73, in *Early Medieval Kingship*, P. H. Sawyer and I. N. Wood (eds.), Leeds: University of Leeds, 1979.

18 John of Fordun, *Chronica Gentis Scotorum*, 1384–7.

19 Stewart Jnr, footnote 15, p. 121.

20 Caldwell and Ewart, p. 164.

21 *James I: The True Law of Free Monarchies and Basilikon Doron*, Daniel Fishlin and Mark Fortier (eds.), Toronto: Victoria University, 1996, pp. 27–8.

22 Lisa Hopkins, *Shakespeare on the Edge: Border-crossing in the Tragedies and the Henriad*, Farnham: Ashgate, 2005, p. 89.

23 Stewart Jnr, pp. 116–56.

24 Boswell's *Life*, 16 March 1759; quoted in Philip Pullman, *Daemon Voices: On Stories and Storytelling*, Oxford: David Finkling Books, 2017, p. 339.

25 'The Seafarer', lightspill.com/poetry/oe/seafarer.html.

26 Carole Pateman, *The Sexual Contract*, Cambridge: Polity Press, 1988; Hannah Dawson (ed.), *The Penguin Book of Feminist Writing*, London: Penguin Classics, 2021. See also Eleanor Scott, from the Introduction to *Invisible People and Processes: Writing Gender and Childhood into European Archaeology*, Jenny Moore and Eleanor Scott (eds.), Leicester: Leicester University Press, 1997, p. 9. King James VI/I published *Daemonologie* in 1597.

27 Silvia Federici, *Caliban and the Witch*, London: Pluto, 2004, p.185.

28 *An Leabhar Mòr: The Great Book of Gaelic*, Malcolm Maclean and Theo Dorgan (eds.), Edinburgh: Canongate, 2002, p. 54. Reproduced in Gaelic (without commentary) in E. C. Quiggin, *Poems from the Book of the Dean of Lismore with a Catalogue of the Book and Indexes*, J. Fraser (ed.), Cambridge: Cambridge University Press, 1937, 'LXII, MS.p.251.', p. 78.

29 Thomas Owen Clancy, 'Women poets in early medieval Ireland', in Christine Meek and Katharine Simms (eds.), *The Fragility of Her Sex'? Medieval Irishwomen in Their European Context*, Dublin: Four Courts Press, 1996, pp. 43–72, at p. 56.

30 William Gillies, 'Gaelic literature in the later Middle Ages', in *The Edinburgh History of Scottish Literature*, Vol. 1, Ian Brown (ed.), Edinburgh: Edinburgh University Press, 2007, p. 224.

31 Clancy, p. 57.

32 George Geddes and Angela Gannon, *St Kilda: The Last and Outmost Isle*, Edinburgh: Historic Environment Scotland, 2015.

33 This word is spelt 'sheiling' and 'shieling'. See: 'SHIELING, n. Also shielin, -en, sheal(l)ing, †schealling, sheelin(g), sheil(l)in(g), †shilin; ¶shielding. ['ʃilɪn] 1. A hut or rude shelter, a temporary house of stones, sods, etc., esp. one built for the accommodation of shepherds and dairy maids in the higher or more remote areas used as summer grazing ground for sheep and cattle, = Shiel, n., 1. (Sc. 1808 Jam.). Gen. Sc., hist., and in n.Eng. dial. Also attrib.', *Scottish National Dictionary*, https://www.dsl.ac.uk/entry/snd/shieling.

34 We sailed past Faslane (HMNB Clyde) on our training voyage, the home of Britain's Trident missiles; that was even stranger.

35 Martin Henig, 'The mosaic pavements: their meaning and context', in Barry Cunliffe, *The Roman Villa at Brading, Isle of Wight: The Excavations of 2008–10*, Oxford: Oxford School of Archaeology, 2013, p. 217.

36 MacPhee, p. 112.

9. Rathlin

1 Whether Somerled is Norse or Gaelic in origin still causes contention; see https://clandonald-heritage.com/somhairlidh-or-somerled/.

2 Wallace Clark, *Rathlin: Its Island Story*, Co. Londonderry: North-West Books, 1988 (first edition called *Rathlin: Disputed Island*, 1971), p. 87.

3 Ibid., p. 81.

4 *An Leabhar Mòr/The Great Book of Gaelic*, Malcolm Maclean and Theo Dorgan (eds.), Dublin: O'Brien Press, 2008, pp. vi–vii.

5 Clark, p. 79.

6 The McDonnell clan, for example, were said to have been the custodians of St Columba's gold pectoral cross – until 1584, when the English seized it in a raid, it was sent south to London and lost. Ibid., p. 104.

7 John Dee, *The Limits of the British Empire*, Ken MacMillan with Jennifer Abeles (eds.), Westport, CT: Praeger, 2004, pp. 3–4, 6, 10.

8 Clark, p. 85.

9 Jonathan Bardon, *The Plantation of Ulster: The British Colonization of the North of Ireland in the Seventeenth Century*, Dublin: Gill and Macmillan, 2011, p. 2.

10 Richard Bagwell, *Ireland under the Tudors*, Vol. 2. London: Longmans, 1885, p. 244.

11 *Annals of the Four Masters*, celt.ucc.ie/published/T100005E/text008.html.

12 Clark, p. 93.

13 Bagwell, p. 302.

14 Ramsay Colles, *The History of Ulster: From the Earliest Times to the Present Day*, London: Gresham Publishing, 1919, Vol. 1, pp. 236–7.

15 Elizabeth I to the Earl of Essex, 12 Aug. 1575: *Calendar of the Carew Manuscripts,* J. S. Brewer and William Bullen (eds.), London: Longmans, 1868, p. 21.

16 Bagwell, p. 324.

17 Sir Henry Sidney's *Memoir of His Government of Ireland, Ulster Journal of Archaeology,* First Series, Vol. 5, 1857, pp. 299–323.

18 Clark, footnote 3, p. 96, quoting O'Laverty, 1878–95: 'Some years ago great quantities of human bones were found in a piece of boggy ground a few perches west of the castle'.

19 Such as Lambert Simnel, the anti-Tudor puppet who in 1487 was crowned King Edward IV in Dublin.

20 *Camden's Britannia newly translated into English, with large additions and improvements; publish'd by Edmund Gibson,* London: F. Collins, 1695, pp. 967–8: https://quod.lib.umich.edu/e/eebo2/B18452.0001.001/1:77?rgn=div1;view=fulltext.

21 Lisa Hopkins, *Shakespeare on the Edge: Border-crossing in the Tragedies and the Henriad,* Farnham: Ashgate, 2005, p. 90.

22 Hopkins, p. 87. Achin is an old spelling of this province in Indonesia. It is now known as Aceh. Dee also described his maps metaphorically, in terms of the queen's enthroned body, Dee, p. 5.

23 Kilcolman Castle History, http://core.ecu.edu/umc/Munster/settlement_situation.html.

24 The lake that Guyon journeys across is not Malory's clean, benevolent place of female magic, which renders up sacred weapons and transports a king away for healing. It is 'slow and sluggish', 'Engrost with mud, which did them foule agrise', treacherously 'misty', 'a wide inland sea'.

25 The twelfth-century epic *The Destruction of Eochaid mac Mairidh* tells of how Liban, daughter of the king of Ulster, escaped death in a flood by becoming a salmon-tailed mermaid and living for centuries thereafter in Lough Neagh. 'Irish Muirgen, one of the names of the aquatic lady Liban', Lucy Allen Paton, *Studies in the Fairy Mythology of Arthurian Romance,* Boston: Ginn & Company, 1903, p. 9. (Reprinted by Alpha Editions, 2019.)

26 Philip Watson, *Rathlin Nature and Folklore*, Glasgow: Stone Country Press, 2011, p. 165.

27 And later 'the term for courtesan or common prostitute': Linda Phyllis Austern, 'Women's musical voices in sixteenth-century England', *Early Modern Women*, Vol. 3, 2008, pp. 127–52.

28 *The Faerie Queene*, 2.12.83.

29 'Spenser could never rid his mind of what he witnessed in the Ulster famine; the remarkable number of images of starvation in *The Faerie Queene* attest to its hold on the imagination': Philip Schwyzer, 'Exhumation and ethnic conflict: from St Erkenwald to Spenser in Ireland', *Representations*, 95 (1), 2006, pp. 1–26. Seamus Heaney writes that 'In Elizabethan English, bawn (from the Irish *bó-dhún*, a fort for cattle) referred specifically to the fortified dwellings that the English planters built in Ireland to keep the dispossessed natives at bay . . . I cannot help thinking of Edmund Spenser in Kilcolman Castle, reading the early cantos of *The Faerie Queene* to Sir Walter Raleigh, just before the Irish would burn the castle and drive Spenser out of Munster back to the Elizabethan court': in his translation of *Beowulf*, London: Faber & Faber, 1999, p. xxx. M. M. Gray writes that while Spenser 'advocated severe measures of repression' in Ireland (in his prose work, *A View of the State of Ireland*), 'the misery he had seen in Munster throws its shadow over the *Faerie Queene*': 'The influence of Spenser's Irish experiences on *The Faerie Queene*', *Review of English Studies*, Oxford: Oxford University Press, Vol. 6, No. 24 (Oct. 1930), pp. 413–28, p. 426.

30 '[O]ne of the most politically significant mass migrations to have taken place in western Europe since medieval times': Philip Robinson, *Plantation of Ulster: British Settlement in an Irish Landscape, 1600–1670*, Dublin: Gill and Macmillan, 1984, p. 1.

31 James A. Stewart Jr, 'War and peace in the Hebrides: the origin and settlement of the "Linn Nan Creach"', *Proceedings of the Harvard Celtic Colloquium*, 16/17, 1996, pp. 116–56, p. 147.

32 Augustus McCurdy, *Rathlin's Rugged Story: From an Islander's Perspective*, Coleraine and Ballycastle, self-published, 2000, p. 29.

33 One of them, Brigadier Gage, wrote a Foreword in 1971 to Wallace Clark's history of the island in which he acclaimed the island's lack of 'demonstrations, hippies or layabouts'. In Wallace Clark, *Rathlin: Disputed Island*, Londonderry: North-West Books, 1988, p. 7.

34 Stewart Dalby, *The Friends of Rathlin Island*, Clifton upon Teme: Polperro Heritage Press, 2004, p. 70.

35 Xiaojie Liu et al., 'Seaweed reproductive biology: environmental and genetic controls', *Botanica Marina*, 60 (2), 2017, pp. 89–108.

36 John Henry MacAuley, Notes on 'Ould Lammas Fair', countysongs.ie.

37 Martin Martin, *A Description of the Western Islands of Scotland circa 1695 and a Late Voyage to St Kilda*, Edinburgh: Birlinn, 1999, p. 31; Alexander Carmichael, *Carmina Gadelica*, Edinburgh: Floris Books, 1992 [1900], I.63.

38 *The Tempest*, II.i.

39 Jonathan Bate, 'Shakespeare's islands', in *Shakespeare and the Mediterranean: The Selected Proceedings of the International Shakespeare Association World Congress, Valencia 2001*, Tom Clayton, Susan Brock and Vicente Forés (ed.), Newark: University of Delaware Press, 2004, p. 290.

40 Faith Nostbakken, *Understanding the Tempest: A Student Casebook to Issues, Sources and Historical Documents*, Westport, CT: Greenwood, 2004, p. 31.

41 Silvia Federici, *Caliban and the Witch*, London: Pluto, 2004, p. 106.

10. *Scilly*

1 Charles Thomas describes 'surges' when the tide not only reaches the top of its usual range but is caused to exceed itself further by 'unusual combinations of prolonged spells or high Atlantic winds, falls in barometric pressure and peaks in the lunar-month cycle'. Scilly has experienced surges in recent memory, when, in Thomas's words, 'granite boulders of half-ton weight' were tossed about the island of St Martin, and two feet of sand and weed were deposited on the Old Town road: Thomas, *Exploration of a Drowned Landscape: Archaeology and History of the Isles of Scilly*, London: B. T. Batsford, 1985, pp. 48–9.

2 James W. Meeker, 'Subtleties of the isle: islands of the imagination', *Interdisciplinary Studies in Literature and Environment*, 18 (1), Winter 2011, pp. 197–202.

3 Thomas writes that there had been a real inundation, in historical memory – the 'island' starts being referred to as the 'islands' by the eleventh century; probably the inundation happened 'between the times of King Alfred and the Tudor monarchs'; Thomas, pp. 8, 34.

4 Ibid., pp. 55–8.

5 'Sometimes I glimpse my friend / glinting beneath / the shape-shift silvers / of the waves . . . so near and far from the blessed isles . . . pacing the boulevards of Lyonesse', Penelope Shuttle, *Lyonesse*, Hexham: Bloodaxe, 2021.

6 Thomas, p. 265.

7 Ibid., p. 275.

8 https://poly-olbion.exeter.ac.uk/the-text/full-text/song-1/.

9 Thomas, pp. 61, 154, 159.

10 The writer William Borlase, who published a book on Scilly in 1756, drew on the writing of Diodorus Siculus in 30 BC to suggest (tentatively, in a footnote) that all Cornish islands may once have been home to a sun cult: 'St Michael's Mount was originally called in British Dinsul, ie the Hill belonging or dedicated to the Sun; and the vast flat Rocks common in these Islands . . . formerly the floor of a great Temple, are no improbable arguments that they might have had the same dedication . . . for Diodor. Sicul . . . says, "it was dedicated to the Sun . . ."; and there can be no doubt but this was one of the British Islands': William Borlase, *Observations on the Ancient and Present State of the Islands of Scilly, and their Importance to the Trade of Great-Britain*, Oxford: W. Jackson, 1756, p. 25.

11 They had been accused in 384 of the Priscilline heresy, according to Sulpicius Severus. Clive Mumford, *Portrait of the Isles of Scilly*, London: Robert Hale, 1967, p. 59. Jessie Mothersole, *The Isles of Scilly: Their Story, Their Folk and Their Flowers*, London: Religious Tract Society, 1910, pp. 19–20.

12 Scilly and Cornwall came under the dominion of the English crown as early as the reign of King Athelstan in the tenth century. But

when the duchy was created, Scilly, some thirty miles from Cornwall, was so insignificant and far away it was missed off the original grant. There were now two *Domini de Scilly*: spiritual lords, the abbots of Tavistock Abbey, who controlled Scilly through the priory on Tresco, and temporal lords, who extracted a rent which ranged from '300 puffins at Michaelmas' in 1345, to only fifty puffins by the reign of Henry VI. Daniel Lysons and Samuel Lysons, 'The Scilly Islands', in *Magna Britannia: Volume 3, Cornwall*, London: T. Cadell and W. Davies, 1814, pp. 330–37. With the Dissolution, the Crown took back the spiritual possession of the islands, acquiring 'lordship' of it in 1540. N. J. G. Pounds, *The Parliamentary Survey of the Duchy of Cornwall*, Part II: Isles of Scilly – West Antony and Manors in Devon, Devon and Cornwall Record Society, Exeter, 1984, p. 131.

13 D. and S. Lysons, pp. 330–37.

14 Mumford, p. 61.

15 Ann Fanshawe, also spelt Anne: Anne Harrison, Lady Fanshawe, *Memoirs of Lady Fanshawe*, Dodo Press reprint, pp. 20–21. See also Lucy Moore, *Lady Fanshawe's Receipt Book: An Englishwoman's Life During the Civil War*, London: Atlantic Books, 2017.

16 Robert Heath, *A Natural and Historical Account of the Islands of Scilly*, London, 1750; reprinted as *The Isles of Scilly by Robert Heath: The First Book on the Isles of Scilly, Written . . . 1750*, Newcastle upon Tyne: R. Manby and H. S. Cox, 1967, pp. 51 ff.

17 By the mid-eighteenth century, other subversive traditions are recorded on Scilly, such as 'goose-dancing' at Easter, when 'the maidens are dressed up for young men and the young men for maidens'; Natalie Zemon Davis, *Society and Culture in Early Modern France*, Cambridge: Polity Press, 1965/87, p. 139. In 1890, Walter Besant had the heroine of his Scilly-based story *Armorel of Lyonesse* (London: Chatto & Windus) gaze south-west to 'the broad mouth of Oroonooque and the shores of El Dorado.' By this time, at least, the perspectives of island women had become important, even to mainstream Britain.

18 R. C. Anderson, 'Operations of the English fleet: 1648–52', *English Historical Review*, 31 (123), July 1916, p. 408.

19 Sean Kelsey, 'King of the sea: the Prince of Wales and the Stuart monarchy', *History*, 92 (4), 2007, p. 440.

20 Ibid., pp. 428–48.

21 Mary Coate, 'The Duchy of Cornwall: its history and administration 1640–60', *Transactions of the Royal Historical Society*, 10, 1927, pp. 135–69, at p. 162. Andrew Marvell, who later worked in Westminster for the staunchly Parliamentarian Latin Secretary to Cromwell, John Milton, wrote a poem in 1649, 'The Unfortunate Lover', which, it has been suggested, is a nautical allegory of the 'Prince of Wales, "cast away in the Scilly Isles after the failure of the Royalist cause in the West in 1646" ': J. M. Newton, 'What do we know of Andrew Marvell?', *Cambridge Quarterly*, 6 (2), 1973, pp. 125–43, at p. 138, quoting R. H. Syfret's 1940 work on Marvell's poem.

22 See Sid Lonegren, *Labyrinths: Ancient Myths and Modern Uses, revised and updated fourth edition*, Glastonbury: Gothic Image Publications, 1991/2007: 'Oliver Cromwell delivered the death knell to sacred space in England', p. 13.

23 It was possibly, as Mark Stoyle writes, 'concealed resentment against English cultural hegemony – accentuated in 1648 by the protestantising, centralising policies of the parliamentary regime' that led to Cornwall rising again in the second Civil War: Stoyle, 'The Cornish Rising of 1648 and the Second Civil War', *Albion*, 32 (1), spring 2000, pp. 37–58, at p. 56. In 1887 M. A. Courtney emphasized the lasting Royalist sympathies of the islands by quoting a ballad sung by Scillonians of the Cornish: 'In Cromwell's days I was for him, / But now, my boys, I'm for the king; / For I can turn, boys, with the tide, / And wear my coat on the strongest side': Courtney, 'Cornish Folk-lore', *Folk-Lore Journal*, 5 (1), 1887, pp. 14–61, at p. 44.

24 John Putley, *The Isles of Scilly in the English Civil Wars*, Bristol: Stuart Press, 2003, p. 5.

25 Ibid., pp. 13–15.

26 John Taylor, *Wandering to See the Wonders of the West*, London, 1649, pp. 17–18 (republished in *The Old Book Collector's Miscellany*, Vol. 3, London: Reeves & Turner, 1873). He rhymes: 'I do give you good account / From London unto Cornwall's Michael's Mount, / Of all my journey, and what news I found . . . Seven times at Sea I served Eliza Queen . . . Last (to the King) at the Isle of Wight I went, / Since when my best content, is discontent: / Thus having travelled North, and South, and East / I mean to end my travels with the West.'

27 R. L. Bowley, *Scilly at War*, St Mary's: Bowley Publications, 2001, p. 85.

28 Thomas, p. 251.

29 In the words of his descendant, 'In 1647 Parliament nominated Colonel John St Aubyn . . . to be Captain of the Mount . . . In 1659 he purchased the Mount from the Basset family, who, at that time, had been impoverished on account of their loyalty to the King'; John St Aubyn, *St Michael's Mount: Illustrated History and Guide*, St Ives: J. St Aubyn, 1978, pp. 22–3.

30 R. L. Bowley, *The Fortunate Islands: The Story of the Isles of Scilly* (based on 1945 edition of E. L. Bowley), St Mary's, Isles of Scilly: Bowley Publications, 2004, p. 40.

31 During the Interregnum, when Parliament surveyed the islands (two years later than the rest of Cornwall because of the resistance put up by Royalist forces), they were described as 'late parcell of the possessions of Charles Stuart late King of England', Pounds, p. 131.

32 Borlase, p. 39.

33 Pounds, p. 133.

34 Mumford, p. 77.

35 Lisa Hopkins, *Shakespeare on the Edge: Border-crossing in the Tragedies and the Henriad*, Aldershot: Ashgate, 2005, p. 89.

36 Thomas, p. 232.

37 Lonegren, p. 51.

38 Quoted in William Henry Matthews, *Mazes and Labyrinths: A general account of their history and development*, independently published [subsequently by London: Longmans & Co], 1922, pp.160–1.

39 Ronald Hutton, *Pagan Britain*, Yale: Yale University Press, 2013 (reprint 2014), p. 353.

40 By 1648, the courtier Richard Fanshawe, exiled with the nascent King Charles II to Scilly and mainland Europe, was awash with nostalgia for pre-war England, in which an isle was as blessed as those of Horace's sixteenth ode: see Syrithe Pugh, 'Fanshawe's critique of Caroline pastoral: allusion and ambiguity in the 'Ode on the Proclamation', *Review of English Studies*, 59 (240), 2008, pp. 379–91. Later, reflecting on those years in a poem written under house arrest near Sheffield, he also called himself 'a pilgrim of the seas'. Edward Hyde, Earl of Clarendon, may have begun his iconic six-volume *History of the Rebellion* in Scilly; as Nigel Smith writes, it was these islands – the enforced island eyrie – that imbued the books with their 'sea imagery, itself both biblical, epic and romantic in origin': Smith, *Literature and Revolution in England*, Yale: Yale University Press, 1994, p. 347.

41 See Ann Hughes, *Gender and the English Revolution*, London: Routledge, 2011.

42 Quoted in Melinda J. Gough, ' "Not as myself": the queen's voice in 'Tempe Restored', *Modern Philology*, 101 (1), 2003, pp. 48–67, n. 12, p. 54.

43 As Gough writes, *Tempe Restored* 'celebrated to an unprecedented degree the prerogatives of elite and nonelite women alike to participate centrally in the social, political, and increasingly theatrical functions of majesty', p. 67.

44 Dolores Palomo, 'The halcyon moment of stillness in Royalist poetry', *Huntington Library Quarterly*, 44 (3), 1981, pp. 205–21, p. 221.

45 Quoted in Louis B. Wright, 'The reading of plays during the Puritan Revolution', *Huntington Library Bulletin* (6), 1934, pp. 73–108, p. 101.

46 It opens with a Prologue condemning censorship: 'An Ordinance from our pretended State, / Sowes up the Players mouths, they must not prate / Like Parrats what they're taught upon the Stage, / Yet we may Print the Errors of the Age.'

47 Wright, p. 100.

48 Barbara G. Walker, *The Woman's Encyclopaedia of Myths and Secrets*, New York: HarperCollins, 1983, p. 854.

49 Silvia Federici, *Caliban and the Witch*, London: Pluto, 2004, p. 102.

50 Ann Fanshawe, *Memoirs of Lady Fanshawe*, London: Henry Colburn, 1829, p. 47.

51 During the Civil War, Bermuda had been controlled by Royalists – privateering, as usual. But by the 1650s, when Marvell wrote his poem, Bermuda had become a destination for convicts, providing a sink for England's unwanted criminalized, but also functioning, in the imagination, as a place yet unsullied. There has been much scholarly debate about the precise meaning of Marvell's poem – is it Puritan or political propaganda; is it ironic and ungodly? The key lines are surely those early ones about 'an Isle so long unknown, / And yet far kinder than our own?'. See Timothy Raylor, 'The instability of Marvell's *Bermudas*', *Andrew Marvell Newsletter*, 6 (2), winter 2014, https://marvell.wp.st-andrews.ac.uk/newsletter/the-instability-of-marvells-bermudas/.

52 The 'floating islands a new hatchéd nest', a reference, Palomo contends, that looks back as far as Ben Jonson's masques *Neptune's Triumph* (1624) and *Fortunate Isles* (1625), both of which have floating islands, as does Strode's *The Floating Island*, of course; Palomo, p. 214.

53 This famous image first appeared on a copper coin in 1665, during the reign of Charles II. Pepys wrote in his diary for 25 February of 'The king's new medall, where, in little, there is Mrs Stewart's face . . . and a pretty thing it is that he should choose her face to represent Brittannia by', *The Diary of Samuel Pepys*, London/Glasgow: Collins' Clear-Type Press, 1933, p. 178.

54 There was Francis Lee's Christian-throwback *Antiquity Revived: or the Government of a Certain Island Antiently Called Astreada* (1693); the politically left-wing tract by Gabriel Plattes called *A Description of the Famous Kingdown of Macaria* (1641), based on an island from More's *Utopia*; fantastical islands such as Henry Schooten's *The Hairy-Giants, or, A Description of Two Islands in the South Sea* (1671); Henry Neville's male-titillating polygamy fantasy, *The Isle of Pines* (1668). As Gregory Claeys writes in his study, *Restoration and Augustan British Utopias*, 'the utopian desire' burned brightly 'in mid-seventeenth-century Britain to an inordinate extent'. Gregory Claeys (ed.), *Restoration and Augustan British Utopias*, Syracuse: Syracuse University Press, 2000, p. xi.

55 Erin Lang Bonin, 'Margaret Cavendish's dramatic utopias and the politics of gender', *Studies in English Literature, 1500–1900*, 40 (2), Spring, 2000, pp. 339–54.

56 Margaret Cavendish, *The Convent of Pleasure and Other Plays*, Ann Shaver (ed.), Baltimore: John Hopkins University Press, 1999, pp. 240–41.

57 Cavendish in Gregory Claeys (ed.), pp. 60–61.

11. Man

1 In *Portraits of Islands*, Eileen Molony (ed.), London: Dennis Dobson, 1951, p. 23.

2 Peter J. Davey and James R. Roscow, *Rushen Abbey and the Dissolution of the Monasteries in the Isle of Man*, Isle of Man: Natural History and Antiquarian Society, 2010, p. 9.

3 Here 'most valleys meet and here surrounding mountains hide the sea', wrote John Betjeman in Molony (ed.), p. 19.

4 Peter Davey, personal correspondence.

5 John Belchem's review of Roger Dickinson's *The Lordship of Man under the Stanleys: government and economy in the Isle of Man, 1580–1704*, *English Historical Review*, 114 (458), Sept. 1999, pp. 985–6.

6 R. H. Kinvig, *The Isle of Man: A Social, Cultural and Political History*, Liverpool: Liverpool University Press, 1975, p. 119.

7 Quoted in John A. Thomson, *The Smuggling Coast: The Customs Port of Dumfries, Forty Miles of the Solway Firth*, Dumfries: T. C. Farries, 1989, p. 24.

8 *The History and Description of the Isle of Man* was published first along with his panegyrics and political treatise; and then again, in 1744, as a stand-alone volume.

9 Author of works such as 'A Poem Humbly Inscribed to His Majesty, Prince of Wales' ('When first Britannia's slavish Chain was broke, / And her gall'd Neck eas'd of the Roman Yoke'), who makes free with emotive island metaphors in his political encomiums ('Our Halcyon Days renew'd their welcome Date, / And we esteem'd our Happiness

compleat: / His timely Aid repell'd the swelling Tide / Of raging Rome, for Pity, not for Pride). George Waldron, *The Compleat Works in Verse and Prose of George Waldron, Gent., Late of Queen's College, Oxon*, Theodosia Waldron (ed.), printed for the Widow and Orphans, London: Cengage Gale, 1731, p. 3; 'Christianity without persecution', p. 30.

10 George Waldron, *The History and Description of the Isle of Man: viz, Its Antiquity, History, Laws, Customs, Religion and Manners of its Inhabitants, Minerals, Curious and Authentick Relations of APPARITIONS OF GIANTS that have liv'd under the Castle Time immemorial. Likewise many Comical and Entertaining Stories of the Pranks play'd by Fairies, &c.*, London: W. Bickerton, 1744, pp. 15–16.

11 Waldron, p. 21.

12 Anon., 'Observations upon the antient state, and rise of the trade of the Isle of Mann', Manx Museum Archives [MMA]: nd [1721–1736], MS 09707/1/20; AP 60 (2nd)-16.

13 MMA, AP 60 (2nd)-19.

14 MMArchives, AP 60 (2nd)-9.

15 Neville Williams, *Contraband Cargoes: Seven Centuries of Smuggling*, London: Longman, Green & Co., 1959, pp. 95–6.

16 In Scilly I heard people referring to FMLs: fucking mainlanders.

17 *London Magazine*, November 1754.

18 Williams, p. 124.

19 Gareth Pugh, Manx National Heritage Project Archivist (The Atholl Papers), 31.03.22, https://www.imuseum.im/the-atholl-papers-the-revestment/.

20 gov.im/about-the-government/departments/cabinet-office/external-relations/constitution/.

21 Wikipedia [https://en.wikipedia.org/wiki/Lord_of_Mann#cite_note-5; 12.3.23], quoting Edward Callow, *From King Orry to Queen Victoria: A Short and Concise History of the Isle of Man*, London: Elliot Stock, 1899, "Preface", p. x.

22 Kinvig, p. 121.

23 Walter Scott, *Guy Mannering*, London: Adam and Charles Black, 1913, Ch. 9, p. 74.

24 John Feltham, *A Tour through the Island of Mann, in 1797 and 1798; comprising sketches of its ancient and modern history, constitution, laws, commerce, agriculture, fishery etc. including whatever is remarkable in each parish, its population, inscriptions, registers etc.*, Bath, 1798, p. 136.

25 Thomson, p. 25.

26 C. W. Gawne, *The Isle of Man and Britain CONTROVERSY 1651–1895: From Smuggling to the Common Purse*, Douglas: Manx Heritage Foundation, 2009, p. 8.

27 See Isle of Man Government, 'What "Brexit" means for the Isle of Man', p. 7, https://www.gov.im/media/1353298/brexit-faqs-final.pdf.

28 http://www.abdullahquilliam.org/about-abdullah-quilliam-society/

29 From William Harrison's edition of Waldron's *A Description of the Isle of Man*, originally published for the Manx Society in 1865, *Vol. 11, Waldron's History*, and transcribed and edited for the website *Isle of Man.com* by F. Coakley, 2001.

30 Williams, p. 128.

31 'The shadow cast by Revestment on these coastal communities was dark deep and long': Frances Wilkins, 'The impact of the Revestment on the history of Dumfries and Galloway', *Isle of Man Natural History and Antiquarian Society Revestment Symposium 2015*, recorded talk.

32 MMA, MD 514/6722, Liverpool. Collector to Board, 3 March 1788.

33 Thompson, pp. 26, 29.

34 John Pinfold, who edited the Bodleian Library's edition of the memoirs of the Manx slave captain Hugh Crow also estimated that 'a considerable proportion of them [slave captains] were fellow Manxmen': Introduction to *The Memoirs of Captain Hugh Crow*, Oxford: Bodleian Library, 2007, p. vii.

35 Frances Wilkins, *Manx Slave Traders: A Social History of the Isle of Man's Involvement in the Atlantic Slave Trade*, Kidderminster: Wyre Forest Press, 1999, p. 129.

36 Ibid., p. 15.

37 John Pinfold, Introduction to *The Memoirs of Captain Hugh Crow*, p. vi. Crow describes how 'Bermudean, or, as our sailors called them, the *Bermugian* fishermen, are said, as soon as they see a dolphin, to put the

fire on the pot to cook him, so sure are they of killing the fish . . . On the homeward passage, when passing through the gulph of Florida, my services in securing many a supply of dolphin, which were very acceptable as a change of food, and an addition to our stock, were most thankfully considered both by the captain and the crew: and we frequently served up a mess called *chowder*, consisting of a mixture of fresh fish, salt pork, pounded biscuit and onions', pp. 26–7.

38 *The Memoirs of Captain Hugh Crow*, pp. 100–101.

39 Williams, p. 128.

40 Lucy Warwick-Ching, 'Clock ticks on Isle of Man tax', *Financial Times*, 19 Feb. 2013.

41 Gaut's Cross, no. 99, St Andreas Church.

42 *Skeealyn Vannin/Stories of Mann: The Complete Collection of Manx Language Archive Recordings Made by the Irish Folklore Commission in 1948*, Douglas: Manx National Heritage, 2003, p. 6.

43 'This may explain why so many of the recitations recorded in 1948 are religious texts', *Skeealyn Vannin*, p. 8.

44 Preface to *Manx Ballads and Music*, A.W. Moore, Douglas: Manx National Heritage, 1896, p. xi.

45 Feltham, p. 136.

46 Ibid., pp. 35–7.

47 Mona Douglas, *Twelve Manx Folk Songs: with Manx, Gaelic and English Words*, trans. M. Douglas. Arranged with Pianoforte accompaniment by A. Foster. [Airs chiefly from A. W. Moore's *Manx Ballads and Music*.] 2 sets. London: Stainer & Bell, 1957, pp. 20–23.

48 Waldron, 1731, p.104. Barbara Walker writes that the island used to have 'an "enchanted palace" with a crypt chapel of thirteen pillars, the sacred number of the old lunar year': Barbara G. Walker, *The Woman's Encyclopaedia of Myths and Secrets*, New York: HarperCollins, 1983, p. 574.

49 And again in 1744.

50 N. D. Quilliam, *Keys and Cuffs: The Inside Stories; The History of the Isle of Man/Manx Prisons, 1417–2008*, self-published, Isle of Man, 2009, p. 13.

51 ' "I thought they could capsize the boat": orcas on the attack', *The Week*, 10 Oct. 2020, taken from *Observer*.

52 Tom Mustill's recent book, *How to Speak Whale: A Voyage into the Future of Animal Communication*, London: William Collins, 2022, shows that marine mammals live in families and clans, have fights and love each other.

53 Mona Douglas, for example, was named for the island. *Mona* is also what the Romans said the island of Anglesey was called. The medieval Latin name for the Isle of Man was Eubonia, but the two islands were also known by the name Mona. Bede conjoins them as the 'Mevanian Isles', and this twinning lasted into the eighteenth century, with Henry Rowlands, in *Mona Antiqua Restaurata*, calling Man the 'sister' of Mona. Tim Clarkson, *Columba*, Edinburgh: John Donald Publishers Ltd, 2011, p. 65. 'Edwin . . . brought under English rule the British Mevanian Isles, which lie between Ireland and Britain', Bede, *Ecclesiastical History of the English People*, Leo Sherley-Price (trans.), Harmondsworth: Penguin, 2003, II.5, p. 108. 'Mona . . . and her sister the isle of Man', Henry Rowlands, *Mona Antiqua Restaurata. An Archæological Discourse on the Antiquities, Natural and Historical, of the Isle of Anglesey*, London: J. Knox, 1766, p. 70.

54 Feltham, pp. 7–8.

55 J. M. Jeffcott, 'Mann, its names and their origin', *Manx Miscellanies*, II, William Harrison (ed.), Douglas, Isle of Man, Printed for the Manx Society, 1880, p. 10.

56 She gives as reference Johannes C. H. R Steenstrup, *The Medieval Popular Ballad*, trans. from the Danish by Edward Godfrey Cox, Boston, MA: Ginn & Co., 1914, p. 105: '*mon* is probably Old Norse *man* (girl), whence *mareminde* (mermaid), which corresponds to the German *mereminne*.'

57 Walker, p. 574.

58 Matthias Egeler, *Islands in the West: Classical Myth and the Medieval Norse and Irish Geographical Imagination*, Turnhout: Brepols, 2017, pp. 56–7. Myles Dillon and Nora Chadwick described how, in the Welsh stories, Bran is the brother of Manannán, from a family 'not native to any one Celtic country but to the Irish sea, and all its surrounding

coasts, with its nucleus in the Isle of Man': *The Celtic Realms*, London: Weidenfeld and Nicolson, 1967, pp. 150–51.

59 Michael Newton's translation; 'Poem in praise of Raghnall of Man', *Exploring Celtic Civilizations: An Online Celtic Studies Coursebook*, 2016, https://exploringcelticciv.web.unc.edu/prsp-record/text-poem-in-praise-of-raghnall-of-man/. See also Egeler: 'the poem *Baile suthach sith Emhna (A Fertile Place is the Elf-Mound of Emain)* . . . completely and in great detail equates Emain with the Isle of Man', p. 57.

60 John Rhys, *Celtic Folklore Welsh and Manx*, Oxford: Oxford University Press, 1901. See: sacred-texts.com/new/cfwm/cf109.htm: 'This was written in the sixteenth century, and based probably on Higden's *Potychronicon*, book 1, chap. xliv.' J. G. Frazer, *The Golden Bough* (1922; reprint 1971), p. 107. Frazer also noted that wrens were hunted at Christmas time, at least 'down to the eighteenth century', pp. 703–704. He called wrens 'the little king', but Barbara Walker writes that the island belief was that the Fairy Queen inhabited the body of a wren – she was said to have 'sometimes led the whole male population into the sea where they perished' (her source here is W. Carew Hazlitt, *Faiths and Folklore of the British Isles*, New York: Benjamin Blom, 1965, pp. 387–90). The wren was said to be a druidic bird – in the tenth-century Welsh poem 'The prophecy of Britain' from the *Book of Taliesin*, the 'word which is cognate with druid is *dryw*, which also means 'wren' – and wrens again 'came to be equated with druid in the eighteenth century' (see Anne Ross in Miranda J. Green (ed.), *The Celtic World*, London: Routledge, 1995, pp. 429–30). The Manx tale sounds like a local folk version of the *Voyage of Bran*.

61 Margaret Fay Shaw, *Folksongs and Folklore of South Uist*, London: Routledge and Kegan Paul, 1955, p. 7.

62 Barbara Walker writes that 'calendar consciousness developed first in women, because of their natural menstrual body calendar'. In Gaelic, she adds, the words for menstruation (*miosach*) and calendar (*miosachan*) 'are the same'. And in English, too. Walker, pp. 645–6.

63 Mona Douglas, *The Secret Island: Poems and Plays in Verse*, Douglas: Victoria Press, 1943, pp. 41–2.

12. *Western Isles*

1 'Western Isles' has historically meant all of the islands west of Scotland, or all of the Hebrides (Outer and Inner). Today Comhairle nan Eilean Siar (the Western Isles Council) represents only the Outer Hebrides, Barra north to Lewis.

2 There is also one like this near Sheenaghan Point in Ireland: James O'Laverty: *An Historical Account of the Diocese of Down and Connor, Ancient and Modern*, Dublin: James Duffy & Sons, 1878–95, Vol. 3, p. 142: 'supposed to have been so poised for the performance of some forgotten religious rites'.

3 Canmore website archaeological fieldnotes, 2018. 'Tiree, Balephetrish: Clach Na Choire ... Ringing Stone' canmore.org.uk/site/21529/tiree-balephetrish.

4 Eric Cregeen and Donald W. Mackenzie, *Tiree Bards and their Bardachd: The Poets in a Hebridean Community*, Isle of Coll: Society of West Highland & Island Historical Research, 1978, p. 20.

5 King James VI was perhaps the first – sending planters over to Lewis in 1605, and 'finally licensing a huge military invasion of the area in 1608'. Lisa Hopkins, *Shakespeare on the Edge: Border-crossing in the Tragedies and the Henriad*, Farnham: Ashgate, 2005, p. 93.

6 Even Samuel Johnson recognized the perniciousness of this, writing in *A Journey to the Western Islands of Scotland* (1775) of how, 'Their chiefs . . . have . . . lost much of their influence; and as they gradually degenerate from patriarchal rulers to rapacious landlords, they will divest themselves of the little that remains.'

7 T.M. Devine, *The Scottish Clearances: A History of the Dispossessed, 1500–1900*, London: Penguin Books, 2018, pp. 243–6.

8 J. M. Bumsted, *The People's Clearance: Highland Emigration to British North America, 1770–1815*, Edinburgh: Edinburgh University Press, 1982, p. 100.

9 So, too, the bard of Coll: 'The proud, handsome youths today are evicted, / . . . cold and empty the homes;/I see not the maid of an evening go milking . . ./ The folk of the kilt and the hose and cocked

bonnets . . . are sent overseas to climates unwholesome / With no end in view but to lay the land bare.' Cregeen and Mackenzie, p. 20.

10 John Prebble, *The Highland Clearances*, Harmondsworth: Penguin, 1963, p. 249.

11 James Hunter, *The Making of the Crofting Community*, New Edition, Edinburgh: John Donald Publishers, 2000 (1976), pp. 53ff.

12 Or the village of Imber on Salisbury Plain, cleared in 1943 and now open to the public only during Easter weekend. Matthew Green has other evocative examples in *Shadowlands: A Journey Through Lost Britain*, London: Faber & Faber, 2022.

13 John Lorne Campbell (ed.), *The Book of Barra*, London: George Routledge, 1936.

14 Keith Branigan. *From Clan to Clearance: History and Archaeology on the Isle of Barra, c.850–1850 AD*, Oxford: Oxbow, 2005, p. 140.

15 Donald Macleod quoted in Alexander Mackenzie, *The History of the Highland Clearances: containing a reprint of Donald Macleod's Gloomy memories of the Highlands; Isle of Skye in 1882; and a verbatim report of the trial of the Braes crofters*, Inverness: A. & W. Mackenzie, 1883, p. 256.

16 Ben Buxton, *The Vatersay Raiders*, Edinburgh: Birlinn, 2008, pp. 68ff.

17 Hugh S. Roberton, 'Mingulay Boat Song', *Songs of the Isles: A Collection of Island and Highland Tunes from Various Sources, Set to English, or to Anglo-Scottish*, London: J. Curwen & Sons, 1938, no. 2749, pp. 2–3.

18 Nan MacKinnon, quoted in Buxton, p. 208.

19 Buxton, p. 2.

20 Ibid., p. 118.

21 Quoted in Buxton, p. 135.

22 Monbiot, in his Foreword to Alastair McIntosh's *Soil and Soul: dispatches of a Celtic ecowarrior*, London: Aurum, 2001; online at https://www.alastairmcintosh.com/soilandsoul/samples-soilsoul.htm

23 Buxton, p. 22.

24 Quoted by Compton Mackenzie in *The Book of Barra*, John Lorne Campbell (ed.), pp. 6–7.

25 Carmichael, *Carmina Gadelica*, Edinburgh: Floris Books, 1992 (reprint), p. 19.

26 The Irish Folklore Commission recorded conversations between Manx speakers about fairies – one man records not seeing the fairies since he stopped speaking Manx regularly, thirty years back, *Skeealyn Vannin*, p.11; pp. 80–83.

27 Fiona Mackenzie, 'Margaret Fay Shaw's Hebridean Odyssey', BBC Radio 3, Jan. 2021.

28 From South Uist, in particular, come the Selkie songs, women's songs which purport to be in seal language and to speak to the mythical relationship between these enigmatic creatures, with their huge humanoid eyes, and their human admirers. From the island of Eigg (Eilean nam Ban Mora, the island of big women) come the songs of Cuchullan, sun-god and fighting hero; Parsifal, or Amadan Mòr. From this same island, too, has come a lot of contemporary music, some via the recording studio of Johnny Lynch of Lost Map Records. In 2016, ten Scottish and English female musicians recorded a beautiful album, *Songs of Separation*, based mostly on folk material from either side of the border, including the song 'Soil and Soul', with the line 'There's a woman in the mountain, there's a woman in the hill . . .'

29 *Sea Tangle: Some More Songs of the Hebrides Collected, Edited, Translated, and Arranged for Voice and Pianoforte by Marjory Kennedy-Fraser and Kenneth Macleod*, London: Boosey, 1913.

30 Marjory Kennedy-Fraser, *Songs of the Hebrides*, Vol. 2, https://electric-scotland.com/history/women/MKFSongsOfTheHebridesBVolTwo02.pdf.

31 Probably the authorship, if one could be said to exist in this primarily oral culture, was collective and diffused over many years. India's great epic, the Mahabharata, was an organic, fluid text, to which many people contributed, until the moment when it came to be written down. In the Mahabharata this moment becomes part of the story: when the epic's author, the human sage Vyasa, enlists the elephant-headed god Ganesh as his scribe.

32 Martin Martin claimed that women, in particular, were 'anciently denied the use of writing in the islands to prevent love-intrigues'. Martin Martin, *A Description of the Western Islands of Scotland circa 1695 and a Late Voyage to St Kilda*, Edinburgh: Birlinn, 1999, p. 85.

33 Quoted in Claire McEachern, *The Poetics of English Nationhood, 1590–1612*, Cambridge: Cambridge University Press, 1996, p. 144.

34 '[K]nowledge of the past and the ancestors was a vital part of Highland consciousness': Fiona Stafford, *The Sublime Savage: James Macpherson and the Poems of Ossian*, Edinburgh: Edinburgh University Press, 1988, p. 13.

35 She, too, linked this traditional Celtic art to that of the 'ancient Hindoos'. Marjory Kennedy-Fraser, p. 82.

36 Fiona Mackenzie, 'Margaret Fay Shaw's Hebridean Odyssey', BBC Radio 3, Jan. 2021.

37 'The feminine embodied in the landscape', Alastair McIntosh, *Poacher's Pilgrimage: An Island Journey*, Edinburgh: Birlinn, 2018 [2016], p. 72.

38 Quoted in Lewis Spence, *The History and Origins of Druidism*, London: Rider, 1949, p. 63. See *Popular Tales*, Vol. I, p. 24, XCIII.

39 As Sam Knight recently pointed out in his book on twentieth-century prophecy – drawing on the writings of Martin Martin in 1695 – 'it appeared to be a social phenomenon . . . when people moved away from the Hebrides, the future no longer appeared to them': *The Premonitions Bureau: A True Story*, London: Faber & Faber, 2022, p.143. Happily, Martin Martin writes, 'upon their return to England, the first night after their landing they saw the second-sight.' Martin Martin, Chapter XIV: 'An Account of the Second Sight', p. 215.

40 Roger Hutchinson, *The Soap Man: Lewis, Harris and Lord Leverhulme*, Edinburgh: Birlinn, 2003, p. 153.

41 Alastair McIntosh, pp. 46–8.

42 With views, she observed, east to Skye, 'which may have been used for solar or lunar observations': Margaret Curtis, 'Archaeology Notes (2016)', https://canmore.org.uk/site/346392/holasmul.

43 Duncan Garrow, Fraser Sturt and Mike Copper, *Submerged Neolithic of the Western Isles, Interim Report (March 2017)*, http://crannogs.soton.ac.uk/wp-content/uploads/sites/220/2018/09/Lewis_Lochs_Interim_Report_March_2017.pdf.

44 Alastair McIntosh, p. 13.

45 Barbara G. Walker, *The Woman's Encyclopaedia of Myths and Secrets*, New York: HarperCollins, 1983, pp. 645–6.

46 https://www.legislation.gov.uk/ukpga/1981/69.

47 Reverend George Tulloch, 'Edderachillis', New Statistical Account, Edinburgh: W. Blackwood and Sons, 1845.

48 See the description in Robert Atkinson, *Island Going, to the remoter isles, chiefly uninhabited, off the north-western corner of Scotland*, London: Collins, 1949, p. 36.

13. Channel Islands

1 Rebecca Wragg Sykes, *Kindred: Neanderthal Life, Love, Death and Art*, London: Bloomsbury, 2020, p. 150.

2 Though the islands were once part of the Duchy of Brittany, in 933 they were annexed by the Duchy of Normandy. Raoul Lempriere, *History of the Channel Islands*, London: Robert Hale Limited 1974 [1980], Wikipedia, https://en.wikipedia.org/wiki/Bailiwick_of_Guernsey.

3 'As late as the coronation of King George III in 1761', the representative of the Duke of Normandy 'walked in the Abbey procession taking precedence over the Archbishop of Canterbury': ibid., p. 29. As Tim Thornton writes in *The Channel Islands 1370–1640: Between England and Normandy*, Woodbridge, Martlesham: Boydell & Brewer, 2012: 'The key theme of the local historiography of the Channel Islands from the 17th century onwards is the claim of their unbending loyalty to the English Crown', p. 1.

4 Simon Watkins, *We remember the Occupation by the Nazis: Memories of the German Occupation of the British Channel Islands 1940–45 by the People Who Lived through It*, CD Audiobook, read by Roy McLoughlin, St. John, Jersey: Channel Island Publishing, 2010.

5 He referred twice to Napoleon (still the bogeyman in Britain), and to the unchanged geographical conditions which rendered Britain strong and vulnerable ('the same wind which would have carried his transports across the Channel might have driven away the blockading fleet').

6 Churchill's Writing and Speeches, '1940: The Finest Hour', International Churchill Society, https://winstonchurchill.org/resources/speeches/1940-the-finest-hour/we-shall-fight-on-the-beaches/.

7 Marie de Garis, *Folklore of Guernsey*, self-published, Guernsey, 1975 [1986], p. 114.

8 T. X. H. Pantcheff, *Alderney: Fortress Island*, Chichester: Phillimore & Co., 1981, p. 3.

9 Paul Sanders, *The Ultimate Sacrifice: The Jersey Islanders who Died in German Prisons and Concentration Camps during the Occupation 1940–1945*, Jersey: Jersey Heritage Society, 2004 (1998), p. 18.

10 David Wingeate Pike, Review [Untitled] in *Guerre mondiales et conflits contemporains* (258), April–June 2015, p. 138.

11 Philip Bailhache, Foreword to Sanders, p. ix.

12 Madeleine Bunting, *A Model Occupation: The Channel Islands Under German Rule, 1940–45*, London: Pimlico, 1995, 2004.

13 Sanders, p. 108.

14 Ibid., p. 129.

15 Ibid., p. 131.

16 Just as the British incarcerated Napoleon on St Helena, and in 1945 Maréchal Pétain would be banished to the island of Yeu after being found guilty of high treason for collaboration with the Nazis, so the Germans used islands as prisons – some more intensely than others. Ibid., p. 153.

17 Ibid., p. 131.

18 Mary Liff to her friend Grace Salisbury, Jersey Museum; see Jacqueline King's *A Cake for the Gestapo*, London: ZunTold, 2020, for a vivid fictional rendition of a childhood during occupation.

19 'A directory of Europe's royalty and higher nobility', https://en.wikipedia.org/wiki/Almanach_de_Gotha.

20 Sibyl Hathaway, *Dame of Sark: An Autobiography*, Jersey: La Haule Books, 1961, p. 114.

21 Ibid., p. 118.

22 Bunting, pp. 58–9.

23 Solomon H. Steckoll, *The Alderney Death Camp*, Granada: Mayflower, 1982, quoting 'War Office document 199/214', pp. 117–18.

24 Somewhat contradicting Louise Willmot's argument in her essay 'Women and resistance' that Bunting et al.'s focus on Jerry-bags exaggerates the issue. Whether it exaggerates it or not, these women were

by default in the spotlight for their sexual behaviour. Louise Willmot, 'Women and resistance' in Gillian Carr, Paul Sanders and Louise Willmot (eds.), *Protest, Defiance and Resistance in the Channel Islands: German Occupation, 1940–45*, London: Bloomsbury Academic, 2014.

25 Solomon H. Steckoll, *The Alderney Death Camp*, London: Granada, 1982, p. 119.

26 Sanders, p. 177, n. 342.

27 Steckoll, p. 119.

28 Wilmot, 2014, p.184.

29 Sanders, p. 113.

30 Sanders, p. 97.

31 Bunting, p. 6.

32 Bunting, p. 263.

33 Michael Shea, in '*The Country Life Book of*' *Britain's Offshore Islands*, Richmond upon Thames: Country Life, 1981, p. 21.

34 Bunting, p. 261. Bob le Sueur died in 2022 aged 102.

35 Wingeate Pike, p.129. He is quoting Steckoll here: 'Steckoll dénonce le fait que leur rapport fut classé sans suite et qu'il «reste introuvable aujourd'hui».'

36 David Fraser, *The Jews of the Channel Islands and the Rule of Law, 1940–45: 'Quite Contrary to the Principles of British Justice'*, Brighton: Sussex Academic Press, 2000, p. 14.

37 Sanders, p. 8.

38 Guernsey is due one when the current bailiff retires.

39 Sanders, p. 17.

40 Steckoll, p. 122.

41 Bunting, pp. 107, 318, 344. Technically, Hathaway's North American husband was the ruler, as she explained to him after their wedding day: ' "Under our old feudal laws a husband owns everything that his wife possesses and this applies to the lordship of the island. You are Seigneur of Sark *à cause de sa femme*." ' But Sibyl, who spoke German and was an islander by birth, ruled in reality. Hathaway, p. 81.

42 Alderney Museum display, visited 14 Dec. 2015.

43 Steckoll, p. 17.

44 Ibid., p. 156.

45 Ibid., p. 179.

46 Ibid., p. 22; Pantcheff, p. 65.

47 Bunting, p. 183.

48 Steckoll, p. 86. A German soldier, Gustav Dahmer, wrote in his diary, 'It certainly was a godforsaken island': Alderney Museum.

49 Steckoll, pp. 90, 99.

50 Ibid., p. 103.

51 John Dalmau, *Slave Worker in the Channel Islands*, Guernsey: Guernsey Press Co., 1956, p. 18.

52 Pantcheff, p. 70.

53 Wingeate Pike, p. 128.

54 Ibid., pp. 129–30.

55 Steckoll, pp. 21, 37.

56 Ibid., p. 39.

57 Bunting, p. 285.

58 Interview with Trevor Davenport, Alderney, 16 Dec. 2015.

59 Steckoll, p. 20.

60 Wingeate Pike, p. 128: 'L'histoire de l'occupation allemande des îles anglo-normandes attend toujours son auteur'.

61 C. Sturdy Colls and Kevin Colls, 'Reconstructing a painful past: a non-invasive approach to reconstructing Lager Norderney in Alderney, the Channel Islands', in Eugene Ch'ng et al. (eds.), *Visual Heritage in the Digital Age*, London: Springer-Verlag, 2013, pp. 120–21. She has since released a documentary about Alderney, *Adolf Island* (2019).

62 Bunting, p. 34. The Alderney cow was famous before the war; in *Emma* (1816), Jane Austen described how the Martin family had 'eight cows, two of them Alderneys, and one a little Welch cow' – apparently inspired by her own mother's herd of Alderney cows, one of which 'makes more butter than we use': https://janeaustensworld.com/tag/alderney-cows/. During the First World War, Virginia Woolf 'bicycled through a herd of Alderney cows' in Sussex; Harriet Baker, *Rural Hours: The Country Lives of Virginia Woolf, Sylvia Townsend Warner and Rosamond Lehmann*, London: Allen Lane, 2024, p. 51. A. A. Milne even gave the Alderney cow Royal patronage in his poem 'The King's Breakfast' (1925): 'The Dairymaid / She curtsied, / And went and told

The Alderney: / "Don't forget the butter for / The Royal slice of
bread".'

63 Alderney Museum display.

64 *Alderney Press*, Interview, 11–21 Dec. 2015, p. 4.

65 The name probably derived from the French, *butte*, hillock.

66 Willmot, p. 195.

67 'It was finally Britain's Cold War enemy, the Soviet Union, who opened
up the issue.' Sanders, p. 82.

68 Kristine von Oehsen, 'The lives of Claude Cahun and Marcel Moore',
in Louise Downie (ed.) *Don't Kiss Me: The Art of Claude Cahun and
Marcel Moore*, Tate 2006, p. 20.

69 It is interesting to note the findings of *The Report of the Independent Jersey Care
Inquiry 2017* (into abuses in Jersey's childcare system, from 1945 onwards).
The report identified what it termed 'the Jersey Way': 'At best the "Jersey
Way" is said to refer to the maintenance of proud and ancient traditions and
the preservation of the island's way of life. At its worst, the "Jersey Way" is
said to involve the protection of powerful interests and resistance to change,
even when change is patently needed', p. 3. http://www.jerseycareinquiry.
org/Final%20Report/Volume%201%20Combined.pdf.

70 Claire Follain in Downie (ed.), p. 92.

71 'This seems a sad disregard for the courageous actions of the two
women, whose impact over the five years of occupation appears to
have been acknowledged only by the Nazi occupiers themselves.'
Downie (ed.), p. 94.

72 Downie, in ibid., pp. 7–8.

73 Bunting, p. 317.

74 There are divergent spellings: La Roche Qui Sonne, Le Roque Qui Sonne;
see http://www.megalithicguernsey.co.uk/le_rocque_qui_sonne/.

75 Guernsey Museum display, visited 24 Sept. 2021.

76 Edgar MacCulloch, *Guernsey Folk Lore: A Collection of Popular Superstitions, Legendary Tales, Peculiar Customs, Proverbs, Weather Sayings, etc.,
of the People of that Island*, Edith Carey (ed.), London: Elliot Stock,
1903, p. 114.

77 http://www.megalithicguernsey.co.uk/le_rocque_qui_sonne/. Darrel
Manitowabi, 'Sinmedwe'ek: The other-than-human grandfathers of

North-central Ontario', in Papers of the 39th Algonquian Conference, Karl S. Hele and Regna Darnell (eds.), 2008, pp. 444–458.

78 Interview with Phil de Jersey, 23 Sept. 2021.

79 Kevin Jelly and George Nash, 'New over old: an image-based reassessment of Le Déhus passage grave's "Le Gardien du Tombeau", Guernsey', *Time and Mind*, Vol. 9 (3), 2016, pp. 245–65, at p. 259. See also Philip de Jersey (2017): 'Stretching credulity: the 'Christianisation' of the figure in the Déhus passage grave, Guernsey,' *Time and Mind*, London: Taylor & Francis Online; https://www.tandfonline.com/doi/full/10.1080/1751696X.2017.1310569.

80 Barry Cunliffe, *Facing the Ocean: The Atlantic and Its Peoples, 8000 BC to AD 1500*, Oxford: Oxford University Press, 2001, p. 238.

81 Jelly and Nash, p. 260.

14. *Westminster*

1 https://www.canveyisland.org/category/history-2/oldphotos/photos-from-oikos-archives.

2 Camden's *Britannia* 'newly translated into English, with large additions and improvements; publish'd by Edmund Gibson', 1748. https://quod.lib.umich.edu/e/eebo2/B18452.0001.001/1:77?rgn=di vi;view=fulltext.

3 William Thomson, *The Book of Tides: A Journey through the Coastal Waters of Our Island*, London: Quercus, 2016, p. 14.

4 Several female contemporary artists have responded to Britain's political isolationism by making pieces of art that explore this subject – Cornelia Parker's installation *Island* (2022), which encases encaustic tiles from the House of Commons and Lords in a greenhouse painted with chalk from the White Cliffs of Dover; Nye Thompson's *Insulae* (2019), a film of the waters just off the British coastline; Julie Brook's *Firestacks* in the tides of the Outer Hebrides.

5 Quito Swan, *Black Power in Bermuda: The Struggle for Decolonization*, New York: Palgrave Macmillan, 2009, pp. 1–2.

6 Later, Walton Brown would become Home Minister of Bermuda, before suddenly passing away in October 2019.

7 Eva N. Hodgson, *Second-class Citizens; First-class Men*, Bermuda: The Writers' Machine, 1988, p. 11. Eva Hodgson passed away in 2020.

8 In many ways it was more totalitarian than the United States – segregation lasted in Bermuda until the Theatre Boycott of 1959; in the 1960s, works such as Fanon's *Wretched of the Earth* were banned here. Swan, p. 8.

9 It was her education and work in the United States during the 1960s and '70s that made her realize two things: in many ways racial apartheid was even worse in British Bermuda than in the States, and that in both places white women were more oppressed by their own society than black women by theirs. Eva N. Hodgson, 'Bermuda and the search for blackness', in *Is Massa Day Dead? Black Moods in the Caribbean*, Orde Coombs (ed.), New York: Anchor Press/Doubleday 1974, pp. 143–63, at pp. 147, 161.

10 'Bermudians, under white tutelage, have always prided themselves on *not* being West Indian', Hodgson, 'Bermuda and the search for blackness', p. 143.

11 https://www.virginislandsnewsonline.com/domains/virginisland-snewsonline.com/en/news/economy-bust-layoffs-continue-following-hurricane-irma.

12 Interview with Professor Andrew Le Sueur, 17 July 2015.

13 For example, 'Russian dirty money has favored Cyprus, Gibraltar, and Nauru, all with strong historical British links', Nicholas Shaxson, *Treasure Islands: Uncovering the Damage of Offshore Banking and Tax Havens*, New York: Palgrave Macmillan, 2012 [2011], p. 27. See also Oliver Bullough, *Money Land: Why Thieves and Crooks Now Rule the World and How to Take It Back*, London: Profile, 2018.

14 Nicholas Barton and Stephen Myers, *The Lost Rivers of London: Their Effects upon London and Londoners, and Those of London and Londoners upon Them*, Whitstable, Kent: Historical Publications, 2016 [update of Barton's 1962 edition], Ch. 3, 'The River Tyburn', pp. 54–68. Also: https://thethorneyislandsociety.org.uk/ttis/index.php/thorney-tales/35-thorney-tales-2-the-river-tyburn.

15 *In Our Time*, 'The Great Stink', Melvyn Bragg and guests, BBC Radio 4, 29 Dec. 2022.

16 *The Chronicle of Henry of Huntingdon*, Thomas Forester (trans.), London: H. G. Bohn, 1853, p. 199.

17 Moelfre's nearby chambered cairn and early Christian chapel proved that this thoughtful and accomplished island society both drew on prior sanctity and bequeathed it to ensuing generations.

18 As Compton Mackenzie (resident in the Hebrides) wrote in 1936, 'The knowledge that there are still many who believe that it would serve the state to allow the Islands to become a wilderness for sportsmen like so much of the Highlands is always bitter with those of us who would rather see London a heap of ruins', in his 'Catholic Barra', in *The Book of Barra*, John Lorne Campbell (ed.), Stornoway: Acair, 1998, p. 25.

19 See also 'Shelling the Houses of Parliament', 1893, reproduced in Alex Butterworth's *The World That Never Was: A True Story of Dreamers, Schemers, Anarchists and Secret Agents*, London: Bodley Head, 2010, plate 8. Matthew Gandy writes about this too, including a Museum of London exhibition from 2010 which projected Parliament Square full of rice paddies: 'Fears, Fantasies and Floods: the Inundation of London' in *The Fabric of Space: Water, Modernity and the Urban Imagination*, Cambridge, Mass: MIT Press, 2014, pp. 209–10.

20 Sitting on a concrete bench on Clink Street, outside the remnant of Winchester Palace, were four retirees, all from Surrey, who had met for the first time on the train up that morning: female twins, and a married couple, he adorned with medals from his naval service in the Falklands and other wars, she aglow with the wonderful time they were having. Chertsey, Surrey, is a Thames island – Cerotaesei, Cerot's island, according to Bede; it housed two monasteries, one for bishop Earconwald, and one for his sister. Bede, 1968, IV.6. That evening, to my astonishment, as I was standing watching the lying-in-state pilgrims exiting from Westminster Hall with my children, I saw the four folk from Surrey whom I had talked to in the morning. The orderliness! They had just emerged, at 6.15 p.m., dazed and moved, after queuing for exactly twelve hours.

21 Nat Guest @unfortunatalie, 8 Sept 2022.

22 'The subject can be identified as Neptune, or, alternatively, as a river god – perhaps a personification of the local river, the Thames.' Another statue was found in Southwark. Penny Coombe et al., *Roman Sculpture*

from London and the South-East, Oxford: Oxford University Press, 2015, pp. 3–4, 37. The Romans, notably, kept their rivers clean.

23 From Cecilia Vicuña's words of thanks on a signboard at 'Brain Forest Quipu', Tate Modern, dated 10 September 2022.

24 Helena Horton, 'Source of the River Thames dries out "for first time" during drought', *Guardian*, 4 August 2022.

25 As at Maeshowe and the Ness of Brodgar, which are mirrored by salt-sweet lochs: Nick Card et al., 'The situation of the buildings on the Ness of Brodgar emphasizes the axial role this spit of land may have played both as a causeway between the two henges and other monuments, and as a barrier between two different environments or habitats – that is the salt water of Stenness Loch and the fresh water of Harray Loch', Nick Card et al, 'Heart of Neolithic Orkney World Heritage Site: Building a landscape' in Larsson, M. and Parker Pearson, M. (eds) *From Stonehenge to the Baltic: Living with Cultural Diversity in the Third Millennium BC*, Brit Arch Report Inter Series 1692, pp. 221–231.

26 Christopher Thomas, Robert Cowie and Jane Sidell, *The Royal Palace, Abbey and Town of Westminster on Thorney Island: Archaeological Excavations (1991–8) for the London Underground Limited Jubilee Line Extension Project*, London: Museum of London Archaeology Service, 2006, p. 1: 'Westminster is important . . . also for the evidence it provides . . . of habitation stretching back more than 7000 years'; also pp. 146–7: 'the sea around Westminster and Southwark suddenly became much more important at the end of the Neolithic'.

Bibliography

—*Of works cited and consulted*

Abram, David, *Becoming Animal*, Vintage: London, 2011.

Ackroyd, Peter, *Albion: The Origins of the English Imagination*, London: Chatto & Windus, 2002.

—, *Thames: Sacred River*, London: Chatto & Windus, 2007.

Adam, Robert M., *Sgàile Is Solas: Lasting Traces, Mingulay to Scarp*, Stornoway: Acair, 2007.

Adams, Jonathan and Katherine Holman (eds.), *Scandinavia and Europe 800-1350: Contact, Conflict and Coexistence*, Turnhout, Belgium: Brepols Publishers, 2004.

Adomnán of Iona, *Life of St Columba*, Richard Sharpe (trans.), Harmondsworth: Penguin, 1995.

—, *De Locis Sanctis*, Denis Meehan (ed.), Dublin: Dublin Institute of Advanced Studies, 1958; http://research.ucc.ie/celt/document/T201090

Aldhouse-Green, Miranda, *Celtic Goddesses: Warriors, Virgins, Mothers*, London: British Museum Press, 1995.

Aldhouse-Green, Miranda J., *Exploring the World of the Druids*, London: Thames & Hudson, 1997.

Aldhouse-Green, Miranda and Stephen, *The Quest for the Shaman: Shapeshifters, Sorcerers and Spirit-healers of Ancient Europe*, London: Thames & Hudson, 2005.

Aldhouse-Green, Miranda, *Boudica Britannia: Rebel, Warleader and Queen*, Harlow: Pearson Education Limited, 2006.

Aldridge, Wendy, *Hobnails and Sea-Boots: Flower-farming in the Isles of Scilly*, London: Harrap, 1956.

Allen Paton, Lucy , *Studies in the Fairy Mythology of Arthurian Romance*, Boston: Ginn & Company, 1903 [Reprinted by Alpha Editions, 2019].

Anderson Graham, P., *Lindisfarne or Holy Island Its Cathedral, Priory and Castle AD 635-1920*, London, 1920.

Bibliography

Anderson, Judith H., 'Androcentrism and Acrasian Fantasies in the Bower of Bliss', in *Reading the Allegorical Intertext: Chaucer, Spenser, Shakespeare, Milton*, Ashland, Ohio: Fordham University Press, 2008.

Anderson, Perry, *Passages from Antiquity to Feudalism*, London: Verso, 1974.

Anderson, R. C., 'Operations of the English fleet: 1648–52', *English Historical Review*, 31 (123), 1916, pp. 406–428.

Andersson, Gunnar (ed.), *We Call Them Vikings*, Stockholm: Statens historiska museer, 2016.

Anckar, Dag, 'Westminster Democracy: A Comparison of Small Island States Varieties in the Pacific and the Caribbean', *Pacific Studies*, 23 (3/4), 2000.

Anon, *Annals of the Four Masters*, celt.ucc.ie/published/T100005E/text008.

Anon, *Annals of Ulster (to AD 1131)*, Seán Mac Airt and Gearóid Mac Niocaill (eds.): Part 1: Text and Translation, Dublin: Dublin Institute for Advanced Studies, 1983; also: https://celt.ucc.ie/published/T100001A/index.html

Anon, *Beowulf*, Seamus Heaney (trans.), London: Faber & Faber, 1999.

Anon, *Duchy Tenants Association Newsletter*, Isles of Scilly, 2004–11.

Anon, *Historia Norwegie*, Peter Fisher (trans.), Inger Ekrem and Lars Boje Mortensen (eds.), København: Museum Tusculanum Press, University of Copenhagen, 2003.

Anon, *Laxdale Saga*, Muriel A.C. Press (trans.), Peter Foote (ed.), London: Dent, 1964; https://sagadb.org/laxdaela_saga.en

Anon, *Old English Chronicles including Ethelwerd's Chronicle, Asser's Life of Alfred, Geoffrey of Monmouth's British History, Gildas, Nennius together with the spurious chronicle of Richard of Cirencester*, J. A. Giles (ed.), London: G. Bell and Sons Limited, 1910.

Anon, *Orkneyinga Saga: The History of the Earls of Orkney*, trans. Hermann Pálsson and Paul Edwards, London: Hogarth Press, 1978 [Penguin, 1981].

Anon, 'Poem in praise of Raghnall of Man', Michael Newton (trans.), in *Exploring Celtic Civilizations: An Online Celtic Studies Coursebook*, 2016, https://exploringcelticciv.web.unc.edu/prsp-record/text-poem-inpraise-of-raghnall-of-man/.

Anon, *Rites of Durham being a description or brief declaration of all the ancient monuments, rites, and customs belonging or being within the monastical*

*Church of Durham before the suppression; Written 1593;*https://archive. org/details/ritesofdurhambeioocathrich/page/n5/mode/2up.

Anon [Heldris of Cornwall], *Silence: A Thirteenth-Century French Romance*, Sarah Roche-Mahdi (trans. and ed.), East Lansing, Michigan: Michigan State University Press, 1992 [2007].

Anon, *The Annals of Clonmacnoise being Annals of Ireland from the Earliest Period to AD 1408*, Conell Mageoghagan (trans.), 1627, Denis Murphy (ed.), Dublin, 1896 [facsimile reprint 1993 by Llanerch Publishers, Somerset].

Anon, *The Annals of St-Bertin*, Janet L. Nelson (trans.), Manchester: Manchester University Press, 1991.

Anon, *The Earliest Life of Gregory the Great, by an anonymous monk of Whitby*, Bertram Colgrave (trans.), Lawrence: University of Kansas Press, 1968 [Cambridge, 1985].

Anon, *The Mabinogion*, Charlotte Guest (trans.), 1849, transcribed 2004 by Project Gutenberg: gutenberg.org/files/5160/old/mbng1oh.htm.

Anon, *The Orkneyinga Saga*, Alexander Burt Taylor (trans.), Edinburgh: Oliver and Boyd, 1938.

Anon, 'The Seafarer', in George Philip Krapp and Elliot Van Kirk Dobbie (eds.), *The Exeter Book*, New York: Columbia University Press, 1936; light-spill.com/poetry/oe/seafarer.html.

Ari, the Learned, *The Book of the Settlement of Iceland*, T. Ellwood (trans.), Kendal: T. Wilson, 1898.

Armitage, Marian, *Shetland Food and Cooking*, Lerwick: The Shetland Times, 2014.

Ashbee, Paul, 'Culture and Change in the Isles of Scilly', in Colin Renfrew (ed.), *The Explanation of Culture Change: Models in Prehistory*, London: Duckworth, 1973, pp. 521–7.

Aspinall-Oglander, Cecil, *The Roman Villa at Brading*, Newport, Isle of Wight: J. Arthur Dixon, c.1950.

Atkinson, Robert, *Island Going*, London: Collins, 1949.

Aubrey, John: *Brief Lives*, Richard Barber (ed.), London: Folio Society, 1975.

Austen, Jane, *Emma*, London: John Murray, 1816.

Austern, Linda Phyllis, 'Women's musical voices in sixteenth-century England', *Early Modern Women*, 3, 2008, pp. 127–52.

Avienius [Avienus], *Ora Maritima*, J. P. Murphy (ed.), Chicago Ridge, IL: Ares Publishers, 1977.

Badcoe, Tamsin, '"The Compasse of That Islands Space": Insular Fictions in the Writing of Edmund Spenser', *Renaissance Studies*, 25 (3), 2011, pp. 415–32.

Bagwell, Richard, *Ireland under the Tudors*, Vol. 2. London: Longmans, 1885.

Bailhache, Philip, Foreword to Paul Sanders, *The Ultimate Sacrifice: The Jersey Islanders who Died in German Prisons and Concentration Camps during the Occupation 1940–1945*, Jersey: Jersey Heritage Society, 1998 [2004].

Ballard, J. G., *Concrete Island*, London: Jonathan Cape, 1974.

Ballard, Linda-May, 'Le Lac et l'ile: quelques traditions des pecheurs du Lough Neath et l'ile de Rathlin, Irlande due Nord,', *Ethnozootechnie*, 90, 2011.

Balter, Michael, 'Monumental Roots', in *Science*, 343 (3), 2014.

Bambery, Chris, *A People's History of Scotland*, London: Verso, 2014.

Bardon, Jonathan, *The Plantation of Ulster: The British Colonization of the North of Ireland in the Seventeenth Century*, Dublin: Gill and Macmillan, 2011.

Barkham, Patrick, *Islander: A Journey Around Our Archipelago*, London: Granta, 2017.

Barton, Nicholas, and Stephen Myers, *The Lost Rivers of London: Their Effects upon London and Londoners, and Those of London and Londoners upon Them*, Whitstable: Historical Publications, 2016 [update of Barton's 1962 edition].

Basin, Fenella, 'Viking Women', Lecture at Peel Heritage Trust, Centenary Centre, Isle of Man, 2014.

Bate, Jonathan, 'Shakespeare's islands', in *Shakespeare and the Mediterranean: The Selected Proceedings of the International Shakespeare Association World Congress, Valencia, 2001*, Tom Clayton, Susan Brock and Vicente Forés (eds.), Newark: University of Delaware Press, 2004.

Bathurst, Bella, *The Wreckers: A story of killing seas, false lights and plundered ships*, London: HarperCollins Publishers, 2005.

Beard, Mary, John Norton and Simon Price, *Religions of Rome: Volume 2, A Sourcebook*, Cambridge: Cambridge University Press, 2001.

Bede, *The Pan-Anglican Synod before 'St. Augustine's Chair'; or, Venerable Bede's Account of the Christianity that came from Rome*, London: Hardwicke & Bogue, 1878.

—, *Life of Cuthbert*, in *The Age of Bede*, J. F. Webb (trans.), Harmondsworth: Penguin, 1965 [reprint 1985].

—, *History of the English Church and People*, Leo Sherley-Price (trans.), R. E. Latham (ed.), London: Penguin, 1968 [later editions known as *Ecclesiastical History of the English People*].

—, *The Reckoning of Time*, translated, with introduction notes and commentary by Faith Walls, Liverpool: Liverpool University Press, 1999.

Belchem, John, review of Roger Dickinson's *The Lordship of Man under the Stanleys: government and economy in the Isle of Man, 1580–1704*, *English Historical Review*, 114 (458), 1999, pp. 985–6.

—, (ed.), *A New History of the Isle of Man, Volume 5: The Modern Period 1830–1999*, Liverpool: Liverpool University Press, 2000.

Bellows, Henry Adams, *The Poetic Edda, Volume 1: Lays of the Gods: Voluspo*, New York: American-Scandinavian Foundation, 1936.

Benwell, Gwen, and Arthur Waugh, *Sea Enchantress: The Tale of the Mermaid and Her Kin*, London: Hutchinson, 1961.

Besant, Walter, *Armorel of Lyonesse: a romance of to-day*, London: Chatto & Windus, 1890.

Black, Maggie, *The Medieval Cookbook*, London: British Museum Press, 1993.

Black, Stephen F., 'Coram Protectore: The Judges of Westminster Hall under the Protectorate of Oliver Cromwell', *The American Journal of Legal History*, 20 (1), 1976, pp. 32–64.

Blackie, C., *A Dictionary of Place-Names Giving Their Derivations*, London: John Murray, 1887.

Blackie, Sharon, *If Women Rose Rooted: A life-changing journey to authenticity and belonging*, London: September Publishing, 2016.

Bonin, Erin Lang, 'Margaret Cavendish's dramatic utopias and the politics of gender', *Studies in English Literature*, 1500–1900, 40 (2), 2000, pp. 339–54.

Bonner, Gerald, D.W. Rollason and Clare Stancliffe (eds.), *St Cuthbert His Cult and His Community to AD 1200*, Woodbridge: Boydell Press, 1989.

Borlase, William, *Observations on the Ancient and Present State of the Islands of Scilly, and their Importance to the Trade of Great-Britain*, Oxford: W. Jackson, 1756.

Bowden, Mark and Allan Brodie, *Defending Scilly*, Swindon: English Heritage, 2011.

Bowers, Susan R., 'Medusa and the female gaze', *NWSA Journal*, 2 (2), 1990.

Bowley, R. L., *Scilly at War*, St Mary's: Bowley Publications, 2001.

—, *The Fortunate Islands: The Story of the Isles of Scilly* [based on 1945 edition of E. L. Bowley], St Mary's, Isles of Scilly: Bowley Publications, 2004.

Bradley, Richard, *An Archaeology of Natural Places*, London: Routledge, 2000.

Bragg, Melvyn, and guests, *In Our Time*, 'The Great Stink', BBC Radio 4, 29 Dec. 2022.

Branigan, Keith, *From Clan to Clearance: History and Archaeology on the Isle of Barra, c.850–1850 AD*, Oxford: Oxbow, 2005.

Braund, David, *Ruling Roman Britain: Kings, Queens, Governors and Emperors from Julius Caesar to Agricola*, London: Routledge, 1996.

Breay, Claire and Joanna Story (eds.), *Anglo-Saxon Kingdoms: Art, Word, War*, London: British Library, 2018.

Brenton, Howard, *Plays: Two*, London: Methuen Drama, 1989.

Brereton, Georgine E., *Des Grantz Geanz: An Anglo-Norman Poem*, Oxford: Society for the Study of Medieval Languages and Literature, 1937.

Brewer, J. S., and William Bullen (eds.), *Calendar of the Carew Manuscripts*, London: Longmans, 1868.

Briffault, Robert, *The Mothers: A Study of the Origins of Sentiment and Intentions*, New York, Macmillan, 1928.

Brinklow, Laurie, Frank Ledwell and Jane Ledwell, *Message in a Bottle: The Literature of Small Islands* [proceedings from an international conference, Charlottetown, Prince Edward Island, Canada, June 28 to 30], 1998.

Brown, Michelle P., *The Lindisfarne Gospels: The British Library Treasures in Focus*, London: The British Library, 2006.

—, *The Lindisfarne Gospels and the Early Medieval World*, London: The British Library, 2011.

Brown, Walton Jr, *Bermuda and the Struggle for Reform, Race, Politics and Ideology, 1944-1998*, Bermuda: Cahow Press, 2011.

—, 'Terry Tucker and the Poverty of History: A Book Review', Blog, 2013, http://respicefinemi.blogspot.com/search?q=Terry+Tucker.

—, 'Bermuda: We are not a tax haven', *Guardian*, 27th June 2013.

Bullough, Oliver, *Money Land: Why Thieves and Crooks Now Rule the World and How to Take It Back*, London: Profile, 2018.

Bumsted, J. M., *The People's Clearance: Highland Emigration to British North America, 1770–1815*, Edinburgh: Edinburgh University Press, 1982.

Bunting, Madeleine, *A Model Occupation: The Channel Islands Under German Rule, 1940–45*, London: Pimlico, 1995.

Burns, A. R., 'Procopius and the Island of Ghosts', *English Historical Review*, Oxford, 70 (275), 1955, pp. 258–61.

Butterworth, Alex, *The World That Never Was: A True Story of Dreamers, Schemers, Anarchists and Secret Agents*, London: Bodley Head, 2010.

Buxton, Ben, *The Vatersay Raiders*, Edinburgh: Birlinn, 2008.

Caesar, *The Gallic War*, H. J. Edwards (trans.), London: William Heinemann, 1919.

Caldwell, David H., and Gordon Ewart, 'Finlaggan and the Lordship of the Isles: an archaeological approach', *Scottish Historical Review*, 72 (194), 1993, pp. 146–66.

—, 'The Scandinavian Heritage of the Lordship of the Isles', in *Scandinavia and Europe 800-1350: Contact, Conflict and Coexistence*, Jonathan Adams and Katherine Holman (eds.), Turnhout, Belgium: Brepols Publishers, 2004.

Callaghan, Steve, and Bryce Wilson (eds.), *The Unknown Cathedral: Lesser-known Aspects of St Magnus Cathedral in Orkney*, Kirkwall: Orkney Islands Council, 2001.

Camden, William, *Britannia newly translated into English, with large additions and improvements; publish'd by Edmund Gibson*, London: F. Collins, 1695: https://quod.lib.umich.edu/e/eebo2/B18452.0001.001/1:77?rgn=div1;view=fulltext.

Campana, Joseph, 'Boy Toys and Liquid Joys: Pleasure and Power in the Bower of Bliss', *Modern Philology*, 106 (3), 2009, pp. 465–496.

Campbell, Ewan, *Saints and Sea-Kings: The First Kingdom of the Scots*, Edinburgh: Birlinn, 1999.

Campbell, J. F., *Popular Tales of the West Highlands orally collected*, Edinburgh: Edmonston & Douglas, 1860–2.

—, *More West Highland Tales: Volume 1* [orally collected by J.F. Campbell, translated by John G. MacKay], Edinburgh: Birlinn, 1994 [based on Oliver and Boyd edition, 1940].

Campbell, J., 'Elements in the background to the life of St Cuthbert and his early cult,' in Gerald Bonner, D.W. Rollason and Clare Stancliffe (eds.), *St Cuthbert His Cult and His Community to AD 1200*, Woodbridge: Boydell Press, 1989.

Campbell, John Lorne (ed.), *The Book of Barra*, London: George Routledge, 1936 [Stornoway: Acair, 1998].

Canmore, National Record of Historic Environment [The online catalogue to Scotland's archaeology, buildings, industrial and maritime heritage], https://canmore.org.uk/

Card, Nick et al., 'Heart of Neolithic Orkney World Heritage Site: Building a landscape' in Larsson, M. and Parker Pearson, M. (eds.) *From Stonehenge to the Baltic: Living with Cultural Diversity in the Third Millennium BC*, Brit Arch Report Inter Series 1692, 2007, pp.221-231.

Card, Nick, 'Neolithic temples of the Northern Isles: stunning new discoveries in Orkney', *Current Archaeology*, 2010, https://archaeology.co.uk/articles/news/neolithic-temples-of-the-northern-isles.htm.

Card, Nick, and Antonia Thomas, 'Painting a picture of Neolithic Orkney: decorated stonework from the Ness of Brodgar', in Andrew Cochrane and Andrew Meirion Jones (eds.),*Visualising the Neolithic: Abstraction, Figuration, Performance, Representation*, Oxford: Oxbow, 2012.

Carmichael, Alexander, *Carmina Gadelica. Hymns and incantations with illustrative notes on words, rites, and customs, dying and obsolete: orally collected in the Highlands and Islands of Scotland and translated into English* [Gaelic & English], Edinburgh: Norman Macleod, 1900; reprint, Edinburgh: Floris Books, 1992.

Carr-Gomm, Philip and Stephanie, *The Druid Craft Tarot Deck*, London: Connections Book Publishing, 2004 [Eddison Books Limited, 2016].

Carruthers Sellar, Walter and Robert Julian Yeatman, *1066 and All That : A Memorable History of England, Comprising All the Parts You Can Remember, Including 103 Good Things, 5 Bad Kings and 2 Genuine Dates*, London: Methuen and Co., 1930.

Carruthers, Martin, 'The Life and Death of a Broch', Lecture, Kirkwall, Orkney, 2017.

Carson, Rachel, *The Sea Around Us*, Oxford: Oxford University Press, 1950 [2018].

Carthy, Eliza, et al., *Songs of Separation: Reflections on the Parting of Ways*, Album, 2016; https://www.songsofseparation.co.uk/.

Dio, Cassius, *Dio's Roman History*, Earnest Cary (trans.), London: Heinemann, 1914; http://penelope.uchicago.edu/Thayer/E/Roman/Texts/Cassius_Dio/62*.html.

Cavendish, Margaret, *The Convent of Pleasure and Other Plays*, Ann Shaver (ed.), Baltimore: John Hopkins University Press, 1999.

Chambost, Edouard, *Guide des paradis fiscaux face à 1992*, Paris: Sand, 1989.

Chazelle, Celia, 'The power of oratory: rereading the Whitby Liber Beati Gregorii', *Traditio*, 76, Cambridge: Cambridge University Press, 2021, pp. 29–77.

Chadwick, Nora, *The Celts*, Harmondsworth: Penguin, 1970.

Chaucer, Geoffrey, *The Riverside Chaucer*, Larry D. Benson (ed.), Oxford: Oxford University Press, 1987.

Churchill, Winston, *Churchill's Writing and Speeches*, '1940: The Finest Hour', International Churchill Society, https://winstonchurchill.org/resources/speeches/1940-the-finest-hour/we-shall-fight-on-the-beaches/.

Cicero, Marcus Tullius, *Cicero on divinatio : De divinatione*, David Wardle (trans.), Oxford: Clarendon Press, 2006; http://penelope.uchicago.edu/Thayer/e/roman/texts/cicero/de_divinatione/1*.html.

Claeys, Gregory (ed.), *Restoration and Augustan British Utopias*, Syracuse: Syracuse University Press, 2000; *Utopia: The History of an Idea*, London: Thames &Hudson, 2011 [2020].

Clancy, Thomas Owen, 'Women poets in early medieval Ireland', in Christine Meek and Katharine Simms (eds.), *The Fragility of Her Sex'? Medieval Irishwomen in Their European Context*, Dublin: Four Courts Press, 1996.

Clark, Wallace, *Rathlin: Its Island Story*, Co. Londonderry: North-West Books, 1988 [first edition: *Rathlin: Disputed Island*, 1971].

Clarke, Hyde, et al. 'The Picts and Pre-Celtic Britain', *Transactions of the Royal Historical Society*, 3, 1886, pp. 243–80.

Clarkson, Tim, *Columba*, Edinburgh: John Donald Publishers Ltd, 2011.

Coakley, Frances (ed.), 'A Manx Note Book: An Electronic Compendium of Matters Past and Present Connected with the Isle of Man', http://www.isle-of-man.com/manxnotebook/

Coate, Mary, 'The Duchy of Cornwall: its history and administration 1640–60', *Transactions of the Royal Historical Society*, 10, 1927, pp. 135–69.

Cohen, Colleen Ballerino, *Take Me to Paradise: Tourism and Nationalism in the British Virgin Islands*, New Brunswick: Rutgers University Press, 2010.

Cohen, Jeffrey Jerome, *Of Giants: Sex, Monsters and the Middle Ages*, Minneapolis, Minn.: University of Minnesota Press, 1999.

Colles, Ramsay, *The History of Ulster: From the Earliest Times to the Present Day*, London: Gresham Publishing, 1919, Vol. 1.

Coombe, Penny, et al., *Roman Sculpture from London and the South-East*, Oxford: Oxford University Press, 2015.

Cope, Julian, *The Modern Antiquarian: A Pre-millennial Odyssey through Megalithic Britain*, London: Thorsons, 1998.

Corrigan, Felicitas (ed.), *More Latin Lyrics: From Virgil to Milton*, Helen Waddell (trans.), London: Victor Gollancz, 1985.

Courtney, M. A., 'Cornish Folk-lore', *Folk-Lore Journal*, 5 (1), 1887, pp. 14–61.

Cowper, B. H., *A Descriptive and Statistical Account of Millwall, commonly called the Isle of Dogs; including notice of the founding, opening, etc., of the West India Docks and City Canal; and notes relating to Limehouse, Poplar, Blackwall and Stepney*, London: Robert Gladding, 1853.

Crawford, Barbara, Review, in *Scottish Historical Review*, 60 (170), Oct. 1981, pp. 205–8.

—, Review of Brian Smith and John Ballantyne (eds.), *Shetland Documents 1195–1579*, Lerwick: Shetlands Islands Council and The Shetland Times, 1999, https://www.euppublishing.com/doi/pdfplus/10.3366/nor.2000.0012.

Crawford, Julie, 'Convents and Pleasures: Margaret Cavendish and the Drama of Property', *Renaissance Drama*, 32, 2003, pp. 177–223.

Cregeen, Eric and Donald W. Mackenzie, *Tiree Bards and their Bardachd: The Poets in a Hebridean Community*, Isle of Coll: Society of West Highland & Island Historical Research, 1978.

Creighton, John, *Coins and Power in Late Iron Age Britain*, Cambridge: Cambridge University Press, 2000.

Criado Perez, Caroline, *Invisible Women: Exposing Data Bias in a World Designed for Men*, London: Vintage, 2020.

Cromarty, Charles, *The Lindisfarne Story: A Saga of Island Folk*, Newcastle upon Tyne: Graham, 1971.

Crow, Hugh, *The Memoirs of Captain Hugh Crow*, John Pinfold (ed.), Oxford: Bodleian Library, 2007.

Cummings, Vicki, and Amelia Pannett, 'Island views: the settings of the chambered cairns of southern Orkney', in *Cummings and Pannett* (eds.), *Set in Stone: New Approaches to Neolithic Monuments in Scotland*, Oxford: Oxbow, 2005.

Cunliffe, Barry, *Facing the Ocean: The Atlantic and Its Peoples, 8000 BC to AD 1500*, Oxford: Oxford University Press, 2001.

—, *The Extraordinary Voyage of Pytheas the Greek*, London: Penguin, 2001.

—, *Druids: A Very Short Introduction*, Oxford: Oxford University Press, 2010.

—, *The Roman Villa at Brading, Isle of Wight: The Excavations of 2008–10*, Oxford: Oxford School of Archaeology, 2013.

Curphey, Robert A., *Ancient centres of government of the Isle of Man: an illustrated guide to Peel Castle, Castle Rushen and Tynwald Hill*, Douglas: Isle of Man Government, 198–.

Dalby, Stewart, *The Friends of Rathlin Island*, Clifton upon Teme: Polperro Heritage Press, 2004.

Dalmau, John, *Slave Worker in the Channel Islands*, Guernsey: Guernsey Press Co., 1956.

Darling, Frank Fraser, *Island Years, Island Farm*, Toller Fratrum: Little Toller Books, 2011.

Davenport, Trevor, *Festung Alderney: The German Defences of Alderney*, Alderney: Alderney Society, 2003.

Davey, Peter J. and James R. Roscow, *Rushen Abbey and the Dissolution of the Monasteries in the Isle of Man*, Isle of Man: Natural History and Antiquarian Society, 2010.

Davidson, Alan, *North Atlantic Seafood*, Totnes: Prospect Books, 2003.

Davidson, J. L. and A. S. Henshall, *The Chambered Cairns of Orkney*, Edinburgh: Edinburgh University Press, 1989.

Davies, R. T. (ed.), *Medieval English Lyrics: A Critical Anthology*, London: Faber & Faber, 1963.

Davis, Craig R., 'Cultural assimilation in the Anglo-Saxon royal genealogies', *Anglo-Saxon England*, 21, 1992, pp. 23–36.

Davis, Natalie Zemon, *Society and Culture in Early Modern France*, Cambridge: Polity Press, 1965 [1987].

Dawson, Hannah (ed.), *The Penguin Book of Feminist Writing*, London: Penguin, 2021.

Deavin, Mark-Kevin, 'Ulysses in the north? The Yggdrasill myth re-considered', in *Rivista di cultura classica e medioevale*, 55 (2), 2013, pp. 517–38.

Dee, John, *The Limits of the British Empire*, Ken MacMillan with Jennifer Abeles (eds.), Westport, CT: Praeger, 2004.

Defoe, Daniel, *A Tour Through the Whole Island of Great Britain*, Pat Rogers (ed.), Harmondsworth: Penguin, 1971.

de Garis, Marie, *Folklore of Guernsey*, Guernsey: de Garis, 1975 [1986].

de Jersey, Philip, 'Stretching credulity: the 'Christianisation' of the figure in the Déhus passage grave, Guernsey,' *Time and Mind*, 2017, https://www.tandfonline.com/doi/full/10.1080/1751696X.2017.1310569.

De Luca, Christine, *Dat Trickster Sun: Poems*, Edinburgh: Mariscat Press, 2014.

Demetriou, Tania, '"Essentially Circe": Spenser, Homer, and the Homeric Tradition', *Translation and Literature*, 15 (2), 2006, pp. 151–176.

Deneault, Alain, *Offshore: Tax Havens and the Rule of Global Crime*, George Holoch (trans.), New York: The New York Press, 2011.

Deschamps, Eustache, 'Sur les divers noms de l'Angleterre': MCLIV in *Oeuvres*,

Devine, T.M., *The Scottish Clearances: A History of the Dispossessed, 1500–1900*, London: Penguin Books, 2018.

Dickens, Charles, *Oliver Twist, Great Expectations; A tale of two cities*, London: Octopus, 1981.

Dictionaries of the Scots Language, https://www.dsl.ac.uk.

Dillon, Myles, and Nora Chadwick, *The Celtic Realms*, London: Weidenfeld and Nicolson, 1967.

Siculus, Diodorus, *The Library of History*, C. H. Oldfather (trans.), Cambridge, Mass.: Harvard University Press, 2004–.

Donahue, Charles, 'The Valkyries and the Irish war-goddesses', *DMLA*,. 56 (1), 1941, pp. 1–12.

Donald Monro, *Monro's Western Isles of Scotland and Genealogies of the Clans, 1549*, R. W. Munro (ed.), London/Edinburgh: Oliver & Boyd, 1961.

Donne, John, *John Donne*, John Carey (ed.), Oxford: Oxford University Press, 1990.

Douglas, Mona (trans.), *The Secret Island: Poems and Plays in Verse*, Douglas, Isle of Man: Victoria Press, 1943.

—, *Twelve Manx Folk Songs: with Manx, Gaelic and English Words*, [Arranged with Pianoforte accompaniment by A. Foster. Airs chiefly from A. W. Moore's Manx Ballads and Music.], 2 sets. London: Stainer & Bell, 1957.

Downie, Louise (ed.), *Don't Kiss Me: The Art of Claude Cahun and Marcel Moore*, London: Tate, 2006.

Drayton, Michael, *Poly-Olbion:* https://poly-olbion.exeter.ac.uk/the-text/full-text/song-1/.

Dressler, Camille, *Eigg: The Story of an Island*, Edinburgh: Polygon, 1998.

Duffy, Eamon, *The Stripping of the Altars: Traditional Religion in England c.1400-c.1580*, New Haven/London: Yale University Press, 1992.

Dumville, David N., 'Echtrae and Immram: some problems of definition', in *Ériu*, Dublin: Royal Irish Academy, 27, 1976, pp. 73–94.

Dunleavy, Gareth W., *Colum's Other Island: The Irish at Lindisfarne*, Madison: University of Wisconsin Press, 1960.

Dunn, Douglas (ed.), *Twentieth-Century Scottish Poetry*, London: Faber & Faber, 1992 [2006].

Eckenstein, Lina, *Woman under Monasticism: Chapters on Saint-Lore and Convent Life between AD 500 and AD 1500*, Cambridge: Cambridge University Press, 1896.

Economist: 'Island mentality: bad schools and low aspirations used to be inner-city problems', 27 Jan. 2014.

Edmonds, Mark, *Orcadia: Land, Sea and Stone in Neolithic Orkney*, London: Head of Zeus, 2019.

Egeler, Matthias, *Islands in the West: Classical Myth and the Medieval Norse and Irish Geographical Imagination*, Turnhout: Brepols, 2017.

—, 'Iceland and the Land of Women: The Norse Glæsisvellir and the Otherworld Islands of Early Irish Literature', in Aisling Byrne and Victoria Flood (eds.), *Crossing Borders in the Insular Middle Ages*, Turnhout: Brepols, 2019.

Eliot, T.S., *The Four Quartets*, London: Faber & Faber, 1959.

Elmham, Thomas of, *Speculum Augustinian: History of St Augustine's Abbey of Canterbury*(MS1):https://cudl.lib.cam.ac.uk/view/MS-TRINITYHALL-00001/159.

Evans, Ruth, 'Gigantic Origins: an Annotated Translation of *De Origine Gigantum*', *Arthurian Literature*, 16, 1988, pp. 197–211.

Fajut, Noel, *Prehistoric and Viking Shetland*, Lerwick: Shetland Times Ltd, 2006.

Fanshawe, Anne Harrison, *Memoirs of Lady Fanshawe*, London: Henry Colburn, 1829 [Dodo Press Reprint, 2007].

Fay, Jessica, 'Wordsworth's Northumbria: Bede, Cuthbert, and Northern Medievalism', in *The Modern Language Review*, 111 (4), 2016, pp. 917–935.

Fell, Christine, *Women in Anglo-Saxon England: and the impact of 1066*, London: British Museum, 1984.

Feltham, John, *A Tour through the Island of Mann, in 1797 and 1798; comprising sketches of its ancient and modern history, constitution, laws, commerce, agriculture, fishery etc. including whatever is remarkable in each parish, its population, inscriptions, registers etc.*, Bath, 1798.

Field, John, *Kingdom, power and glory : a historical guide to Westminster Abbey*, London: James & James, 1997.

Field, P. J. C. 'Caxton's Roman War', *Arthuriana*, 5 (2), 1995, pp. 31–73.

Finnemore, Peter, https://peterfinnemore.com/About.

Flaws, Margaret and Gregor Lamb, *The Orkney Dictionary*, Kirkwall: The Orcadian, 1996 [2001].

Florance, Arnold, *Queen Victoria at Osbourne* [Foreword by the late Earl Mountbatten of Burma], London: English Heritage, 1987.

Flower, Barbara, and Elisabeth Rosenbaum, *The Roman Cookery Book: A Critical Translation of 'The Art of Cooking' by Apicius for Use in the Study and the Kitchen*, Edinburgh: Harrap, 1958.

Follain, Claire, in Louise Downie (ed.), *Don't Kiss Me: The Art of Claude Cahun and Marcel Moore*, London: Tate, 2006.

Fordun, John of, *Johannis de Fordun Chronica gentis Scotorum*, William F. Skene (ed.), Edinburgh: Edmonston and Douglas, 1871.

Fraser, David, *The Jews of the Channel Islands and the Rule of Law, 1940–45: 'Quite Contrary to the Principles of British Justice'*, Brighton: Sussex Academic Press, 2000.

Frazer, J. G., *The Golden Bough: a study in magic and religion*, London: Macmillan, 1915.

Freeman, Philip, *Ireland and the Classical World*, Austin: University of Texas Press, 2001.

Fuchs, Barbara, 'Conquering Islands: Contextualising *The Tempest*', *Shakespeare Quarterly*, 48 (1), 1997, pp. 45–62.

Gaiman, Neil, *Norse Mythology*, London: Bloomsbury Publishing, 2017.

Gameson, Richard (ed.), *St Augustine and the Conversion of England*, Stroud: Sutton Publishing, 1999.

Gandy, Matthew, *The Fabric of Space: Water, Modernity and the Urban Imagination*, Cambridge, Mass: MIT Press, 2014.

Gannon, Angela and George Geddes, *St Kilda: The Last and Outmost Isle*, Edinburgh: Historic Environment Scotland, 2015.

Garnham, Trevor, *Lines on the Landscape, Circles from the Sky: Monuments of Neolithic Orkney*, Stroud: The History Press, 2004.

Garrow, Duncan, and Fraser Sturt, 'Neolithic crannogs: rethinking settlement, monumentality, and deposition in the Outer Hebrides and beyond', *Antiquity*, 93 (369), 2019, pp. 664–84.

Garrow, Duncan, Fraser Sturt and Mike Copper, 'Submerged Neolithic of the Western Isles, Interim Report (March 2017)', http://crannogs.soton.ac.uk/ wp- content/uploads/sites/220/2018/09/Lewis_Lochs_Interim_Report_March_2017.pdf.

Gavey, Ernie, *German Tunnels in Guernsey, Alderney & Sark*, Guernsey: Festung Guernsey/Channel Island Art & Books, 2012.

Gawne, C. W., *The Isle of Man and Britain Controversy 1651–1895: From Smuggling to the Common Purse*, Douglas: Manx Heritage Foundation, 2009.

Gibson, Julie, 'Tourism and archaeology in Orkney: the Ness Effect', *Archaeologist*, 91, 2014.

Giles, Melanie, 'Iron Age bog bodies of North-western Europe: representing the dead', *Archaeological Dialogues*, 16 (1), pp. 75–101.

Gill, Crispin, *The Isles of Scilly*, Newton Abbot: David & Charles, 1975.

Gillies, William, 'Gaelic literature in the later Middle Ages', in *The Edinburgh History of Scottish Literature*, Ian Brown (ed.), Edinburgh: Edinburgh University Press, 1, 2007.

Gimbutas, Marija, *The Living Goddesses*, Miriam Robbins Dexter (ed.), Berkeley: University of California Press, 2001.

Ginns, Michael, *The Organisation Todt and the Fortress Engineers in the Channel Islands*, St John, Jersey: Channel Islands Occupation Society, 1994 [2006].

Golliher, Jeffrey Mark, 'Leylines in modern Britain: the sacred geography of a pilgrimage site as an expression of folk protest', *New York Folklore*, 13 (3), 1987.

Goodacre, S., et al., 'Genetic evidence for a family-based Scandinavian settlement of Shetland and Orkney during the Viking periods', *Heredity*, 95, 2005, pp. 129–35.

Gore, Derek, 'A Review of Viking Attacks in Western England to the Early Tenth Century: Their Motives and Responses' in Ryan Lavelle and Simon Roffey (eds.), *Danes in Wessex*, Oxford: Oxbow Books, 2015.

Gough, Melinda J., '"Not as myself ": the queen's voice in *Tempe Restored*', *Modern Philology*, 101 (1), 2003, pp. 483–67.

Graves, Robert, *The White Goddess: A historical grammar of poetic myth*, London: Faber & Faber, 1961 [1988].

Gray, M. M., 'The influence of Spenser's Irish experiences on *The Faerie Queene* ', *Review of English Studies*, Oxford: Oxford University Press, 6 (24), 1930, pp. 413–28.

Green, J. R., *A Short History of the English People*, London: Macmillan, 1874.

Green, Matthew, *Shadowlands: A Journey Through Lost Britain*, London: Faber & Faber, 2022.

Gregory I, Pope, *The Book of Pastoral Rule and Selected Epistles of St Gregory the Great, Bishop of Rome*, Revd James Barmby (trans.), Buffalo, NY: Christian Literature Publishing Co., 1895.

Grigson, Geoffrey, *The Scilly Isles*, London: Paul Elek, 1948.

Grimond, Jo, *Memoirs*, London: Heinemann, 1979.

Grocock, Christopher, and Sally Grainger, *Apicius: A Critical Edition with an Introduction and English Translation of the Latin Recipe Text Apicius*, Totnes: Prospect, 2006.

Hagen, Ann, *Anglo-Saxon Food and Drink*, Ely: Anglo-Saxon Books, 2006.

Halliday, Josh and Sally Weale, 'Ofsted chair apologises for calling Isle of Wight a ghetto full of inbreeding', *Guardian*, 5th August 2016; https://

www.theguardian.com/uk-news/2016/aug/05/ofsted-chair-david-hoare-isle-of-wight-poor-ghetto.

Hamer, Richard, *A Choice of Anglo-Saxon Verse*, London: Faber & Faber, 1970.

Harden, Jill, *The Picts*, Edinburgh: Historic Scotland, 2010.

Hardyng, John, *The Chronicle of Iohn Hardyng*, London: F. C. & J. Rivington, 1812 [New York: AMS Press, 1974].

—, *Chronicle: edited from British Library MS Lansdowne 204*, James Simpson and Sarah Peverley (eds.), Kalamazoo: Medieval Institute Publications, 1, 2015.

Harrington, Sue, 'Stirring women, weapons, and weaving: aspects of gender identity and symbols of power in early Anglo-Saxon England', in *Archaeology and Women: Ancient and Modern Issues*, Sue Hamilton, Ruth D. Whitehouse and Katherine I. Wright (eds.), Walnut Creek, California: Left Coast Press, 2007.

Harris, Barbara J., 'A New Look at the Reformation: Aristocratic Women and Nunneries, 1450-1540', *Journal of British Studies*, 32 (2),1993, pp. 89–113.

Hart, Jonathan, *Columbus, Shakespeare and the Interpretation of the New World*, Basingstoke: Palgrave Macmillan, 2003.

Haswell-Smith, Hamish, *The Scottish Islands*, Edinburgh: Canongate, 2004.

Hathaway, Sibyl, *Dame of Sark: An Autobiography*, Jersey: La Haule Books, 1961.

Hazlitt, W. Carew, *Faiths and Folklore of the British Isles*, New York: Benjamin Blom, 1965.

Heale, Martin, 'The late Middle Ages, 1380–1539', in David Brown (ed.), *Durham Cathedral: History, Fabric and Culture*, New Haven: Yale University Press, 2014.

Heath, Robert, *A Natural and Historical Account of the Islands of Scilly*, London: R. Manby and H. S. Cox, 1750 [reprinted as *The Isles of Scilly by Robert Heath: The First Book on the Isles of Scilly*, Newcastle upon Tyne: Frank Graham, 1967].

Hedenstierna-Jonson, C, Kjellström, A, Zachrisson, T, et al., 'A female Viking warrior confirmed by genomics', *American Journal of Physical Anthropology*, 164, 2017, pp. 853–860.

Hemming, Jessica, 'Reflections on Rhiannon and the Horse Episodes in "Pwyll" ', *Western Folklore*, 57 (1), 1998, pp. 19–40.

Henig, Martin, 'The mosaic pavements: their meaning and context', in Barry Cunliffe, *The Roman Villa at Brading, Isle of Wight: The Excavations of 2008–10*, Oxford: Oxford School of Archaeology, 2013.

Higgins, Charlotte, *Under Another Sky: Journeys in Roman Britain*, London: Jonathan Cape, 2013.

Higham, N. J., *The English Conquest: Gildas and Britain in the 5th century*, Manchester: Manchester University Press, 1994.

Hill, Christopher, *The World Turned Upside Down: Radical Ideas During the English Revolution*, London: Penguin, 1972 [1975].

Hill, Stuart, *Stolen Isles: Shetland's True Status*, Shetland: Forvik University Press, 2014.

Hindley, Geoffrey, *A Brief History of the Anglo-Saxons: The Beginnings of the English Nation*, London: Robinson, 2006.

Hingley, Richard, *Roman Officers and English Gentlemen: The Imperial Origins of Roman Archaeology*, London: Routledge, 2000.

Hirshfield, Jane, *Women in Praise of the Sacred: 43 Centuries of Spiritual Poetry by Women*, New York: HarperPerennial, 1994.

Hobbs, Richard and Ralph Jackson, *Roman Britain*, London: British Museum Press, 2010.

Hodgson, Eva N., 'Bermuda and the search for blackness', in *Is Massa Day Dead? Black Moods in the Caribbean*, Orde Coombs (ed.), New York: Anchor Press/Doubleday 1974.

—, *Second-class Citizens; First-class Men*, Bermuda: The Writers' Machine, 1988.

Hollis, Stephanie, *Anglo-Saxon Women and the Church: Sharing a Common Fate*, Martlesham, Woodbridge: Boydell Press, 1992.

—, 'Minister-in-Thanet foundation story', *Anglo-Saxon England*, 27, Michael Lapidge (ed.), Cambridge: Cambridge University Press, 1998.

— (ed.), 'Wilton as a centre of learning' in *Writing the Wilton Women: Goscelin's Legend of Edith and Liber confortatorius*, Turnhout: Brepols, 2004.

Hollo, Kaarina, 'Allegoresis and Literary Creativity in Eight-Century Ireland: The Case of *Echtrae Chonnlai*, in *Narrative in Celtic Tradition: Essays in Honor of Edgar M. Slotkin*, Joseph Eska (ed.), *CSANA Yearbook 8-9*, 2011, pp. 1171–128.

Hopewell, David, 'Tai Cochion Roman settlement, Anglesey 2011–12 (G1632), Summary Report, April 2011–March 2012', http://www.heneb.co.uk/cadwprojs/cadwreview2011-12/taicochion11-12.html.

Hopkins, Lisa, *Shakespeare on the Edge: Border-crossing in the Tragedies and the Henriad*, Aldershot: Ashgate, 2005.

Horace, *Odes and epodes*, Niall Rudd (trans.), Cambridge, Mass.: Harvard University Press, 2004.

Horton, Helena, 'Source of the River Thames dries out 'for first time' during drought', Guardian, 4th August 2022.

Hostettler, Eve, *The Isle of Dogs: a brief history*, London: Island History Trust, 2000.

Howe, Nicholas, *Migration and Mythmaking in Anglo-Saxon England*, New Haven/London: Yale University Press, 1989.

Hrdy, Sarah, *The woman that never evolved*, Cambridge, Mass.: Harvard University Press, 1981.

Hudston, Sara, *Islomania*, Bridport: Agre, 2000.

Hughes, Ann, *Gender and the English Revolution*, London: Routledge, 2011.

Hughes, Philip, *The Reformation in England*, London: Hollis & Carter, 1950-54.

Hughes, Ted, *Shakespeare and the Goddess of Complete Being*, London: Faber & Faber, 1993.

Hunt, Peter, *Jersey: A Crown Peculiar*, Chichester: Phillimore, 2005.

Hunter, James, *The Making of the Crofting Community*, New Edition, Edinburgh: John Donald Publishers, 1976 [2000].

—, 'The 2nd John McEwen Memorial Lecture: Towards a Land Reform Agenda for a Scots Parliament', 22nd Sept 1995.

—, *Last of the Free: A Millenial History of the Highlands and Islands of Scotland*, Edinburgh: Mainstream, 1999.

—, *Aimhreit an Fhearainn: The Land Struggle in Skye and Lewis James Hunter and others describe key episodes in the crofters' campaign for land reform in the 1880s*, Isle of Lewis: The Islands Book Trust, 2011.

Huntington, Henry, *The Chronicle of Henry of Huntingdon*, Thomas Forester (trans.), London: H. G. Bohn, 1853.

Hutchinson, Ann M., in *Nuns' Literacies in Medieval Europe: The Antwerp Dialogue*, Virginia Blanton, Veronica O'Mara and Patricia Stoop (eds.), Turnhout: Brepols, 2017.

Hutchinson, Roger, *The Soap Man: Lewis, Harris and Lord Leverhulme*, Edinburgh: Birlinn, 2003.

Hutton, Ronald, *Pagan Britain*, Yale: Yale University Press, 2013.

—, *The Witch: A History of Fear, from Ancient Times to the Present*, New Haven/London: Yale University Press, 2017.

Imsen, Steinar, 'Introduction', in *The Norwegian Domination and the Norse World c.1100–c.1400*, Steinar Imsen (ed.), Trondheim: Rostra Books/Tapir Academic Press, 2010.

Irish Folklore Commission, *Skeealyn Vannin/Stories of Mann: The Complete Collection of Manx Language Archive Recordings Made by the Irish Folklore Commission in 1948*, Douglas: Manx National Heritage, 2003.

Isidore of Seville, *Etymologies*, https://penelope.uchicago.edu/Thayer/L/Roman/Texts/Isidore/14*.html.

Jackson, Kenneth, *A Celtic Miscellany: Translations from the Celtic Literatures*, Harmondsworth: Penguin, 1971.

Jakobsen, Jakob, *The Place-names of Shetland*, London, 1936 [republished by Lerwick: Shetland Library, 1993].

James I, *The True Law of Free Monarchies and Basilikon Doron*, Daniel Fishlin and Mark Fortier (eds.), Toronto: Victoria University, 1996.

Jamie, Kathleen, *Findings*, London: Sort Of Books, 2005.

Jansen, Sharon L., *Reading Women's Worlds from Christine de Pizan to Doris Lessing*, London: Palgrave Macmillan, 2011.

Jeffcott, J. M., 'Mann, its names and their origin', *Manx Miscellanies*, 2, William Harrison (ed.), Douglas, Isle of Man: Manx Society, 1880.

Jefford, Andrew, *Peat Smoke and Spirit: A portrait of Islay and its whiskies*, London: Headline, 2004.

Jelly, Kevin and George Nash, 'New over old: an image-based reassessment of Le Déhus passage grave's "Le Gardien du Tombeau", Guernsey', *Time and Mind*, 9 (3), 2016, pp. 245–65.

Jenkins, D. E., *Bedd Gelert: Its Facts, Fairies and Folk-lore*, Portmadoc: Llewelyn Jenkins, 1899 [facsimile edition 1999].

Johnson, Lesley, 'Return to Albion, in Arthurian Literature, James P. Carley and Felicity Riddy (eds.), Cambridge: D. S. Brewer, 1995.

Johnson, Samuel and James Boswell, *Johnson's Journey to the Western Islands of Scotland and Boswell's Journal of a Tour to the Hebrides with Samuel*

Johnson, LL.D., R. W. Chapman (ed.), London: Oxford University Press, 1924 [1961].

Johnston, Thomas, *Our Scots Noble Families*, Glasgow: Forward Publishing Co., 1909.

Jones, Barri and David Mattingly, *An atlas of Roman Britain*, Oxford: Basil Blackwell, 1990.

Jones, John, *Speak Welsh: An introduction to the Welsh language combining a simple grammar, phrase book and dictionary*, Cardiff: John Jones Publishing, 1977 [2005].

Judith Jesch, *Women in the Viking Age*, Woodbridge: Boydell Press, 1991.

Kaufman, Amy, 'The law of the lake: Malory's sovereign lady', *Arthuriana*, 17 (3), 2007, pp. 56–73.

Kellett, Katherine R., 'Performance, Performativity, and Identity in Margaret Cavendish's *The Convent of Pleasure*', *Studies in English Literature, 1500-1900*, 48 (2), 2008, pp. 419–442.

Kelsey, Sean, 'King of the sea: the Prince of Wales and the Stuart monarchy', *History*, 92 (4), 2007, pp. 428–448.

Kelvin, Lord Smith, *Report of the Smith Commission for further devolution of powers to the Scottish Parliament*, Edinburgh: The Smith Commission, 27th November 2014.

Kennedy-Fraser, Marjory and Kenneth Macleod (trans. and ed.), *Sea Tangle: Some More Songs of the Hebrides Collected*, Arranged for Voice and Pianoforte, London: Boosey, 1913.

—, *Songs of the Hebrides*, 2, London and New York: Boosey & Co, 1923; https://electricscotland.com/history/women/MKFSongsOfThe HebridesBVolTwo02.pdf.

Kerr, Peter, *The Story of Emigration from Berneray, Harris*, North Uist: Berneray Historical Society, 2012.

King, Anthony and Grahame Soffe, *A Sacred Island: Iron Age, Roman and Saxon Temples and Ritual on Hayling Island*, Winchester: Hayling Island Excavation Project, Winchester: Winchester University Press, 2013.

King, Anthony, 'Reviewing recent findings in Hayling Island and Meonstoke, Hampshire, which have given new insights into Roman sacred landscapes', Lecture at University of Sussex, 2nd May 2019.

King, Jacqueline, *A Cake for the Gestapo*, London: ZunTold, 2020.

King, Tom, *Thames Estuary Trail: A walk around the end of the world*, Westcliff on Sea: Desert Island Books, 2001.

Kinvig, R. H., *The Isle of Man: A Social, Cultural and Political History*, Liverpool: Liverpool University Press, 1975.

Kissack, Annie, *Smuggler's Lullaby*, Recording, British Library Sound Archive.

Kneale, Matthew, *English Passengers*, London: Penguin, 2000.

Knight, Sam, *The Premonitions Bureau: A True Story*, London: Faber & Faber, 2022.

Lapidge, Michael and David Dumville (eds.), *Gildas: New Approaches*, Woodbridge: Boydell Press, 1984.

Lawson, Bill, *Harris in History and Legend*, Edinburgh: John Donald Publishers, 2002.

Le Bas, Damian, *The Stopping Places*, London: Chatto & Windus, 2018.

Le Patourel, J. H., *The Medieval Administration of the Channel Islands 1199-1399*, Oxford: Oxford University Press, 1937.

Le Roux, Charles-Tanguy, *Carnac, Locmariaquer and Gavrinis*, Editions Ouest-France, 2001 [2017].

Le Sueur, Andrew, 'What is the future for the Judicial Committee of the Privy Council?', https://www.ucl.ac.uk/constitution-unit/sites/constitution_unit/files/72_1.pdf.

Le Sueur, Bob, *Growing Up Fast: An Ordinary Man's Extraordinary Life in Occupied Jersey* [As Told To Chris Stone], St Mary, Jersey: Seeker Publishing, 2020.

Lees, Clare A., and Gillian Overing, *A Place to Believe In: Locating Medieval Landscapes*, Pennsylvania: Pennsylvania State Press, 2006.

—, *Double Agents: Women and Clerical Culture in AngloSaxon England*, Cardiff: University of Wales Press, 2009.

Lempriere, Raoul, *History of the Channel Islands*, London: Robert Hale Limited, 1974 [1980].

Lewis-Williams, David, and David Pearce, *Inside the Neolithic Mind: Consciousness, Cosmos and the Realm of the Gods*, London: Thames & Hudson, 2005.

Lightfoot, J. L., *Dionysius Periegetes: Description of the Known World with Introduction, Text, and Commentary*, Oxford: Oxford University Press, 2014.

Linklater, Eileen, 'Udal law: past, present and future?', University of Strathclyde, LLB Hons. Dissertation, 2002.

Liptrot, Amy, *The Outrun*, Edinburgh: Canongate, 2015.

Little, William, H.W. Fowler and Jessie Coulson, *The shorter Oxford English Dictionary on historical principles*, C.T. Onions (ed.), Oxford: Clarendon Press, 1, 1973.

Liu, Xiaojie et al., 'Seaweed reproductive biology: environmental and genetic controls', *Botanica Marina*, 60 (2), 2017, pp. 89–108.

Ljosland, Ragnhild, 'The men in Maeshowe: John D. Mackay Memorial Lecture', Orkney Science Festival Lecture, Kirkwall, 11th September 2017.

—, Blog with Chris Gee: https://brodgar.co.uk/2016/02/24/a-rouge-viking-at-swanbister-orphir/.

Hobhouse, Hermione, *Survey of London: Poplar, Blackwall and Isle of Dogs*, 43 and 44, London: London County Council, 1994.

Lonegren, Sid, *Labyrinths: Ancient Myths and Modern Uses*, revised and updated fourth edition, Glastonbury: Gothic Image Publications, 1991 [2007].

Lyne, Malcolm, 'Roman Wight', Isle of Wight History Centre, 2006, https://oxfordarchaeology.com/images/pdfs/Solent_Thames/County_resource_assessments/Roman_IOW.pdf.

Lysons, Daniel, and Samuel Lysons, 'The Scilly Islands', in *Magna Britannia: Volume 3, Cornwall*, London: T. Cadell and W. Davies, 1814.

Mac Mathuna, Seamus, *Immram Brain: Bran's Journey to the Land of the Women*, Tübingen: M. Niemeyer, 1985.

Mac Mhaighstir Alasdair, Alasdair, *The Birlinn of Clanranald*, Alan Riach (trans.), Newtyle: Kettillonia, 2015.

Macartney, Allan, 'Routes to island autonomy?', *Open UniversityScotland*, 1983, http://www.scottishgovernmentyearbooks.ed.ac.uk/record/22892/1/1983_10_Routestoislandautonomy.pdf.

Macartney, Mac, *The Children's Fire: Heart song of a people*, Practical Inspiration Publishing, 2018.

MacCulloch, Edgar, *Guernsey Folk Lore: A Collection of Popular Superstitions, Legendary Tales, Peculiar Customs, Proverbs, Weather Sayings, etc., of the People of that Island*, Edith Carey (ed.), London: Elliot Stock, 1903.

Macdonald, Angus and Patricia, *The Hebrides: An Aerial View of a Cultural Landscape*, Edinburgh: Birlinn, 2010.

MacDonald, Fraser, 'St Kilda and the sublime', *Ecumene: A Journal of Cultural Geographies*, 8 (2), 2001, pp. 151–174.

Macdonald, Donald, *Tales and Traditions of the Lews*, Edinburgh: Birlinn, 2004 [2009].

Macdonald, R. Andrew, *The Kingdom of the Isles: Scotland's Western Seaboard c.1100-c.1336*, East Linton: Tuckwell Press, 1997.

Macdonell, Margaret, *The Emigrant Experience: Songs of Highland Emigrants in North America*, Toronto: University of Toronto Press, 1982.

Macfarlane, Robert, *The Wild Places*, London: Granta, 2007.

—, *The Old Ways: A Journey on Foot*, London: Penguin, 2012.

Mack, Chris, Executive Chairman of Fresca Group Ltd [Thanet Earth], 'High-tech horticulture sets the tone for the future', Speech at The Oxford Farming Conference, 2011: https://www.ofc.org.uk/sites/ofc/files/papers/chris-mack.pdf.

Mackay Brown, George, *An Orkney Tapestry* [Drawings by Sylvia Wishart], London: Gollancz, 1969.

—, *Greenvoe: a novel*, London: The Hogarth Press, 1975.

—, *The Island of the Women and Other Stories*, London: John Murray, 1998.

Mackenzie, Alexander, *The History of the Highland Clearances: containing a reprint of Donald Macleod's Gloomy memories of the Highlands; Isle of Skye in 1882; and a verbatim report of the trial of the Braes crofters*, Inverness: A. & W. Mackenzie, 1883.

Mackenzie, Fiona, 'Margaret Fay Shaw's Hebridean Odyssey', BBC Radio 3, 2021.

Maclean, Malcolm and Theo Dorgan (eds.), *An Leabhar Mòr: The Great Book of Gaelic*, Edinburgh: Canongate, 2002/Dublin: O'Brien Press, 2008.

MacNeill, F. M., *Iona: A History of the Island*, London: Blackie and Son, 1920.

MacPhee, Kathleen, *Somerled: Hammer of the Norse*, Glasgow: Neil Wilson, 2004.

Macpherson, James, *The poems of Ossian: and related works*, Howard Gaskill (ed.), with an introduction by Fiona Stafford, Edinburgh: Edinburgh University Press, 1996.

Malory, Thomas, *Works*, Eugène Vinaver (ed.), Oxford: Oxford University Press,1954 [1971]; also: https://www.gutenberg.org/cache/epub/1252/pg1252-images.html#chap257.

Manitowabi, Darrel, 'Sinmedwe'ek: The other-than-human grandfathers of North-central Ontario', in *Papers of the 39th Algonquian Conference*, Karl S. Hele and Regna Darnell (eds.), 2008, pp. 444–458.

Manx Museum Archives, 'Observations upon the antient state, and rise of the trade of the Isle of Mann', nd [1721–1736], MS 09707/1/20, AP 60 (2nd)-16; 'An account of smuggling transactions in the Isle of Man in the year 1750', AP 60 (2nd)-19; 'Attorney General's opinion on the Act 7 Geo 1st how East India goods may be seized in the Isle of Mann', AP 60 (2nd)-9; Collector to Board, 3 March 1788, MD 514 /6722; MD 514 / 6722; MD 514 /6722.

Marett-Crosby, Anthony, *The Foundations of Christian England: Augustine of Canterbury and His Impact*, Ampleforth: Ampleforth Abbey Press, 1997.

Mark, Joshua J., 'Thomas Malory', World History Encyclopedia, https://www.worldhistory.org/Thomas_Malory/.

Marsden, John, *Somerled and the Emergence of Gaelic Scotland*, East Linton: Tuckwell Press, 2000.

Marsden, Philip, *The Summer Isles: A Voyage of the Imagination*, London: Granta, 2019.

Marsh, Sarah, 'Eating mackerel no longer sustainable, Good Fish Guide advises', 5th April 2023, https://www.theguardian.com/environment/2023/apr/05/mackerel-loses-sustainable-status-as-overfishing-puts-species-at-risk.

Martin, Arthur Patchett, *The Queen in the Isle of Wight: A Personal Memoir of her Majesty at Osbourne*, London: Henry Sotheran & Co, 1898.

Martin, Dave (ed.), *Isle of Man Studies XVI*, Isle of Man: Isle of Man Natural History and Antiquarian Society, 2019; *Isle of Man Studies XVII*, Isle of Man: Isle of Man Natural History and Antiquarian Society, 2021.

Martin, Martin, *A Description of the Western Islands of Scotland circa 1695 and a Late Voyage to St Kilda*, Edinburgh: Birlinn, 1999.

Marvell, Andrew, *The complete poems*, Elizabeth Story Donno (ed.), Harmondsworth: Penguin, 1972.

Matthews, William Henry, *Mazes and Labyrinths. A general account of their history and development*, London: Longmans & Co, 1922.

Mayr-Harting, Henry, *The Coming of Christianity to Anglo-Saxon England*, Pennsylvania: Penn State University Press, 1972.

McCartan, Sinead B., 'The utilisation of island environments in the Irish mesolithic: Agendas for Rathlin island', *New Agendas in Irish Prehistory: Papers in Commemoration of Liz Anderson*, Angela Desmond et al (eds.), Bray, Co Wicklow: Wordwell, 2000, pp. 15–30.

McCone, Kim, *'Echtrae Chonnlai' and the beginnings of Vernacular narrative writing in Ireland: A critical edition with introduction, notes, bibliography and vocabulary*, Maynooth: Dept of Old and Middle Irish, 2000.

—, *The Celtic Question: Modern Constructs and Ancient Realities*, Dublin: School of Celtic Studies, 2008.

McCurdy, Augustus, *Rathlin's Rugged Story: From an Islander's Perspective*, Coleraine and Ballycastle: McCurdy, 2000.

McEachern, Claire, *The Poetics of English Nationhood, 1590–1612*, Cambridge: Cambridge University Press, 1996.

McGlashan, Derek J., Robert W. Duck and Colin T. Reid, 'The foreshore: geographical implications of the three legal systems in Great Britain', *Area*, 36 (4), 2004, pp. 338–47.

McIntosh, Alastair, *Poacher's Pilgrimage: An Island Journey*, Edinburgh: Birlinn, 2016.

Meehan, Bernard and Claire Breay, 'The St Cuthbert Gospel' in *Anglo-Saxon Kingdoms: Art, Word, War*, Claire Breay and Joanna Story (eds.), London: The British Library, 2018.

Meeker, James W., 'Subtleties of the isle: islands of the imagination', *Interdisciplinary Studies in Literature and Environment*, 18 (1), 2011, pp. 197–202.

Melancholicus, Mercurius, *Craftie Cromwell: or, Oliver ordering our new state.: A tragi-comedie*, London, 1648; https://quod.lib.umich.edu/e/eeb02/A74789.0001.001?view=toc

Milne, A. A., *The King's Breakfast: a selection of verse from 'When we were very young'*, London: Methuen Children's, 1984.

Mitchell, Ian, *Isles of the West: A Hebridean Voyage*, Edinburgh: Canongate, 1999.

Molony, Eileen (ed.), *In Portraits of Islands,* London: Dennis Dobson, 1951.

Momber, Garry, et al (eds.), *Mesolithic Occupation at Bouldnor Cliff and the Submerged Prehistoric Landscapes of the Solent,* York: Council for British Archaeology, 2011.

Monaghan, Patricia, *Encyclopedia of Goddesses and Heroines,* Novato, CA: New World Library, 2014.

Monbiot, George, Foreword to Alastair McIntosh, *Soil and Soul: dispatches of a Celtic ecowarrior,* London: Aurum, 2001; https://www.alastairmcintosh.com/soilandsoul/samples-soilsoul.htm.

—, Prize Lecture, Orwell Society, London, 14th July 2022.

Monmouth, Geoffrey of, *Historia Regum Britanniae,* Sebastian Evans (trans.), London: J. M. Dent, 1912 [1928].

—, *The Vita Merlini,* John Jay Parry (trans.), Urbana: University of Illinois Studies in Language and Literature, 1925; https://www.sacred-texts.com/neu/eng/vm/vmeng.htm

—, *The Life of Merlin,* Paul White (trans.), Launceston: Bossiney Books, 2004.

Montgomery, Janet, et al., 'Finding Vikings with isotope analysis: the view from wet and windy islands', *Journal of the North Atlantic,* 7, 2014, pp. 54–70.

Moore, A.W., *Preface to Manx Ballads and Music,* Douglas: Manx National Heritage, 1896.

—, *A Vocabulary of the Anglo-Manx Dialect,* [with the cooperation of Sophia Morrison and Edmund Goodwin], Oxford: Oxford University Press, 1924 [Isle of Man: Yn Cheshaght Ghailckagh, 1991].

Moore, David W., *The Other British Isles: A History of Shetland, Orkney, the Hebrides, Isle of Man, Anglesey, Scilly, Isle of Wight, and the Channel Islands,* Jefferson, NC: McFarland & Co, 2005.

Moore, Lucy, *Lady Fanshawe's Receipt Book: An Englishwoman's Life During the Civil War,* London: Atlantic Books, 2017.

More, Thomas, *Utopia,* Paul Turner (trans.), London: Penguin, 1965 [2003].

Morris, Joan, *Against Nature and God: The History of Women with Clerical Ordination and the Jurisdiction of Bishops,* London: Mowbrays, 1973.

Mortensen, Andras and Símun V. Arge (eds.), *Viking and Norse in the North Atlantic: Select Papers from the Proceedings of the Fourteenth Viking Congress, Tórshavn 19-30 July 2001,* Tórshavn: Føroya Fróðskaparfelag, 2005.

Mothersole, Jessie, *The Isles of Scilly: Their Story, Their Folk and Their Flowers*, London: Religious Tract Society, 1910.

Muir, Tom, *Tales of Vikings Lands*, Kirkwall: Orcadian Limited, 2015.

Mumford, Clive, *Portrait of the Isles of Scilly*, London: Robert Hale, 1967.

Musson, Nellie E., *Mind the Onion Seed*, Hamilton: Black Roots Bermuda, 1979.

Mustill, Tom, *How to Speak Whale: A Voyage into the Future of Animal Communication*, London: William Collins, 2022.

Nansen, Fridtjof, *In Northern Mists: Arctic Exploration in Early Times*, London: William Heinemann, 1, 1911.

Neal, David S., and Stephen R. Cosh, *Roman Mosaics of Britain: Vol. 1: Northern Britain*, London: Illuminata, 2002; *Roman Mosaics of Britain: Volume III: South-East Britain*: Part I, London: Society of Antiquaries of London, 2009.

Nelson, Maggie, *The Argonauts*, Brooklyn, NY: Melville House, 2016.

Némirovsky, Irène, *Suite française*, Sandra Smith (trans.), London: Vintage Books, 2009.

Nennius, *Historia Brittonum*, *The History of the Britons*, J.A. Giles (trans.), London: James Bohn, 1841. Also: https://www.gutenberg.org/files/1972/1972-h/1972-h.htm.

Newman, Barbara, *God and the Goddesses: Vision, Poetry & Belief in the Middle Ages*, Philadelphia: University of Pennsylvania Press, 2003.

Newman, John Henry, *The Lives of the English Saints*, London: S. T. Freemantle, 3, 1901.

Newton, J. M., 'What do we know of Andrew Marvell?', *Cambridge Quarterly*, 6 (2), 1973, pp. 125–43.

Nicolson, Adam, *Sea Room: An Island Life*, London: HarperCollins Publishers, 2001.

Nicholson, Cornelius, *A Descriptive Account of the recently discovered Roman Villa near Brading, Isle of Wight*, London: Elliot Stock, 1880.

Noises, Full of, [Original Music Inspired by the Isles of Scilly], *en plein air: music made in the open air*, Album, Isles of Scilly, 2016/7.

—, *Islands of Women*, Album: 2023.

Nostbakken, Faith, *Understanding the Tempest: A Student Casebook to Issues, Sources and Historical Documents*, Westport, CT: Greenwood, 2004.

O'Donaghue, Denis, *Brendaniana: St Brendan the Voyager in Story and Legend*, Dublin, 1893 [reprinted by Forgotten Books, 2018].

Oehsen, Kristine von, 'The lives of Claude Cahun and Marcel Moore', in Louise Downie (ed.), *Don't Kiss Me: The Art of Claude Cahun and Marcel Moore*, London: Tate, 2006.

O'Laverty, James, *An Historical Account of the Diocese of Down and Connor, Ancient and Modern*, Dublin: James Duffy & Sons, 1878–95, Vol. 3.

Oldham, Frances QC, *The Report of the Independent Jersey Care Inquiry 2017*, http://www.jerseycareinquiry.org/Final%20Report/Volume%20 1%20Combined.pdf.

Oram, Richard (ed.), *The Lordship of the Isles*, Leiden: Brill, 2014.

Orme, Nicholas, *Medieval Children*, Yale: Yale University Press 2001.

Orosius, *Seven Books of History against the Pagans: The Apology of Paulus Orosius*, Irving W. Raymond (ed.), New York: Columbia University Press, 2002; *Historiae adversum paganos*, http://www.attalus.org/latin/ orosius1.html.

O'Sullivan, Thomas D., *The 'De excidio' of Gildas : its authenticity and date*, Leiden: Brill, 1978.

Ovid, *Metamorphoses*, Arthur Golding (trans.), Madeleine Forey (ed.), London: Penguin, 2002.

Owen, Olwyn, *The Sea Road: A Viking Voyage Through Scotland*, Edinburgh: Historic Scotland/Canongate, 1999.

— (ed.), *The World of the Orkneyinga Saga: 'The Broadcloth Viking Trip'*, Kirkwall: Orkney Islands Council, 2005.

Palomo, Dolores, 'The halcyon moment of stillness in Royalist poetry', *Huntington Library Quarterly*, 44 (3), 1981, pp. 205–21.

Pálsson, Hermann, and Paul Edwards, 'Narrative Elements in the Icelandic Book of Settlements', in *Mosaic: An Interdisciplinary Critical Journal*, 4 (2), 1970, pp. 1–11.

Pantcheff, T. X. H., *Alderney: Fortress Island*, Chichester: Phillimore & Co., 1981.

Pateman, Carole, *The Sexual Contract*, Cambridge: Polity Press, 1988.

Pederson, Tara, '"We shall discover our Selves": Practicing the Mermaid's Law in Margaret Cavendish's *The Convent of Pleasure*', *Early Modern Women*, 5, 2010, pp. 111–135.

Pennick, Nigel, *Celtic Sacred Landscapes*, London: Thames & Hudson, 1996.

Pepys, Samuel, *The Diary of Samuel Pepys*, London/Glasgow: Collins' Clear-Type Press, 1933.

Peterson, George P. S., *The coastal place-names of Papa Stour*, Shetland: George P.S. Peterson, 1993.

Phillips, Graham, *The Marian Conspiracy: The Hidden Truth about the Holy Grail, the Real Father of Christ and the Tomb of the Virgin Mary*, London: Sidgwick and Jackson, 2000.

Pliny the Elder, *Natural History*, H. Rackham (trans.), London: Folio Society, 2012.

Plummer, Charles, *Bethada Náem n Érenn: Lives of Irish Saints. Edited from the original MSS. with introduction, translations, notes, glossary and indexes*, Oxford: Clarendon Press, 1, 1922.

Plutarch, *Life of Julius Caesar*, Loeb Classical Library edition, 7, 1919: http://penelope.uchicago.edu/Thayer/E/Roman/Texts/Plutarch/Lives/Caesar*.html.

Points, Guy, *An Introduction to Anglo-Saxon Church Architecture & Anglo-Saxon & Anglo-Scandinavian Sculpture*, Oxford: Oxbow Books, 2015.

Pounds, N. J. G., *The Parliamentary Survey of the Duchy of Cornwall, Part II: Isles of Scilly – West Antony and Manors in Devon*, Devon and Cornwall Record Society, 1984.

Powell, Hilary, 'Following in the Footsteps of Christ: Text and Context in the Vita Mildrethae ', *Medium Ævum*, 82 (1), 2013, pp. 23–43.

Power, Eileen, *Medieval English Nunneries, c.1275–1535*, Cambridge: Cambridge University Press, 1922.

Prebble, John, *The Highland Clearances*, Harmondsworth: Penguin, 1963.

Price, John E., and F. G. Hilton Price, *A Guide to the Roman Villa Recently Discovered at Morton, between Sandown and Brading, on the Isle of Wight*, Ventnor, Isle of Wight: Briddon Bros, 1887 [12th edition].

Price, T. D., 'Introduction: new approaches to the study of the Viking Age settlement across the North Atlantic', *Journal of the North Atlantic*, 7, 2018, pp. i-xii.

Procopius, 'Thule', *History of the Wars*, taken from H. B. Dewing, *Procopius with an English Translation*, in seven volumes: *History of the Wars*, Books VII (continued) and VIII, 5, London: William Heinemann, 1928.

Pugh, Gareth, Blog as Manx National Heritage Project Archivist (The Atholl Papers), 2022, https://www.imuseum.im/the-atholl-papers-therevestment/.

Pugh, Syrithe, 'Fanshawe's critique of Caroline pastoral: allusion and ambiguity in the 'Ode on the Proclamation', *Review of English Studies*, 59 (240), 2008, pp. 379–91.

Pullman, Philip, *Daemon Voices: On Stories and Storytelling*, Oxford: David Finkling Books, 2017.

Putley, John, *The Isles of Scilly in the English Civil Wars*, Bristol: Stuart Press, 2003.

Qualtrough, John Karran, and William John Scatchard, *"That Island"*, Douglas: Victoria Press, 1965; https://archive.org/stream/thatisland-ooqualiala/thatislandooqualiala_djvu.txt.

Quarrell, Johnnie, *Portrait of Foulness*, Romford: Ian Henry Pub., 1998.

Quiggin, E. C., *Poems from the Book of the Dean of Lismore with a Catalogue of the Book and Indexes*, J. Fraser (ed.), Cambridge: Cambridge University Press, 1937.

Quilliam, N. D., *Keys and Cuffs: The Inside Stories; The History of the Isle of Man/Manx Prisons, 1417–2008*, Isle of Man: Quilliam, 2009.

Raine, James (ed.), *The Inventories and Account Rolls of the Benedictine Houses or Cells of Jarrow and Monkwearmouth in the County of Durham*, London: Surtees Society, 1854.

Rakusen, India, 'Witch', BBC Radio 4, 2023.

Ramos, Aarón Gamaliel and Angel Israel Rivera (eds.), *Islands at the cross-roads: politics in the non-independent Caribbean*, Kingston, Jamaica: Ian Randle Publishers, 2001.

Rawcliffe, Roger, *No Man is an Island: 50 years of Finance in the Isle of Man*, Douglas: Manx Heritage Foundation, 2009.

Raylor, Timothy, 'The instability of Marvell's Bermudas ', *Andrew Marvell Newsletter*, 6 (2), 2014, https://marvell.wp.st-andrews.ac.uk/newsletter/the-instability-of-marvells-bermudas/.

Rees, Alwyn, and Brinley Rees, *Celtic Heritage: Ancient tradition in Ireland and Wales*, London: Thames & Hudson, 1961.

Rendall, Jocelyn, *Exploring Papay*, Papa Westray, Orkney: Papay Publications, 2015.

Renwick, Esther, 'In depth: steatite in Shetland', *Shetland Archaeology*, 2016, https://www.archaeologyshetland.org/post/2016-1-16-in-depth-steatite-in-shetland.

Reynolds, Ffion, Lecture on Bryn Celli Ddu, Societies Pavilion, Anglesey Eisteddfod, 9th September 2017

Rhys, John, *Studies in the Arthurian Legend*, Oxford: Clarendon Press, 1891.

—, *Celtic Folklore Welsh and Manx*, Oxford: Oxford University Press, 1901.

Ritchie, Anna (ed.), *Orkney in Its European Context*, Cambridge: McDonald Institute for Archaeological Research, 2000.

Ritchie, Harry, *The Last Pink Bits*, London: Hodder & Stoughton, 1997.

Rivet, A.L.F. and Colin Smith, *The Place-Names of Roman Britain*, London: B.T. Batsford Ltd, 1979 [1982].

Robb, Graham, *The Ancient Paths: Discovering the Lost Map of Celtic Europe*, London: Picador, 2013.

Roberton, Hugh S., 'Mingulay Boat Song', *Songs of the Isles: A Collection of Island and Highland Tunes from Various Sources, Set to English, or to Anglo-Scottish*, London: J. Curwen & Sons, 1938.

Robertson, T. A., (ed.), *Da Sangs at A'll Sing ta Dee: A Book of Shetland Songs*, Lerwick: Shetland Folk Society, 1973 [reprint 2013].

Robinson, Philip, *Plantation of Ulster: British Settlement in an Irish Land-scape, 1600–1670*, Dublin: Gill and Macmillan, 1984.

Roffey, Monique, *The Mermaid of Black Conch*, Leeds: Peepal Tree, 2020.

Rollason, D. W., *The Mildrith Legend: A Study in Early Medieval Hagiography in England*, Leicester: Leicester University Press, 1982.

— (ed.), *Cuthbert: Saint and Patron*, Durham: Dean and Chapter of Durham, 1987.

—, in David Brown (ed.), *Durham Cathedral: History, Fabric and Culture*, New Haven: Yale University Press, 2014.

Rollason, Lynda, 'Priory's Outreach: Durham's Cells', in David Brown (ed.), *Durham Cathedral: History, Fabric and Culture*, New Haven: Yale University Press, 2014.

Romer, F. E., *Pomponius Mela's Description of the World*, Ann Arbor: University of Michigan Press, 1998.

Ross, Anne, 'The Divine Hag of the Pagan Celts' in *The Witch Figure*, Venetia Newhall (ed.), London and Boston: Routledge and Kegan Paul, 1973.

—, and Don Robins, *The Life and Death of a Druid Prince: The Story of an Archaeological Sensation*, London: Rider, 1989.

—, in Miranda J. Green (ed.), *The Celtic World*, London: Routledge, 1995.

Rowlands, Henry, *Mona Antiqua Restaurata*, Dublin, 1723; *Antiqua restaurata. An Archæological Discourse on the Antiquities, Natural and Historical, of the Isle of Anglesey*, London: J. Knox, 1766.

Ruch, Lisa M., *Albina and Her Sisters: The Foundation of Albion*, Amherst, New York: Cambria Press, 2013.

Rustici, Craig M., *The Afterlife of Pope Joan*, Michigan: University of Michigan Press, 2006.

Sanders, Paul, *The Ultimate Sacrifice: The Jersey Islanders who Died in German Prisons and Concentration Camps during the Occupation 1940–1945*, Jersey: Jersey Heritage Society, 1998 [2004].

Sanger, George, *Seventy Years a Showman: my life and adventures in camp and caravan the world over*[Introduction by Kenneth Grahame], London: J. M. Dent & Sons, 1926.

Sanmark, Alexandra, 'Patterns of assembly: Norse thing sites in Shetland', in *Journal of the North Atlantic*, 5, 2013, pp. 96-110.

Savine, Alexander, *English monasteries on the eve of the dissolution*, in *Oxford studies in social and legal history*, Paul Vinogradoff (ed.), Oxford: Oxford University Press, 1, 1909.

Savory, H. N. , 'Excavations at Dinas Emrys, Beddgelert (Caern.), 1954-6', in *Archaeologia Cambrensis*, Cardiff: Cambrian Archaeological Association, 109, 1961.

Schwyzer, Philip, 'Exhumation and ethnic conflict: from St Erkenwald to Spenser in Ireland', *Representations*, 95 (1), 2006, pp. 1–26.

Scott, Betty, et al., 'A new view from La Cotte de St Brelade, Jersey', *Antiquity*, 88 (339), 2014.

Scott, Duncan Craig, *Quetzalcoatl Rising: A Buddhist Monk in Fifth Century Mexico*, Createspace Independent Publishing Platform, 2012.

Scott, Eleanor, 'Animal and infant burials in Romano-British villas: a revitalization movement', in P. Garwood et al. (eds.), *Sacred and Profane: Proceedings of a Conference on Archaeology, Ritual and Religion*, Oxford: Oxford University School of Archaeology, 1991.

—, *A Gazetteer of Roman Villas in Britain*, Leicester: University of Leicester School of Archaeological Studies, 1993, pp. 101–2.

—, 'Introduction', *Invisible People and Processes: Writing Gender and Childhood into European Archaeology*, Jenny Moore and Eleanor Scott (eds.), Leicester: Leicester University Press, 1997.

Scott, Ian G. and Anna Ritchie, *Pictish and Viking-age Carvings from Shetland*, Edinburgh: Royal Commission on the Ancient and Historical Monuments of Scotland, 2009.

Scott, Manda, *Boudica: Dreaming the Eagle*, London: Bantam Press, 2003.

Scott, Walter, *Guy Mannering: or, the Astrologer*, Edinburgh: James Ballantyne and Co, 1815.

—, *The Pirate*, Edinburgh: Archibald Constable and Co, 1822.

—, *Peveril of the Peak*, Edinburgh: Archibald Constable, 1823.

Self, Kathleen M., 'The Valkyrie's gender: Old Norse shieldmaidens and Valkyries as a third gender', *Feminist Formations*, Baltimore: John Hopkins University Press, 26 (1), 2014, pp. 143–72.

Severin, Tim, *The Brendan Voyage*, London: Hutchinson, 1978.

Shakespeare, William, *The complete works*, Stanley Wells and Gary Taylor (eds.), Oxford : Clarendon, 1986.

Shaw, Margaret Fay, *Folksongs and Folklore of South Uist*, London: Routledge and Kegan Paul, 1955.

Shaxson, Nicholas, *Treasure Islands: Uncovering the Damage of Offshore Banking and Tax Havens*, New York: Palgrave Macmillan, 2011.

Shea, Michael, *The Country Life Book of Britain's Offshore Islands*, Richmond upon Thames: Country Life, 1981.

Shepherd, Alexandra, 'Skara Brae', in Anna Richie (ed.), *Neolithic Orkney in Its European Context*, Cambridge: McDonald Institute for Archaeological Research, 2000.

Shuttle, Penelope, *Lyonesse*, Hexham: Bloodaxe, 2021.

Sidney, Henry, *Memoir of His Government of Ireland: 1583*, *Ulster Journal of Archaeology*, 5, 1857, pp. 299–323.

Silvia Federici, *Caliban and the Witch*, London: Pluto, 2004.

Simeon [Symeon], of Durham, *The historical works of Simeon of Durham*, J. Stevenson (trans.), London: Seeleys, 1855.

Simpson, Charlie, *In Da Galley: Sixty Essays in Seafood Philosophy*, Lerwick: The Shetland Times, 2000.

Sink, *Hoy Sound: Pure improvisation recorded on the morning of 27th October 2017 in the extraordinary acoustic of the empty oil tank at the Lyness Naval Base on the Orkney island of Hoy*, Digital Album, 2019.

Skelly, George, *A Guide to Lindisfarne, Bamburgh, Farne Islands, Dunstanburgh Castle Etc.*, Alnwick: C. E. Moore, 1888.

Smiles, Samuel, *The Huguenots: Their Settlement, Churches, and Industries, in England and Ireland*, London: John Murray, 1895.

Smith, Brian, *Toons and Tenants: Settlement and society in Shetland, 1299-1899*, Lerwick: The Shetland Times, 2000.

Smith, Nigel, *Literature and Revolution in England*, Yale: Yale University Press, 1994.

Smith, T. B., 'The law relating to the treasure', in *St Ninian's Isle and Its Treasure*, A. Small, C. Thomas and D. M. Wilson (eds.), Oxford: Oxford University Press, 1, 1973.

Smith-Mason, Catherine, *The Stones of Laxey*, Dunblane: DOICA Ltd, 2001.

Smyth, Adam, '"Art Reflexive": The Poetry, Sermons, and Drama of William Strode (1601?-1645)', *Studies in Philology*, 103 (4), 2006, pp. 436–464.

Spence, Lewis, *The History and Origins of Druidism*, London: Rider, 1949.

Spenser, Edmund, *The Faerie Queene*, A. C. Hamilton (ed.), London: Longman, 1977 [1995].

—, *A View of the Present State of Ireland* [Edited, principally from MS. Rawlinson B 478 in the Bodleian Library and MS 188.221 in Caius College, Cambridge], W. L. Renwick (ed.), Dublin : L. Flin & A. Watts, 1763.

Spickernell, William, *The Roman Villa, Carisbrooke, Isle of Wight, with ground plan &c.*, Newport, Isle of Wight, 1860.

Spray, Thomas Edward, 'Patterns of nationalist discourse in the early reception of the Icelandic sagas in Britain', Durham University Ph.D. thesis, 2019, http://etheses.dur.ac.uk/12964/.

St Aubyn, John, *St Michael's Mount: Illustrated History and Guide*, St Ives: J. St Aubyn, 1978.

Stafford, Fiona, *The Sublime Savage: James Macpherson and the Poems of Ossian*, Edinburgh: Edinburgh University Press, 1988.

Staley, Lynn, *The Island Garden: England's Language of Nation from Gildas to Marvell*, Notre Dame, Ind: University of Notre Dame, 2012.

Stanton, David W. G., Jacqueline A. Mulville and Michael W. Bruford, 'Colonization of the Scottish islands via long-distance deer (Cervus elaphus)', *Proceedings of the Royal Society B: Biological Sciences*, London, 2016.

Steckoll, Solomon H., *The Alderney Death Camp*, London: Granada, 1982.

Steele, Philip (ed.), *Lyn Cerrig Bach: Treasures from the Iron Age*, Ynys Môn/ Anglesey: Cyngor Sir Oriel Ynys Môn/Isle of Anglesey County Council, 2012.

Steenstrup, Johannes C. H. R, *The Medieval Popular Ballad*, trans. from the Danish by Edward Godfrey Cox, Boston, MA: Ginn & Co., 1914.

Stenton, Dorothy, *The English Women in History*, London: Routledge, 1957.

Stewart Jnr, James A., 'War and peace in the Hebrides: the origin and settlement of the "Linn Nan Creach" ', *Proceedings of the Harvard Celtic Colloquium*, 16/17, 1996, pp. 116–56.

Stewart, George R., 'English Geography in Malory's *Morte D'Arthur*', *The Modern Language Review*, 30 (2), 1935, pp. 204–209.

Stewart Richardson, Iona, 'For the nineteenth year, the Isle of Wight is above the national average for suicides according to the Office for National Statistics': Isle of Wight Radio, 10 Sept. 2020, https://www.iwradio.co.uk/news/isle-of-wight-news/island-suicide-numbers-are-worryingsays-charity-on-prevention-day/.

Stoney, Barbara, *Sibyl, Dame of Sark: a biography*, London: Hodder & Stoughton, 1978.

Story, Joanna, *Lindisfarne Priory*, London: English Heritage, 2005.

Stout, Margaret B., *Cookery for Northern Wives*, Lerwick: T. & J. Manson, 1925 [Lerwick: Shetland Heritage Publications, 2013].

Stoyle, Mark, 'The Cornish Rising of 1648 and the Second Civil War', *Albion*, 32 (1), 2000, pp. 37–58.

—, '"Fullye Bente to Fighte Oute the Matter": Reconsidering Cornwall's Role in the Western Rebellion of 1549', *The English Historical Review*, 129 (538), 2014, pp. 549–577.

Strabo, *The Geography of Strabo*, Duane W. Roller (trans.), Cambridge: Cambridge University Press, 2014.

Strode, *The Floating Island: a tragi-comedy* [in five acts and in verse], London, 1655; https://quod.lib.umich.edu/e/eebo/A94057.0001.001?view=toc.

Sturdy Colls, Caroline and Kevin Colls, 'Reconstructing a painful past: a non-invasive approach to reconstructing Lager Norderney in Alderney, the Channel Islands', in Eugene Ch'ng et al. (eds.), *Visual Heritage in the Digital Age*, London: Springer-Verlag, 2013.

Sumption, Jonathan, *Pilgrimage: An Image of Mediaeval Religion*, London: Faber & Faber, 1975.

Swan, Quito, *Black Power in Bermuda: The Struggle for Decolonization*, New York: Palgrave Macmillan, 2009.

—, 'Smoldering Memories and Burning Questions' in *Politics of Memory: Making Slavery Visible in the Public Space*, Ana Lucia Araujo (ed.), New York/Abingdon: Routledge, 2012, pp. 71–91.

Tacitus, Cornelius, *The Agricola and Germania*, R. B. Townshend (trans.), London: Methuen & Co, 1894; http://www.perseus.tufts.edu/hopper/text?doc=Perseus%3Atext%3A1999.02.0081%3Achapter%3D16.

—, *Annals*, John Jackson (trans.), London: Loeb Classical Library, 1937.

Tatlock, J. S. P., *The Legendary History of Britain: Geoffrey of Monmouth's* Historia Regum Britanniae *and its early Vernacular Versions*, Berkeley: University of California Press, 1950.

Taylor, John, *Wandering to See the Wonders of the West*, London, 1649 [republished in *The Old Book Collector's Miscellany*, London: Reeves & Turner, 3, 1873].

Teather, Anne, 'Neolithic phallacies: a discussion of some southern British artefacts', in Mats Larsson and Mike Parker Pearson (eds.), *From Stonehenge to the Baltic: Living with Cultural Diversity in the Third Millennium BC*, Oxford: Archaeopress, 2007.

Teit, J. A., 'Water-Beings in Shetlandic Folk-Lore, as Remembered by Shetlanders in British Columbia', *The Journal of American Folklore*, 31 (120), 1918, pp. 180–201.

Thacker, Alan, 'Lindisfarne and the origins of the cult of St Cuthbert', in *St Cuthbert, His Cult and His Community to AD 1200*, Gerald Bonner, David W. Rollason and Clare Stancliffe (eds.), Woodbridge: Boydell Press, 1989.

Thomas, Antonia, *Art and Architecture in Neolithic Orkney: Process, Temporality and Context*, Oxford: Archaeopress, 2016.

Thomas, Charles, *Exploration of a Drowned Landscape: Archaeology and History of the Isles of Scilly*, London: B. T. Batsford, 1985.

—, Celtic Britain, London: Thames and Hudson, 1986.

Thomas, Christopher, Robert Cowie and Jane Sidell, *The Royal Palace, Abbey and Town of Westminster on Thorney Island: Archaeological Excavations (1991–8) for the London Underground Limited Jubilee Line Extension Project*, London: Museum of London Archaeology Service, 2006.

Thomas, Julian, 'Identity of place in Neolithic Britain', in *Neolithic Orkney in Its European Context,* Anna Ritchie (ed.), Cambridge: McDonald Institute for Archaeological Research, 2000.

Thomson, John A., *The Smuggling Coast: The Customs Port of Dumfries, Forty Miles of the Solway Firth*, Dumfries: T. C. Farries, 1989.

Thomson, William, *The Book of Tides: A Journey through the Coastal Waters of Our Island*, London: Quercus, 2016.

Thornton, Tim, *The Channel Islands 1370–1640: Between England and Normandy*, Woodbridge, Martlesham: Boydell & Brewer, 2012.

Tomalin, David, *Roman Wight: A Guide Catalogue*, Newport: Isle of Wight County Council, 1997.

—, et al. (eds.), *Coastal Archaeology in a Dynamic Environment: A Solent Case Study*, Oxford: Archaeopress, 2012.

—, *Roman Vectis: Archaeology and Identity in the Isle of Wight*, Isle of Wight: Vectensica Publishing, 2022.

Towrie, Sigurd, 'Orkneyjar: The Heritage of the Orkney Islands',http://www.orkneyjar.com/.

Tsing, Anna Lowenhaupt, *The Mushroom at the End of the World: On the Possibility of Life in Capitalist Ruins*, Princeton: Princeton University Press, 2015.

Tucker, Terry, *Bermuda's Story*, Bermuda: Department of Education, 1959.

—, *Bermuda Today and Yesterday 1503-1980s*, London/Bermuda: Hale, 1983.

Tudor, Victoria, 'The cult of St Cuthbert in the twelfth century: the evidence of Reginald of Durham', in Gerald Bonner, D.W. Rollason and Clare Stancliffe (eds.), *St Cuthbert His Cult and His Community to AD 1200*, Woodbridge: Boydell Press, 1989.

Tulloch, Lawrence, *Shetland Folktales*, Cheltenham: The History Press, 2014.

Tulloch, Reverend George, 'Edderachillis', *New Statistical Account*, Edinburgh: W. Blackwood and Sons, 1845.

Turner, Val E., Julie M. Bond and Anne-Christian Larsen (eds.), *Viking Unst: Excavation and Survey in Northern Shetland 2006–2010*, Lerwick: Shetland Amenity Trust, 2013.

UCL, Judicial Institute, 'The future of the Judicial Committee of the Privy Council: 26 November 2012: programme & background papers', London, 2012.

UK, Parliament, House of Commons Committee of Public Accounts, 'The accounts of the Duchies of Cornwall and Lancaster: Nineteenth Report of Session 2004–05', https://publications.parliament.uk/pa/cm200405/cmselect/cmpubacc/313/313.pdf.

Vennemann, Theo, 'The name of the Isle of Thanet', in *Language and Text: Current Perspectives on English and Germanic Historical Linguistics and Philology*, Andrew James Johnston, Ferdinand Von Mengden and Stefan Thim (eds.), Heidelberg: Universitätsverlag, 2006, pp. 345–74.

Vickers, Miranda, *Eyots and Aits: islands of the River Thames*, Stroud: History, 2012.

Vicuña, Cecilia, 'Brain Forest Quipu', Tate Modern Turbine Hall exhibition board, 2022.

Virgil, *Eclogues*, Len Krisak (trans.), Philadelphia, Pa.: University of Pennsylvania Press, 2012.

Wade-Evans, A.W., *Nennius's 'History of the Britons': together with 'The Annals of the Britons' and 'Court pedigrees of Hywel the Good' also 'The story of the loss of Britain'*, London: S. P. C. K., 1938.

Waldron, George, *The Compleat Works in Verse and Prose of George Waldron, Gent., Late of Queen's College, Oxon*, Theodosia Waldron (ed.), printed for the Widow and Orphans, London: Cengage Gale, 1731.

—, *The History and Description of the Isle of Man: viz, Its Antiquity, History, Laws, Customs, Religion and Manners of its Inhabitants, Minerals, Curious and Authentick Relations of APPARITIONS OF GIANTS that have liv'd under the Castle Time immemorial. Likewise many Comical and Entertaining Stories of the Pranks play'd by Fairies, &c.*, London: W. Bickerton, 1744.

Wales, National Assembly for/Cynulliad Cenedlaethol Cymru, 'Key Statistics of the Isle of Anglesey', April 2008: https://senedd.wales/

NAfW%20Documents/anglesey.pdf%20-%2018042008/anglesey-English.pdf.

Walker, Barbara G., *The Woman's Encyclopaedia of Myths and Secrets*, New York: HarperCollins, 1983.

Walkinshaw, Colin: The *Scots Tragedy: A history of Scottish nationalism*, London: G. Routledge & Sons, 1935.

Warner, Marina, *Monuments & Maidens: The Allegory of the Female Form*, London: Weidenfeld and Nicolson, 1985.

Warwick-Ching, Lucy, 'Clock ticks on Isle of Man tax', *Financial Times*, 19th February 2013.

Watkins, Alfred, *The Old Straight Track: Its Mounds, Beacons, Moats, Sites and Mark Stones*, London: Abacus, 1925 [reprint 1974].

Watkins, Simon, *We remember the Occupation by the Nazis: Memories of the German Occupation of the British Channel Islands 1940–45 by the People Who Lived through It*, CD Audiobook, read by Roy McLoughlin, Jersey: Channel Island Publishing, 2010.

Watson, Aaron and David Keating, 'The architecture of sound in Neolithic Orkney', in *Neolithic Orkney in Its European Context*, Anna Ritchie (ed.), Cambridge: McDonald Institute for Archaeological Research, 2000.

Watson, Philip, *Rathlin Nature and Folklore*, Glasgow: Stone Country Press, 2011.

Watts, Victor (ed.), *The Cambridge Dictionary of English Place-Names*, Cambridge: Cambridge University Press, 2004.

Waugh, Doreen, in *Viking Unst: Excavation and Survey in Northern Shetland 2006–2010*, Val E. Turner, Julie M Bond and Anne-Christian Larsen (eds.), Lerwick: Shetland Amenity Trust, 2013.

Webster, Graham, *The Roman Invasion of Britain*, London: B.T. Batsford, 1980 [1993].

Webster, Jane, 'At the End of the World: Druidic and Other Revitalization Movements in Post-Conquest Gaul and Britain', *Britannia*, 30, 1999, pp. 1–20.

Welsh Government, *Welsh Index of Multiple Deprivation*, 2019: https://gov.wales/sites/default/files/statistics-and-research/2019-11/welsh-index-multipledeprivation-2019-results-report-024.pdf.

Werner, Martin, 'The Madonna and Child Miniature in the "Book of Kells"', *Art Bulletin*, 54 (2), 1972, pp. 129–39.

Wickham-Jones, Caroline, *Orkney: A Historical Guide*, Edinburgh: Birlinn, 2015.

Wilkins, Frances, *The Isle of Man in Smuggling History*, Kidderminster: Wyre Forest Press, 1992.

—, *Manx Slave Traders: A Social History of the Isle of Man's Involvement in the Atlantic Slave Trade*, Kidderminster: Wyre Forest Press, 1999.

—, *The Isle of Man and the Jacobite Network*, Kidderminster: Wyre Forest Press, 2002.

—, 'The impact of the Revestment on the history of Dumfries and Galloway', *Isle of Man Natural History and Antiquarian Society Revestment Symposium 2015*, recorded talk.

Williams, J. ab Ithel (ed.), *The Barddas of Iolo Morganwg: a collection of original documents, illustrative of the theology, wisdom, and usages of the Bardo-Druidic system of the Isle of Britain*, London: Longman, 1862.

Williams, Neville, *Contraband Cargoes: Seven Centuries of Smuggling*, London: Longman, Green & Co., 1959.

Williams, Ronald, *The Lords of the Isles: The Clan Donald and the Early Kingdom of the Scots*, London: Chatto & Windus, 1984.

Willmot, Louise, 'Women and resistance' in Gillian Carr, Paul Sanders and Louise Willmot (eds.), *Protest, Defiance and Resistance in the Channel Islands: German Occupation, 1940–45*, London: Bloomsbury Academic, 2014.

Wingeate Pike, David, Review [Untitled] in *Guerre mondiales et conflits contemporains*, 258, 2015.

Woolf, Alex, 'The song of the death of Somerled and the destruction of Glasgow in 1153', *Sydney Society for Scottish History Journal*, 14, 2013, pp. 1–11.

Woolf, Greg, 'A distant mirror: Britain and Rome in the representation of empire', in Juan Santos Yanguas and Elena Torregaray Pagola (eds.), *Laudes Provinciarum: Retórica y política en la representación del imperio romano*, Vitoria: Universidad del País Vasco, 2007.

Wragg Sykes, Rebecca, *Kindred: Neanderthal Life, Love, Death and Art*, London: Bloomsbury, 2020.

Wright, Louis B., 'The reading of plays during the Puritan Revolution', *Huntington Library Bulletin*, 6, 1934, pp. 73–108.

Index

ALLEN LANE
an imprint of
PENGUIN BOOKS

Also Published

David Sumpter, *Four Ways of Thinking: Statistical, Interactive, Chaotic and Complex*

Philip Gold, *Breaking Through Depression: New Treatments and Discoveries for Healing*

Wolfram Eilenberger, *The Visionaries: Arendt, Beauvoir, Rand, Weil and the Salvation of Philosophy*

Giorgio Parisi, *In a Flight of Starlings: The Wonder of Complex Systems*

Klaus-Michael Bogdal, *Europe and the Roma: A History of Fascination and Fear*

Robin Lane Fox, *Homer and His Iliad*

Jessica Rawson, *Life and Afterlife in Ancient China*

Julian Jackson, *France on Trial: The Case of Marshal Pétain*

Wesley Lowery, *American Whitelash: The Resurgence of Racial Violence in Our Time*

Rachel Chrastil, *Bismarck's War: The Franco-Prussian War and the Making of Modern Europe*

Lucy Jones, *Matrescence: On the Metamorphosis of Pregnancy, Childbirth and Motherhood*

Peter Turchin, *End Times: Elites, Counter-Elites and the Path of Political Disintegration*

Paul McCartney, *1964: Eyes of the Storm*

Theresa MacPhail, *Allergic: How Our Immune System Reacts to a Changing World*

John Romer, *A History of Ancient Egypt, Volume 3: From the Shepherd Kings to the End of the Theban Monarchy*

John Rapley and Peter Heather, *Why Empires Fall: Rome, America and the Future of the West*

Scott Shapiro, *Fancy Bear Goes Phishing: The Dark History of the Information Age, in Five Extraordinary Hacks*

Elizabeth-Jane Burnett, *Twelve Words for Moss*

Serhii Plokhy, *The Russo-Ukranian War*

Martin Daunton, *The Economic Government of the World: 1933-2023*

Martyn Rady, *The Middle Kingdoms: A New History of Central Europe*

Michio Kaku, *Quantum Supremacy: How Quantum Computers will Unlock the Mysteries of Science – And Address Humanity's Biggest Challenges*

Andy Clark, *The Experience Machine: How Our Minds Predict and Shape Reality*

Monica Potts, *The Forgotten Girls: An American Story*

Christopher Clark, *Revolutionary Spring: Fighting for a New World 1848-1849*

Daniel Chandler, *Free and Equal: What Would a Fair Society Look Like?*

Jonathan Rosen, *Best Minds: A Story of Friendship, Madness, and the Tragedy of Good Intentions*

Nigel Townson, *The Penguin History of Modern Spain: 1898 to the Present*

Katja Hoyer, *Beyond the Wall: East Germany, 1949-1990*

Quinn Slobodian, *Crack-Up Capitalism: Market Radicals and the Dream of a World Without Democracy*

Clare Carlisle, *The Marriage Question: George Eliot's Double Life*

Matthew Desmond, *Poverty, by America*

Sara Ahmed, *The Feminist Killjoy Handbook*

Bernard Wasserstein, *A Small Town in Ukraine: The place we came from, the place we went back to*

Mariana Mazzucato and Rosie Collington, *The Big Con: How the Consultancy Industry Weakens our Businesses, Infantilizes our Governments and Warps our Economies*

Carlo Rovelli, *Anaximander: And the Nature of Science*

Bernie Sanders, *It's OK To Be Angry About Capitalism*

Martin Wolf, *The Crisis of Democractic Capitalism*

David Graeber, *Pirate Enlightenment, or the Real Libertalia*

Leonard Susskind and Andre Cabannes, *General Relativity: The Theoretical Minimum*

Dacher Keltner, *Awe: The Transformative Power of Everyday Wonder*

William D. Cohan, *Power Failure: The Rise and Fall of General Electric*

John Barton, *The Word: On the Translation of the Bible*

Ryan Gingeras, *The Last Days of the Ottoman Empire*

Greta Thunberg, *The Climate Book*

Peter Heather, *Christendom: The Triumph of a Religion*

Christopher de Hamel, *The Posthumous Papers of the Manuscripts Club*

Ha-Joon Chang, *Edible Economics: A Hungry Economist Explains the World*

Anand Giridharadas, *The Persuaders: Winning Hearts and Minds in a Divided Age*

Nicola Rollock, *The Racial Code: Tales of Resistance and Survival*

Peter H. Wilson, *Iron and Blood: A Military History of German-speaking Peoples since 1500*

Ian Kershaw, *Personality and Power: Builders and Destroyers of Modern Europe*

Alison Bashford, *An Intimate History of Evolution: The Story of the Huxley Family*

Lawrence Freedman, *Command: The Politics of Military Operations from Korea to Ukraine*

Richard Niven, *Second City: Birmingham and the Forging of Modern Britain*

Hakim Adi, *African and Caribbean People in Britain: A History*

Jordan Peterson, *24 Rules For Life: The Box Set*

Gaia Vince, *Nomad Century: How to Survive the Climate Upheaval*

Keith Fisher, *A Pipeline Runs Through It: The Story of Oil from Ancient Times to the First World War*

Christoph Keller, *Every Cripple a Superhero*

Roberto Calasso, *The Tablet of Destinies*

Jennifer Jacquet, *The Playbook: How to Deny Science, Sell Lies, and Make a Killing in the Corporate World*

Frank Close, *Elusive: How Peter Higgs Solved the Mystery of Mass*

Edward Chancellor, *The Price of Time: The Real Story of Interest*

Antonio Padilla, *Fantastic Numbers and Where to Find Them: A Cosmic Quest from Zero to Infinity*

Henry Kissinger, *Leadership: Six Studies in World Strategy*

Chris Patten, *The Hong Kong Diaries*

Lindsey Fitzharris, *The Facemaker: One Surgeon's Battle to Mend the Disfigured Soldiers of World War 1*

George Monbiot, *Regenesis: Feeding the World without Devouring the Planet*

Caroline Knowles, *Serious Money: Walking Plutocratic London*

Serhii Plokhy, *Atoms and Ashes: From Bikini Atoll to Fukushima*

Dominic Lieven, *In the Shadow of the Gods: The Emperor in World History*

Scott Hershovitz, *Nasty, Brutish, and Short: Adventures in Philosophy with Kids*

Bill Gates, *How to Prevent the Next Pandemic*

Emma Smith, *Portable Magic: A History of Books and their Readers*

Kris Manjapra, *Black Ghost of Empire: The Long Death of Slavery and the Failure of Emancipation*

Andrew Scull, *Desperate Remedies: Psychiatry and the Mysteries of Mental Illness*

James Bridle, *Ways of Being: Beyond Human Intelligence*

Eugene Linden, *Fire and Flood: A People's History of Climate Change, from 1979 to the Present*

Cathy O'Neil, *The Shame Machine: Who Profits in the New Age of Humiliation*

Peter Hennessy, *A Duty of Care: Britain Before and After Covid*

Gerd Gigerenzer, *How to Stay Smart in a Smart World: Why Human Intelligence Still Beats Algorithms*

Halik Kochanski, *Resistance: The Undergroud War in Europe, 1939-1945*

Joseph Sassoon, *The Global Merchants: The Enterprise and Extravagance of the Sassoon Dynasty*

Clare Chambers, *Intact: A Defence of the Unmodified Body*

Nina Power, *What Do Men Want?: Masculinity and Its Discontents*

Ivan Jablonka, *A History of Masculinity: From Patriarchy to Gender Justice*

Thomas Halliday, *Otherlands: A World in the Making*

Sofi Thanhauser, *Worn: A People's History of Clothing*

Sebastian Mallaby, *The Power Law: Venture Capital and the Art of Disruption*

David J. Chalmers, *Reality+: Virtual Worlds and the Problems of Philosophy*

Jing Tsu, *Kingdom of Characters: A Tale of Language, Obsession and Genius in Modern China*

Lewis R. Gordon, *Fear of Black Consciousness*

Leonard Mlodinow, *Emotional: The New Thinking About Feelings*

Kevin Birmingham, *The Sinner and the Saint: Dostoevsky, a Crime and Its Punishment*

Roberto Calasso, *The Book of All Books*

Marit Kapla, *Osebol: Voices from a Swedish Village*

Malcolm Gaskill, *The Ruin of All Witches: Life and Death in the New World*

Mark Mazower, *The Greek Revolution: 1821 and the Making of Modern Europe*

Paul McCartney, *The Lyrics: 1956 to the Present*

Brendan Simms and Charlie Laderman, *Hitler's American Gamble: Pearl Harbor and the German March to Global War*

Lea Ypi, *Free: Coming of Age at the End of History*